Baseball
Hall of Fame
Autographs

Baseball Hall of Fame Autographs

A Reference Guide

RON KEURAJIAN

Foreword by FAY VINCENT

McFarland & Company, Inc., Publishers
Jefferson, North Carolina, and London

LIBRARY OF CONGRESS CATALOGUING-IN-PUBLICATION DATA

Keurajian, Ron, 1967–
Baseball Hall of Fame autographs : a reference guide / Ron Keurajian ;
foreword by Fay Vincent.
p.   cm.
Includes index.

ISBN 978-0-7864-7050-1
softcover : acid free paper ∞

1. Baseball players — United States — Autographs — Collectors and
collecting.   2. Baseball players — United States — Biography.
3. Autographs — United States — Collectors and collecting.
I. Title.
GV875.2.K48 2012   796.357 — dc23   2012038752

BRITISH LIBRARY CATALOGUING DATA ARE AVAILABLE

Front cover photographs: Autographed baseball by Jackie Robinson
(National Baseball Hall of Fame Library Cooperstown, N.Y.);
baseball display case (iStockphoto/Thinkstock)

Manufactured in the United States of America

*McFarland & Company, Inc., Publishers
Box 611, Jefferson, North Carolina 28640
www.mcfarlandpub.com*

To Mom and Dad

Table of Contents

Acknowledgments

Steve Koschal
Benjamin Neely
Adams County Historical Society
Adams County, Recorder of Deeds
Kathy Grillo
Dr. Richard Bagdasarian
John Keurajian
Ronald S. Glaser
Jim Buchanan
Ted Elmo+
Richard Patman
Doug Averitt
Jim Stinson
Harvey Swanebeck
Richard Albersheim
Paul Esacove
John L. Scott
Brenda L. Chenault
Dan O'Brien
ShaRon Taylor
The Family of George Davis
The Family of Sam Thompson
The Family of George Waddell
Ernie Harwell
Robert Lifson
Donald Thompson
Gladys H. Catron
Ed Catron
The Family of J. Leslie Wilkinson
The Public Library of Newark, New Jersey
The Public Library of Lake Orion, Michigan
The Public Library of Oxford, Michigan
Sports Collectors Digest
Rocky Landsverk
T. S. O'Connell
The National Baseball Hall of Fame and Museum
George Hawley
James L. Gates, Jr., Baseball Hall of Fame
Ted Spencer, Baseball Hall of Fame
Lelands.com
Josh Evans

Robert Edwards Auctions
Steve Cyrkin
Robert Schweppe
Peter O'Malley
Brent Shyer
Kimberly Cole
Dan Cariseo
Andy Cooper Jr.
Society for American Baseball Research
Robert Mitchell
Gregory Vartanian, U.S. Marshal
Dr. William R. Cobb
The Public Library of New York
Bryan Dec
The Family of Walter Johnson
The United States Marshals Service
Kevin Burke
Naoki Kamiya
Anne B. Shephard
John Mule Miles
Cincinnati Museum Center
Kirk Krikorian
Peter Nash
Joe Tufano
Suffolk County Probate and Family Court
James Gavaghan
Luella H. Kurkjian
Hawaii State Archives
Commissioner Fay Vincent
Aram Papazian
Richard Simon
Zina Rhone
National Archives — Atlanta
Jerry Casway
Sara E. Brewer
Dr. Richard Saffro
Alfred Angelo
Frank Ceresi
Joe Enos
Bob Eaton

Foreword

Fay Vincent

Willie Sutton, the infamous bank robber, once replied to the question of why he robbed banks with a line that has relevance here. He said, "Because that is where the money is." There is also a lot of money in collecting — and forging — baseball autographs. In this timely book, Ron Keurajian, a nationally known expert in the art and science of fraudulent baseball autographs, exposes in superb detail how forgeries are done, the little tricks to detecting fake autographs, and which autographs make sense to buy and which do not. This is a reference guide sure to take its place as the essential purchase for anyone beginning to establish or trying to build an autograph collection of baseball figures.

I remember how surprised I was when people began to ask me for my autograph. Similarly, my friend and predecessor as commissioner, Bart Giamatti, was amused by the interest in his autograph. We often marveled at our own ineptness as players and at how stunning it was to be treated in the same fashion as those who could play the game. But we soon learned how serious collectors have become and how much money is involved in the business of staging card shows where fans and collectors can buy autographs. Early on I recall the scandal when several prominent players were prosecuted for failure to report their earnings from such shows to the IRS. Today many Hall of Fame baseball players are able to generate a generous annual income from appearances at such card shows. In addition, most players, and even old baseball executives like me, receive mail requests for our signatures and some former players insist on being paid to sign. It is not surprising that a solid reference book has arrived to fill the twin needs of warning the potential buyer of the enormous number of fake autographs and informing the market of important aspects of this business.

Of course the business of fraud is even older than baseball. Almost from the very beginning of the game there were problems. The early autographs of such luminaries as Babe Ruth, Ty Cobb and Harry Heilmann are the focus of much of this book and yet the grim reality is some of the greatest players treated the requests for autographs as a nuisance and had clubhouse boys and others sign for them. I recall being so surprised and disappointed when I learned during our gambling investigation of Pete Rose that he also had others sign for him. In the early days, of course, the players had no basis for appreciating how valuable their

1

autographs would become. As this book points out, the number of forged autographs may amount to the majority of all those in the marketplace for such players as Ruth, Cobb and Lou Gehrig. Moreover, even some authentication firms have been found to be themselves engaged in fraud. With fraud so prevalent, this reference guide will serve to save the eager but not expert collector. There are some delightful lessons in here. I was amused to learn my old friend John Mize never placed a dot over the "i" in his signature but yet there are numerous fake autographs of his with the dot sitting on top of the "i." Good stuff, that.

The collection of baseball autographs is a natural and healthy extension of being a fan of the game. I have a modest collection of signed baseballs, pictures, and other memorabilia and they bring back fond and warm memories. I have some regrets that the business of autograph collecting has come to dominate the fun of it. Somehow we have lost sight of baseball in this. But like the other forms of fraud, money comes to overwhelm just about everything, including the decent basis for collecting autographs. I did not keep my items for their value and the investing aspect never appealed to me. This book is a reminder of the risks of investing even in baseball history. You may strike out. Moreover, the pitcher and ball may be juiced. Remember the old baseball line "Say it ain't so, Joe." That kid — who was hoping Shoeless Joe Jackson hadn't cheated — speaks for me in this arena. I just wish this book were not necessary. But as you read it, you will understand why it is a valuable and necessary work.

Fay Vincent: eighth commissioner of Major League Baseball, September 13, 1989, to September 7, 1992.

Preface

When I grew up in an old baseball town like Detroit, baseball was everywhere. I would hear stories from my uncles about Tom Bridges, Billy Rogell, Pinky Higgins, Billy Pierce, Doc Cramer, and Hank Greenberg. When I was a little kid, my neighbor, Mr. Bill Sinclair, would tell me stories of Ty Cobb, Wahoo Sam Crawford, Twilight Ed Killian, and other Tiger greats from the mythical Dead Ball era. I just fell in love with the grand old game of baseball. I started to collect baseball cards in 1976. Collecting baseball cards exposed me to autographs, which is where this story begins. I collected autographs of all the players I could. The older the player the better. In the September 18, 2011, issue of *Autograph* magazine I wrote a story on the passing of my dear friend Ernie Harwell, where I explained why I collect baseball autographs:

"I have often wondered why I collect baseball autographs. I am sure it is a question every collector asks themselves. At first I thought it is a way of preserving history for future generations or maybe the way autographs display so nicely on the wall. But upon further reflection I think it's something much more personal and maybe even a bit selfish. No, I think I collect baseball autographs because it reminds me of a simpler time when life was free of care and worry

and the only thing that mattered was baseball. That 1978 Detroit Tigers team baseball takes me back to my childhood when Rusty Staub, Milt May, and Mark Fidrych were kings. My 1924 Ty Cobb signed baseball I treasure so transports me back to a time that I have never been to but dearly wish I could visit. I guess I collect simply for those cherished memories of the grand old game and times long since past."

Over the past three decades I have studied baseball autographs, signing habits, and forgeries. I started assembling a reference library of signatures, both originals and copies, for my personal use, many of which you will find illustrated in this book. These days, collecting knowledge is just as important to me as collecting the autographs themselves. About 10 years ago, I started writing signature studies on vintage baseball and golf autographs, nearly 40 of them for *Sports Collectors Digest* and later for *Autographalert.com* and *Autograph* magazine.

I write articles and put relevant information out there and let the collecting public do with it what they will. It is my hope that my words will help educate autograph collectors everywhere. For years I have seen thousands upon thousands of forgeries bought, sold, and traded. I have seen thousands sold by auction houses and thousands more wrongly certified as genuine by the authentication companies.

On occasion, I will speak up when it comes to a significant piece whose authenticity is in question. A case in point is the Ty Cobb golfing diary from 1946 that came out of the collection of the late Barry Halper. Major League Baseball purchased many significant artifacts from the Halper collection and donated them to the National Baseball Hall of Fame. The diary had detailed writings about Cobb and fellow legends like Babe Ruth, Joe DiMaggio, Harry Heilmann and the like. It was crudely written and portrayed Cobb as a petty individual with poor writing skills. In the July 5, 2009, *Detroit Free Press*, retired Detroit Tigers broadcaster Ernie Harwell, who had known Cobb well, broke the story on the diary, writing, "The Cobb diary is a fake and will be forever relegated to the archival basement in Cooperstown." The FBI had examined the diary at the request of the Hall of Fame. Harwell quoted directly from the FBI report: "The written entries are not consistent with the natural writing style of Tyrus R. Cobb." The report also noted "numerous characteristics indicative of simulations/tracings."

The research for this book took me to many unlikely places. Collectors were more than happy to give me access to their collections so I could have suitable illustrations. You will also find many rare signatures reproduced that are directly from the National Baseball Hall of Fame's collection. The Hall granted me access to the Frederick Long collection and the massive August Herrmann collection. Both collections have many letters dating to the 1870s. Local governments also proved invaluable, where municipal employees in more than 30 states searched through court records, probates, and deeds looking for signed documents. Many rare signatures turned up through their efforts and are illustrated in this book. For many illustrations it is the first time they have ever been reproduced.

No book has been published that approaches the detail found herein. I have written this book in such a way that it can be used by the novice autograph hound as well as the most advanced collector. I hope this book will be of use not only to the collecting public but also, in some small way, will help preserve the history that is the game of baseball.

Introduction

When I was in middle school an English teacher, whose name has escaped me, assigned me a book report. The topic: a biography on the life and times of former Detroit Tigers outfielder Ty Cobb. I was more than happy to undertake that task; after all, I was a baseball fan. My other choice was Heinz Guderian.

Ty Cobb was the greatest player in the history of the game. A man that has no equal. He was as fast as lightning on the basepaths and swung a wicked bat. Cobb would retire with 12 batting crowns, a record-setting .367 lifetime average, 4,191 base hits, 1,961 RBIs, and the holder of more records than any other player in history. Cobb, nicknamed "The Georgia Peach," would be among the first men enshrined in the National Baseball Hall of Fame. He would go down in history as the greatest there ever was.

I read everything I could on Cobb. I put pen to paper and reduced my thoughts to writing. Five pages later I had composed a work that rivaled the talents of Charles Dickens himself, or so I thought. I sat back and read my biography of Cobb. "What a wonderful piece of work," I said to myself, but as I neared the end of my literary masterpiece I had an idea. Wouldn't it be nice if I could add something more to my report?

Something that would make my report stand out above the crowd? That something turned out to be former Detroit Tigers legend Charlie Gehringer.

Gehringer was one of the finest infielders in the history of the game and a local legend in Michigan. Born in 1903, he was the product of rural Fowlerville, a small town about 70 miles northwest of Detroit. He was the local-boy-done-good. Gehringer started his career with the Tigers during the Roaring Twenties, 1924 to be precise. He would anchor the Detroit infield for many years. He retired in 1942 with lifetime numbers that would eventually earn him a bronze plaque in Cooperstown.

Even at my young age I knew the name of the great Charlie Gehringer. I also knew that when Gehringer broke into the big leagues then–Tigers manager Cobb took the young rookie under his wing. He showed Gehringer how to refine his playing skills.

Gehringer lived out a quiet retirement in the upscale community of Birmingham. His house was but a stone's throw from where I lived. I got the bright idea of calling him up for some personal accounts of his old manager, one Mr. Cobb, to add to my report. I figured adding the words of a Cobb teammate would enhance my book report greatly.

I phoned Gehringer and explained the

reason I had contacted him. I asked for a few minutes of his time, which he gladly gave me. I think the five minutes I had allotted myself turned into nearly one hour. He had great stories of Cobb. Then we talked about Billy Rogell, Lefty Gomez, Rudy York, Walter Johnson, and on and on. It was a great conversation. It was like taking a trip back in time to the golden age of baseball.

Just before I said good bye, Gehringer gave me one of the biggest thrills of my life. He invited me over to his house to view his collection of mementos. I gladly accepted and spent an hour at his house. What an amazing collection Gehringer had. Books, bats, old, scuffed-up balls, and silver trophies.

After the grand tour I thanked him for sharing his private collection with me. With a firm handshake I said good bye. As I was about to leave he had a strange look on his face. I thought to myself maybe I did something wrong. He looked at me and asked, "Don't you want my autograph?"

"Autograph? Sure!" I replied and with that Gehringer pulled from his cherry wood desk a postcard-sized picture of his Hall of Fame plaque. He signed it and gave it to me. It was my very first Hall of Fame signature. From that point I was hooked. I decided to collect as many Hall of Fame autographs as I could get my hands on.

When I first started collecting back in the late 1970s the baseball autograph hobby was still in its infancy. The collector base was scattered about in a patchwork of unorganized dealers and hobbyists. Back then there were no big auction houses for this material. Values were small. Examples of known signatures were few and far between. In general, the baseball autograph was an insignificant sideshow in the world of sports memorabilia.

I can remember those days long ago when single signed baseballs of Ty Cobb and Babe Ruth could be purchased for $100. I also remember back in 1983 when long time collector Harold Bussey shelled out $300 for a multi-signed Hall of Fame ball. It included such hallowed names as Grover Alexander, Walter Johnson, Ken Williams, Dazzy Vance, Tris Speaker, Connie Mack, as well as Ruth and Cobb. Everybody thought "Doc" Bussey was insane for spending that type of cash but I guess he got the last laugh.

There was a certain innocence to autographs back then. Little value and little demand correlated into very few forgers and forgeries. After all, who would take the time to forge a signature of Cobb only to get $10 for it.

After meeting Tigers legend Charlie Gehringer, I rushed home with my treasured Gehringer signature and made plans to obtain other autographs. I purchased paper, envelopes, stamps, and the bible of autograph collecting, *The Baseball Address List* by Jack Smalling, at my local baseball card store.

I wrote a bunch of letters, dropped them into the hands of the United States Postal Service, and waited patiently. After about a week of checking the mailbox, I received my first reply. I rushed inside the house and feverishly opened the envelope. Inside was an autograph of Gehringer's counterpart and teammate Hank Greenberg, who sent me a signed plaque postcard. I was thrilled to get another Tiger G-Man. Over the next few weeks the names started to roll in. Joe Cronin was next, followed by Lefty Gomez, and so on. I had never seen so many names. They included Al Lopez, Cool Papa Bell, Freddie Lindstrom, George Kelly, Joe Di-Maggio, Burleigh Grimes, and Stan Coveleski, just to name a few. Some included short letters and picture postcards. Joe Sewell wrote me a full-page letter about Cobb! Soon I had more than 30 signatures.

After obtaining all the Hall of Famers I could, I then pursued stars not in the Hall of Fame. It opened up a whole new avenue for my pursuits. Dead Ball Era pitcher George Uhle was my first such signature.

Soon I went to my first baseball card show. The shows back then were a lot different from today. They were small cozy affairs with dealers who were more interested in chatting than making a buck. At my first show, I ran across a dealer who was selling Hall of Fame signatures. I went to the show with $20. I left $20 poorer but had a signed newspaper picture of Lefty Grove, index cards signed by Dizzy Dean, Jesse Haines, and a guy named Eddie Cicotte, who the dealer recommended I buy.

In 1982, I made my first big purchase from long-time collector Ed Budnick. He sold me a promissory note dated 1926 signed by early Tiger slugger Harry Heilmann. That one set me back $30 but I happily shelled out the cash. After all, Heilmann was far and away the rarest signature now residing in my collection.

Well that was then and this is now. The once gentle pursuit of collecting signatures has turned into a high stress endeavor with forgeries lurking around every corner. The once tiny hobby has grown into a big business with followers in the millions. Those Cobb and Ruth autographed balls that once could be had for $100 each are now hitting auction prices of $50,000 to $75,000. I was part of the early days of the baseball autograph hobby. They are fond memories I will cherish. I have come to the realization that it is no longer a quaint hobby. It has become an "industry" where rare signatures are exchanged like precious commodities.

One of the greatest experiences in my early days of collecting was the interaction with the veteran collectors, gentlemen who had been collecting since the 1950s. What a wealth of knowledge I gathered from men like Doug Averitt, Jim Buchanan, Jim Hammond, Kevin Willbond, Dick Patman, Jim Hawkins, Ted Elmo, and Harvey Swanebeck. They were more than happy to pass on their priceless knowledge to me. It is the most important research I have ever done, and likely ever will do, in this field.

While collecting autographs has been the pursuit of the learned man for hundreds of years, collecting baseball signatures did not become fashionable until the 1920s. Before that time a baseball player signing an autograph was a rare event. Baseball autographs signed prior to 1920 are basically non-existent and limited to documents.

The most important statement ever made about baseball autographs comes not from a collector but from former New York Giants outfielder Fred Snodgrass. Snodgrass played big league ball from 1908 to 1916 and was a sure-handed fielder with John McGraw's Giants. Snodgrass was featured in the book *Glory of Their Times*, authored by Larry Ritter. In his interview with Ritter, Snodgrass made perhaps the most important statement regarding baseball autographs. Every collector of vintage baseball signatures should commit Snodgrass's words to memory: "There were no autograph hounds in those days, it hadn't started where boys and people were interested in getting your signature, that wasn't done."

Except for the rare exception, usually limited to signed menus from dinner banquets, people didn't collect baseball autographs at the turn of the twentieth century. This is something to keep in mind the next time you are offered a Rube Waddell signed baseball.

By 1920 autograph collecting went through a monumental change. For decades, collectors were securing signatures of presidents, generals, composers, and authors. But as America entered the Roaring Twenties signatures of athletes, aviators, and entertainers became the "in" thing to collect. All of a sudden Babe Ruth and Hack Wilson were chic. At this junction of the hobby, signatures were obtained exclusively at the ballpark or in person at a hotel. Collecting signatures through the mail was, at this time, basically non-existent.

It is not surprising that most signatures from the 1920s are found on autograph albums and scorecards. Baseballs were also employed to obtain signatures but the cost of a ball made them less often used by the collector of the day. Collecting single-signed balls was really never considered. Back then the goal was to get as many signatures as possible on one ball. Nobody thought of getting a ball signed by *just* Harry Heilmann or Bob Fothergill, that would have been a waste of a good baseball.

Autograph collecting remained basically unchanged in the 1930s. Most signatures were still obtained in person, although one noticeable difference was the increase in obtaining signatures on photographs.

The big change in the hobby came in the 1940s when signatures were being requested through the mail. This was the biggest change in the hobby and the birth of modern day autograph collecting. Collectors would exchange addresses and slowly but surely the old-time ballplayers were tracked down and that elusive signature was secured. Many letters exist from the old-time stars that instruct a collector on how to locate a long retired player. One of the favorite pieces in my collection is a letter from the legendary Flying Dutchman, Honus Wag-

ner, written to an early collector. In the letter, Wagner lists the whereabouts of some of his former teammates. It is simply a great letter and offers keen insight into the early days of the hobby.

The 1940s also saw the birth of a new phenomenon in the hobby, the government postcard. Penny postcards that were purchased from the United States Post Office helped collectors greatly. Back in the 1940s and 1950s these cards became very popular for obtaining autographs. A collector would mail the card to the player who would sign it and then drop it in the mail. The best part was that the card would be postmarked from the player's hometown.

By the 1960s the hobby saw an influx of many new collectors as autographs started to build value. The death of Ty Cobb in July 1961 was a turning point in the hobby. With the passing of one of the greatest players in history, many collectors entered the hobby. I cannot tell you how many times I have heard that the death of Cobb inspired fans to obtain autographs.

Things remained essentially unchanged until the 1980s when players started to sign at baseball card shows and charge a fee for signing an autograph. When I was a young kid such things were unheard of. In the mid–1970s my mom drove me and some friends to a local window store where Tigers first baseman Jason Thompson was signing autographs for free. All we had to do was wait in line for an hour or two. Nobody then would even think of paying for a signature.

Well it is now the twenty-first century and the baseball autograph hobby has evolved. The superstars charge $500 to sign a baseball bat. Skilled forgers have flooded the market with fake material. Rare signatures now sell for big money. There is a general loss of the innocent and gentle days of a hobby that will never return.

Today, vintage Hall of Fame signatures are as valuable as precious gemstones and that invites fraud. I am not sure what happened to my innocent little hobby but it is a far different ballgame than it was just a few years back. Forgeries, scams, theft, and controversies seem to be lurking everywhere.

One story puts the hobby in perspective. For many years signatures purportedly written by Hall of Fame legend Rube Waddell have been bought and sold. Waddell, who died in 1914 of consumption, is an extremely rare autograph. About six years ago I wrote an article stating that no genuine Waddell signatures existed. I was attacked by many authenticators and dealers who claimed many genuine specimens did exist. On the other side of the coin, long-time collectors sided with me. While doing research for this book I tried to locate a confirmed Waddell specimen for illustration. For years I searched and had all but given up. One day I read that Waddell had filed for divorce around 1910 or so. Back then divorce was a rare event but I did some detective work and found that the divorce was handled in St. Louis. I picked up the phone, called the courthouse, and spoke to one of the clerks to ask how long they kept the legal files. "We keep them forever" was the reply. I then asked if they would check and see if there

were any documents associated with George Edward Waddell. The court clerk called me back the next day and stated she found Waddell's divorce file. When I asked if there was anything signed by him, the reply was "yes." I was shocked. An old forgotten legal file sitting in some dank oubliette was uncovered. I received a copy of the file and sure enough the Waddell signatures on the divorce documents did not match the autographs sold over the past 50 years, save one piece.

The interest in Hall of Fame autographs have put institutional archival collections at risk. Several years ago some individuals gained access to these collections. They claimed that they needed to look at the collections for research purposes. Many rare and valuable letters and documents have been stolen out of libraries, government offices, and even the Baseball Hall of Fame.

The above is what you, as a collector, will be up against — this is *not* bottle cap collecting. Forgeries, incompetent authenticators, stolen documents, and the like are rampant. Autographs are one of the most complex of all collectibles. It is imperative that you build a foundation of knowledge that will allow you to assemble a valid collection of Hall of Fame autographs. This book will enable you to pursue a hobby that will give you enjoyment, and profit, for years to come.

♦ ONE ♦

Mediums to Collect

So now you have decided to start collecting baseball autographs. At first the task may seem overwhelming. There are thousands of baseball players and countless more non-players whose signatures are just as collectible. Then there are the mediums to collect. Will it be signed gum cards? Photographs? Baseballs? Index cards? What teams? What positions? The potential combinations are endless.

Like anything else in life, when you start something new take it slow. Collect what you like but don't bite off more than you can chew. Don't throw around big money, at least not yet. Remember you are a rookie and until you become seasoned in the science of signature analysis you need to keep it simple.

Initially, avoid the rare Hall of Fame signatures. Concentrate on the more inexpensive items. There are plenty of great signatures out there for the taking. Quite a nice signature library can be assembled and you don't have to spend a lot of money to do it. For example, Hall of Fame members that passed away after 1970 are available whose signatures cost relatively little. Jesse Haines, Ford Frick, Lefty Grove, Joe Medwick, and other legends of the game come to mind. They generally cost less than $50 per signature.

You should focus on two key areas. First, collect what you like; if it appeals to you then by all means start accumulating signatures that you like. Second, keep in the back of your mind the rate of return. Autographs are not only fun but they can also be financially rewarding. Investment potential is just as important as the fun of collecting. If you make money at something you like, then it is even more enjoyable.

Before you start collecting be mindful that the majority of baseball autographs are not truly collectible. Most signatures exist in mass quantities; in other words there is simply too much supply. How many signatures of George Kell, Bobby Doerr, Andre Dawson, and Cal Ripken are available? Ten thousand? Fifty thousand? One hundred thousand? Five hundred thousand? The exact number is not certain; one thing is certain: there is so much out there that these signatures will never be worth anything of significance, at least not in our lifetimes. If you are buying up signatures of these players with the idea of making money, you're in for a rude awakening.

If the common signatures interest you, then be my guest. There is nothing wrong with this type of material, just remember it will always be common.

This chapter examines a variety of mediums that are widely collected, where a nice collection of signatures can be assembled with little effort.

Baseball Cards

The most popular collecting medium is the signed baseball card. There are countless collectors that collect signed gum cards. Some collectors focus on completing a signed set from a particular year, while others try to obtain multiple signatures on team cards. Either way, collecting signed cards is very rewarding and creates a fabulous and colorful display.

Early Topps gum card issues from 1952 through 1976 are the most popular among collectors. There are cards of many fine players including Mickey Mantle, Stan Musial, Ted Williams, Sandy Koufax, and many others. The rarest and highest demand cards are the vintage signed cards, those issued before World War II. The 1940 Play Ball set seems to be favorite among collectors because it incorporates not only active players of the day but also retired stars such as Nap Lajoie, Grover Cleveland Alexander, and George Sisler.

The most popular of the old-time sets to obtain signatures on is 1933 Goudey gum cards. These are very desirable and coveted by collectors. The cards themselves are beautifully illustrated. The set includes many of the biggest names in baseball history, such as Babe Ruth, Lou Gehrig, Waite Hoyt, Hack Wilson, Kiki Cuyler, and Eddie Collins. When these cards were issued they were rarely presented to players for signature. Signed cards of the long deceased players are very rare to non-existent. The two exceptions to this rule are Ruth and Gehrig, since these men were giants of the game and fans

of the day sought out their signatures on anything they could get signed. Today, signatures of both these Yankees greats can be found on Goudey cards, though they are still considered rare.

Collectors did not really start to obtain signatures on Goudey or Play Ball cards until the mid–1960s. Today, many of the more recently deceased players exist on signed cards, such as Gabby Hartnett, Goose Goslin, Hank Greenberg, and Pie Traynor, but are uncommon to scarce. Any signed Goudey card of a player that died before 1965 must be studied carefully as it is most likely a forgery. If you see a Hack Wilson or Arky Vaughan signed Goudey card, chances are close to 100 percent that they are forged.

For all practical purposes the earliest set you will be able to collect is the 1933 Goudey set. Any cards issued before the Goudey set cannot be assembled as most cards don't exist signed. However, the chances of completing a signed Goudey set is highly unlikely, even excluding the ultra rare Nap Lajoie card from the mix. Obtaining 50 percent to 60 percent of the set signed is likely if you have the financial wherewithal. Certain signed specimens can be very expensive. For example, a choice 1933 Lou Gehrig Goudey card sold for $7,000 in 2006 and a Jimmie Foxx 1933 Goudey, with superior display value, sold for $3,000 in 2008 (Mastro).

Then there is the most famous set in the history of baseball cards, the one referred to as the "monster," the legendary T-206 set. Issued between 1909 and 1911, this set contains 523 cards with 16 different tobacco brands advertised on the back of the cards. This set contains many obscure stars of the Dead Ball Era and many unknown Southern League players. Most of the turn-of-the-century Hall of Famers are featured in the T-206 set. All the mythical figures can be found in the set from Cy Young to Honus Wagner to Willie Keeler to Jack Chesbro.

Many collectors have tried to secure signed T-206 cards or other early tobacco issues but their efforts have been in vain. My advice to collectors that wish to collect signed T-cards is: Don't. Signed T-cards are very rare and limited to those players who lived into the late 1960s. By this time most of the players featured on these cards had passed away. You will not be able to find more than a handful of genuinely signed T-cards. Sam Crawford, who died in 1968, is very rare, as I have seen only two genuine specimens in my 30 years of searching. Larry Doyle, Fred Snodgrass, Rube Marquard, and a select few other players are available but that is it. If you are looking for signed T-cards of John McGraw, Cy Young, Joe Tinker, Johnny Evers, and the other long deceased players you will unequivocably fail. There may be the occasional rarity that surfaces but for all practical purposes signed cards of these legends should be considered non-existent.

For years forgers have been buying up the low-grade T-cards and applying fake signatures upon them. I have seen "signed" T-206 cards of Tinker, Waddell, Young, Chesbro, Germany Schaefer, Wild Bill Donovan, and Walter Johnson for example. With just one exception, I have yet to see a genuine signed T-206 card of any Hall of Famer that died before 1968.

The exception, and there is only one, is Ty Cobb. Cobb was such a giant of the game that even back when sports memorabilia was worthless, people were collecting Cobb material. All the way back in 1910 fans were saving items of the Georgia Peach. Cobb was the one player from the Dead Ball Era that

Exhibit 1: signed T-206 Ty Cobb card

was presented with T-cards to sign. Today the handful of genuinely signed Cobb T-206 cards that exist are true gems of the hobby. I have examined four genuine specimens. Exhibit 1 is a nicely signed T-206 specimen. These are very rare and have an estimated value of $20,000 to $25,000, but in an auction could go much higher. A rare T-202 triple fold card of Cobb and George Moriarty signed by Cobb sold for $17,300 in 2009 (SCP Auctions).

Single-Signed Baseballs

Single-signed baseballs are to the baseball autograph field what handwritten letters of

George Washington and Abe Lincoln are to the presidential signature hobby. These are the most valuable of any signed medium. Prices, in recent years, have gone through the roof.

Before you start collecting single-signed baseballs I must add a word of caution. This is the one area where the truly skilled forgers have concentrated their efforts. Baseballs are where you find the very well executed forgeries in large quantity. Baseballs with stunning forgeries of Tris Speaker, Roger Bresnahan, Herb Pennock, "Shoeless Joe" Jackson, Dazzy Vance, and other old-time legends are common in the market. Though many signatures have been targeted, three names seem to be the main focus of skilled forgers: Ty Cobb, Babe Ruth, and Lou Gehrig.

If you contemplate purchasing a museum-grade Ruth or Gehrig ball be very cautious as they are likely forged. Museum-grade specimens do exist but they are *so* few and far between. The hobby did not become structured until the 1950s, well after Ruth and Gehrig had passed on. In other words collectors did not specifically go out of their way to buy items to get signed in the 1930s. Can you imagine a boy, during the Depression, buying an official league ball just to get it autographed? I saw about 10 Ruth balls in pristine condition at a recent national baseball card convention but only one of them was genuine. The others were questionable. As to the genuine one, it wasn't all that pristine but it was still very nice.

I have come to the conclusion that most of these museum-grade Ruth and Gehrig single-signed baseballs are fake. A lot of long-time collectors have pointed out something very important about the museum-grade Ruth and Gehrig balls and it is worth noting. Back in the 1980s and early 1990s

these gem signed baseballs were nowhere to be found. I have been in this hobby for 30-plus years and I don't ever recall seeing these pristine balls, except on *very* rare occasions. It was only in the last 10 or so years, when prices skyrocketed, did these museum-grade specimens surface in quantities.

Ty Cobb is a slightly different story. The Georgia Peach lived into the early part of the 1960s well after the hobby became organized in the 1950s. Hence, post–1950 museum-grade Cobb singles are available, but the vast majority of these are likely forgeries. If you made a big enough donation to the Cobb Educational Foundation, Cobb would mail you a signed baseball along with a nice letter. Accordingly, I can remember museum-grade single-signed Cobb balls being available in the 1980s. There are many nice Cobb balls in the market. In recent years values have seen a material increase. A signed Cobb ball sold for $5,300 in 2011 (Legendary Auctions), despite the fact that the signature was somewhat faded.

Single-signed balls really did not become the "in thing" to collect until the 1950s and then only the stars were presented with balls to sign. Single-signed balls of Rogers Hornsby, Cy Young, Tris Speaker, Nap Lajoie, and Honus Wagner are available but rare. Single-signed balls of most Hall of Famers that died before 1950 are exceedingly rare and many don't exist at all. If you are looking for Amos Rusie, Mickey Welch, Bid McPhee, Joe Kelley, and the like you will be looking until the day you die.

The only Hall of Famers that died before 1945 that you may find on single-signed balls are those that stayed close to the game. John McGraw who died in 1934, Charlie Comiskey who died in 1931, and Roger Bresnahan who died in 1944 are very rare on single-signed balls but a specimen or two exist of each. These men were involved with the game after their playing careers ended, providing an opportunity for a forward-thinking collector to obtain a signed ball. Lou Gehrig is another exception. He was such a popular star that fans were obtaining his signature on balls for years.

For those players that retired long ago and drifted into obscurity, locating a single-signed ball of say Rusie or McPhee is very unlikely. One, single-signed balls were not actively collected before the 1950s. Two, the whereabouts of these long retired players were not known. These two factors should logically tell you that single-signed balls of the old-timers just aren't around.

The following is a list of Hall of Famers, based on my observations, whose signatures do not exist on single-signed balls: Cap Anson, Jacob Beckley, Dan Brouthers, Ray Brown, Morgan Bulkeley, Alexander Cartwright, Henry Chadwick, Frank Chance, Oscar Charleston, Jack Chesbro, John Clarkson, Jimmy Collins, Roger Connor, Andy Cooper, Arthur Cummings, George Davis, Ed Delahanty, Martin Dihigo, Barney Dreyfuss, Buck Ewing, Rube Foster, Willie Foster, Pud Galvin, Josh Gibson, Frank Grant, Billy Hamilton, Ed Hanlon, Pete Hill, William Hulbert, Hugh Jennings, Addie Joss, Tim Keefe, Willie Keeler, Joe Kelley, Mike Kelly, Biz Mackey, Christy Mathewson, Tom McCarthy, Joe McGinnity, Bid McPhee, Jose Mendez, Jim O'Rourke, Ed Plank, Alex Pompez, Cum Posey, Charles Radbourn, Amos Rusie, Louis Santop, Frank Selee, Albert Spalding, Mule Suttles, Ben Taylor, Sam Thompson, Cristobal Torriente, Rube Waddell, John Ward, Mickey Welch, Sol White, J. L. Wilkinson, Vic Willis, Jud Wilson, George Wright, Harry Wright, and Ross Youngs.

Miller Huggins and Ban Johnson are not on this list because they were close to the game until their deaths and thus had opportunities to sign baseballs, though I have never seen a genuine single-signed baseball of either man.

It should be further noted that most of the above Hall of Famers cannot be found on any baseballs, single-signed or otherwise. From the above list I have examined genuine signed baseballs of Chesbro, Jennings, Dihigo, Gibson, Plank, Youngs, and McGinnity. Recently, I saw a multi-signed Mathewson ball that I would pronounce as genuine, but it is the only one I know of.

For many years there was a story floating around that the Hall of Famers would sign dozens of baseballs when they visited the Hall of Fame. The collection at Cooperstown is said to have many single-signed baseballs of Burkett, Nichols, Alexander, and the rest of the Hall of Famers. Jim Gates, library director at the Baseball Hall of Fame, confirmed this practice does occur but that it did not start until 1960.

The main focus of collectors has always been members of the Hall of Fame. So if you think single-signed baseballs of the long deceased Hall of Famers are tough, then non–Hall of Famers are even tougher. Very few collectors were wise enough to obtain signatures of the non–Hall of Fame stars on a baseball. Collecting the non–Hall of Fame signatures as singles did not become fashionable until the mid–1970s. A few collectors were collecting singles before that time but there was only a handful of them.

Your focus should be on players that are generally known to have signed balls. A reputable dealer can point you in the right direction. In general, stay away from the Hall of Famers that died before 1950. There are plenty of signed baseballs of Hall of Famers that lived into the 1970s. These balls can be purchased for $1,000 or less. Rube Mar-quard, Max Carey, Freddie Lindstrom, and Jesse Haines come to mind. I would also advise you not to spend a lot of money on either current Hall of Famers or recently deceased players like Jim Palmer, Cal Ripken, Enos Slaughter, Rod Carew, and Rick Ferrell. The supply is just too great.

The Ultimate Collection

For those of you that are trying to complete a signed Hall of Fame set, my advice to you is don't. This is an impossible task. No one has a complete set and no one will ever have one. It is not possible to assemble a complete set, since it is easier to find a cure for cancer than it is to obtain a signature of every Hall of Famer.

There are certain signatures that are so rare they have never been offered in the market and likely never will. There is great debate as to what these signatures actually look like. Franklin Grant and Tim Keefe are good examples.

In recent years the Baseball Hall of Fame has cataloged collections that were donated years ago, such as the Frederick Long and August Herrmann collections. Many ultra rare signatures have been found in these collections. These signatures, of course, are not, nor will they ever be, available in the market. It is very possible that the Hall has many more rare signatures. As collections are documented, more signatures will, no doubt, be discovered.

Team-Signed Baseballs

Team-signed baseballs are very popular among collectors as they are an excellent way to obtain many signatures on one item. Like single-signed baseballs, though, this area of collecting is fraught with danger. Skilled forgers have focused on vintage team baseballs simply because they are so valuable. In general, collecting entire teams on baseballs did not become fashionable until the 1920s when the "rabbit" ball was introduced.

During my 30-plus years of collecting I have examined at least 100 pre–1920 signed team balls, either by physical examination or through detailed photographs. Many came with certificates of authenticity. Many have been sold by the major auction houses. However, I have examined only three pre–1920 signed team balls that I would pronounce as genuine.

The 1930s saw the popularity of signed team balls increase. Clubs would have balls signed by the entire team, which were given to VIPs and sportswriters as gifts. Former Tigers shortstop Billy Rogell once told me that he and his teammates would sign dozens of balls at one sitting for management to distribute.

Today, signed team balls are a treasured part of the national pastime and are in high demand. World Series signed team balls are in the most demand, for example the 1984 Detroit Tigers. A signed team ball of the 1984 Tigers is valued at approximately $500. On the other hand, a 1983 or 1985 Tigers ball, which basically had the same roster, is worth only about $100. The difference is the World Series that the 1984 team captured. The most treasured World Series ball is the 1927 Yankees, which contains many stars including Ruth and Gehrig. In 2008 a nice specimen sold for $38,000 (Robert Edward Auctions). A similar ball sold for $37,000 in 2005 (Mastro).

It is a good idea to focus on team balls that contain major stars or those teams that had a star player die young. I know that sounds cold and unfeeling but the market is the market. A baseball signed by the minor league 1937 Newark Bears sold for $705 in 2009 (Robert Edward Auctions). It contained a rare signature of future Reds catcher Willard Hershberger, who committed suicide in 1940. The scarcity of his signature enhanced the value of an otherwise worthless ball.

Yankees team balls are consistently the highest valued simply because of the unending supply of great stars. The signatures of Gehrig, Ruth, Shocker, Berra, Dickey, Pennock, Lazzeri, DiMaggio, Mantle, Maris, Munson, Ruffing, and Ford make a New York Yankees team ball so valuable.

A ball signed by an entire team is worth the most. If a signed team ball is missing a minor star, then the value will still hold. However, if a major star has not signed the ball, then the value is cut significantly. As an illustration, a 1926 Detroit Tigers team ball would have been signed by Ty Cobb, Harry Heilmann, Heinie Manush, Lu Blue, and Bob Fothergill. These are all desirable names, especially Cobb, who is the key signature on the ball. A complete signed 1926 Detroit Tigers team ball is worth about $3000 to $4000. If the ball is missing a signature of Frank O'Rourke or Ed Wells, both minor stars, the value of the ball would not decrease. On the other hand, if the ball is missing Cobb's signature, then the value drops markedly and is worth no more than $1000. It is a good idea to study teams and make sure when you purchase a signed team ball that all the major stars have signed.

Even though a lackluster team is of lesser value its team ball is still worth collecting and still holds lots of memories. My favorite team ball is a 1978 Tigers ball. Nothing great but it brings back many fond memories of my youth.

Sometimes really bad teams are worth a lot simply because they were so bad. The St. Louis Browns are always a valuable ball no matter what year. A team-signed baseball of the 1952 Browns sold for $747 in 2006 (Mastro). That is a strong price considering the forgettable nature of the team. The 2003 Tigers, with their record breaking loss season, is another good ball to obtain. These teams attain a cult status of sorts.

Many team balls have been produced by forgers. I have seen hundreds of fake balls over the years, from the 1910s to the 1970s and all years in between. Based on my observations the following are the most commonly forged team baseballs:

- 1933 American League All-Star team. Many forgeries exist and the ones I have seen are signed by Ruth on the sweet spot. Some of these balls seem to be overly browned as if they were stained by tea.
- 1920s New York Yankees. These teams are the most forged of any team balls. Ruth, Gehrig, Huggins, Lazzeri, and Pennock are highly valued as is the very rare Urban Shocker signature. Shocker died of pneumonia in 1928. His lifetime record of 187 wins against only 117 losses makes him a prime candidate for the Hall of Fame.
- 1912–1920 Detroit Tigers. Many forged Dead Ball Era team balls of the Bengals exist. It is likely the combination of Ty Cobb, Sam Crawford, Harry Heilmann, and the very rare Hugh Jennings signature that attracts forgers. The signatures on these balls appear thicker. Some signatures, like Wally Pipp, are signed in print rather than in cursive. The forger also signs Cobb's name with an ugly and labored paraph that goes back and forth three to four times. These balls contain forgeries that are rudimentary in con-

struction. Some have a drawing of a tiger's head on a side panel. Given that these baseballs all exhibit a similar hand, it is clear that one forger is responsible for producing them.

- 1929–1931 Philadelphia Athletics. The great Athletic teams of the Depression era with an assortment of Hall of Famers such as Mickey Cochrane, Al Simmons, Jimmie Foxx, and Lefty Grove are frequently targeted. It should be noted that one forger also creates signed team sheets as well.

- 1926–1928 Philadelphia Athletics. These balls are a favorite target of forgers simply because of the multitudes of major stars: Ty Cobb, Tris Speaker, Eddie Collins, Zack Wheat, Connie Mack, Mickey Cochrane, Al Simmons, Lefty Grove, and Jimmie Foxx. It should be noted that one forger also creates signed team sheets as well.

- 1919–1920 Chicago White Sox. Probably the highest valued team ball in the hobby. Many forged balls exist with Manager William Gleason's signature penned on the sweet spot. Some signatures are signed in print rather than in cursive. Joe Jackson, though illiterate, could, at this time, sign his name but rarely did so. Jackson, later in life, delegated autograph duties to his wife. As of 2012, I know of no confirmed examples of a 1919 or 1920 Chicago White Sox signed team ball. If any were signed, they are probably lost to history.

- 1914 Boston Red Sox: This was Babe Ruth's rookie year, so it is another ball that is commonly forged. A genuine team ball with a Ruth rookie signature would be national treasure. Unfortunately, they likely do not exist. I have examined three specimens that all were poorly executed forgeries. The signatures are shaky in appearance and were executed by the same forger.

There are several things to look for when examining signed team balls. First, the flow of the ink. Forged balls will typically evidence signatures with a labored appearance. The forgeries will lack rapid flow found in genuine signatures. Due to the labored appearance, the thickness of ink will be wide and uniform among all the forgeries. This is a telltale sign that the autographs were methodically signed by the same hand. A genuine signed team ball should have ink strokes of various thickness, some thin, some fat, some in between as each person signs differently. These forged balls will typically lack the racing effect — that is, ink strokes that touch down and leave the paper, creating a tailing effect (see chapter 2 for a full discussion of the racing effect).

Another error many forgers make, or I should say used to make, is they evenly space the forgeries from one another. On a genuine signed team ball some signatures will touch each other. Ink lines will cross, evincing a rapid signing hand as one would expect. A lot of forged team balls will have signatures that are evenly spaced apart. The signatures do not touch each other. It gives the ball a slightly uniform look. Recently, forgers have corrected this error as I have examined forged balls where the signatures touch each other.

If you examine a signed team ball that exhibits any of the above flaws, it should be considered suspect and purchase avoided.

Potential Hall of Famers

A player that is granted entrance into the Hall of Fame stands among the immortals of the game and shall be forever remembered. Throughout the years only a scarce few men, and one woman, have been so honored with a bronze plaque in Cooperstown. Once a player achieves the Hall of Fame the demand for his signature explodes. Many old-time stars of the game still patiently wait for induction into the Hall of Fame. The possible induction of a player will increase the value of his signature, as collectors often speculate on who will be the next inductee. It is always a good idea to stock up on players that will eventually make the Hall of Fame.

The financial rewards can be great. Take, for example, Vic Willis who died in 1947. For years his signature could be purchased for under $100. Willis, a 249-game winner, was often mentioned as a potential Hall of Famer. When he was finally inducted in 1995 the value of his signature increased. In 2008, a Willis-signed business card sold for $9,075 (Lelands.com).

Before his induction into the Hall of Fame Barney Dreyfuss was of little interest. Signed letters could be purchased for a couple of hundred dollars. He was inducted into the Hall of Fame in 2008. Shortly thereafter an exceptional signed letter sold for $9,000 (Mastro). Dreyfuss letters of average disposition still command good prices. A signed typed letter from 1930 sold for $1,875 in 2009 (Lelands.com).

Those often mentioned as future members of the Hall of Fame are Bobby Veach, Ed Reulbach, Urban Shocker, Sam Leever, Mel Harder, Roger "Doc" Cramer, Tony Mullane, Deacon Phillippe, Frank Navin, Lefty O'Doul, President George W. Bush, Ken Williams, Babe Herman, Steve Garvey, General Abner Doubleday, Buzzy Bavasi, Jim Kaat, Charlie Finley, Ron Guidry, Harvey Kuenn, Allie Reynolds, Billy Rogell,

Riggs Stephenson, Rusty Staub, Gus Weyhing, Jess Tannehill, Tommy John, Gil Hodges, Pete Browning, and George Van Haltren. Also many umpires are on the list including Tim Hurst, Shag Crawford, Beans Reardon, Hank O'Day, Silk O'Loughlin, Bill Summers, and Negro League umpire Bob Motley. It is also a good idea to obtain signatures of baseball commissioners and league presidents such as Bart Giamatti, Bud Selig, Fay Vincent, Bobby Brown, John Heydler, Leonard Coleman, Gene Budig, and Chub Feeney.

Game-Used Bats

What area of sports memorabilia is the most frequent target of fraud? The answer is easy: game-used bats.

Back in the mid–1980s I spoke with Hall of Famer Joe Sewell. During our phone conversation the question of game-used equipment came up. I asked him if he had any old bats that he used in the big leagues. His answer surprised me. He said that once your bat was cracked, "it was used as kindling wood." Sewell further stated that he never saved any of his bats.

In a letter I received from Bobby Doerr in June 2011, Doerr confirmed fellow Hall of Famer Sewell's statement. In regards to broken bats, Doerr stated: "Bat boys threw them out, I never kept mine." Doerr further wrote that "players did not care about broken bats."

These statements contradict the experts of the game-used bat trade. For years I have seen many store-bought bats and bats that were never within 500 miles of a major league game sold as game-used in the big leagues. I have spoken to many honest dealers who sell vintage game-used bats and they will admit that there is no way to tell for sure if a bat was game-used. Think about it, how can you tell if a bat was used in the major leagues? It is a bit like saying that a bat was, at one time, in the state of Michigan. There is no way to prove it, so a collector must take a leap of faith.

Bats that were used by the old-time stars likely do not exist. I often shake my head at collectors that spend big money on game used bats of the old-time Hall of Famers. The chances of obtaining a genuine used major league bat from the 1930s and before are slim.

Modern game-used bats are another story, since these can be verified. Today, Major League Baseball understands the need for this type of collectible so clubs will release bats with proper documentation. Another thing that can be done is to have the game-used bat signed by the player and have him notate on the bat that it was used in major league play. Since handwriting can be verified, this will confirm major league use.

Famous Hair

This is actually an odd collectible and seems to go hand in hand with the autograph hobby. For years some collectors have tried to accumulate hair of famous men and women of history. I have seen hair that purportedly came from Cobb, Ruth, Napoleon, Adolf Hitler, Abe Lincoln, Mozart, James Dean, and the like. For those of you who collect hair I would strongly urge you to watch the barbershop scene in the movie *The Shootist*, starring John Wayne and Lauren Bacall, as it will answer all questions regarding celebrity hair.

Multi-Signed Items

Multi-signed items are extremely popular with collectors and one of my personal favorites. It takes an autograph collector more effort to collect multiple signatures on one item. The supply of this material is small when compared to other collecting mediums. In addition multi-signed items make an attractive display.

My suggestion is to collect material signed by players linked by some event or team in the game's past. For example, items signed by members of the 1968 Detroit Tigers or the 1961 New York Yankees make fine collectibles and can be picked up at a reasonable price. Many collectors concentrate on obtaining pitchers that have thrown a no-hitter. Items signed by members of the 500-home-run club or the 3000-hit club are also highly treasured.

A museum-grade Babe Ruth and Lou Gehrig signed baseball sold for $95,000 in 2006 (Robert Edward Auctions). A baseball signed by 11 members of the 500-home-run club sold for $1,200 in 2011 (Legendary Auctions). A baseball signed by 25 Cy Young winners, including seven Hall of Famers, sold for $840 in 2009 (Legendary Auctions).

Infamous Games

Infamous games is a fascinating area of collecting and another of my personal favorites. When I was young, two games stuck in my mind. First was the now infamous Disco Demolition Night at Comiskey Park and the other was the George Brett pine-tar game. Collecting material associated with historic games is popular and will always be in demand. In addition to the above games, another popular game is the Marichal/Roseboro game where pitcher Juan Marichal was at the plate and whacked Dodgers catcher Johnny Roseboro over the head with a bat.

In the final game of the 1976 season, the Twins were playing the Kansas City Royals. Entering the game three men were vying for the American League batting crown, Hal McRae, George Brett, and Rod Carew. It all came down to one hit. The manager of the Twins was Gene Mauch. To make a long story short Brett got a hit and McRae did not. Brett won the crown. McRae later accused Mauch of allowing Brett to get a hit so the title would go to the white ballplayer. Though nonsense, the ensuing controversy became part of baseball lore. The Mauch-McRae batting crown scandal is now a very collectible event in the history of baseball.

By way of example, George Brett's signature is worth $10. A Brett-signed ticket stub from the pine-tar game sold for $580 in 2005 (Robert Edward Auctions). A signed letter of Lee MacPhail discussing the pine-tar game sold in 2011 for $85 on eBay. That is a high price for a MacPhail letter.

The rogues of the game are always collectible. Anything signed by members of the Chicago Black Sox will always be in demand. So too will the gamblers like Hal Chase and William Cox. Pete Rose committed the ultimate baseball sin and was banished from Major League Baseball for betting on his own team. Rose will sign items associated with his gambling, including copies of the Dowd Report. These players will be of value in the years to come. Oscar Felsch was a member of the Black Sox. While his career was lackluster at best, his signature is valuable simply by association with the World Series fix of 1919. A signed index card sold for $2,900 in 2005 (MastroNet).

Memorabilia from notable games are highly desired by collectors. The more controversy the more demand. Anything associated with famous or infamous games in baseball will be a good addition to your collection.

Letters

Letters are a great way to collect signatures and are also a way to preserve baseball history. Letters that discuss aspects of the game, player trades, rulings, or an old-time player recalling some long-forgotten story are always in demand.

In the *Sanders Autograph Price Guide—7th Edition* authored by Dr. Richard Saffro (Autograph Media 2009), contributing writer Steven Raab writes: "A good content piece is one in which the writer either tells you something of great interest or significance about himself or a primary field of his endeavor, or provides valuable descriptions or information about an important event." Jerry Patterson in *Autographs: A Collector's Guide* (Crown Publishers 1973) neatly describes letters that are pedestrian in nature: "Content is of very great importance in pricing manuscripts and letters. The most derogatory statement that can be made about an ALS is that it is 'a dinner invitation.'"

Letters are a keyhole look back into the history of the game. If you run across a letter with good baseball content, try to secure it. Content letters are always in demand and will increase in value in the years to come. Back in 1990, I purchased a letter signed by Cy Young. It was dated in the 1950s and written on his personal letterhead. The body of the letter was dictated by Young and written by someone else. The content was phenomenal. He stated that he never faced Babe Ruth and denied ever throwing the spitball. Now if the content of this letter was routine it would be valued at $1,000 to $1,250. Because this letter has some important content, it is easily worth $3,000 to $4,000 despite the fact that the body of the letter was written by someone other than Young. Had this letter been accomplished entirely in Young's hand it would likely sell for at least $7,500.

By way of example, a rare Joe Kelley handwritten letter dated 1940 sold for $10,000 in 2008 (Robert Edward Auctions). The content related to Willie Keeler enhanced the letter's value greatly.

A Sam Crawford letter, signed with his first name only, discussing Shoeless Joe Jackson and Charlie Comiskey sold for $1,880 in 2010 (Robert Edward Auctions). The same letter with routine content would sell for around $150. A Christy Mathewson letter that offered advice on pitching from 1925 sold for $16,700 in 2011 (Legendary Auctions).

If your budget does not allow you to buy expensive letters, there is a great alternative. You can start your own collection of content letters by simply writing players yourself. A letter from Lee MacPhail discussing his decision in the George Brett pine-tar game. Or a letter from Brooks Robinson where he lists his all-time team.

Another type of letter that is collectible are letters signed by those individuals that were a small part of the game. Take, for example, Hugo Friend. Friend was a circuit court judge in Chicago and presided over the trial of the Black Sox. Because he was involved in the trial and linked to Shoeless Joe Jackson, his signature is valuable and very rare.

One of the favorite letters in my collec-tion is from Supreme Court Justice John Paul Stevens, who attended the 1932 World Series. He states that Babe Ruth did, in fact, call his shot and pointed to the bleachers before hitting a home run.

These letters are not only desired by collectors. Researchers, historians, and authors also find them a valuable tool. I will often receive requests from researchers asking for a photocopy of a letter from my collection, which I am more than happy to provide.

There are three different types of letters: Typed Letter Signed (TLS), Letter Signed (LS), and the most valuable Autographed Letter Signed (ALS). TLS is self explanatory and is common for the more modern players. An LS is a letter that is signed by the player but the body is in another's hand. The above referenced Cy Young letter is considered an LS. An ALS is the highest valued of all letters, since it is a letter written and signed by the player (note: a handwritten short letter, or note, signed by the player is denoted ANS). Fortunately for collectors of vintage signatures, most of the retired players can be found on ALsS. It was easier to write a letter than to place paper in a typewriter. In the studies in Part II, I will sometimes refer to an ALS as a "handwritten letter," but there is no difference.

Take, for example, Ty Cobb. A TLS of Cobb is rare while an ALS is common, relatively speaking. Yet the ALS is worth far more than a TLS. As a collector, you will note the significant difference in the values between TLS/LS and the coveted ALS.

Ty Cobb and Babe Ruth

I have often said that the world could be coming to an end and the value of Cobb and Ruth material would continue to increase.

These are *the* two giants of baseball and demand is so great it cannot be quantified. There is Cobb and Ruth, then everyone else. While the demand for signed material of Gehrig, Mathewson, Wagner, and Young is strong, it is nothing when compared to the Georgia Peach and the Sultan of Swat.

When I started collecting, autographs of these two were, and still are, plentiful. Neither signature is scarce. There are literally tens of thousands of their signatures in the market. Signed balls, photos, Hall of Fame plaque postcards, government postcards, gum cards, T-cards, you name it they have signed it. I am often asked the question who signed more autographs, Ruth or Cobb? Given the fact that Cobb lived a lot longer there are *far* more Cobb signatures in the market. His signature is on the common side. A search conducted on November 13, 2011, showed, what appeared to be, 62 genuine Cobb signatures posted for sale on eBay. The demand for these two signatures lies not in rarity but in the insurmountable demand for their autograph.

Years ago I spoke with Ty Cobb's daughter, Beverly McLaren. Beverly was running the Cobb Educational Foundation for under-privileged kids, which Cobb set up in honor of his father, Professor William Herschel Cobb. Beverly would seek donations for the Foundation. If a donor sent in $20 or more, she would send back a canceled bank check bearing Cobb's signature. It was a nice memento that would encourage donations.

During our conversation Beverly informed me that she released countless checks, "over five thousand of them" she told me. Whether this is an accurate number I do not know. I can tell you that there is a seemingly endless supply of Cobb checks in the market. In the mid–1980s Cobb checks were of little value and were quickly absorbed into the market. Today, those same checks, which cost $20 back in the 1980s, are now valued close to $1,000 with checks dated in the 1920s approaching $2,000.

Museum-grade single-signed balls of Cobb used to sell for $5,000 in the year 2000. Now a mere decade later that same ball is worth $40,000 to $50,000. The same can be said for Ruth material as well. Back in the early 1980s Ruth single-signed balls were selling for about $100 to $200. Today that same ball now sells for 5,000 to $10,000. A Ruth museum-grade ball typically sells for $50,000.

The beautiful thing about the signatures of Cobb and Ruth is that they are recession proof and discovery proof. Due to the tremendous demand, economic conditions do not affect values related to these two greats. In good times or in bad, the value seems to always increase.

Another benefit of collecting these two is that the word "supply" has no meaning. If you own something rare, a discovery of the same item will decrease the value of your cherished piece. I cannot tell you how many times I have seen signed bank checks fall in value because the supply seems continuous.

When Honus Wagner checks first hit the market, they were selling for over $2,000. They were billed by dealers as "very rare." It became apparent that they were not rare and there was a good supply. The prices began to fall. Today, that same Wagner check, which cost $2,000 in the early 1990s, can now be purchased for $1,250. The supply adversely affected the value.

On the other hand if 100, or even 1,000, checks signed by Cobb or Ruth were discovered, they would quickly be absorbed into the market. The demand would be unaffected and the value of existing checks would not fall.

Limited-Edition Cards

The limited-edition area of collecting increased greatly in the early 1980s with the introduction of the Perez-Steele art postcard set. Limited to 10,000 sets, this issue featured all the members of the Hall of Fame. The Dick Perez artwork is fabulous and makes for a fine collectible. When this set first came out, very few people collected them. Cards signed by Hall of Famers that died in the mid–1980s are scarce and command good money. The two key signed cards from this set are Lloyd Waner and Satchel Paige, who both died shortly after the release of the set. The Paige and Waner cards would likely sell for over $5,000 each.

Other Perez-Steele limited-edition cards include the Great Moments set. Limited to 5,000 sets, these cards are fashioned after the early T3 Turkey Red tobacco cards. These cards are highly desirable and also make for a fine display.

There are various other limited-edition sets that are lesser known but just as collectible. Limited-edition cards are not limited to baseball. The Goal Line Art cards are popular with football collectors. The Mueller Enterprise Golf cards are coveted by golfing buffs especially since they contain cards of President Gerald Ford and entertainer Bob Hope.

Hall of Fame Plaque Postcards

Postcards that feature a Hall of Famer's bronze plaque are typically signed along the top or bottom boarder and make for an excellent display. There are five distinct groupings of these plaques: Albertypes, Artvue, Brown/Gold Plaques, Multi Colored Dexter Press, and Metallic Plaques cards (which are actually smaller than postcards and made of thin metal). When the "metals" were first issued, they were met with much resistance and sales were poor. Today, though, metallic plaques are gaining in popularity.

The Albertypes were first issued in the 1930s. Starting in the 1950s Artvue black and white plaque postcards replaced the Albertypes. In the 1960s the Brown/Gold Plaques entered the market and are still being produced to this day.

Much controversy exists as to what cards could be signed. There are several Albertypes that could have been signed but many do not exist in signed format. For example, I have never seen genuine signed Albertype cards of Honus Wagner, Jesse Burkett, Johnny Evers, Joe Tinker, and Walter Johnson. Others, while they do exist, are very rare, such as Eddie Collins, Babe Ruth, Larry Lajoie, Grover Alexander, Connie Mack, and Tris Speaker. The same can be said for the Artvue cards as well. Many are very rare, such as Tom Connolly. As for Honus Wagner, I have never seen a genuine front signed card.

For certain rare plaque postcards the value can be great. An Eddie Collins signed plaque sold for $13,000 in 2011 (Hunt Auctions). A Babe Ruth signed plaque sold for $62,150 in 2009 (Philip Weiss Auctions). The latter was the highest price ever paid for a plaque postcard.

As to the Brown/Gold plaques, some are very scarce signed. Goose Goslin, for example, is rare and he typically signed the reverse of the card. There is great controversy as to whether genuinely signed plaque cards of George Weiss exist. I have seen a few examples that are signed as "George M. Weiss." It is said these were obtained directly in the mail. Be warned: probably no genuine Weiss-signed plaque postcards exist.

Signed Books

Signed books are extremely popular. They are a good way to build a displayable collection of baseball memories. Many players have written books and will gladly sign them. Cal Ripken, Ryne Sandberg, and Fergie Jenkins are just some of the baseball greats that have authored books. There are also many older editions in the market that make for great additions to any collection. Babe Ruth, Connie Mack, Ty Cobb, and Jack Coombs come to mind. If you have the money, you can secure some superior signed baseball books for your collection.

Some of the more well known books are in good demand. *Commy*, the biography of Charles Comiskey, was published in 1919. A signed limited edition sold for $2,400 in 2010 (Legendary Auctions). A nice copy of *My War with Baseball*, written and signed by Hall of Famer Rogers Hornsby, sold for $2,130 in 2010 (Legendary).

Another great idea is to obtain multiple signatures in a baseball-related book. Years back Detroit card show promoter Bruce Mugerian had some copies of the book *Cobb Would Have Caught It*, authored by Richard Bak, signed by eight members of the 1945 Detroit Tigers.

Signed books, whether baseball-related or not, are widely collected. Presidents, exploration, sci-fi, astronauts, and World War II signed books will increase in value in the years to come.

Exhibit 2: Joe DiMaggio signed World War II photograph

Other Mediums

There are various other mediums to collect signatures on, such as first-day postal covers, scorecards, picture postcards, home plates, and helmets. An area that seems to be getting a lot of attention of late is baseball and World War II. As these heroes pass on, the demand for their autographs have increased greatly. While many baseball players fought in the war, signed war-related material from these greats is in high demand. Illustrated is a nice signed photo of Joe DiMaggio in uniform (see Exhibit 2). This is simply a great picture and a great image linking baseball and World War II. If you run across this type of material, it is a good idea to purchase it as the supply is relatively small and demand seems to be growing.

♦ TWO ♦

Forgeries and Authentication

Over the years I have invested in many things from stocks to bonds to real estate, but the best investments I have made are in autographs. The rates of return have been phenomenal and consistently outperform all other investments I own. Year after year autographs increase in value.

I started collecting autographs in the 1970s. Back then signatures had relatively little value. At a card show in Southfield, Michigan, Willie Mays was signing autographs for $5 each. While I purchased a signed photo of Mays, I realized early on that I liked the old stuff. As my friends bought rookie cards of Fred Lynn and Alan Trammell, I was drawn to a table of antique wire-service photos, some signed, some not. I struck up a conversation with the seller about old-time baseball. I told him I had $50 to spend and asked him what I should buy.

I informed him I was trying to collect signatures of the Hall of Fame greats. He thumbed through his books and pulled out two photos; one was of Rabbit Maranville and the other was of Harry Hooper. Both signed in blazing fountain pen ink. The seller told me he wanted $60 for both but he cut me a break and sold me both for $50. I was happy as a lark. After I showed the purchases to my friends, my joy quickly

faded at least for a moment, anyway, as I was ridiculed for spending money on some guy named Rabbit Maranville! However, just a few years later I sold the Maranville autograph for $600 while my friends are, to this day, still waiting for their Fred Lynn rookie cards to jump in value.

The days of worthless signatures are long gone. What was once worth little is now of great value. Back in the old days that signature you purchased was very likely genuine. There was no real money involved, hence forgeries were very limited. In fact the only forgery that occurred, to a measurable degree, was with the ultra-rare signatures like Rube Waddell and Addie Joss, but more about that later.

In 2012, forgeries are a huge problem in the field of autographs and it is not limited to baseball signatures. Forged material exists in all fields of collecting from Presidential to Hollywood and all points in between. I have come to the conclusion that the majority of the long-deceased Hall of Fame signatures in the market are forgeries; with the really popular signatures such as Ty Cobb, Babe Ruth, and Lou Gehrig the vast majority are forged.

It is the nature of this collectible that easily enables the creating of a spurious item. Counterfeiting a coin, stamp, or rare beer can would take a lot of effort and money. You would need a great deal of expertise and expensive machinery to replicate these items. But to forge an autograph, all you need is some old paper and a writing instrument and you're in business. For those forgers that think forgery is a good way to make some quick cash, remember this: while producing forgeries is very easy, passing them off as genuine is extremely hard. An expert, well versed in autographs, can spot a fake signature with ease.

Any good signature expert will tell you that there is no such thing as a perfect forgery. It is just about impossible to slip a forgery by an experienced expert. The problem is there are many experts in this field who are not experts at all, and many of these people often end up as authenticators.

Forged signatures come in all shapes and sizes. There are forged photographs, fake team baseballs, and even fake bank checks, so caution is warranted at every turn. The autograph hobby is not for the faint of heart.

Levels of Forgery

There are many forgers with various skill levels. Fortunately for collectors, the vast majority of forgers have limited skill and their work is amateurish in nature. The vast majority of the forgeries in the market today are executed in a crude fashion and are easily recognized as bogus.

Forgeries fall into five categories, with the first category termed Poorly Executed. Most forgeries in the market today fall into this category. Poorly executed implies just that. These forgeries are marked with unsteady lines and shakiness of hand. Much hesitation is evident. These forgeries appear labored in appearance as if signed by a child. Exhibit 3

Exhibit 3: poorly executed Ty Cobb forgeries

shows fine examples of poorly executed forgeries of Ty Cobb. Note the unsteady lines and shakiness of hand.

The second category is known as Traced Forgeries. This forgery is created when paper is placed over a genuine example and traced onto the paper. Traced signatures look exactly like the real thing, but as with poorly executed forgeries there is evidence of unsteady lines. The unsteadiness of the lines is less pronounced than those found in category-one poorly executed forgeries. This is a result of the trace following an actual signature. However, the unsteadiness still is relatively easy to spot. Exhibit 4 shows good examples of traced signatures. Note the methodical appearance and hesitation in the lines. These forgeries will typically be exposed without much trouble.

The third category is the Freehand Forgery. This is where the forger does not know what the target signature he is attempting

Exhibit 5: freehand forgeries of Ty Cobb

Exhibit 4: traced Ty Cobb forgeries

to duplicate looks like and does not care. These forgeries typically flow nicely but do not look anything like the target signature. These are very easy to spot due to the lack of accuracy. This style of forgery is probably the least utilized today but I am still surprised at the amount of freehand forgery I see. I am even more surprised at the number of collectors that are fooled by them. Freehand forgery is typically limited to the really rare signatures. Take, for example, Cobb. A freehand Cobb forgery will be discovered because there are well-documented examples of Cobb's signature and handwriting. Exhibit 5 illustrates freehand forgeries of Cobb. They look nothing like the real thing. However, genuine signatures of Fred Waterman or "Germany" Schaefer or Edgar Willett are very rare. If nobody really knows what a Waterman signature looks like, then one can forge his autograph any old way. It won't be disputed by known examples because, quite frankly, nobody really knows what a Waterman signature looks like.

The fourth category of forgery is the most ominous group of forgeries, classified as Well Executed. These are the forgeries that create havoc in the market and will typically be

certified as genuine by many authentication companies. I have often wondered how many people are forging signatures, but I am sure they number in the hundreds. Only a handful of them are so good that their work fools most of the so-called experts in the industry. Based on what I have examined over the past 20 years I would say the number of truly skilled forgers of vintage baseball material is between 5 and 10. These are the forgers whose work appears in major auctions and comes complete with ill-issued certificates of authenticity. This makes the well executed forgery so ominous.

Exhibit 6 has various Cobb forgeries done by a forger of skill. Note that the handwriting appears smooth and flowing. Hesitation

Exhibit 6: well executed forgeries of Ty Cobb

or unsteadiness of hand is non-evident. These are really good forgeries and will typically fool all but the most trained of eyes. Most, if not all, authentication companies will give these forgeries a "genuine" stamp of approval.

Well executed forgeries are found on all collecting mediums from baseballs to photos to full handwritten letters and are typically limited to the more valuable names. There are no well executed forgeries of Ed Barrow in the market today. Why? Because Barrow is a low demand signature. Bank checks can be purchased for a mere $50. It's not worth the time or effort for such a small return.

Well executed forgeries are created by forgers who not only have excellent physical skills but also study writing habits and idiosyncrasies of the target signature. Well executed forgeries will not only have the appearance of a genuine signature but also copy other aspects of the target signature. Back around 1983, I went to a baseball card show in Royal Oak, Michigan, where former St. Louis slugger Johnny Mize was signing autographs, and I wanted a ball for my collection. I purchased my autograph ticket, which at the time was $2, and headed towards the table where the Big Cat was seated. I approached Mize and asked him to sign my ball, which he signed "To Ron, with best wishes." I was thrilled and thanked him. Mize was a kindly gent who still retained his bone-crushing physique even at the age of 70 or so.

Since nobody else was in line, I struck up a conversation, and we talked for 15 minutes. During our conversation Mize mentioned to me that he never dotted the "i" in his last name but rather would drag the pen to make the dot look more like a dash. I'm not sure how that point came up, but it was interesting to me and his words stuck in my head. Ever since I always check Mize signa-

tures I come across just to see if I can find one with a dotted "i." Some 30 years later, more than 99 percent of the Mize signatures I have run across have a dash above the letter "i." This is something that is not well known about Mize's signature. Were Mize forgeries to enter the market, they likely would not incorporate this aspect of the signature. A really good forger, on the other hand, would catch this quirk and incorporate it into his forgeries.

A good forger will study genuine material and glean certain nuances and then add them to his work. For example, copying inscriptions from a target signature is common. Cobb used to sign a lot of his inscriptions "To Joe Doe, From His Friend." Hall of Famer Rabbit Maranville liked the phrase "Yours in Sports." The skilled forger will add these words to his forgeries to give them a flavor of genuineness.

A skilled forger will go to great lengths to give his work an edge. A forger will search for postmarked envelopes and forge the target signature with the player's return address. Since former Detroit slugger Harry Heilmann lived in the Detroit area, I have seen forgeries of Heilmann placed next to postmarks struck in Detroit. The postmark was removed from a generic envelope and the Heilmann forgery was simply added. The postmark gives the forgery a feeling of genuineness.

The final type of forgery is one authorized by the signer. These are referred to as Secretarial Signatures or Ghost Signed. Some stars would delegate the task of signing autographs to a secretary, spouse, or clubhouse attendant. While these signatures were authorized by the celebrity, they have no value. Some players that were known to employ ghost signers are Lou Gehrig, Joe DiMaggio, Ty Cobb, Babe Ruth, Earle Combs, Red

Faber, Joe Jackson, Cap Anson, Mordecai Brown, and Christy Mathewson. Team and league executives were liberal in their use of ghost signers. There are many letters that bear secretarial signatures of Connie Mack, Frank Navin, Kenesaw Landis, Joe Tinker, Charlie Comiskey, August Herrmann, John Heydler, and Ban Johnson. Ghost-signed material was not meant to trick anyone when they were accomplished, but today many are sold as genuine. Typically, secretarial signatures are not signed to mimic the target signature. The deviation of hand is great so they are easily identified as fake. On rare occasions a secretary can produce a convincing forgery. For example, Frank Navin's secretary could duplicate Navin's signature with a high degree of accuracy.

The key in the autograph field is experience. As a collector you should always look at things with a critical eye. In an industry loaded with forgeries, a little pessimism can go a long way. Collect examples of known signatures and keep them for reference and study. Experienced collectors will build a reference library of signatures to use as exemplars. The more you know about a signature and the particulars of it, the less likely you will purchase a forgery.

Handwriting is something personal to all of us. We cherish our handwriting. It is what defines us, shows our personality, and tells the world who we are. It is also something we aggressively protect. Society could not exist without the written word. Handwriting is as precious a commodity as gold. People do not want their signature copied or used for illegal purposes.

A person's handwriting is second nature. It is something you really don't have to think about. When you sit down and write a letter, your hand just takes over and effortlessly you sign away. Only you and no one else can write like you. A forger can attempt to copy your handwriting, but the key word here is "copy." Forgery is a form of mimicry. The crime of forgery is a laborious process. Sit down and try writing in someone else's hand. After a short time, your hand becomes cramped and painful. Forgery is actually a tiresome job. It is this great effort that is the downfall of any forger, since this labor creates a forgery that will evidence methodical strokes and hesitation of hand.

As Kenneth Rendell writes in *Autographs and Manuscripts: A Collector's Manual* (Charles Scribner's Sons 1978): "Normal handwriting (with the exception of writing severely affected by age or illness) is produced with relative speed, consistency, uniform strength, and, normally, a degree of carelessness and a lack of attention to detail. The most immediate characteristic of forged writing is the care taken in the execution that results in slow, hesitating strokes giving the appearance of being drawn."

There are well executed forgeries that exhibit no hesitation at all, but the strokes will appear slightly different from the target signature. The absolute rule is that any forgery, no matter how good, will always have some small defect that will tell the trained eye it's a forgery. It may be a small defect, but a defect nevertheless.

For a forger to create a signature and make it look convincing, he must not only get down the physical appearance of the target signature but also sign it in a flowing hand. That is extremely hard. The forger's hand wants to sign in its own style, not in the style of another person's hand. A signature is virtually as unique as a fingerprint. There are no two fingerprints that are alike and no two people have the same exact handwriting.

Do not be swayed by the old adage "The

only way to be absolutely certain the signature is genuine is to watch it be signed." The analysis of signatures can be done with absolute certainty. The average person cannot tell the difference between a genuine signature and a forgery. Most collectors cannot detect a well executed forgery. But there is one signature that, no matter how well forged, will never fool you. You don't have to be an expert or even an autograph collector. And what signature am I talking about? The answer is: your own. Your signature has been with you your entire life. You constantly study it. If you can study your own signature, then with prolonged exposure you can study *any* signature to detect whether it is genuine or a forgery.

Reckless Flow

A genuine signature is signed in a free flowing manner that exhibits effortless lines. A genuine signature has a nice bouncy feel to it. A genuine signature is accomplished, for lack of a better phrase, in a reckless manner.

Ty Cobb 1 and Ty Cobb 2 are genuine signatures of Ty Cobb. Note how the strokes are fast and exhibit a wonderfully smooth flow. The curves are nice and lack any hesitation whatsoever. Upon enlargement, as shown in Ty Cobb 3 and Ty Cobb 4, the ink strokes appear smooth. Ty Cobb 5 and Ty Cobb 6 are forgeries of Cobb. Under magnification, the ink strokes appear slightly

Ty Cobb 1: genuine signature

Ty Cobb 2: genuine signature

Ty Cobb 3: enlargement of a genuine signature

Ty Cobb 4: enlargement of a genuine signature

labored and evidence shakiness. This is very common among most forgeries.

The genuine signatures shown in Ty Cobb 3 and Ty Cobb 4 are rapidly signed. The pen almost rises above the paper, leav-

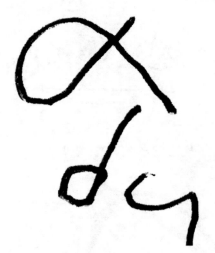

Ty Cobb 5: detail of a forged signature

Exhibit 7: racing start

Ty Cobb 6: detail of a forged signature

Exhibit 8: racing finish

ing strokes of various thicknesses. A forger will have trouble copying this characteristic with any degree of accuracy. The variant thickness in ink strokes indicates rapid movement and it usually occurs in the same areas of the signature.

A genuine signature should exhibit Racing Starts and Racing Finishes. A signature should begin with a faint ink stroke that becomes more pronounced. The end result is a tailing effect from very thin to very thick ink strokes. Exhibit 7 is a fine example of a racing start. On the other side of the coin, the ending of the stroke should have a racing finish. The ink stroke will go from a bold and thick stroke to an ever thinning line until it leaves the paper. Exhibit 8 is a nice example of a racing finish. The overall result is a signature that appears fast on paper and pleasing to the eye.

There is one exception to this rule. If the signer's hand is affected by infirmity, due to illness or palsy, then the racing effect may not be exhibited.

Partial Analysis

A trap that most collectors fall into is to analyze only certain portions of a signature and not the signature as a whole.

At a baseball card show back in the early 1980s, I overheard two autograph dealers having a conversation about autographs and how to analyze handwriting. One of the fellows was lecturing the other. You know, the so-called expert that knows everything but in reality knows very little. It was this expert's opinion that the best way to authenticate a signature was to examine it letter by letter; for example, the top of the "T" crosses over the "C" and so on.

This type of analysis is the easiest way to be fooled by a forgery. You cannot accurately judge a signature by this method. A signature is always the same and always different. In other words, even though a particular signature is always signed in the same hand, every signature will vary somewhat. Try signing your autograph the exact same way. You will find it an impossible task. I don't care if you sign your name a million times, no two will be alike. You are a human, not a robot.

By way of illustration, look at Babe Ruth 1. This is the letter "B" from a signature of Babe Ruth. Most autograph collectors that look at this letter would say that it is a for-

Babe Ruth 2: genuine signature

gery, since the "B" is slightly quirky. Babe Ruth 2 is the same signature in full. This is a genuine Ruth signature, quirky "B" and all. A collector using partial analysis would deem this signature a forgery, which would be incorrect. The opposite is also true. A forger could hit almost precisely on a letter or two of the target signature. Using partial analysis, you may be fooled into thinking it is a genuine signature.

The only way to determine the authenticity of a signature is to learn a signer's handwriting and judge the entire signature.

Then and Now — The Hands of Time

Forgeries in more modern autograph fields are much more common than in the older and more established fields. A modern field is where most autographs were accomplished after 1900. In the older more established fields, the signatures were created before 1900.

Presidential signatures exist in quantities for every president that served before 1900. It is rare to find a well executed forgery of George Washington. Washington's signature is extremely valuable, but forgers avoid his signature like the plague. I have only seen one well executed Washington forgery in the past 10 years. To forge any of the earlier presidents, a forger of great skill is needed to make a convincing forgery.

It is not so much that the forgery is harder to create. The difficulty comes in creating the vintage look and feel of the piece. A

Babe Ruth 1: genuine signature in detail

document signed by Washington is over 200 years old. Therefore, a forger must make the item look 200 years old. This is no easy task, since faking the aging process is extremely hard. How do you age vellum to make it look ancient? Or make ink look a century old? It cannot be done to a degree that would fool an expert. There are ways of faking the aging process by adding certain chemicals. But the addition of a chemical always leaves fingerprints that the trained eye can find.

The gentle hands of time are the only thing that can properly age a document. A forger, no matter how good, cannot match what can only be done by nature. That is why the majority of forgeries in the market today are in fields of the more modern, post–1900 names. It is much easier to create a forgery of Jimmie Foxx or Ted Williams than it would be to create a forgery of a Hall of Famer that died in the 1890s. Most baseball autographs were accomplished after 1900. A forger does not have to fake the aging process to any measurable degree. All a forger needs is a pencil and an old album page.

In my 30-plus years of collecting, I have seen some really bizarre examples of artificial aging, everything from staining paper with tea to burning the edges with a match to rubbing dirt into paper.

Reptile Ink

A few years back I came across a dealer at a baseball card show who was selling an album page with many rare Detroit Tiger signatures. The most notable signature was that of Hall of Fame manager Hughie Jennings. The page was signed in the 1910s, or so the dealer told me. Jennings is a really

rare signature, and when accompanied by signatures of other old-time Tiger greats would be a treasured prize. The asking price was $3,000. As I kept studying the signatures, something looked funny. It did not pass the smell test. Something was wrong with those rare scrawls of ink. Upon closer examination, it was apparent that the ink was artificially aged to make the signatures appear vintage.

Chemicals have long been a forger's friend. The right cocktail of chemicals, ammonia, and sugars can do some pretty amazing things. I have examined many forgeries that used some form of chemical soup to accelerate the aging process. With all of them, one thing stands out: Fountain pen ink, which is usually smooth and flowing, will appear uneven and rough.

Chemicals have long been added to fountain pen ink to change the shades of color. Vibrant hues of new ink turn into more gentle shades of vintage ink. The two most popular colors of fountain pen ink are black and blue. Once signed, the ink will go through an aging process. Depending on the type of paper used and the storage conditions, the ink will change colors. Black ink will typically turn into a dark gray or sometimes a brown tone. Blue ink will shade into a lighter blue with tones of gray. Over the years, the fountain-pen ink will become a vintage color that is pleasing to the eye. Certain paper will pronounce the toning. For example, black ink placed on cheap newspaper will turn a deep rustic brown, whereas the same ink on high-quality bank document paper will exhibit a lesser amount of toning.

Now enters the forger with his bag of tricks. Certain chemicals mixed the right way can vastly accelerate the aging process. Years turn into seconds. Black ink turns brown and gray and blue ink turns into gray.

It will literally happen before your eyes. Chemicals to accomplish forgery are not limited to paper mediums. These chemicals can also be applied to baseballs. Given the baseball's uneven leather surface, the chemical alteration is harder to detect. Upon close study, however, chemically aged ink will reveal its flaws.

I have always admired old documents, the feel, the vintage take-you-back-in-time look, even the musty smell of old paper. There is just something wonderful about antique documents. Touched by time, they have a regal presence. When examining old ink, you should look for two things. First, the nice mellow shades of color and, second, the flow of the ink. Whether something was signed in 2010 or 1910, the ink flow will never change, at least not to the naked eye. The flow of an ink stroke, on a properly stored document, is as beautiful as the day it was created. Some iron gall ink will corrode paper and vellum, but this is generally limited to ink that was applied several hundred years ago. As a collector of baseball autographs, this will not be an issue.

When chemicals are added to accelerate the aging process, it not only changes the shading of the ink but also its texture. Altered ink, if you look closely, will lack the smooth flowing strokes. No magnification is needed, though it would certainly enhance the flaws. Exhibit 9 is a nice ink flow of an unaltered signature. However, in Exhibit 10 and Exhibit 11, note how the ink appears slightly cracked and evidences a clumping effect. The ink looks like the skin of a reptile. This is a telltale sign that something has been added to the ink or applied to the paper directly.

Chemically altered ink is not limited to fountain-pen ink. Chemicals can also change the appearance of ball-point ink, which

Exhibit 9: flowing ink stroke

Exhibit 10: chemically altered ink

Exhibit 11: chemically altered ink

tends to give it a faded or washed-out appearance. The end result makes the ink appear older than it is. Since a ball-point pen uses a different type of ink than a fountain pen does, the cracking or clumping effect is not evident.

Bleeding Signatures

The easiest way to make a forgery look old is to simply place it on old paper. Most forgeries are applied to old book paper. If you get that old edition of *Alice in Wonderland* off the book shelf and rip out the end paper, the paper looks old because it is old. It is nicely brown with a touch of brittleness.

Back in the late 1980s I was offered some rare signatures. All were signed on old brown paper. There was Kid Nichols, Joe Tinker, Jesse Burkett, and Harry Heilmann. I concluded, quite correctly, that they were all forgeries. I politely declined this treasure trove of vintage signatures and walked away. Upon observation I did realize something: the older the paper the more brittle it becomes. This is key in spotting forgeries.

Retrieve a piece of paper lying around, any paper will do. Take it in your hands and bend it. It is nice and flexible. Now try that same test with 150-year-old book paper. The paper does not bend, it cracks. Old paper, because of time, begins to decay. What was once flexible paper is now weak and dry.

When fountain-pen ink is applied to new paper, it easily absorbs into the fiber of the paper and the ink is held in place. But when fountain-pen ink is applied to old paper, the absorbency is compromised by the paper's decay factor. The fibers of old paper simply cannot hold the ink, resulting in an overflow of sorts. Newly applied fountain-pen ink on old paper will cause a seeping effect that allows the signature to bleed into the paper. It makes the signature look slightly fuzzy. Exhibit 9 is a genuine signature, in which you will note the clean smooth flow of the ink strokes. Exhibit 12 is a forgery accomplished in fountain pen that was applied to old book paper. This is a good illustration of the bleeding effect. Exhibit 13 is a forgery

Exhibit 12: bleeding ink

Exhibit 13: forgery of President Adams with bleeding effect

of President John Adams. The bleeding effect here is strong, resulting in a signature that appears blurred. This effect is limited to fountain-pen ink and will not appear with forgeries accomplished in ball point or pencil.

The bleeding effect is also exacerbated or mitigated by the type of paper used. There are different grades of paper. The general rule is the higher the quality of paper the less pronounced the bleeding will be. United States currency is of the utmost quality and its unidentified blend makes for a very durable paper. A crisp antique note will hold its flexibility well. When ink is applied to old bank notes, it will evidence little sign of bleeding. The same is true for high gloss photographs, little bleeding effect is evident.

Scale

Most of us sign our names in the same manner and size. Take a look at all those canceled bank checks you have lying around. Place them next to each other and compare the signatures. Not only do the signatures look alike, they are approximately the same size. The length, height, and slant are very similar; in other words, they all have the same scale.

Many forgeries fail because they lack the proper scale. Sometimes forgeries are too big, but mostly they are too small. Forgeries tend to be cramped. The smaller the forgery, the less effort it takes to create it. In *The Negro Leagues Autograph Guide* (Tuff Stuff Publications 1999), authors Kevin Keating and Michael Kolleth write: "Many amateur forgers tend to produce writing that is smaller than what would naturally be expected. Some have theorized that this is an unconscious attempt to hide the imperfection of the forgery."

Always study known exemplars of signatures and the mediums they are placed on. Ty Cobb government postcards that were signed in the 1950s should all have roughly the same sized signature. Cobb's hand changed throughout his life. A signed government postcard from the 1930s will evidence a signature shorter in height. All postcards signed by Cobb at this time should have signatures of about the same size. This, of course, varies by the medium it is placed on. The smaller the medium, the smaller the signature; however, the scale should always be the same. Charlie Gehringer signed many Goudey gum cards, and he always signed these cards in the same fashion and the same size. Learning proper scale of a signature can go along way to detecting forgeries.

Point Construction

A signature is not only signed in the same scale but also usually in the same manner with consistent breaks in the hand. I sign my name with no breaks in the signature. Rick Ferrell's signature is different, as there are two distinct breaks in his autograph. He signs his name as R-ick F-errell. Thus all Ferrell signatures should exhibit the same break points. A Ferrell signature where a break occurred between the "e" and "r" should cause you concern.

The Evolving Forger

Today, forgery entails not only faking a signature but also devising counterfeit mediums to place the forgeries on. Today's forger is a lot more sophisticated, moving from signing unconvincing forgeries on scorecards and scraps of paper to more elaborate counterfeits.

A few years back I was at a card show and came across a dealer selling baseball autographs, including Sam Crawford, Goose Goslin, and Pie Traynor. He had a couple of signed government postcards that were dated in the 1940s. One of the postcards was signed by the great Philadelphia Phillies hurler Grover Cleveland Alexander. The price was $400. Alexander is considered rare on postcards so I began to negotiate a price. We went back and forth but could not come to terms. I walked away dejected. Later on I went back to the Alexander piece and studied it some more. The more I looked at it, the more suspicious I became. The card was nice and clean, maybe just a bit too clean. I was a bit confused and glad the dealer rejected my offer.

This Alexander postcard is a prime example of how the forgery trade has transformed. Forgers are producing fake documents, phony stock certificates, and the like to enhance their work. There are many bogus mediums that forgers have created to enhance their craft.

Government Postcards

Forged government postcards are in the market. These postcards first surfaced in the early 1990s and come complete with postmarks that make them convincing. It is not so much the forgeries are of great caliber, but the postmark typically lulls the unsuspecting collector into a false sense of security.

Finding unused government postcards is not hard at all. Unused Jefferson and Lincoln penny postcards are available at any stamp store. Creating an old postmark is not a problem either. Any rubber stamp maker can create one. Add a basic fountain pen into the mix and the forger is in business. These forgeries are particularly damaging to the autograph hobby because of their sophisticated nature.

These cards are very nice and neat. They look too clean. They don't look like they are 60 to 70 years old. The paper is fresh and bright with sharp corners. Some of these postcards have scotch tape around the edges. The tape is discolored a dark brown to further enhance the forgery. However, the tape has been artificially aged. The signatures are neatly centered and exhibit a slight labored appearance. They lack the free flowing nature of a genuine signature. While the postmarks are very close to the real thing, the stamp lines appear just a shade thicker. The postmarks are clearly counterfeit. All the cards I have examined do not have the ocean-wave postmark as seen in Exhibit 14 but rather have a hand-cancel postmark that is commonly obtained at the post office window. Exhibit 15 is the style of postmark used

Exhibit 14: machine cancel postmark

Exhibit 15: hand-cancel postmark

on the forged postcards. Note the football-shaped stamp at the end of the postmark. If you examine a government postcard with this cancel, study it very carefully before buying. The signatures most commonly forged are Lou Gehrig, Ty Cobb, Babe Ruth, Grover Alexander, Cy Young, Amos Rusie, and Jimmie Foxx.

Rent Receipts and Bills of Sale

Another common trick is to purchase old documents such as rent receipts and bills of sale and place a forgery on it. These papers are in good supply and can be purchased at any flea market.

The forger will apply the term "O.K." or "approved" then add a forged signature. I have seen many genuine rental receipts with forged signatures. Common target names are Babe Ruth, Eddie Plank, and Frank Chance.

Pay Receipts

Pay receipts are a medium that must be studied carefully. Though they may look like bank checks, they are not official documents. A good percentage contain secretarial signatures usually signed for the player by his wife. Pay receipts were common around the turn of the twentieth century. A pay receipt evidenced an on-site cash payment, where the player would sign the receipt when the payment was handed to him. Many pay receipts exist that were signed by someone other than the player. Secretarial-signed pay receipts exist especially for Christy Mathewson and Tony Mullane.

File Contracts

File contracts cause a lot of confusion in the hobby. A file contract is one that is kept with the team as a duplicate. Back in the old days, generally two contracts were signed, one for the team and one for the player. Since the copy machine had not yet been created, a team secretary would rewrite the original contract on a blank contract form. The file contract would replicate the original, word for word, including the signature. Years later, file contracts entered the market. They are sold as genuine to unsuspecting collectors. Many file contracts exist including those relating to Charles Radbourn, Christy Mathewson, John McGraw, and other early stars of the game. Fortunately, the scrivener, in no way, tried to replicate the player's signature, so file contracts are easily exposed as spurious with little effort.

Notarized Documents

A notarized document is one where a signature is witnessed by a notary public. Once witnessed, the signature is certified as genuine with a signature of the notary and sometimes with an impressed seal. Notarized documents are a good source of signatures, but there is a caveat. I have been in banking since 1993 and have seen cases where a notarized document contains a forged signature. On occasion, I do examine a notarized baseball document with a secretarial signature. This seems to be more common, for some reason, with Negro League material. Notarized documents will, on occasion, contain forgeries. The same rule applies for medallion guarantees.

Bank Checks

About ten years ago I ran across a dealer selling a few bank checks signed by Babe Ruth. There is nothing odd about that, but one of the checks caught my eye. Something did not look right. The Ruth checks turned out to be fake. Fake canceled checks do exist for Ruth, Mathewson, Gehrig, and Cobb. A lot of these Ruth checks are made payable to country clubs. No doubt other names exist as well.

When examining a signed check or any bank document, look for high quality print on high quality paper. The printing on a genuine check is crisp and clear, since financial documents are of high quality. The print lines on the counterfeit Ruth checks were thicker than those found on a genuine check. The printing was also slightly fuzzy, evidencing a poorer quality of print. These Ruth forgeries were poorly executed. The collector is lulled into a false sense of security because the forgery is on a bank check.

Another common practice is to make a high quality print of the target check and sell it as genuine. This started with Cobb checks back in the early to mid–1990s. Recently, facsimile checks have appeared on eBay. Babe Ruth, Roberto Clemente, Christy Mathewson, Honus Wagner, Lou Gehrig, and Walter Johnson are commonly targeted. Facsimile checks are not limited to baseball. Ronald Reagan, Marilyn Monroe, Charles Lindbergh, Dean Martin, and other non–sports figures have been targeted. They are usually framed with a picture. The glass helps conceal that the check is fake. Never buy a framed signature. You want to examine any signature free from encumbrances such as glass or plastic.

Letters

Like anything else, letters are a target of forgers. Forgers have gone to great lengths to counterfeit old letterhead.

A common method is to obtain some old stationery and place a letterhead on it using a rubber stamp. There are confirmed examples for both Cobb and Ruth. I am sure that it has been done for other players as well. Examine letterhead carefully; if it looks slightly fuzzy or blurred, that is a telltale sign that a rubber stamp has been used.

Another common method is to create letterhead using a computer printer. Unlike the low-grade quality of the rubber stamp, these are much more precise. They are too precise and too clear. Computer-generated letterhead looks too neat and uniform. During the 2004 presidential election, a counterfeit letter regarding President George W. Bush's military record surfaced weeks before the election and caused a firestorm. The letter was quickly dismissed as a forgery simply because the typed script looked too neat.

Another common practice is to locate old business or hotel stationery. Flea markets are a good source for this stationery. This is tricky because the stationery is genuine and has a nice vintage look. Many of the forged letters are accomplished in pencil to avoid the above-referenced bleeding effect. It should be noted that many early baseball players would write letters while on the road and thus did use hotel stationery. Careful study is needed.

In the past two years a flood of forged Cobb letters, on hotel letterhead, have entered the market. These are accomplished in green ink and green-colored pencil. The forger usually addresses the letter "Dear Ron:—" (note the colon and the dash).

Printed Signatures

Printed signatures are those that were applied during the photographic process and are not accomplished by the signer. The most common place to find printed signatures is on baseball cards. Printed signatures can be found on a wide assortment of items. Team-issued picture postcards and the annual *Baseball Register* are good places to find them.

While these facsimiles look like the genuine signature, they have no value. A printed signature is easily identified by examination. A genuine signature will exhibit nice ink flows with subtle changes to shades, pressure, and width. It is always a good idea for any collector to purchase a magnifying glass. Under magnification a facsimile signature will appear as a uniform solid color, usually black. The facsimile will lack ink flows and shading. Also some, but not all, of the facsimiles will lack change in the width of the ink lines, evidencing a machining process. The racing effect is also usually lacking.

Another area where printed signatures

have been used are on team-signed balls issued by the team. Many clubs will issue baseballs that have printed signatures of the team members. This practice became popular in the 1950s. These balls fool a lot of people but have little to no value. The tip-off is the thick uniform signatures. These printed signatures will be strikingly bold. The signatures are usually evenly spaced from each other giving the ball a very precise look. They are usually found on balls with the team logo. If you have a team-signed baseball and the ball has the team's logo printed on it, examination is needed. The signatures may be stamped. It is said that official American League or National League balls never contain printed signatures, but I have run across both with facsimile signatures, so caution is warranted

The Auto-Pen

Robots have made life easier for mankind and they do many wonderful things. One area where the robot is not welcome is in the field of autographs. The auto-pen is a machine that replicates a signature. Instead of having the celebrity sign, just place the paper under the machine and press a button. The auto-pen will produce a signature. Presidents, starting with Dwight Eisenhower, made liberal use of the auto-pen. The convenience of this device is best described in *Presidents of the United States Autopen Guide* (2009) where authors Stephen Koschal and Andreas Wiemer write: "The Autopen easily and quickly reproduces a signature using almost any type of writing instrument including pencils. Thousands of signatures can be applied to letters, photographs, books, souvenir items and more in a single working day."

The modern auto-pen first appeared in the late 1940s and became widely used in the 1950s. Baseball players did not start using the auto-pen until the 1960s but then it was limited to a couple of major stars. Today, the auto-pen is used by players that receive a lot of autograph requests. If you are a collector of the vintage baseball signatures, the auto-pen will not be a problem. You will not find an auto-pen signature of the old-time greats.

Auto-pen signatures are easily spotted. The signatures are uniform and methodic. They will evidence a thick, labored appearance. The racing effect is also lacking. Because they are accomplished by a machine, the signatures are basically identical. If you place two auto-pen signatures next to each other, there will be no noticeable differences. Exhibit 16 is a fine example of an auto-pen signature of retired Supreme Court justice Sandra Day O'Connor. Note the uniform thickness of the strokes and the lack of reckless flow.

Exhibit 16: typical auto-pen of Sandra Day O'Connor

Commingling of Signatures

Another common practice among forgers is to intermix forgeries with real signatures. This is most often found on multi-signed baseballs and album pages. Many forgers will buy album pages or balls that contain several genuine signatures, then add a forgery or two to enhance the value. Exhibit 17 is a genuine signed album page by three members of the 1939 Detroit Tigers. Exhibit 18 is the same sheet with a forgery of Ty

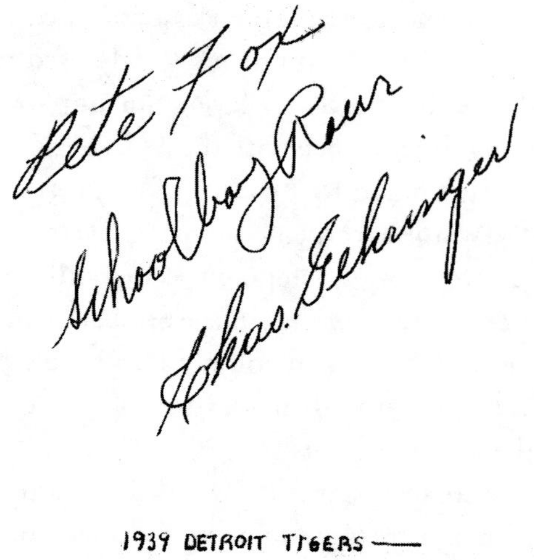

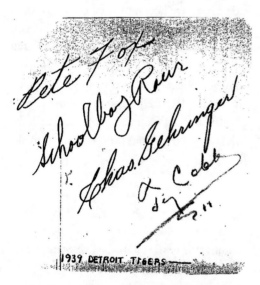

1939 DETROIT TIGERS ——

Exhibit 17: genuine signed album page

Exhibit 18: genuine signed album page with Ty Cobb forgery added

Cobb added. The value has ostensibly increased from $100 to $1,000. The lesson here is to study all signatures carefully regardless of the medium or the number of signatures on a particular piece. Many times I have examined a genuine multi-signed ball with a forged Ruth, Gehrig, or Cobb signature.

In *Forging History* (University of Oklahoma Press, 1994), Rendell writes: "Sections of forged writing added to genuine docu-

ments are usually detected if the forgery was added sometime later, as is usually the case, by the feathering effect of writing on old porous paper."

Authentication Companies

The two greatest threats to the hobby are (or I should say were) forgers and ignorant collectors. It is a combination that affects the hobby as a whole. Collectors such as myself are not directly affected by forgeries. We have none in our possession. But when a collector gets stuck with a fake piece, it places a damper on the hobby as a whole. That collector usually exits the hobby.

If forgery wasn't enough of a problem, another threat has entered the field. It has become the unwitting ally of the forger and today helps forged material enter the market. It has become one of the biggest threats to the autograph field. I speak of the Authentication Companies.

During the past few years many companies have sprung up that will, for a fee, examine a signature. They issue a Certificate of Authenticity (COA) that certifies the signature as genuine. This is a good idea, in theory, but in practice it has turned out to be a disaster. The problem is that an authentication company is only as good as the authenticator behind it. Many collectors and experts genuinely believe they understand signature analysis, but in reality they don't. This leads to countless errors whereby forged material is wrongly certified as genuine. In the *Standard Catalog of Sports Memorabilia—3rd Edition* (F+W Publications, 2003) long-time *Sports Collectors Digest* editor Rocky Landsverk gives this important advice: "COAs are only as good as the company that backs them. A lot of fake material comes with a great looking COA."

As of today, there are many authentication companies of various shapes and sizes. Unfortunately, the authentication companies are making countless errors as thousands upon thousands of forgeries have been wrongly certified as genuine and are sold to unsuspecting collectors.

I am often asked which authentication company I recommend. Currently, I do not recommend any of the authentication companies. The amount of errors made by these companies is unacceptable and tells me that these experts are not really experts at all. I wish I could say there is one company that is the gold standard in the industry, but, unfortunately, I can't. The true experts are the long-time collectors who have nothing to do with the authentication companies.

Most authentication companies are good for weeding out the most rudimentary of forgeries but many well executed and even not-so-well-executed forgeries are being wrongly certified as genuine. I am amazed at how many collectors purchase signatures and merely rely on the COA it comes with. They have no idea whether the signature is genuine or not. They blindly rely on a silly piece of paper. In short, a COA has no meaning or value whatsoever. The only COA that should count is the one in your head that is formulated by experience.

Authentication companies make most of their errors in two categories The first area is the very rare signatures, those players that died before 1940. The second area is museum-grade signed baseballs such as those signed by Wagner, Cobb, Ruth, Gehrig, and Mathewson, and various team balls like the 1927 Yankees and 1929 Athletics.

The very rare signatures are ones that are few and far between. I have seen many forgeries of Hughie Jennings, Jack Chesbro, Christy Mathewson, and Joe Kelley certified as genuine by the authentication companies. This is an area where skilled forgers have concentrated their efforts. They are creating some rather convincing forgeries. Based on my years of observation, I would estimate that the majority of all the rare signatures certified as genuine by the authentication companies are forgeries.

Regarding museum-grade signed baseballs, the sad reality is that most of these pristine vintage baseballs, which I term museum-grade, are nothing more than forgeries. Whenever you hear of a signed baseball selling for $25,000 or more, the chances are it is a forgery. These rare balls come with multiple COAs issued by the authentication companies, but are nothing more than nicely accomplished forgeries.

It is time for federal law enforcement to step in and actively investigate the problem of authentication companies. In my opinion, it would be very simple to bring this fragile house of cards crashing down. There are two things going on here. First, I believe a lot of the errors in certifying forgeries as genuine are not good faith mistakes but more along the lines of reckless behavior in order to generate revenues. I could be wrong, but there is just too much certified forged material in the market. I have always believed law enforcement should employ the services of a skilled forger and then randomly submit forged work to the major authenticators and see what comes back as certified. If my guess is correct a whole lot of fake material will come back certified as genuine.

The problem is the authentication process, which works in the following manner. A collector submits a signature or a group of signatures to an authentication company. A fee is charged, which varies; the rarer and more valuable the signature, the more the fee. Fees generally start in the $20 to $25 range. Once submitted, the signature is examined by an expert or someone labeled as such. After about 15 to 25 days, the signature is returned with a letter. The letter will either state the autograph is genuine or that it is not.

The heart of the problem is that the authentication company's policies are drafted in such a way that they are not liable for anything. They give only an "opinion." If you look at the fine print, these companies require you to waive all liability. If they make a mistake and certify a forgery as genuine, then the collector is out of luck.

Gregory Vartanian, a long-time United States marshal has stated: "Rare autographs, like fine works of art, have long been targeted by the criminal element and many convincing forgeries have entered the market with the help of wrongly issued certificates of authenticity."

Is there some standard to the authentication system? The answer is, unfortunately, no. Here is the crux of the problem. There are ten of thousands of COAs in the market, many of which are associated with a forged item. If one, or all, of the authentication companies fall, then there are countless COAs that will be deemed worthless. Then what? Many signatures will be in limbo and thousands of collectors will be stuck. I cannot tell you how many times a signature that comes complete with a COA is later deemed a forgery or the authenticity is challenged. Instead of the signature being returned for a refund, it is simply dumped back into the market. It is sold again and some other collector gets burned. It's their problem now. An authentication company that makes an error can simply state, "This was our opinion."

For more information on authentication companies and COAs, see the December 16, 2005, issue of *Sports Collectors Digest*. In this edition long-time autograph dealer Stephen Koschal gives detailed insight into the whole authentication process, both good and bad.

Old Collections

There is a big misconception that if a signature came out of an old collection then it must be real. If a signature has been resting in a collection for 50 years, then chances are pretty good it is genuine. If you think about it, why would a collection that was assembled in the 1950s have a fake Cobb signature in its inventory? Back then you could write Cobb through the mail and he would sign. There is no need to forge that which is of little value.

However, there is one flaw to the logic of old collections and that is when it comes to the really rare names. Signatures of Rube Waddell, Adrian Joss, George Mullin, and Ray Chapman have been forged for decades. I cannot tell you how many times I have examined an old collection from the 1950s that was filled with forgeries of the ultra-rare signatures. If an Adrian Joss signature comes out of an old collection, it is very likely fake. Even back then the ultra-rare signatures were being forged. Old collections are filled with forgeries of the really rare names.

◆ THREE ◆

Obtaining Signatures and the Auction Process

Mail

While there are many ways to obtain signatures, the most common method is through the mail. Sit at your desk, write a letter to your favorite player, and ask him for an autograph. Wait a week or so and see what comes back. Sometimes you will get a treasured signature, but sometimes you will not.

When I started requesting signatures, in the 1970s, just about all the Hall of Famers at that time were willing signers, even the big names like Ted Williams, Joe DiMaggio, and Stan Musial. If you sent out requests to 50 Hall of Famers, you were likely to receive 47 or 48 positive responses. There were a few holdouts like Mantle, Mays, and Aaron who were never really responsive to mail requests. Today, it is a bit tougher and many Hall of Famers do not sign through the mail. Some Hall of Fame members, like Andre Dawson, will request a donation to their favorite charity.

Here are four helpful tips when requesting a signature through the mail:

1. Enclose a short letter. It should be addressed to "Sir" or "Mr." When asking for a signature always be polite and use the word "please." A handwritten letter is always better than a letter generated on a computer. It is more personal and you are more likely to get a positive response. In *the Standard Catalog of Sports Memorabilia—3rd Edition*, collector Bryan Petrulis offers the following advice: "In your letter add something that is unique to that particular player. It lets the player know you care about him/her and are not just using them ... players love to reminisce about the past accomplishments."

2. Always enclose a self addressed stamped envelope (SASE). You, the collector, should not expect a player to pay for postage in honoring *your* request. A SASE makes it easy for the player to return. If you do not enclose a SASE, you will not get a response.

3. Limit your request to two or three items. Anything over that amount and you will appear to be a professional dealer. This decreases your chance of a positive response.

4. Send only flat items like index cards, picture postcards, and baseball cards. This makes it easy for return. Do not send bats, books, or baseballs as they may be refused. If you wish to send bulky items, make arrangements with the signer beforehand.

The most important book to assist you in obtaining signatures through the mail is *The Baseball Autograph Collector's Handbook* by

Jack Smalling. This book contains the addresses of just about anybody associated with Major League baseball, including Hall of Fame members, umpires, managers, executives, and coaches.

In Person

Another way to obtain autographs is in person. This is mostly limited to current players. Hall of Famers do, however, show up at old-timer's games and the annual Hall of Fame induction ceremony at Cooperstown. First, be courteous, do not approach a player at a restaurant or in the bathroom. If you are eating out, would you like someone to bother you for an autograph during dinner? Secondly, only request one signature, maybe two at the most. Anything more and you will appear to be a profiteer and likely walk away empty-handed. Moreover, bring a pen and something to sign. I have seen a fan request an autograph only to be rejected because he lacked the above. This seems elementary, but it happens a lot.

Card Shows

Other venues for autographs are card shows and private signings. Most Hall of Famers and stars do engage in these events. A fee is usually charged for an autograph and that fee is usually tiered. To sign a flat item will cost, say, $20. Jerseys, balls, and bats will carry a higher fee. I have seen some card show promoters charge $300 to $400 for a signature.

Inscriptions

Is it better to get the signature personalized? For the living Hall of Famers, the answer is no. They sign so much material that collectors will want a signature that is not inscribed. The opposite is true for the rarer signatures. It is much more desirable to have a signature of Cy Young or Christy Mathewson signed *and* inscribed. The more handwriting the better.

Auctions

What about the rare and vintage material? Honus Wagner isn't signing anymore. The best way to get the vintage material is through a trusted dealer or an auction house. Auctions come in all forms and sizes, from the established houses to the home seller using an online site like eBay. Auction houses are a good way to obtain rare signatures, since they have many wonderful and rare items for sale. But signatures up for bid must be studied. Countless times I have seen forged items for sale in major auctions.

Because auctions are so important for obtaining the rare material, here is some advice from two veteran auctioneers, Josh Evans, founder of Lelands.com auction house in Bohemia, New York, and Robert Lifson, founder of Robert Edward Auctions in Watchung, New Jersey, in response to a number of frequently asked questions.

Q: What signed items are the easiest to sell and what signed items are the hardest to sell?

EVANS: "The better the quality the easier it is to sell. The interesting part is that the more expensive material is actually easier to sell than the less expensive material. Smart buyers want great stuff rather than bargains."

LIFSON: "Autographed items that are most popular with bidders tend to be those of all-time great legends such as Ty Cobb, Babe Ruth, Christy Mathewson, Walter Johnson, and really just about any of the top tier Hall of Famers from the olden days.... In a well-run auction with great circulation, every item finds its audience. Lesser Hall of Famers and obscure rare non–Hall of Famers can be very desirable on the right items, but both supply and demand can sometimes be low. For example, over the past forty years we have never had anyone call us up and say 'What do you have coming up for auction on Rabbit Maranville?' No one has ever called to ask us about what Al Lopez items we have. But if we had single-signed balls of either of these Hall of Famers, they would do great. On the other hand, we get calls asking about Babe Ruth and Lou Gehrig items every day; authentic Ruth and Gehrig items of any quality are always in high demand."

Q: In terms of demand, how do vintage baseball autographs compare to other fields such as presidential, Hollywood, or literary?

EVANS: "Baseball has the largest audience in terms of buyers, and has the greatest liquidity because of the strong dealer market. Because of this, baseball material has had greater growth than other fields but is also more expensive overall. However, the really important written 'content' pieces don't compare to say presidential or historical autographs. That is because in the end what Babe Ruth has to say will never have the importance of the words of George Washington or Albert Einstein."

LIFSON: "We are pretty much a baseball auction house so I'm not sure we are qualified to comment on the relative demand of the different fields. All of these other fields (presidential, Hollywood, historical, etc.) I assume have their own active collecting communities. That is certainly the case in the baseball collecting world, in part due to

conventions, Internet sites, and trade publications. Baseball is a fairly narrow field that is very popular with collectors. But I'm sure there has been a great deal of collector interest in presidential autographs, for example, for a much longer time than baseball autographs."

Q: Where do you see the value of vintage Hall of Fame signatures going in the next five to ten years?

EVANS: "Overall, growth will be steady in the next five to ten years. But specifically the more pedestrian material will plateau while the better material will achieve great growth."

LIFSON: "I've always been surprised at the resiliency of the baseball autograph market. I used to think that all the fraud and fakes, all the honest differences of opinions regarding authentication, and all the conflicts of interest that are inherent with dealers selling autographs would negatively affect collector enthusiasm and prices, but after all these years, I have to say that I just don't see it. I see collectors as enthusiastic as ever, prices higher than ever, and collectors getting more knowledgeable and sophisticated in response to authenticity and authentication issues. With autographs, there are always going to be authentication issues that come up, but collectors are more aware and sophisticated today than ever before. That's why we see certain auctions offering forgeries that sell for pennies on the dollar. Sophisticated collectors know to stay away from many bad items. So the answer to the question really is that I see the value of vintage Hall of Fame signatures continuing to increase in future years, and will all the more so as authentication becomes more sophisticated, and collectors and authenticators become more knowledgeable. That doesn't mean that collectors and authenticators will ever always 'get it right' but the greater the confidence of sophisticated buyers, the more comfortable the buyers are, this is supportive to higher prices. Not only does greater knowledge and confidence support greater demand, but as forgeries are taken out of the marketplace, the supply of believed-to-be-authentic signatures naturally decreases. The laws of supply and demand will always rule. I see increased values for authentic vintage Hall of Fame autographs in the future."

Q: What should a potential bidder look for in a money-back guarantee?

EVANS: "Length of time, any terms or limitations, the reputation of the auction house itself, and their longevity in the marketplace.... However, the bidder should rely on himself more on his own due diligence than on the auction house itself or any written guarantees. Auction houses seem to come and go these days while the pieces themselves last forever. The first thing a buyer should do is try to get a consensus of opinion from as many people as possible that have a reliable knowledge in that particular branch of material. Then become as knowledgeable as possible yourself in the piece itself. That is something that will benefit you for years to come and will benefit you immeasurably in the long term."

LIFSON: "Every autographed item is different and every auction has different terms. I would encourage bidders not to rely on a 'money-back guarantee' as in most cases the term is meaningless. The buyer has to have some type of criteria that he or she is using to assess authenticity. There is always the possibility that one person will like an autograph and another will not. No one is going to sell an autographed item with the understanding that if anyone ever in the future expresses that they do not like a signature, the buyer may return the item. Given enough time, every signed item ever sold might qualify for a return! I've never understood the criteria by which an item could be returned under a 'money-back guarantee.' If it's not spelled out precisely, then the guarantee doesn't have any meaning. Also, the finances and longevity of a seller providing a guarantee is inherently related to the value of the guarantee. If the seller dies or goes out of business, what is the value of the guarantee? (Note: All sellers eventually die or retire or go out of business.) If the seller does not have the funds to honor a guarantee, what is the value of the guarantee? Now I'm not saying that a buyer should expect no protection. If you buy a Jackie Robinson check, you should get a real Jackie Robinson check, not a color Xerox of a Jackie Robinson check. That's a given. But my advice to collectors is to only consider buying items that, after doing their own research, or choosing to rely on the expertise of a third party whose expertise you have confidence in (or preferably both), you have no need for a 'money back guarantee.' If the authenticity of the item (and hence value) is totally reliant on the guarantee of the seller and you would otherwise not have reason to think the item is real or not real, don't buy it. There are plenty of great items out there that are universally recognized as authentic, that you could take anywhere on any day and show them to any knowledgeable collector or dealer and get a resounding positive opinion. Why waste your time and money on items that are questionable? I think all collectors would rather have a real item for a strong price than a fake item for a 'bargain.' It takes thought and discipline. This doesn't mean you can eliminate all risk of buying a forgery with a snap of the fingers, by willing it. But a knowledgeable collector can easily avoid almost all, if not all, forgeries. A 'money back guarantee' sounds great, but it can be an illusion and can even encourage collectors to have a false and unwarranted sense of security. Do some work upfront. Learn about your hobby before spending money. Understand and be comfortable with what you are buying before you buy it. Remember, you should be buying an item, not an opinion. If the only thing that makes an item authentic and therefore valuable in your eyes is the opinion of 'XYZ,' and otherwise you would not think it's real, then maybe you should not be buying that item. Someday 'XYZ' may not be around to vouch for the item, or 'XYZ's' opinion will not be held in as high a regard. The answer, of course, is to stick with items that you are confident are authentic, even if you have to pay a premium for them. The market may go up or down, but when it's time to sell them, everyone will want them, and with good reason."

Q: What is your opinion of certificates of authenticity?

EVANS: "They are only as good as the person that is standing behind them."

LIFSON: "Collectors should not put too much stock in certificates of authentication. They should ideally take stock in their own opinions and the confidence they have in dealers, collectors, and authenticators whose opinions they believe have value. That can, of course, involve a letter of authenticity. But all letters of authenticity are not created equal. If you have great respect for the opinion of authenticator XYZ, and authenticator XYZ likes a given autograph that is of interest to you and writes a letter, of course that is great. Give this opinion the value and respect that you believe is warranted. Authenticators are human. They can make

mistakes. If an authenticator that you respect and whose opinion you hold in high regard likes an item that you have interest in and writes a letter on it, especially if the authenticator specializes in the type of signature or item in question, it is logical that this is very confidence inspiring. It should! But the letter itself does not make the item authentic or not authentic. So the bottom line is: there is risk that naturally accompanies the field of autographs. Do your work. Learn about what you are collecting. Seek the opinions of others, especially those whose knowledge you respect. There's nothing wrong with a certificate of authenticity but understand it is not a guarantee of authenticity. Over-reliance on a letter of authenticity is a mistake. All of these vintage signatures have one thing in common: neither you nor any of the authenticators who have an opinion regarding authenticity were personally there to see the item signed. If you believe a given authenticator is very knowledgeable about a particular signature of interest (say Babe Ruth, for example), and that authenticator has a positive opinion about the Babe Ruth signature in question, that would be very positive. That's common sense. It's not a guarantee of authenticity. I'm not sure a guarantee is possible. It's a knowledgeable person's opinion. Similarly, if a Babe Ruth autograph is of interest and it looks good to your eye, but an authenticator whose knowledge you respect regarding Babe Ruth signatures is not comfortable writing a letter on it (or even worse, states that he believes it to be a forgery), that should be of great concern. Of course, the authenticator could be wrong. My recommendation is for buyers to not blindly accept any opinion or letter of authentication, but to take the opinion into account and give it the respect that you feel is appropriate. It's a personal decision how much weight you wish to put on the opinion of others, whether it is expressed verbally or in an accompanying letter."

Q: Where do you see the value of Ty Cobb and Babe Ruth signatures going in the next five to ten years?

EVANS: "Ty Cobb is probably one of the more undervalued signatures in the market and I only see growth in the future. This is regardless of the fact that Ty Cobb is somewhat forgotten by baseball fans in comparison to the notoriety and weight he held when they first began Hall of Fame voting in 1936. At the time he was #1 in voting, surpassing even that of Babe Ruth. But collectors have a sophistication the general public or the normal baseball fan does not have. Therefore, they will see Ty Cobb as what he truly is, the greatest of his time and perhaps of all time. Babe Ruth is in many ways the most overvalued signature. Conversely, there was a joke going around the opening of the National Baseball Hall of Fame in 1939 that the rarest thing in Cooperstown was a baseball "not signed by Babe Ruth." However, the demand for his signature is so great that it continues to outstrip this earlier supply. But I do see the better Ruth items continuing to pull away from the more pedestrian material. You will see the better pieces (things that have good 'content' and true signed 'gems') ever increasing in price and leaving the more common material in the dust."

LIFSON: "Historically, Ruth and Cobb signatures have consistently risen in value. My best guess is that signatures of these immortals will slowly continue to rise in value, just as they have in years past. Ty Cobb and Babe Ruth are never going out of style."

Q: What is your opinion about buying signatures over the Internet?

EVANS: "If we are talking about eBay, it is a jungle out there. I would be very careful and stick only to people who are known to you or have been recommended by reliable sources. There are some good sellers but they are a far smaller percentage than the norm. But everyone makes mistakes so keep that in mind. Always do your due diligence. And remember most of all, the adage 'too good to be true' applies best here. Don't be greedy; as brutal as this sounds, pigs do get slaughtered."

LIFSON: "Collectors should be very careful about where they buy autographs. Buying autographs on eBay or from unknown sellers on the Internet can be very dangerous. Anyone can set up an Internet site. Anyone can list anything they want on eBay. Including criminals. There is enough danger in the collectibles world, in general, and the rare autograph world, in particular, without sending money to people that are not known with certainty to be reliable and established. And remember: on eBay a picture can be taken from any source. A letter of authenticity can be photoshopped. If you have a problem, you may not even be able to reach the seller. We've seen websites devoted to selling autographs where we believe every item is a forgery. And they all come with 'letters of authenticity.' Do your homework. It's not that hard to stay away from most of the out-and-out criminals. There are many established and reliable sellers on the Internet. There are many quality sellers on eBay. A little networking among fellow collectors, a little reading up on who are reliable sellers, a little common sense will all pay big dividends in helping you to avoid the problems that are so common with buying collectibles (especially autographs) over the Internet."

Q: What is a reasonable buyer's premium?

EVANS: "You are asking the wrong guy here. A good auctioneer knows buyer's premiums are a necessary evil in today's hobby climate in order to compete for consignments. As a buyer, simply factor the buyer's premium in when you buy. In the end, you have the power as the buyer as you can simply say 'yes' or 'no.'"

LIFSON: "There is no such thing as a reasonable buyer's premium. Most buyer's premiums for auctions are somewhere between 10 percent and 20 percent. But the precise level of the buyer's premium should be of no concern to the buyer as the buyer can adjust his or her bidding to account for the buyer's premium. If the buyer's premium is 20 percent, the buyer will bid a little less than if the buyer's premium is 10 percent. It won't affect what the buyer pays."

◆ FOUR ◆

Provenance, the Black Market and Other Things

Some things in life are overblown, where people throw around words not really knowing what they mean. "Provenance" is one such word. It is a silly little word that has taken on a life of its own in the sports memorabilia market. Provenance has led many a collector down a path of ruin.

The game-used bat trade employs "provenance" a lot. In fact I can't think of an area of sport memorabilia that uses it more. Is it not odd that the game-used bat market is where the most fraud occurs? Provenance has grown into the uncontrollable 90-ton brontosaur — with an attitude.

Provenance according to *Webster* means nothing more than "origin" or "derivation." Where did the item you are about to purchase come from? What is its origin? That is easy enough. But for provenance to work, one must assume the world is free from fraud and that simply is not so. If someone wishes to pass a forgery, then does it not make sense that they will fabricate a story to go along with the forgery? If a forger can create a signature, then he can create a story behind it. I often shake my head at how many collectors fall for a bogus story when purchasing a forgery.

Should provenance be considered when purchasing a signature? In general, the an-

swer is no. I have never understood those who use provenance to authenticate signatures. It is merely a crutch used by those who don't really understand signature analysis. The study of signatures is based on the physical construction of the autograph and nothing more. Bob Eaton, president of RR Auction in Amherst, New Hampshire, states: "The 30 years that I've been authenticating handwriting, I have learned that the *most* important step is to inspect the signature itself."

In the December 23, 2005, *Sports Collectors Digest*, autograph dealer Stephen Koschal offers his thoughts on provenance. Koschal, who is generally considered the nation's leading authority on presidential autographs, states: "Provenance is a major problem today with authenticators because too many authenticators can use the provenance to make their decision for them." The story behind a signature has no relevance. Either the signature is genuine or it is not. Far too many times material that once came with iron-clad provenance later was proved to be forged.

Back in the 1930s the Sinclair Oil Company gave out a certain number of baseballs signed by Babe Ruth. For years these balls were circulating and all you had to say was

"This is a Sinclair Oil Contest ball" and it was deemed genuine. Many of us knew that these balls were secretarially signed. Today these baseballs, with the iron-clad provenance, are worthless.

Back around 1910, Hall of Famer Christy Mathewson authored two books, *Pinching in the Pinch* and *Won in the Ninth*. Whether Mathewson ever wrote these books is doubtful. More likely he just lent his name to the publisher. The actual writer was probably an O.B. Keeler type of author.

These books sold fairly well. A certain number of copies were signed. *Won in the Ninth* was issued in what is termed "presentation copies." These were limited-edition books that Mathewson supposedly signed and they were given out as gifts. Presentation copies of *Won in the Ninth* have been circulating for years and because of that fact they gained a semblance of authenticity. In actuality these books were not signed by Mathewson, but rather by a secretary. Provenance was used to authenticate a signature that deviated greatly from Mathewson's signature.

The Black Market

Starting in the late 1970s many institutions were raided and priceless signed documents were stolen. I did not realize how big a problem this was until very recently when I ran across a website called *Haulsof shame.com*. This site is dedicated to tracking down stolen baseball artifacts. The founder of this site is Peter Nash. He has done an effective job in locating these items and having them returned to the rightful owners.

When considering a new accession to your collection, be mindful of its origin.

Consider possible title issues before you purchase. Now you might think that is an impossible task. How can you tell if something is stolen? In many cases you can't, but certain factors should send up warning flags.

In general, be leery of official government documents such as signed customs forms. In the summer of 2010 one such form signed by astronaut Neil Armstrong entered the market and was quickly seized by law enforcement. Another document that should raise suspicions are signed wills and testaments of any kind. These should not be in the market. If you happen to see one, it was likely stolen from the courthouse where it was filed. This has become a huge problem whereby court archives have been raided. Wills of many Hall of Fame members have disappeared. If you have a will in your collection, it is likely stolen. While some have been recovered, many are still missing in action. It is possible that an old version of a will was released by the player's estate but highly unlikely. A will that is replaced by an updated will will most likely be destroyed by the drafting attorney. In general, I consider wills of any kind to be toxic, so I advise collectors to avoid them in total.

The National Baseball Hall of Fame has numerous collections that contain material from the present day and go back to the pioneer days of baseball. The amount of signed material in these collections is mind boggling. These collections contain many rare and unique pieces. It appears that these collections were pillaged and many rare signatures were stolen, in particular the Herrmann Collection and the Frederick Long Collection.

August "Garry" or "Gary" Herrmann was a long-time baseball executive. He was president of the Cincinnati ballclub around the turn of the twentieth century, and he served as director of the National Commission from 1902 to 1920, which was organized by Major League Baseball to settle disputes. During Herrmann's tenure, the commission dealt with thousands upon thousand of issues. It appears just about all of the writings were saved. They were donated to the Hall of Fame.

Today, any letter or document addressed to Herrmann, the National Commission, Tom Lynch, Ban Johnson, Harry Pulliam, Frank Navin, John Heydler, John Tener, John Brush, or Nick Young should be considered suspect and its origins must be investigated carefully as it may be a stolen. Moreover, any letter that is addressed to a league executive that involves payment of salary, salary disputes, suspensions, and games that were protested should also be scrutinized as well. These too may have been stolen. My advice is to avoid any of the above referenced items.

Another smaller, but much older, collection housed at Cooperstown is the Frederick Long collection. Long was the treasurer of the Boston ballclub from 1871 to 1888 and later the Boston club in the Players League in 1890. Every now and then a letter addressed to Long will appear in the market. I have seen one two-page letter written to Long from Hall of Famer Harry Wright. I suspect these letters are also stolen from this collection, so proceed with caution.

A group of letters that should be considered suspect is any letter written by Ty Cobb to the editor of *The Sporting News*, especially long-time editor and friend of Cobb, Taylor Spink. While *The Sporting News* did sell off some of its archives, there is no record of the Cobb letters being sold. In the summer of 2010 one such letter was posted on eBay. It was quickly seized by the Chesterfield, Missouri, police department. If you run across

any Cobb letter addressed to Spink, proceed with caution.

While Abner Doubleday may have invented the game of baseball, Alexander Cartwright is considered to be the Father of Modern Baseball. His involvement in the game dates back to the 1840s. Cartwright is credited with creating the 9-inning game and setting the bases 90 feet apart. After Cartwright retired from the game, he headed west to Hawaii. He remained there until his death in 1892. Cartwright, a learned man, wrote many letters. He wanted to record his writings so he used a letter press, the nineteenth century version of a photocopy machine. He would place a thin piece of paper, known as an onion skin, on top of a letter he had just written. Both would be placed on a press and the wet ink from the freshly penned letter would transfer to the onion skin. It created a readable copy. Cartwright kept these copies and long after death they were donated the state archive of Hawaii. Recently it has been discovered that some of these letter press documents have been stolen from the archives and made their way into the market. Many documents were stamped with an official oval-shaped stamp that reads "Archives of Hawaii." Unfortunately, it appears the stamps were placed at the edge of the letters and are thus easily cut off. If you see a Cartwright letter press copy, proceed with caution especially if the paper is irregularly shaped, since this is evidence that the government stamp was removed.

The Wright brothers of baseball fame were George and Harry. Both the Wright brothers were pioneers of the game. Both are members of the Hall of Fame. George died in 1937 so he did sign some autographs towards the end of his life. Harry, on the other hand, died in 1895 and you would think his signature would be one of those non-existent autographs. Surprisingly there is a good supply of autographed letters signed in the market, relatively speaking.

The A.G. Spalding collection housed at the New York Public Library contains many rare writings that document the pioneer days of baseball. In this collection are many letters written by the Wrights, particularly Harry. But like the above-referenced collections, the Spalding papers have also been raided. James Margolin, special agent for the FBI, has issued the following statement: "The FBI in New York is actively investigating the theft of items of the Albert Spalding baseball memorabilia collection from the New York Public Library."

Many Wright letters were stolen and have since made their way into the market. After looking into this matter closely, I wonder if there are *any* Harry Wright letters in the market that are not stolen. Any Wright signature dated before 1900 should be examined closely as it may be the product of theft.

Values and the Rate of Return

In the signature studies presented in Part II, I reference sales prices of certain signatures. Autographs have proven to be a great investment vehicle and always seem to be on the upswing. While signatures of the current players will have little value in the years to come, many of the vintage signatures have rates of return that are stunning. In the early to mid–1980s signatures of Cy Young, Ty Cobb, Honus Wagner, and Nap Lajoie could be purchased for $10 to $15. Today those same signatures are valued between $500 to $1,000. I can remember signed index cards of Sam Crawford, Paul Waner, Jimmie Foxx, and Eppa Rixey selling in the $5 range.

Strong rates of return are not limited to the Hall of Fame signatures. Material signed by non–Hall of Fame stars and journeymen have great investment potential as well. Back in the mid–1980s signatures of Eddie Cicotte, Dickie Kerr, Pepper Martin, and Ed Reulbach were selling under $10. In 1986, I purchased a signed 1933 Goudey gum card of Pepper Martin for $5. Today that card would probably sell in auction for $500 to $600.

Focus on the quality material. It may cost a little extra but over time your investment will prove wise. The individual studies in Part II will discuss the supply and demand of a particular signature. If you are savvy, you can assemble a fine collection that will increase in value over the years. I know collectors that assembled collections in the late 1950s and early 1960s by simply writing the players an asking for autographs. Fifty years later, their collections were worth over $500,000 and all it cost them was postage.

Autographs, like any other investment, are subject to the current economic conditions. In the Great Recession of the early twenty-first century, the economy was hit hard and spiraled downward, taking many investments with it and autographs were no exception. A 1938 Yankee-signed team ball with Gehrig's autograph was valued at $4,000 to $5,000 before the Great Recession. In 2012 it could be picked up for about $2,000.

Any time a signature is adversely affected by the economy is a good time to buy. When times recover, the value of autographs will rise again. Once again that 1938 Yankee ball will sell for $5,000.

If you look back at the past 30 years, autographs have gone up and down in value. But overall, the rate of return has been highly positive. I see no reason why this should not continue for decades to come.

◆ FIVE ◆

Signature Studies

In the following studies of signatures of Hall of Fame ballplayers, I have tried to find optimal specimens for illustration. I have also tried to include examples of a player's signature throughout his lifetime, if a change in writing style warrants it. Some players' handwriting remained relatively constant, while others exhibit noticeable change. Some signatures are so rare that I was only able to find one signature to illustrate; for a few players, no specimens could be found.

The most challenging aspect to this book was finding suitable specimens for illustration. I spent many years assembling a reference library of great depth. I would have loved to have obtained original signatures for illustration, but that turned out to be an impossible task. Most signatures illustrated herein are from photocopies of good and clear quality. My intention is that no copies of reproduced signatures (such as those already printed in a book) have slipped by, but it is possible given that I, in many cases, did not examine the original. If that occurred, my apologies.

These studies include a cross section of recent prices realized by Hall of Fame signatures. For many of the rare signatures, this is not possible. Certain Hall of Fame signatures have not been sold in over 20 years. A few, such as Hoss Radbourn and John Clarkson, likely have never been offered for sale. The common signatures, such as George Kell and Willie Mays, have a value of under $100 on just about any medium, as noted in the studies.

The opinions contained herein are based on my 30 years of collecting baseball signatures. Use these opinions as a tool to evaluate Hall of Fame signatures, as part of an ongoing education in the field of autographs.

Hank Aaron

Signature Study: Aaron's signature is legible and plain. His hand is bold and has a rather sloppy appearance. Signatures accomplished early in his career are more reserved and smaller in size. The display value is marginal. As of 2012 Aaron's hand remains strong. A genuine signature will evidence no shakiness of hand and one that does should be considered suspect and avoided.

Signature Population: There is good demand for Aaron's signature. The supply of Aaron signatures in the market is great. He has been signing

Aaron 1: 1981 check endorsement

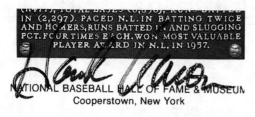

IN (2,297). PACED N.L. IN BATTING TWICE
AND HOMERS, RUNS BATTED IN AND SLUGGING
PCT. FOUR TIMES EACH. WON MOST VALUABLE
PLAYER AWARD IN N.L. IN 1957.

NATIONAL BASEBALL HALL OF FAME & MUSEUM
Cooperstown, New York

Aaron 2: common secretarial

autographs for years at trade shows and through private signings. Mail requests generally go ignored. His signature can be found on photos, baseballs, Hall of Fame plaque postcards, bats, gum cards, and the like. Signed letters of any kind are scarce.

Known Forgeries: Aaron's hand is easy to replicate. Many well executed forgeries exist. Forgeries are typically limited to multi-signed 500-home-run items. It should be further noted that secretarial signatures exist and were sent to satisfy mail requests for his autograph. Many signatures obtained through the mail in the last 20 years have been secretarially signed, as illustrated in Aaron 2.

Sales: Aaron's signature is available. His autograph generally sells for under $100 on most mediums.

Grover Alexander

Signature Study: Alexander signed in a rudimentary hand. There are generally two breaks in the last name of his signature. Letter construction is poorly formed, which marginalizes the display value of the autograph. Most autographs are signed "G.C. Alexander." On occasion, Alexander would sign using his full name "Grover Cleveland Alexander." This latter form of his signature should be considered rare. Alexander was a drinker throughout his life, which resulted in a

Alexander 1: circa 1940s government postcard

Alexander 2: undated signature

Alexander 3: undated signature in full

Alexander 4: undated signature

relative early death at the age of 63. Since he did not reach old age his hand was never affected by infirmity. A genuine signature will evidence no shakiness of hand and one that does should be considered suspect and avoided.

Signature Population: The demand for Alexander's signature is very strong. Alexander's signature is considered scarce on a per se basis. Premium signed items are rare to very rare. He was generally an accommodating signer through the mail but was considered reclusive. Alexander's signature is generally limited to index cards, small book photos, and material signed at the ballpark, mostly in the 1920s. Government postcards are seldom seen and should be considered rare. 8 × 10 photos and letters are rare and highly desirable. The best way to obtain an Alexander signature on a baseball is to locate a signed team ball from the 1920s. It is about the only way to find Alexander on this medium. Single-signed baseballs are in a different league all their own. I have been collecting for 30 years and have only examined three genuine specimens. It goes without saying that most single-signed baseballs offered in the market today are forgeries. I have seen only one genuinely signed Hall of Fame plaque postcard. I know of only one signed bank check. In 1952 future President Ronald Reagan portrayed Alexander in the motion picture *The Winning Team*. President Reagan coveted this role and in later years signed a few Alexander-related items. Reagan-signed Alexander material is very rare and highly coveted by collectors.

Known Forgeries: Replication of his hand is relatively easy. Many well executed forgeries exist. Many forged Alexander government postcards are in the market so caution is warranted. They come complete with a hand-cancel postmark. Another type of Alexander forgery that entered the market in the past 10 years is the Baseball Centennial first-day postal covers, postmarked in 1939. I have examined a few examples with forged Alexander signatures signed "G.C. Alexander" in fountain pen. The forgeries are nicely executed but upon close examination they lack flow. The racing effect is missing. Many of these covers also contain a patriotic looking red, white, and blue airmail sticker affixed to them.

Sales: Short ALS accomplished in pencil sold for $1,763 (Robert Edward Auctions, Spring 2010). Choice ball-point ink signature sold for $770 (RR Auctions, July 2011). Multi-signed baseball sold for $1,993 (Lelands.com, June 2010). Very rare Hall of Fame plaque postcard sold for $26,000 (Hunt Auctions, July 2011).

Roberto Alomar

Signature Study: Alomar signs in a bold and aggressive hand. His signature evidences good flow. Letter construction is marginal. The signature is basically illegible. Display value is moderate at best. As of 2012 Alomar's hand remains strong. A genuine signature will evidence no shakiness of hand and one that does should be considered suspect and avoided.

Signature Population: This is signature where a strong supply outweighs demand. Alomar's signature is common and can be found on most mediums including baseballs, bats, photos, and gum cards. Letters of any kind should be considered scarce.

Known Forgeries: Alomar is a fairly easy signature to replicate. Producing a well executed forgery can be accomplished with little effort. Due to the nominal value of Alomar's signature, he is not the target of skilled forgers.

Sales: Alomar's signature is available. His autograph generally sells for under $100 on most mediums.

Alomar 1: undated signature

Walter Alston

Signature Study: Alston signed in a legible hand with nicely constructed letters. His hand exhibits excellent flow and a certain sophistication.

Alston 1: 1962 signature

Alston 2: 1973 signature

His signature has good eye appeal. On occasion he signed autographs with his nickname "Smokey" but this form of his signature is considered uncommon. Alston's hand remained strong his entire life. A genuine Alston signature will exhibit no shakiness of hand and one that does should be considered suspect and avoided.

Signature Population: The demand for Alston's signature is good and balanced with supply. Alston material is available but there does not seem to be a large supply in the market. He died shortly after his induction into Cooperstown so mass signings were very limited. Alston's signature is generally found on index cards, gum cards, government postcards, and photos. Letters, Perez-Steele cards, 8 × 10 photos, and baseballs are uncommon and desirable. A good number of canceled bank checks are in the market. These are a fine source of Alston signatures.

Known Forgeries: Alston's signature is rather difficult to forge. Most forgeries are rudimentary in construction and evidence a labored appearance. Alston forgeries are generally limited to baseballs and Perez-Steele cards. Genuine Perez-Steele cards are usually signed in black sharpie. If you run across one of these cards signed in blue sharpie proceed with caution as it is likely a forgery.

Sales: Alston's signature is available. His autograph generally sells for under $100 on most mediums.

Sparky Anderson

Signature Study: Anderson signed in an aggressive and nonconforming hand. His signature

Anderson 1: 1984 signature

Anson 1: TLS dated 1906 (courtesy National Baseball Hall of Fame and Museum)

Anson 2: undated signature

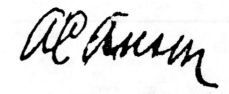

Anson 3: undated ALS (courtesy National Baseball Hall of Fame and Museum)

Anson 4: undated ALS

evidences good flow. Hesitation is lacking. Letter construction is fairly sound but some letters blend together which impairs legibility. Signatures accomplished in the last few years of his life evidence a labored and very shaky appearance. This was due to Parkinson's disease.

Signature Population: There is marginal demand for Anderson's signature. Anderson material is limitless. He was a willing and gracious signer throughout his life. His signature can be found on most mediums including baseballs, photos, bats, gum cards, and the like. Signed letters of any kind are scarce.

Known Forgeries: Anderson is a fairly easy signature to replicate. Producing a well executed forgery can be accomplished with little effort. Due to the nominal value of Anderson's signature, he is not the target of skilled forgers.

Sales: Anderson's signature is available. His autograph generally sells for under $100 on most mediums.

Cap Anson

Signature Study: Anson signed in a rather unattractive hand though it is fairly legible. His signature lacks rapid flow. The signature looks ever so slightly labored. Just about all of the Anson signatures in the market are signed "A.C. Anson." It appears that Anson's hand remained strong until his death in 1922. A genuine Anson signature will exhibit no material shakiness of hand and one that does should be considered suspect and avoided. There seems to be great debate as to whether Anson signed using a capital "A" as opposed to the large lower case "a" exhibited in the illustrations. I have examined a few Anson signatures accomplished with a capital "A" but this form of signature is excessively rare. Just about all signatures are signed with a large lower case "a." I know of no signatures where he has signed with either of his nicknames "Cap" or "Pop."

Signature Population: Anson's signature is in much demand and clearly outweighs the minute supply. After retirement from baseball Anson was elected the city clerk for Chicago. He served one term beginning in 1905. During his time as clerk he signed many documents and letters. Had he not held this position his signature would be near non-existent. Another letter that surfaces, but only rarely, is written on "Capt. Adrian C. Anson — The Grand Old Man of Base Ball" letterhead. These are very attractive as they feature a large photo of Anson in the upper-left-hand corner. Over the years I have seen many signed baseballs, both as single-signed and multi-signed, cabinet-style photographs, and gum cards. I have yet to examine a real one. About the only non-document medium that Anson's signature can be found on are banquet menus that were signed in early 1900s. I know of two that exist. Both are signed in pencil by various baseball figures of the day.

Anson 5: common secretarial

Anson 6: common secretarial

Known Forgeries: Due to the slower nature of Anson's hand, his signature is easy to forge. There are many well executed forgeries in the market. Anson signed many letters and documents as city clerk. The majority are secretarially signed. There are two known secretarial signatures, as illustrated in Anson 5 and Anson 6. If you are looking for an Anson signature my advice is to secure one of the City of Chicago documents or letters. There are also many endorsements signed by Anson. These endorsements are on the reverse of letters sent to the clerk's office. I have concerns regarding the title of signed Anson endorsements of any kind. There are also a few theatrical contracts in the market. Anson was known to do some acting with women billed as his daughters. The contracts are signed as "Captain Anson and Daughters." I have seen two of them. Both were signed by someone other than Anson.

Sales: ALS dated 1907 on City of Chicago letterhead sold for $2,580 (Lelands.com, April 2007). Two-page ALS dated 1907, blank stationery, sold for $4,403 (RR Auctions, August 2010). Short TLS on City of Chicago letterhead sold for $1,972 (Robert Edward Auctions, Spring 2005).

Luis Aparicio

Signature Study: Aparicio signs in a neat and confined hand. His signature lacks hesitation. Flow is impaired by the various breaks in the signature. Letter construction is marginal at best. The signature is mostly illegible. As of 2012 Aparicio's hand remains strong. A genuine signature will exhibit no signs of unsteadiness.

Signature Population: There is marginal demand for Aparicio's signature. There is a strong supply of material available to collectors. His signature can be found on baseballs, bats, gum cards,

Aparicio 1: 2010 signature

Perez-Steele cards, photos, and the like. Signed letters of any kind are scarce.

Known Forgeries: Due to the various breaks in the hand, Aparicio's signature is rather easy to replicate. Producing a well executed forgery would be easy. Due to the nominal value of Aparicio's signature, he is not the target of skilled forgers.

Sales: Aparicio's signature is available. His autograph generally sells for under $100 on most mediums.

Luke Appling

Signature Study: Appling signed in a very legible and rather plain hand. His signature lacks sharp angles. Letter construction is sound. The signature has a high degree of legibility. A signature with average display value. Signatures accomplished later in life evidence a moderate amount of unsteadiness due to infirmity.

Signature Population: There is a tremendous supply of Appling material which clearly outweighs demand. Appling was a willing signer throughout his life. His signature can be found on most mediums including gum cards, baseballs, photos, bats, Perez-Steele cards, and the like. Letters of any kind should be considered uncommon to scarce.

Known Forgeries: Appling's hand lacks rapid flow. His signature would be fairly easy to forge. Due to the nominal value of Appling's signature, he is not the target of skilled forgers.

Appling 1: undated signature

Appling 2: 1990 signature

Sales: Appling's signature is available. His autograph generally sells for under $100 on most mediums.

Richie Ashburn

Signature Study: Ashburn signed in a very aggressive and illegible hand. His signature is unappealing and messy. His signature tends to dominate the medium it is placed on. The display value is marginal, at best. Ashburn died at the age of 70 from a heart attack. A genuine Ashburn signature will exhibit no signs of shakiness and one that does should be considered suspect and avoided.

Signature Population: A signature where demand is balanced with an ample supply. Ashburn was considered a sure bet for induction into Cooperstown. Collectors stocked up on his signature for years. Ashburn's signature can be found on most mediums without any effort. Single-signed baseballs are uncommon. Perez-Steele art cards are also somewhat difficult to find. Some dealers had advertised them as rare but that is a gross overstatement. There is a small supply of bank checks in the market. Letters of any kind are scarce.

Ashburn 1: 1968 signature

Known Forgeries: Due to impaired structure of his hand, Ashburn is a fairly easy signature to forge. There are well executed forgeries in the market but limited to premiums items such as baseballs and Perez-Steele cards.

Sales: Ashburn's signature is available. His autograph generally sells for under $100 on most mediums.

Earl Averill

Signature Study: Averill signed in a very nice and effortless hand. His signature has nice eye appeal. His signature is marked with nice flow. Letter construction is sound. The signature is legible. The display value is sound. Averill's hand

changed little throughout his life. More modern signatures tend to be a bit smaller and more compact. Towards the end of Averill's life, his hand slowed somewhat, evidencing a slightly labored appearance.

Signature Population: A signature of average demand that is well balanced with supply. Averill was an accommodating signer throughout his entire life. He died just before the era of mass signings. Most signatures were obtained through the mail. Averill's signature is common on index cards, Hall of Fame plaque postcards, and smaller-sized photos. His signature is considered less common on baseballs, letters, and 8 × 10 photos. Single signed baseball bats should be considered rare. Additionally, a small supply of bank checks were released by the family but were quickly absorbed. His son, Earl D. Averill, played Major League Baseball in the late 1950s. His signature, as illustrated in Averill 3, should not be confused with that of his famous father.

Known Forgeries: Due to the nice flow and lack of hesitation, vintage signatures are difficult to replicate. Well executed forgeries are very limited. Signatures accomplished later in life are rather easy to copy. Many well executed forgeries exist. In recent years premium items have been targeted by forgers. Forgeries are typically limited to single-signed baseballs and Perez-Steele art postcards. It should further be noted that many forged 1933 Goudey and 1960/1961 Fleer cards are in the market so caution is warranted.

Sales: Averill's signature is available. His auto-

Averill 1: undated signature

Averill 2: 1980 signature

Averill 3: Averill, Earl, Jr.

graph generally sells for under $100 on most mediums.

Frank Baker

Signature Study: Baker signed in a very nice and legible hand. His signature is flowing and lacks hesitation of any kind. Letter construction is sound. The signature has excellent display value. Baker was one of those players that understood the value of an autograph. He would strategically place his signature on a particular medium for maximum appeal. Most signatures are signed "Frank Baker" or "J. Franklin Baker." On occasion he would sign with his nickname as "Frank 'HR' Baker."

Baker's hand remained strong throughout most of his life. Shortly before death he suffered a stroke which debilitated his writing hand. He did sign a few signatures using his other hand, as shown in Baker 4. Note this form of the signature looks nothing like a pre-stroke signature. It is often erroneously pronounced as a forgery. This form of signature is extremely limited and rarely surfaces. It is of little value to collectors.

Signature Population: There is strong demand for Baker's signature. Baker was a good signer throughout his life. Supply and demand are well balanced. There is a surprising number of nicely signed items available. His signature is available on material that could be signed through the mail hence there is a good supply of index cards and government postcards. Higher-grade mediums such as single-signed baseballs, checks, and 8 × 10 photos are considered rare. Letters in any form should also be considered rare. I have never seen a genuinely signed tobacco card. Signed material from Baker's days as a Philadelphia Athletic should be considered excessively rare. Most signed material from his playing days is limited to his tenure

Baker 1: album page dated 1922

Baker 2: teamsheet circa 1930

Baker 3: signed bank check circa 1950s

Baker 4: 1962 post stroke signature

as a New York Yankee in the early 1920s. In the years after her husband's death, Mrs. Baker would honor signature requests by clipping Baker's signature from a check and mailing it to a collector. While signatures cut from checks are fairly common, full checks are rare and highly sought-after.

Known Forgeries: Due to the sophisticated nature of Baker's signature, producing a well executed forgery is difficult. Most forgeries are rudimentary in construction and evidence a labored appearance. About 20 years ago a large cache of forged black-and-white Hall of Fame plaque postcards entered the market. Baker was a target of this forger. Today these plaque postcards are circulating as genuine. Many have been wrongly certified as genuine by the authentication companies. These plaques were signed as "Frank Baker" or "Frank 'HR' Baker." A slight hesitation is noted in the forgeries.

Sales: Hall of Fame plaque postcard sold for $1,385 (Lelands.com, Spring 2006). 5 × 7 photo signed to Mickey Vernon sold for $354 (Hunt Auctions, February 2010). Index card sold for $294 (RR Auctions, June 2011). Signature removed from a check sold for $357 (RR Auctions, October 2010). Signature removed from a check sold for $204 (eBay, December 2011).

Dave Bancroft

Signature Study: Bancroft signed in a neat and legible hand. Marked with a right slanting angle, Bancroft's signature is very pleasing to the eye. His hand lacks rapid flow. The signature appears pensive. Bancroft's hand remained strong for most of his life. In the last few years of his life his signature became slightly unsteady but still maintained nice eye appeal. True shakiness of hand is non-evident and a signature that evidences such should be considered suspect and avoided.

Bancroft 1: ALS dated 1927 (courtesy National Baseball Hall of Fame and Museum)

Signature Population: Demand for Bancroft's signature is marginal at best. The supply of his signature is ample. Bancroft was a good signer throughout his entire life and received many requests even before his induction into the Hall of Fame. Most signatures available in the market exist on index cards, government postcards, and small picture postcards. Bancroft's signature is scarce on premium items such as 8 × 10 photos, candy cards, and exhibit cards. Single-signed baseballs are rare. In 30 years of collecting I have only seen about half a dozen genuine examples. Letters are also very tough to find.

Known Forgeries: Due to the lack of rapid flow, Bancroft is a rather easy signature to replicate. Well executed forgeries are in the market but mostly limited to premium items such as 8 × 10 photographs and baseballs. There are many nicely forged Hall of Fame plaque postcards in the market. Remember that Bancroft was inducted into the Hall in 1971. He died in October 1972. That gave him less than a year to sign plaque postcards. Genuine signed plaque postcards are rare. Most of the ones you see in the market are forged. The majority of those certified as genuine by the authentication companies are in fact forged.

Bancroft 2: undated signature

Sales: Bancroft's signature is available. His autograph generally sells for under $100 on most mediums. Of note: Hall of Fame plaque postcard sold for $1,242 (RR Auctions, August 2010).

Ernie Banks

Signature Study: Banks signs in a vertical hand. His signature is fairly legible but at times can present itself as unappealing. Letters in the

Banks 1: circa 1980s signature

first name morph into indistinguishable lines. The signature is flowing. Hesitation of any kind is lacking. As of 2012 Banks' hand remains strong. A genuine signature will exhibit no shakiness of hand and one that does should be considered suspect and avoided.

Signature Population: A signature of average demand that is outweighed by supply. Banks does many mass signings. He generally does not honor requests for his autograph through the mail. There is a strong supply of photos, balls, bats, baseball cards, and Perez-Steele cards. Signed letters of any kind are considered scarce.

Known Forgeries: Banks is a fairly easy signature to forge. Many nicely executed forgeries exist. Forgeries are generally limited to multi-signed 500-home-run items.

Sales: Banks' signature is available. His autograph generally sells for under $100 on most mediums.

Al Barlick

Signature Study: Barlick signed in a plain and practical hand. His signature lacks aggressive strokes. Letter construction is sound with good formation. Legibility is high. Pre-induction signatures tend to include quote marks around the first name. He would underscore the entire signature with a paraph. After his induction into Cooperstown, Barlick abandoned the quotes and paraph. Barlick died of cardiac arrest, resulting in a hand that remained strong his entire life. A genuine Barlick signature will exhibit no material shakiness of hand and one that does should be considered suspect and avoided.

Barlick 1: 1980 signature with paraph

Barlick 2: circa late 1980s signature

Barrow 2: bank check dated 1951

Signature Population: The demand for Barlick's signature is marginal at best. Though he died relatively shortly after his induction, Barlick did many mass signings. In addition collectors had targeted him for years as an umpire destined for Cooperstown. There is a sound supply of Barlick material available for purchase. His signature is common on index cards, photos, baseballs, Hall of Fame plaque postcards, and Perez-Steele cards. Barlick's signature is less common on bats, letters, and bank checks.

Known Forgeries: Due to the lack of rapid flow, Barlick's signature is easy to forge. Generally, Barlick is not the target of forgers due to the lack of value. Recently many forged National League (Bill White, President) baseballs have entered the market. The forgeries are placed on the sweet spot and evidence a slight shakiness of hand. The first name of "Al" appears smaller next to a very large sized "B." The forgeries are rather rudimentary in construction and one would think easily detected. Many of these forgeries have been certified as genuine by the authentication companies so caution is warranted.

Sales: Barlick's signature is available. His autograph generally sells for under $100 on most mediums.

Edward Barrow

Signature Study: Barrow signed in a strikingly bold hand. His hand is extremely flowing. Signatures tend to be large and reckless in construction. His signature dominates the medium it is placed on. Letter construction is sound but rapid strokes result in a signature with a busy appearance. Barrow's signature exhibits good display value. Most items are signed "E.G. Barrow." Full signatures are scarce. His hand changed little throughout his life. Signatures from the early part of the twentieth

century exhibit little difference from those signed in the 1950s. Barrow died in 1953 and his hand remained strong until his death. If you see a Barrow signature that evidences any amount of shakiness, it should be considered a forgery and avoided.

Signature Population: The demand for Barrow's signature is outweighed by supply. Due to his long association with baseball, numerous signed documents, payroll checks, and letters exist. Letters from his days with the International League are rare and highly desirable. I know of no genuinely signed material from his days with the Detroit Tigers. Personal checks are also available in quantities and can be purchased for a reasonable price. Photos and baseballs are considered rare. I have examined only a couple of single-signed balls in my 30 years of collecting. Barrow is probably the easiest of the long deceased Hall of Fame signatures to obtain.

Known Forgeries: Due to the rapid and complex nature of Barrow's signature, replication of his hand is very difficult. Well executed forgeries are rare. Due to the rarity of photos and baseballs, many forgeries exist but easily standout. Forgeries typically evidence a labored appearance. Additionally, Barrow managed the Boston Red Sox for two years. In 1918 the Red Sox won the World Series. Many forged baseballs from this team are in the market and some are nicely executed. These balls sell for several thousands of dollars because they contain the signature of Babe Ruth. I have examined at least half a dozen signed 1918 Red Sox team balls. I have yet to see a genuine specimen. Finally, while most letters were signed by Barrow, a few were signed by a secretary. A common secretarial signature is illustrated in Barrow 3.

Barrow 1: TLS circa 1910

Barrow 3: common secretarial

Sales: 1924 contract signed with Miller Huggins sold for $2,644 (Robert Edward Auctions, Spring 2011). Bank check sold for $100 (RR Auctions, February 2010). 1930 Yankees payroll check, endorsed by Heb Pennock, sold for $1,100 (Hunt Auctions, March 2009). Letter dated 1936 sold for $124 (eBay, November 2011). 1933 signed document sold for $140 (eBay, January 2012).

Jake Beckley

Signature Study: Beckley signed in a simple and pensive hand. The signature has good letter construction. The resulting signature is fairly legible. The hand lacks crisp angles and rapid flow. Average display value is noted. All signatures I have examined are signed as "J.P. Beckley" and one ALS signed as "Jake." It is unclear whether infirmity of hand existed later in life.

Signature Population: For many years there was much dispute as to what a genuine Beckley signature looked like. The only signatures I know of exist on a couple handwritten letters and that is about it. There are probably under five signatures in the open market. I have never seen a genuinely signed baseball, photo, pay receipt, or card of any kind. It is very likely that his signature does not exist on these mediums. Autographically, an extreme rarity.

Known Forgeries: Due to the rudimentary nature of Beckley's signature, replication of his hand is easy. There is a common forgery of Beckley and it is often signed "J. Beckley" or "J.P. Beckley" with a long paraph that underlines the signature. One of these forgeries can be seen in Beckley 4. These forgeries have been circulating for decades,

Beckley 1: ALS dated 1904 (courtesy National Baseball Hall of Fame and Museum)

Beckley 2: ALS circa 1905 (courtesy National Baseball Hall of Fame and Museum)

Beckley 3: ALS dated 1908 (courtesy National Baseball Hall of Fame and Museum)

Beckley 4: common forgery

so caution is warranted. Another common forgery exists as a payroll endorsement. A genuine pay receipt issued to a Cincinnati player is cut apart and a Beckley forgery is added. These forgeries are usually signed in pencil. The forgeries are slightly labored in appearance and are signed on an angle. It should be further noted that title issues may exist with Beckley signed items.

Sales: Due to the rarity, there have been no recent sales of Beckley's signature.

Cool Papa Bell

Signature Study: Bell's signature is very legible and lacks any sort of flamboyance. Signatures penned during his playing days are accomplished in a slightly larger hand and lack the length of modern signatures. Material signed during his playing days is very rare. Modern autographs are signed in a neat and small hand resulting in a signature without much height. They are very elongated. Though his signature is plain looking, it has good display value. Most signatures are signed in full as "James "Cool Papa" Bell." In the last five or so years of his life, Bell's health declined. He was affected by illness and blindness. Signatures accomplished towards the end of his life are extremely sloppy. Many are just a bunch of jumbled

Bell 1: 1940s signature

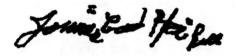

Bell 2: circa 1980s signature

Bell 3: post-blindness signature

lines. Post-illness signatures, for lack of a better phrase, have little to no value and are generally not collected. Bell 3 illustrates a post-illness signature.

Signature Population: There is good demand for Bell's signature. Bell was a willing and gracious signer throughout his life. Bell's pre-illness signature is available but I would not call this form of signature common, at least not on premium items. His signature can be found on index cards, Hall of Fame plaque postcards, and photos. Baseballs, Perez-Steele art cards, and 8 × 10 photos are uncommon. Bats are considered scarce and commonly forged. Letters are also difficult to locate. I am told that a dozen or so canceled bank checks are in the market, though I have never seen one.

Known Forgeries: Bell's hand is rudimentary in construction and is a very easy signature to forge. In the last few years many well executed forgeries have entered the market. Baseballs, bats, and Perez-Steele cards are common targets.

Sales: Bell's signature is available. His autograph generally sells for under $100 on most mediums.

Johnny Bench

Signature Study: Bench signs in a very powerful and aggressive hand. His signature is marked with reckless flow. Hesitation of hand is non-ex-

istent. Letter construction is fairly sound with large and bold letters that tend to be compact. The letters in the first name blend together, which slightly impairs legibility. The signature dominates the medium it is placed on. Overall, a signature with good display value. As of 2012 Bench's hand remains strong. A genuine signature will exhibit no shakiness of hand and one that does should be considered suspect and avoided.

Signature Population: The demand for Bench material is good but the supply seems limitless. Bench's signature can be found on most mediums including gum cards, photos, baseballs, Perez-Steele cards, Hall of Fame plaque postcards, and the like. Letters of any kind are scarce. There is a small supply of genuinely signed 8 × 10 photos by both Bench and President Gerald R. Ford. These are highly desirable and are considered rare. Overall, a very common signature.

Known Forgeries: Given the rapid and complex nature of Bench's hand, his signature is difficult to replicate Well executed forgeries do not exist. Due to the nominal value of Bench's signature, he is generally not the target of skilled forgers. There is one exception, the above-referenced Gerald Ford photos which have been targeted by forgers and many exist. Both the Ford and Bench forgeries that appear on these photos are labored in appearance.

Sales: Bench's signature is available. His autograph generally sells for under $100 on most mediums.

Chief Bender

Signature Study: Bender signed in a nice flowing hand. His signature is marked with nice strokes. The signature has excellent display value. Letter construction is sound. The signature has good legibility. Most signatures are signed "Chief Bender" but some early specimens, those signed before 1940, were signed "Chief C.A. Bender." Bender liked to sign autographs. He would strategically place his signature in the right place on the right item, making for a nice supply of quality material. Bender died shortly after his 70th birth-

Bench 1: 1975 signature

Bender 1: 1931 signature

Bender 2: 1944 signature

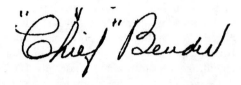

Bender 3: undated signature

day, hence never reached old age. A genuine Bender signature will exhibit no unsteadiness of hand and one that does should be considered suspect and avoided.

Signature Population: There is moderate demand for Bender's signature when compared to the limited supply. His signature should be considered uncommon to scarce. Signatures are generally limited to index cards, album pages, and government postcards. Signed 8 × 10 photos are scarce but some nice specimens do exist. Typed letters signed are scarce. Handwritten letters are rare. Single-signed baseballs do exist but are also considered rare. A few years back a small cache of bank checks were released into the market. Today they are hard to find. Team-signed baseballs from Bender's playing days (excluding the one inning he pitched in 1925) likely do not exist.

Known Forgeries: Bender's signature is moderately difficult to forge, but a few forgers have mastered his hand. Well executed forgeries exist. Many low-grade T-206 cards, complete with forgeries, are in the market so caution is warranted. I have seen many single-signed baseballs over the past 30 years. I have only examined three or four genuine specimens. In his later years Bender worked at Howard Clothes in Upper Darby, Pennsylvania. Several years back countless Bender business cards were released into the market. They came directly from the Bender estate. These are a common target of forgers. If you see a signed business card, proceed with extreme caution as it is very likely forged. Bender's business card can be seen in Bender 4.

Sales: ALS dated 1939, signed first name only, sold for $385 (Hunt Auctions, July 2010). Index card sold for $393 (RR Auctions, January 2011). Contract dated 1944, also signed by Connie Mack, sold for $1,293 (Robert Edward Auctions, Spring, 2011). Full-page ALS, undated, sold for $1,410 (Robert Edward Auctions, Spring 2010).

Yogi Berra

Signature Study: Berra signed in a small and rather aggressive hand. His signature is marked with many curves and is artistic in nature. Letter construction is sound. The signature is fairly legible. Later signatures tend to be more rounded than their vintage counterparts. Overall, his signature is pleasing to the eye. Signatures tend to be fairly consistent throughout the years. As of 2012 infirmity of hand is non-existent. A genuine Berra signature will exhibit no shakiness of hand and one that does should be considered suspect and avoided.

Signature Population: Berra is a very popular sports figure and the demand for his signature is strong. Berra engages in many mass signings. He is a frequent guest at baseball card shows. His sig-

Tel. Boulevard 5430

HOWARD CLOTHES
67 SIXTY-NINTH STREET
Upper Darby, Pa.

"CHIEF" BENDER

Bender 4: business card

Berra 1: album page dated 1966

Berra 2: government postcard dated 1997

Berra 3: common 1950s rubber stamp

nature is common in most forms. Berra's signature can be found on baseballs, bats, photos, baseball cards, Hall of Fame plaque postcards, and the like. Signed letters of any kind should be considered uncommon to scarce.

Known Forgeries: Berra's signature is moderately difficult to replicate. Well executed forgeries are limited. There are no specific forgeries to note. It should be noted that during his playing days Berra employed the use of a rubber stamp when answering requests for his autograph through the mail. The stamp is illustrated as Berra 3.

Sales: Berra's signature is available. His autograph generally sells for under $100 on most mediums.

Bert Blyleven

Signature Study: Blyleven signs in a non-conforming hand. His signature evidences good flow. Hesitation is lacking. The signature is slightly unstructured, lacking precise angles. The signature has a fair degree of legibility. Display value appears average. As of 2012 infirmity of hand is non-existent. A genuine Blyleven signature will exhibit no shakiness of hand and one that does should be considered suspect and avoided.

Signature Population: A signature of marginal demand that is outweighed by supply. Blyleven's signature can be found on most mediums including baseballs, photos, gum cards, and bats. Letters of any kind should be considered scarce.

Known Forgeries: Blyleven's hand is fairly easy to replicate. Creating a well executed would be

Blyleven 1: undated signature

rather easy. Given the nominal value of Blyleven's signature, he is not the target of skill forgers.

Sales: Blyleven's signature is available. His autograph generally sells for under $100 on most mediums.

Wade Boggs

Signature Study: Boggs signs in a non-conforming hand. The signature is signed in a rapid fashion and evidences sharp turns, resulting in a signature that appears choppy. Letter construction is poor. Legibility is impaired. The display value is marginal. As of 2012 Boggs' hand remains sound. A genuine signature will evidence no shakiness of hand and one that does should be considered suspect and avoided.

Boggs 1: circa 1980s signature

Signature Population: There is marginal demand for Boggs' signature. The supply is great. Boggs is a very common signature. His signature can be found on most mediums including photos, baseballs, gum cards, bats, and the like. Signed letters of any kind are scarce.

Known Forgeries: Boggs' hand is fairly easy to replicate. Creating a well executed would be very easy. Given the nominal value of Boggs' signature, he is not the target of skill forgers.

Sales: Bogg's signature is available. His autograph generally sells for under $100 on most mediums.

Jim Bottomley

Signature Study: Most people sign their names in a consistent manner. Every once in a while a person will come along, such as Honus Wagner or Christy Mathewson, who sign with variant forms of handwriting. Jim Bottomley is one of those individuals that had varying signatures. In general, his signature is legible with a splash of sloppiness. Bottomley's signature is bold and strong. As the

Bottomley 1: album page dated 1933

examples illustrate, his signature varies greatly. Hurried signatures, usually signed at the ballpark, are typically signed "J. Bottomley." I have never seen a genuine signature where he signed with his nickname "Sunny Jim." Bottomley died at the relatively young age of 59. Since he never reached old age, infirmity of hand was non-existent. A genuine Bottomley signature will exhibit no signs of shakiness and one that does should be considered suspect and avoided.

Signature Population: Bottomley's signature is in much demand. His signature is uncommon to scarce, at least on a per se basis. Most Bottomley material in the market today was signed during his playing days. His signature can be found on team-signed baseballs, album pages, and scorecards. Signed photos and government postcards are rare, albeit borderline. A handful of signed bank checks and letters are in the market but both should be considered rare. About the only way to

Bottomley 2: postal cover circa 1940

Bottomley 3: undated signature

obtain Bottomley on a baseball is on a team-signed ball. Single-signed baseballs are extremely rare. I have never seen a genuine one in over 30 years of searching.

Known Forgeries: Bottomley's signature is fairly hard to replicate. Well executed forgeries are limited. Bottomley is commonly targeted by skilled forgers. A forgery that has recently entered the market are baseballs. I have examined three of them. These are cream-white baseballs that evidence no use. The forgeries are placed on the side panel. They are signed on a downward angle and accomplished in black fountain pen. The ink is artificially aged to a lighter brown color. The forgery is signed in a slower hand and lacks the recklessness of a genuine signature. Either one or two small paraphs are added under the signature.

Sales: 1931 Major League contract, countersigned by Branch Rickey, sold for $3,525 (Robert Edward Auctions, Spring 2011). Government postcard sold for $481 (Lelands.com, November 2010). ANS, dated 1948, sold for $325 (Hunt Auctions, November 2010). Cardinals reunion ball, signed by nine players including Bottomley, sold for $755 (Lelands.com, Spring 2006).

Lou Boudreau

Signature Study: Boudreau signed in a very flowing hand. His signature is marked with a right angle. The signature is extremely legible. Display value is superior. Boudreau signed in a consistent hand that varied little throughout his life. Signatures from his playing days mirror those signed in retirement. Boudreau's hand remained strong throughout his entire life. A genuine Boudreau signature will exhibit no shakiness of hand and one that does should be considered suspect and avoided.

Signature Population: The demand for Boudreau's autograph is average at best. He was a will-

Boudreau 1: government postcard dated 1950

ing signer throughout his life, resulting in a seemingly endless supply of material. Boudreau's signature can be found on baseballs, photos, Hall of Fame plaque postcards, gum cards, Perez-Steele cards, and the like. His signature is less common on letters but by no mean should letters be considered scarce. A small supply of bank checks are in the market.

Known Forgeries: Boudreau's signature is very hard to forge. No well executed forgeries exist. Due to the nominal value of Boudreau's signature, he is not the target of skilled forgers.

Sales: Boudreau's signature is available. His autograph generally sells for under $100 on most mediums.

Roger Bresnahan

Signature Study: Bresnahan signed in a very refined and eloquent hand. His signature is marked with tight strokes. His signature evidences good flow. Sound letter construction is evident. His signature has good display value. Bresnahan typically signed with his full name "Roger P. Bresnahan" all with one stroke. Most signatures feature no break in the writing. Bresnahan would finish off his signature with a long flowing paraph. Further note the poorly constructed second "n" in the last name. Almost all signatures feature a malformed "n" that converts into the paraph. Bresnahan's hand remained strong his entire life. A genuine signature will exhibit no shakiness of hand and one that does should be considered suspect and avoided.

Signature Population: This is a signature that is in good demand. Bresnahan is a per se scarce signature that boarders on the rare side. On non-

Bresnahan 1: TLS dated 1910 (courtesy National Baseball Hall of Fame and Museum)

Bresnahan 2: ALS dated 1912 (courtesy National Baseball Hall of Fame and Museum)

Bresnahan 3: postal cover circa 1940

Bresnahan 4: undated signature

document-related items, his signature is generally found on album pages. Premium items are extremely rare. Fortunately for collectors, Bresnahan's association with the Toledo Mud Hens and the Detroit Tigers provides the vast majority of material in the market. Many Toledo documents exist in the form of contracts and player-transfer forms. These are an excellent source of Bresnahan signatures. Photos are extremely rare and generally limited to smaller signed books photos. I have never seen a genuinely signed 8 × 10 photo of Bresnahan. Letters are rare to very rare. I have only examined a few genuine letters of any kind. If you are looking for a signed baseball, the best way to obtain Bresnahan is to find a 1930 or 1931 Detroit Tigers team baseball when Bresnahan coached for the Tigers. These team baseballs are an excellent source of Bresnahan signatures. It is about the only way you will find Bresnahan on a baseball. Single-signed baseballs are a different matter altogether. In over 30 years of collecting I have only examined one genuine single-signed baseball. Team-signed baseballs from Bresnahan's days as a player very likely do not exist.

Known Forgeries: Bresnahan's signature is rather difficult to forge. Well executed forgeries are limited. There is a small group of forged singled-signed Bresnahan balls in the market. They have been circulating for years. These are typically signed on the sweet spot of older multi-colored

Bresnahan 5: common secretarial signature (courtesy National Baseball Hall of Fame and Museum)

stitched balls. They are either signed "Roger Bresnahan" or "Rog. Bresnahan." Another commonly
forged item is low-grade T-206 cards that contain
a forgery accomplished in fountain pen or pencil.
In the past couple of years a new type of Bresnahan forgery has entered the market. The forgery
is fairly well executed. This forger takes autograph
albums that contain genuinely signed pages then
adds forgeries to the blank pages of the album.
The forger typically signs seven or eight names
and usually with one rare Hall of Fame signature.
This forger has targeted Bresnahan. While the forgeries are nicely signed, they evidence an ever so
slight hesitation of hand. Another tip off are the
breaks in the signature. With the genuine Bresnahan signature, there is no break in the hand.
With the forgeries there are two distinct breaks
between the "r" and the "P." and the "B." If you
happen to see a Bresnahan with the above-referenced breaks, proceed with caution. This forger
seems to always include a forgery, crudely constructed I might add, of Heinie Mueller on his
pages.

Sales: 1920 Toledo club document, countersigned by Jacob Ruppert, sold for $1,044 (Robert
Edward Auctions, Spring 2006). TLS to *The
Sporting News,* undated, sold for $1,400 (Hunt
Auctions, November 2006). 1919 Toledo club
document, countersigned by Jacob Ruppert, sold
for $929 (RR Auctions, November 2007).

George Brett

Signature Study: George Brett signs in a very
vertical and illegible hand. Letter construction is
substandard. His signature has marginal display
value. His signature is one of the more unattractive autographs of the Hall of Fame members. As
of 2012 Brett's hand remains strong, resulting in
a signature that exhibits no shakiness of hand.

Signature Population: A signature of average
demand that is outweighed by supply. Brett material is common. His signature can be readily
found on photos, balls, bats, gum cards, and the
like. Letters of any kind are scarce. Signed material associated with the infamous pine-tar game
is always in high demand.

Known Forgeries: Brett's signature is rather
easy to forge. Producing a well executed forgery
would take little effort. Due to the nominal value
of Brett material, he is not the target of skilled
forgers.

Sales: Brett's signature is available. His auto-

Brett 1: undated signature

graph generally sells for under $100 on most medi-
ums.

Lou Brock

Signature Study: Brock signs in a large and
flowing hand. Letter construction is fairly sound.
His signature is legible. The display value is high.

Brock 1: undated signature

Overall a nice signature. As of 2012 no infirmity of hand exists. A genuine Brock signature will exhibit no shakiness of hand and one that does should be considered suspect and avoided.

Signature Population: The supply of Brock material outweighs demand. Brock engages in mass signings. Mail requests for his autograph generally go unanswered. Brock signatures exist on most mediums including balls, bats, gum cards, photos, and Perez-Steele cards. Letters of any kind are scarce.

Known Forgeries: Brock's signature is difficult to forge. No well executed forgeries exist in the market. Due to the nominal value of Brock material, he is not the target of skilled forgers.

Sales: Brock's signature is available. His autograph generally sells for under $100 on most mediums.

Dan Brouthers

Signature Study: Brouthers signed in a very clean and refined hand. His signature evidences good flow without recklessness. Hesitation of any kind is lacking. Letter construction is fairly sound, but individual letters tend to blend together. His signature has good display value and is pleasing to the eye. It is not known whether infirmity of hand ever existed.

Signature Population: Brouthers is an extremely rare signature. I estimate a total market population of less than five genuine specimens. There are a couple signed letters in existence. They are written on the "Dan Brouthers' Colts" letterhead. The Frederick Long collection housed at the Baseball Hall of Fame has a few endorsed team payroll checks from the 1890s. The endorsements are signed as "D. Brouthers." These are not available in the open market. I know of no signed photos, baseballs, or nineteenth-century baseball cards.

Known Forgeries: Since Brouthers signed in a more pensive hand, replication is easy. Many well executed forgeries exist in the market. Just about 100 percent of Brouthers signatures in the market are forgeries. For years a common type of forgery signed as "D. Brouthers" has been in the market. The hand is more vertical and rudimentary as if a child penned it. Many of these forgeries are accomplished in pencil.

Sales: Due to the rarity, there have been no recent sales of Brouthers' signature.

Mordecai "Three Fingers" Brown

Signature Study: Brown signed in choppy hand. His signature has many breaks in the first name. Legibility, for the most part, is sound. Brown's signature has good display value, but is not eloquent by any means. Brown's hand remained strong until death. A genuine signature exhibits no shakiness of hand and one that does should be considered suspect and avoided.

Signature Population: Brown's signature is in strong demand. His signature is considered rare, albeit borderline. Signatures are typically limited to index cards, government postcards, and business-related material. Premium items are extremely rare and border on the non-existent. I have never seen a signed T-card. I have examined only one genuinely signed 8 × 10 photograph. Team-signed baseballs from Brown's playing days very likely do not exist. Locating a Brown signature on a baseball is a daunting task. In my 30 years of collecting I have only seen two genuine examples. Both were multi-signed balls, likely autographed in the 1930s or 1940s. Both contained many signatures of players from various teams and eras. A single-signed baseball is a true rarity. I

Brouthers 1: payroll check endorsement dated 1890 (courtesy National Baseball Hall of Fame and Museum)

Brown, M. 1: TLS dated 1919

Brouthers 2: ALS dated 1917

Brown, M. 2: government postcard dated 1935

Brown, M. 3: undated government postcard

Brown, M. 4: undated signature

have never seen a genuine example, though many forged balls exist. Letters of Brown are also very rare. I have examined only a handful of genuine TLsS and maybe two or three handwritten specimens. All letters were business related. I have never seen a genuine signature where it was signed with either of his nicknames. It is often said that Brown detested the nickname "Three Fingers." In reality, he was fond of the name and his business cards read "Mordecai (Three Fingers) Brown." A few signed specimens of these business cards exist.

Known Forgeries: Brown's habit of letter separation results in a signature that is quite easy to forge. It goes without saying that there are many well executed forgeries in the market. After baseball Brown owned and operated a full-service gas station in Terre Haute, Indiana. The fact that he owned a business correlates into many signed documents, but there is a caveat.

Unfortunately, Brown employed the use of a secretary or more likely a relative or an employee to sign business documents and receipts, and endorse checks. The vast majority of signed business documents are not signed by Brown at all. They have been circulating for years and have been sold to many unsuspecting collectors. There are essentially two variant secretarial signatures to watch for. The first is a very legible and plain signature. They are signed "Mordecai Brown" while many check endorsements are signed simply "M. Brown." These signatures are easily spotted as they in no way resemble a genuine Brown signature. There is no attempt, in any way, to copy Brown's handwriting. Another secretarial signature, commonly found on check endorsements and bluish/green station receipts, resemble a genuine signature but are labored in appearance evidencing a slow methodical hand.

Sales: Government postcard sold for $1,655

(RR Auctions, December 2005). 1930 check endorsement sold for $1,410 (Robert Edward Auctions, Spring 2008). Personal business card sold for $2,115 (Robert Edward Auctions, Spring 2007). 1932 check endorsement sold for $1,560 (Mastro, May 2008).

Ray Brown

Signature Study: Brown signed in a flowing hand resulting in a large and bold signature. Letter construction is sound. The signature is very legible with a distinctive "y" in the first name. The display value of his autograph is sound. Towards the end of his life, his hand was affected by infirmity. Signatures accomplished late in life evidence shakiness of hand.

Signature Population: This is a signature of average demand. The population of Brown's signature is extremely limited. A handful of genuine specimens exist. I know of only eight to ten confirmed signatures in the market. One index card, one album page, and maybe five or so contracts. It is fair to say that most collections will never secure a genuine Brown signature. His signature must be considered one of the true rarities of the Hall of Fame members.

Known Forgeries: The rapid nature of Brown's hand makes for a signature that is difficult to replicate. Forgeries are limited to later-in-life signatures. Many album pages have entered the market

Brown, R. 1: ALS dated 1939 (courtesy Newark Public Library, The Newark Eagles Papers)

Brown, R. 2 contract dated 1940

Brown, R. 3: undated signature, post retirement

since his induction that contain Brown forgeries purportedly signed during his career. These forgeries evidence a labored appearance.

Sales: 1939 baseball contract sold for $12,760 (Robert Edward Auctions, Spring 2006).

Willard Brown

Signature Study: Brown's hand seems to have gone through significant changes, most likely due to illness in later years. Early specimens are signed more aggressively and more angled to the right. Later signatures tend to be more rounded. The rough edges are removed. His hand is legible and lacks any sort of flamboyance. One common characteristic is that the "n" in his last name is more wide than it is high. Though he died in 1996, Brown essentially stopped honoring autograph requests right around 1990 due to the onset of Alzheimer's disease. Signatures signed in the mid-to-late–1980s exhibit a fair amount of unsteadiness. The two illustrated specimens were obtained in the mail from Brown in the late 1980s.

Signature Population: His signature is in good demand simply because he played for the St. Louis Browns. When he first entered the Hall of Fame, many dealers advertised Brown as a "very rare" signature. This is incorrect. His signature is scarce but only moderately so. There is a good supply of Brown material in the market and most are in the form of signed index cards. The occasional multi-signed baseball surfaces but Brown's signature on a baseball must be considered rare. A single-signed baseball is very rare. I have never seen one. Photos, letters, and government postcards are also rare and highly desired. Signatures from his playing days are very rare. A signature penned as a player for the St. Louis Browns would be excessively rare.

Known Forgeries: Early signatures are difficult to forge. Signatures signed during the last years of his life are much easier to replicate. Since Brown entered the Hall of Fame, he has been the target of forgers. One common forgery are index cards signed in felt-tip pen. Most of them are signed "Willard J. Brown." In general, Brown ceased using the letter "J." in his signature years before the felt tip was created. If you examine a Brown signature signed with his middle initial, proceed with caution as it is likely a forgery.

Sales: Index card, choice specimen, sold for $451 (eBay, March 2008). Index card sold for $700 (RR Auctions, December 2007). 1941 baseball contract sold for $2,817 (Lelands.com, November 2007).

Morgan Bulkeley

Signature Study: Bulkeley signed in an aggressive and confident hand. The boldness of his signature evidences a man of power. His signature, which is almost always signed "M.G. Bulkeley," is large and illegible. His signature lacks good display value. Towards the end of his life, Bulkeley's hand deteriorated. Signatures accomplished after the World War I era exhibit a labored appearance, evidencing infirmity of hand.

Signature Population: Since Bulkeley was not a player, the demand for his signature is marginal. Bulkeley would be a very rare signature but for the fact that he held many elected positions. He even served as president of Aetna Life Insurance Company. These prominent positions correlate into many signed documents and letters. This is about the only way to obtain a Bulkeley signature. Many signed letters, checks, and other documents exist and have made this long deceased Hall of Famer accessible to most collectors. His signature should still be considered a scarce to borderline rare autograph. About the only other Bulkeley signatures available in the market are signed blank

Brown, W. 1: circa 1980s signature

Bulkeley 1: military document dated 1862

Brown, W. 2: circa 1980s signature

Bulkeley 2: TLS dated 1909

Morgan G. Bulkeley

Bulkeley 3: common secretarial signature dated 1865 by Captain William R. Hunter

Bunning 2: 2000 signature

cards. In the last few years of his life collectors started to mail requests for his signature, not because of his association with baseball but because of his tenure as a governor. Most signatures obtained through the mail evidence a shakiness of hand. I have never seen a signed baseball. As to photos, I have never seen a genuine one. It is very possible that he was presented with a cabinet-style photograph for signature, again simply because of his stature as a public official.

Known Forgeries: Forging Bulkeley's signature requires little effort. There are many well executed forgeries in the market. Many forged album pages exist in the market, so caution is warranted. They are usually signed "M.G. Bulkeley, Conn." and dated. There are a few Bulkeley signatures in the market that were signed during his military service. A few secretarial signatures do exist that were penned by Captain William R. Hunter of the Union Army. The secretarial signature deviates greatly from the genuine specimen. Bulkeley 3 illustrates Hunter's hand.

Sales: Short TLS dated 1910 signed as senator sold for $1,040 (Lelands.com, Spring 2007). Bank check dated 1911 sold for $1,292 (Robert Edward Auctions, Spring 2008). ALS dated 1906 signed as senator, routine content, sold for $1,044 (Robert Edward Auctions, Spring 2006).

Jim Bunning

Signature Study: Bunning signed in a very rapid and aggressive hand. His signature is marked with fast flowing lines. Hesitation of any kind is lacking. Letter construction is marginal at best.

Jim Bunning

Bunning 1: team sheet circa 1960s

Legibility is impaired. The signature has a very tangled appearance where letters morph into indistinguishable lines. Material signed in the 1950s and 1960s is signed in a slower and more legible hand, which differ greatly in appearance from more modern specimens. As of 2012 Bunning's hand remains strong. A genuine signature will exhibit no shakiness of hand and one that does should be considered suspect and avoided.

Signature Population: This is a signature where supply outweighs a marginal demand. With the exception of letters and checks, Bunning's signature is common in all forms. There is a strong supply of balls, gum cards, photos, Hall of Fame plaque postcards, Perez-Steele art cards, and the like.

Known Forgeries: Given the rapid nature of his hand, Bunning's signature would be very difficult to replicate. Due to the nominal value of Bunning material, he is not the target of skilled forgers. It is likely that letters sent while he held political office were signed by secretaries and/or auto-pen.

Sales: Bunning's signature is available. His autograph generally sells for under $100 on most mediums.

Jesse Burkett

Signature Population: Burkett signed in a pensive and thoughtful hand. His signature evidences average flow without a rapid appearance. Hesitation of hand is nominal but a very slight shakiness exists. Letter construction is sound. A signature with above average legibility and display value. There are many variant forms of signatures

Jess C. Burkett

Burkett 1: contract dated 1917 (courtesy College of the Holy Cross Archives)

Burkett 2: ALS dated 1923 (courtesy National Baseball Hall of Fame and Museum)

Burkett 3: document circa 1930s (courtesy collection of Alfred Angelo)

with different letter construction. Burkett made liberal use of secretaries to sign his name. They look nothing like the illustrated specimens. I have tried to locate a signed Burkett document that exhibits a signature penned later in life but I have been unable to find one. I have always been leery of Burkett signatures penned in the 1940s and typically avoid them as suspect. Though there are many signatures in the market that evidence various levels of shakiness, it is unclear to me whether true material infirmity of hand existed.

Signature Population: A signature which is in good demand when compared to a very small supply. Burkett is one of the great mysteries in the field of baseball autographs. He lived into the 1950s and remained close to the game, yet his signature is rare on a per se basis. Premium items are extremely rare to non-existent. Burkett is typically limited to signatures removed from letters. I have never seen a signed photo, baseball, or Hall of Fame plaque postcard of any kind. I have only seen five or six genuine specimens in my lifetime.

Known Forgeries: The lack of recklessness of his hand results in a signature that is easily replicated. Burkett forgeries are common and found on most mediums. It is safe to say the nearly all of the signatures offered for sale are forgeries. Forged Hall of Fame plaque postcards are common. They are signed in a very tremulous hand and are typically signed as "Sincerely" or "Yours Truly, Jesse Burkett." Burkett letters exist in quantities. He was president of the Worcester ballclub in the New England League during the 1910s. I have seen no less than six variant signatures penned on these letters. Most Burkett letters, even handwritten ones, were accomplished by a secretary.

Sales: Due to the rarity, there have been no recent sales of Burkett's signature.

Roy Campanella

Signature Study: Campanella signed in a nice angled and compact hand. His signature is flowing and strokes are pronounced. There is no hesitation evident. Letter construction is sound, resulting in a signature with strong eye appeal. His hand remained relatively constant throughout the years until January 28, 1958, when he was involved in an automobile accident that left him paralyzed from the chest down. For years Campanella could not sign until very late in life when he gained enough use of his hand. He signed with the aid of an arm brace. Post-accident signatures are sloppy and illegible. They are of little value for analysis purposes. Before the automobile accident Campanella's hand remained strong. A pre-accident signature will exhibit no signs of unsteadiness and one that does should be considered suspect and avoided.

Signature Population: Pre-accident signatures are in high demand and limited in supply. Signatures from his Negro League days are rare. Campanella signed many team-related items. There is a good supply of Brooklyn Dodgers signed team balls in the market. His signature is available on scorecards and album pages, which were typically signed at the stadium. Government postcards do exist but must be considered scarce. Signed 8 × 10 photos, letters, and gum cards are rare, albeit borderline. Single-signed baseballs are rare. Most Campanella single-signed balls are forged. I have examined only about a dozen specimens in 30-plus years of collecting.

Known Forgeries: Given the precision of hand, Campanella's signature is somewhat difficult to forge. There are some well executed forgeries in the market. Most signed Perez-Steele cards in the market are forged. It should be noted that Mrs. Campanella would, on occasion, fulfill au-

Campanella 1: circa late 1940s

Campanella 2: contract dated 1948

Campanella 3: secretarial signature by wife

tograph requests for her husband; an example is shown in Campanella 3. Many have been sold as genuine. Campanella is a highly desired name and forgeries abound, so caution is warranted.

Sales: Brooklyn scorecard, signed in pencil, sold for $393 (RR Auctions, January 2009). 1953 government postcard sold for $768 (Lelands.com, November 2009). Hardcover baseball book sold for $850 (Hunt Auctions, February 2010). 1949 government postcard sold for $595 (Hunt Auctions, November 2010). 1952 postal cover sold for $575 (eBay, December 2011).

Rod Carew

Signature Study: Carew has one of the most unappealing signatures of any member of the Hall of Fame. His signature is basically a scrawl with poor letter construction. The signature is illegible. Display value is poor. As of 2012, Carew's hand remains sound. A genuine signature will exhibit no shakiness of hand and one that does should be considered suspect and avoided.

Signature Population: The demand is marginal for Carew-signed material and clearly outweighed by supply. Carew engages in mass signings. His signature is available on most mediums including photos, gum cards, balls, and Perez-Steele cards. Letters of any kind are scarce.

Known Forgeries: Due to the unstructured nature of Carew's hand, his signature is easy to replicate. Creating a well executed forgery would be very easy. Due to the nominal value of Carew's signature, he is not the target of skilled forgers.

Sales: Carew's signature is available. His autograph generally sells for under $100 on most mediums.

Max Carey

Signature Study: Carey signed in an incredibly consistent and bold hand. His signature has very good display value and flows well. His signature is signed in a rapid nature where hesitation of hand is lacking. Letter construction is sound. His signature has a high degree of legibility. Signatures signed throughout the years evidence little change. Signatures from 1930 look the same as those signed shortly before his death. Most of the time he would end his signature with a poorly defined paraph. Carey's hand remained strong his entire life. A genuine signature will exhibit no shakiness of hand and one that does should be considered suspect and avoided.

Signature Population: The demand for Carey's signature is sound. Carey was a generous signer throughout his entire life. The supply of Carey signatures is very strong. His signature exists on most mediums including index cards, Hall of Fame plaque postcards, photos, and Fleer cards. Single-signed baseballs are uncommon to scarce. About 20 years ago a large supply of bank checks entered the market, which date to the 1930s. Signed team balls from Carey's playing days are limited to post–1920 teams. Signed team balls from early in Carey's career very likely do not exist.

Carey 1: album page dated 1933

Carey 2: circa 1970 signature

Carew 1: undated signature

Known Forgeries: Carey's striking hand is very difficult to forge. There are no well executed forgeries in the market. Due the nominal value of his signature, Carey is not the target of skilled forgers. The one exception is single-signed baseballs where forgeries exist.

Sales: Carey's signature is available. His autograph generally sells for under $100 on most mediums. Of note: A museum-grade single-signed National League (John Heydler, President) baseball, circa 1932, sold for $7,121 (Lelands.com, November 2010).

Steve Carlton

Signature Study: Carlton signs in a bold and strong hand. His signature exhibits excellent flow. No hesitation is noted. Letter construction is sound. Good legibility is evident. His hand evidences nice sweeps, creating a signature with superior eye appeal. As of 2012 Carlton's hand remains sound. A genuine signature will exhibit no shakiness of hand and one that does should be considered suspect and avoided.

Carlton 1: undated signature

Signature Population: The demand for Carlton signatures is outweighed by the supply. He engages in many mass signings. Carlton's signature can be found on most mediums including photos, Hall of Fame plaque postcards, baseballs, bats, jerseys, and the like. Signed letters of any kind are considered scarce.

Known Forgeries: Due to the sophisticated nature of Carlton's signature, replication of hand would be difficult. Due the nominal value of Carlton's signature, he is not the target of skilled forgers.

Sales: Carlton's signature is available. His autograph generally sells for under $100 on most mediums.

Gary Carter

Signature Study: Carter signed in a bold and flashy hand. Letter construction is fairly sound.

Carter 1: undated signature

His signature is legible for the most part, though the "er" in his last name tends to be poorly constructed. Acceptable display value is noted. Carter's hand remained sound his entire life. A genuine signature will exhibit no shakiness of hand and one that does should be considered suspect and avoided.

Signature Population: Demand for Carter's signature is marginal and outweighed by supply. His signature can be found on most mediums including bats, balls, photos, gum cards, and the like. Letters of any kind should be considered scarce. Overall, a common signature.

Known Forgeries: Carter would be a rather easy signature to forge. Due to the nominal value of Carter's signature, he is not the target of skilled forgers.

Sales: Carter's signature is available. His autograph generally sells for under $100 on most mediums.

Alexander Cartwright

Signature Study: Cartwright signed in a wonderfully ornate hand. His signature is one of the most artistic signatures around, baseball or otherwise. His signature is marked with crisp strokes and wonderfully flowing lines. His signature displays large capital letters and is finished with a stunning paraph. Cartwright 1 illustrates a choice specimen with a well formed paraph. Typically he signed "Alex J. Cartwright" and other times as "Alx. J. Cartwright." Cartwright's hand remained strong his entire life. A genuine signature will ex-

Cartwright 1: circa 1860 signature

Cartwright 2: ADS dated 1867

hibit no shakiness of hand and one that does should be considered suspect and avoided.

Signature Population: Demand remains sound for this early baseball pioneer. Cartwright is a rare signature and generally limited to just three mediums: letters, documents, and checks. I have never seen a genuinely signed cabinet photo, though I am told one exists. I have never seen a genuinely signed ball and it is very unlikely that one exists. Cartwright was an avid reader and had an extensive library. Most books in his library are identified by bookplate. A few were hand signed by Cartwright, and a couple survive to this day. Signed books are an extreme rarity and are treasured by book collectors. There are also a few handwritten receipts accomplished entirely in Cartwright's hand and usually signed in text.

Known Forgeries: Due to the complex and whimsical nature of Cartwright's hand, his signature is one of the most difficult to forge. Well executed forgeries are extremely limited. Cartwright has become the target of at least one very skilled forger, who I believe resides in Germany. A couple of years back some really nice presidential signatures appeared in auction on eBay. Most were the early presidents and they were nicely accomplished. Also offered by this seller was a signature of Cartwright dated "July 1861." The forger used Cartwright 1 as a template. All the signatures were well executed forgeries and very convincing. The Cartwright signature was well structured and the forger really came close to Cartwright's hand. The one flaw that stood out was the lack of flow in the signature. Cartwright signed in a nice flowing hand and the forger could not quite replicate that aspect of the signature, though he came close. The forgery evidenced a very slight hesitation. The other presidential forgeries were also very well constructed and would fool most experts.

Cartwright 3: bank check dated 1878

Another type of counterfeit to watch out for are period pieces that were never intended to deceive anyone. Cartwright was a prolific letter writer and penned mass quantities of them throughout his life. Cartwright wanted a copy of his letters but they hadn't yet invented the copy machine. In any event he made copies using a letter press. The freshly penned letter was placed in a manual press, a very thin sheet of paper known as "onion skin" was placed atop the original letter, then pressure was applied. The wet ink of the original was transferred to the blank onion skin. The letter-pressed onion skins have been circulating for years. Many are sold as genuine, but they of course are not, and have little value. A couple things to watch out for as these are easily spotted. First, the paper is very thin and fragile. It is called onion skin because of its delicate nature. It is somewhat translucent just like a peeled onion. Second, the writing appears thicker and ever so slightly blurred. This is caused by the press. The lines will evidence no flow of ink when magnified. The general rule is that if you see a Cartwright letter is it probably a letter-press copy and not genuine.

At least one historically significant pressed letter was stolen out of the state Archives of Hawaii, that being a letter written to fellow Knickerbocker Charles DeBost and dated 1865. It is possible many more were taken. Many of the Archive letters feature an oval stamp near the top or bottom of the letter that reads "Archives of Hawaii." If you happen to see one of these letters, you should avoid purchasing it and notify law enforcement. According to Luella Kurkjian, Branch Chief of Historical Records for the state of Hawaii, many letters in the possession of the state were not stamped.

Cartwright letters should be carefully scrutinized as they may be stolen. See the stolen document section in Chapter 4.

Sales: Receipt dated 1877 signed in the text sold for $1,720 (Lelands.com, June 2005). Onion skin copy of a letter dated 1879 sold for $300 (Hunt Auctions, July 2009). 1876 bank document sold for $1,304 (Legendary Auctions, May 2010). Bank check sold for $11,404 (Mastro, Winter 2006).

Orlando Cepeda

Signature Study: Cepeda's signature is rather unattractive and rudimentary in construction. His signature leaves out many letters and in general lacks eye appeal. Many signatures evidence a

Cepeda 1: bank check dated 1989

slightly labored appearance. One of the less appealing signatures of the Hall of Fame members.

Signature Population: The demand for Cepeda's signature is marginal and clearly outweighed by supply. Cepeda engages in mass signings. Cepeda's signature is common on most mediums including balls, bats, photos, and the like. A decent amount of bank checks are in the market. Letters of any kind should be considered scarce.

Known Forgeries: The plain nature of Cepeda's hand makes his signature easy to forge. Due to the nominal value of Cepeda's signature, he is not the target of skilled forgers.

Sales: Cepeda's signature is available. His autograph generally sells for under $100 on most mediums.

Henry Chadwick

Signature Study: Chadwick signatures come in various shapes and sizes. Much debate exists as to what is genuine and what is not. I have seen four completely different hands accepted as genuine. This, of course, cannot be the case. Some have a backwards slant, while some are in printed script. I only accept one form of signature as genuine, which is illustrated. Chadwick signed in a labored and tempered hand. His signature evidences hesitation and unsteadiness. The signature evidences a right slant. Letter construction is marginal, where some blending of letters is evident. His signature is fairly legible, but the sloppy nature of his hand makes for a signature with marginal display value.

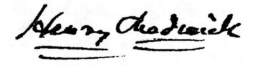

Chadwick 1: circa 1860s signature (courtesy A.G. Spalding Collection, Manuscripts and Archive Division, the New York Public Library, Astor, Lennox, and Tildon Foundations)

Chadwick 2: undated signature (courtesy A.G. Spalding Collection, Manuscripts and Archive Division, the New York Public Library, Astor, Lennox, and Tildon Foundations)

Chadwick 3: ALS dated 1907

Signature Population: The demand for Chadwick material is only fair, likely because of the poor eye appeal of his signature. Chadwick is a rare signature per se and generally limited to letters, documents, and the occasional signed book. I have never seen a genuinely signed baseball or photograph of any kind, though many forgeries exist. Many Chadwick letters are held in institutional collections. It is simply one of the rarer Hall of Fame signatures.

Known Forgeries: The lack of rapid flow makes replication of hand easy. Well executed forgeries exist in quantities. Many signatures exist in printed script. In general, collectors should avoid any signature that is not accomplished in cursive. Any signature that exhibits a left-leaning slant should also be considered suspect. These signatures deviate too much from the confirmed specimens. There are many books that were said to originate from Chadwick's personal library, where a forgery of Chadwick was placed on the front end page. Title issues may exist with many Chadwick letters in the market. See the stolen document section in Chapter 4.

Sales: Due to the rarity, there have been no recent sales of Chadwick's signature.

Frank Chance

Signature Study: Chance signed in an extremely refined and flowing hand. Letter construction is sound. The signature is legible. A sound display value is noted. His signature is marked with crisp lines. On occasion, Chance would sign in a smaller and less flamboyant hand, as illustrated in Chance 3. This variant signature

Chance 1: ALS circa 1910

Chance 3: ALS circa 1915

Chance 2: ALS circa 1910

Chance 4: common forgery

still has nice eye appeal. Chance died at the relatively young age of 47. It is unclear whether infirmity of hand existed in the last years of his life. Given the fact that he never reached old age and that no genuine Chance signatures have surfaced with a labored appearance, it is most likely that infirmity of hand was non-existent.

Signature Population: There is good demand for Chance signatures. Very few specimens exist. The total population is likely under ten genuine signatures in the open market. The only genuine Chance items I know of are all handwritten letters and a signed banquet program or two. I have never seen a genuine signed ball, photo, album page, or tobacco card. Signed team balls from Chance's playing days very likely do not exist. He did manage the Red Sox in 1923 so it is possible that one of these team balls exist, though I know of no genuine specimens. Chance is simply a very rare signature.

Known Forgeries: Chance's signature is very flashy and extremely hard to forge. There are no well executed forgeries in the market. Most forgeries lack the nice flow and the "F" lacks the ornate loop. Chance 4 shows a common forgery; note the slight hesitation and common looking nature of the signature. Many lesser grade T-206 cards with forgeries accomplished in pencil and fountain pen exist. The forgeries are signed "Frank Chance" or "Frank L. Chance" and placed vertically along the left or right side of his head. Another common forgery that entered the market about 15 years ago were generic rent receipts from the turn of the twentieth century. A forged Chance signature is signed near the bottom with the word "O.K." or "Approved" below or above the forgery.

There is also the most treasured signed combination piece, which is signed by all three infield legends Tinker, Evers, and Chance. Many a collector has searched for an item signed by all three Hall of Famers. There are only two known items

signed by all three. They are signed banquet programs along with other Cubs of the day. Several years ago a dealer in Wisconsin was selling forgeries of these three greats. I examined one of these forgeries a couple years ago. The forgeries are amateurish in construction and all evidence a labored appearance. They were signed in pencil or fountain pen ink. The paper was very old and deeply toned. Every once in a while one of these forgeries surfaces so caution is warranted. Title issues may exist with signed Chance letters. See the stolen document section in Chapter 4.

Sales: 1909 banquet menu with Chance and other members of the Cubs, signed in pencil sold for $8,225 (Robert Edward Auctions, Spring 2008).

Albert Chandler

Signature Study: Chandler signed in a very choppy and abrupt hand. His signature is marked with bold vertical lines that jut back and forth. His signature lacks good eye appeal. Legibility is impaired. Recent signatures were signed "A.B. Chandler." Material signed as governor of Kentucky were typically signed "Albert B. Chandler." Towards the end of his life Chandler's eye sight began to fail, which affected his handwriting. Signatures accomplished a year or so before his death evidence a very unsteady hand. Many signed baseballs from this period are poorly signed on an angle.

Signature Population: The demand for Commissioner Chandler material is marginal. He was a very gracious signer throughout his life. Most signatures were penned after his induction into Cooperstown. The supply of Chandler material

Chandler 1: government postcard dated 1986

Chandler 2: secretarial signature

is strong. His signature can be found on Hall of Fame plaque postcards, baseballs, and Perez-Steele cards. His signature is less common on bats, 8 × 10 photos, and TLsS. Handwritten letters are scarce. Chandler was a prolific letter writer in his later years. Many nice typed letters exist with good baseball content. Chandler authored an autobiography titled *Heroes, Plain Folks, and Skunks: The Life and Times of Happy Chandler*. Chandler signed these books but relatively few are available. They are uncommon and highly collectible. A small grouping of bank checks are also in the market, but are uncommon. There are many Commonwealth of Kentucky appointment documents signed by Chandler when he was governor. They are nicely signed in bold fountain pen as "Albert B. Chandler" and countersigned by Thelma Stovall, then secretary of state of Kentucky. The affixed gold seal makes for a wonderful display item.

Known Forgeries: Chandler's hand is rather difficult to replicate. There are no well executed forgeries in the market of non-infirmed signatures. Due the nominal value of his signature, Chandler is not the target of skilled forgers. It should be noted that while most letters are signed by Chandler, a few were secretarially signed. Chandler 2 illustrates a secretarial signature, where the hand is more muted and letter formation is smaller and less pronounced. In addition, when Chandler was a United States senator he had franking privileges, where a printed signature was placed on the envelope in lieu of a stamp. Sometimes these facsimile signatures are removed from the envelope and sold as genuine.

Sales: Chandler's signature is available. His autograph generally sells for under $100 on most mediums.

Oscar Charleston

Signature Study: Charleston signed in a plain and legible hand. He wrote his name instead of signing an autograph. The signature has a nice right slant. Letters tend to be uniformed and lack any flamboyance. Letter construction is sound. The signature is very legible. One notable char-

Charleston 1: ALS circa 1940s (courtesy Newark Public Library, The Newark Eagles Papers)

Charleston 2: ALS circa 1940s

acteristic is that the letters "le" in the last name are closely penned together and look like a lower case "b." It is unclear whether infirmity of hand existed in the last years of his life that would result in an unsteady signature. Given the fact that he never reached old age and that no genuine Charleston signatures have surfaced with a labored appearance, it is likely that infirmity of hand was non-existent.

Signature Population: Charleston's signature is in good demand. There is a minute supply. Charleston is a very rare signature. I estimate a total market population of ten specimens or less. His signature is limited to signed documents and endorsed checks from his playing days in the Negro Leagues. I know of no signed photos or baseballs.

Known Forgeries: Due to the unadorned nature of his hand, Charleston's signature is one of the easier names to forge. Many well executed forgeries exist in the market. A very common forgery is endorsements purportedly removed from the back of bank checks. A strip of an antique bank check is cut and then the forgery is added. These Charleston forgeries are typically signed with his middle initial as "Oscar M. Charleston." I have seen these forgeries accomplished in both ball point and fountain pen.

Sales: Due to the rarity, there have been no recent sales of Charleston's signature.

Charleston 3: TLS dated 1941 (courtesy Newark Public Library, The Newark Eagles Papers)

Charleston 4: circa 1940s signature

Jack Chesbro

Signature Study: Chesbro signed in a plain hand. Ink strokes lack rapid motion and appear slightly labored in appearance. His hand has a slight choppiness to it. Letter construction is fairly sound, resulting in a signature that is legible. Display value is marginal. His signature is marked with a large pronounced "J" in the first name but nothing else is extraordinary about his signature. It is unknown whether Chesbro's hand was affected by infirmity. It is said that he died suddenly of a heart attack. I have never examined a genuine Chesbro signature that evidences shakiness of hand.

Signature Population: The demand for Chesbro's signature is very strong and clearly outweighs a minute supply. The only paper specimen I know of in the open market is a signed bank check, which is illustrated as Chesbro 1. This is a superb fountain pen specimen drawn on the Conway National Bank, Conway, Massachusetts. The check is dated December 10, 1907. Note the signature is signed "Jno. D. Chesbro" and not "John D. Chesbro." Typically, the really rare signatures exist only in document form, but Chesbro is the exception to the rule. Most Chesbro signatures in existence are on baseballs. In 1925 at a Pittsburgh game a certain number of National League (John Heydler, Pres.) baseballs were signed by the members of the 1901 Pirates team in attendance that day. These reunion-signed team balls also contain signatures of Honus Wagner, Fred Clarke, Jess Tannehill, Tommy Leach, and other team members. I have seen three separate specimens in 20 years, two of which were in impaired condition. These balls are an incredible source of Chesbro signatures. It is unclear just how many of these reunion balls were signed. It is safe to say that

Chesbro 1: bank check dated 1907

Chesbro 2: World War I draft card circa 1917 (Record Group 163, Records of the Selective Services Division, National Archives at Atlanta)

Chesbro 3: will dated 1926

Chesbro 4: common forgery

there are less than 10 genuine Chesbro specimens in the market. I have never seen a genuinely signed photo, tobacco card, single-signed ball, or letter of any kind.

Known Forgeries: Due to the lack of rapid motion, Chesbro's signature is a rather easy signature to forge. Chesbro has been a target of forgers for decades. Recently many bogus signatures have entered the market and most, but not all, have been placed on antique bank document paper. These are purportedly signatures removed from checks. These forgeries are signed "John D. Chesbro" which differs from the known check specimen that was signed as "Jno. D. Chesbro." A forged check cut can be seen in Chesbro 4. These forgeries have turned up over the past five or so years and have been wrongly certified by the authentication companies, so caution is warranted. Another common forgery that has been around much longer are typed letters signed. The letters are on blank stationery and signed "Jack Chesbro" in fountain pen. The forgery is then underlined with a plain looking paraph. These letters have incredible baseball content where Chesbro purportedly talks about Ty Cobb, Babe Ruth, Honus Wagner, Clark Griffith and other contemporary players of the time. These letters contain spelling errors. The content seems contrived as if the forger labored to find the words to place in the text. They are closed with either "Sincerely yours" or "Very Truly Yours." I know of no genuine Chesbro letters in existence.

Sales: Due to the rarity, there have been no recent sales of Chesbro's signature.

Nestor Chylak

Signature Study: Chylak's hand is very uncommon, as it has a distinct left angle slant similar to that of Duke Snider. Chylak signed in a pensive hand with poorly formed letters that lack rapid motion. His signature has many breaks, resulting in a choppy and less appealing signature. Most signatures are penned as "Nestor Chylak Jr." Chylak died of a heart attack at the age of 59. Since he never reached old age, infirmity of hand did not exist. A Chylak signature that is labored in appearance should be considered suspect and avoided.

Signature Population: The supply of umpire Chylak material is ample but not overly so. It is balanced with a muted demand. Chylak was an accommodating signer throughout his life but died shortly before the era of mass signings. His signature is available per se but premium items should be considered scarce to rare. Most Chylak signatures in the market are found on index cards. Government postcards are available but should be considered scarce. Signed 8 × 10 photos and letters of any kind are scarce to rare and desirable. There is a surprising number of genuine signed baseballs in the market. Single-signed balls should be considered scarce. I have examined at least three dozen genuine specimens. Baseballs were signed on the side panel and he usually added his title of "A.L. Umpire" or "American League." I have never seen a genuine single-signed baseball signed on the sweet spot. Signed 1955 Bowman cards are rare.

Known Forgeries: Chylak's hand is rather easy to copy. Well executed forgeries can be created with little effort. Based on my research there is a lack of Chylak forgeries in the market. The two exceptions seem to be single-signed baseballs and his 1955 Bowman card.

Sales: Index card sold for $291 (RR Auctions, January 2009). Single-signed American League baseball (Lee MacPhail Pres.) sold for $823 (Robert Edward Auctions, Spring 2011). Signed World Series baseball (Bowie Kuhn, commissioner),

Chylak 1: bank check dated 1975 (courtesy collection of Alfred Angelo)

Chylak 2: undated signature (courtesy collection of Alfred Angelo)

choice specimen, sold for $2,643 (Robert Edward Auctions, Spring 2008). Multi-signed ball with other umpires sold for $252 (eBay, November 2011).

Fred Clarke

Signature Study: Clarke signed in a choppy and unappealing hand. His signature is one of the least attractive of all Hall of Fame members. Letter construction is sound. Good legibility is noted. His hand is marked with strong lines that abruptly break. There are many starts and stops. His signature lacks any measurable flow whatsoever. He signed like an old man, even during his playing days. His hand deteriorated in the last years of his life and unsteadiness is evident.

Signature Population: This is a signature of average demand well balanced by a limited supply. Clarke was a willing signer throughout his long life and signed just about until the end. Most signatures offered in the market are index cards and government postcards. Premium items should be considered rare. I have examined two, maybe three, signed 8 × 10 photos in over 30 years. Single-signed baseballs are also a rarity. I have examined only a handful, less than ten genuine specimens. Signed team baseballs from Clarke's playing days likely do not exist. Letters are also scarce but some nice handwritten specimens exist. Clarke had a bad habit of writing to the end of the page. He would place his signature at the edge of the paper. Sometimes his signature would run off the page. I have never seen a genuinely signed tobacco card of any kind. A signed passport of Clarke does exist and it is likely a unique item.

Known Forgeries: Due to the many breaks in Clarke's hand and lack of rapid flow, his signature is very easy to forge. Well executed forgeries exist in quantities. About 20 years ago the market was flooded with forged Hall of Fame plaque postcards. Clarke was a target of this forger. They are fairly well executed. Many of these postcards were signed in red ink so proceed with caution.

Clarke 1: TLS dated 1908 (courtesy National Baseball Hall of Fame and Museum)

Clarke 2: album page circa 1925

Clarke 3: circa 1930s signature

Sales: Hall of Fame plaque postcard, inscribed, sold for $587 (Robert Edward Auctions, Spring 2008). Choice ink signature sold for $200 (RR Auctions, December 2010). Government postcard sold for $125 (Hunt Auctions, November 2010). Single-signed baseball sold for $3,600 (Mastro, April, 2008).

John Clarkson

Signature Study: Clarkson's signature causes great debate. The illustrated specimen has long been held out as genuine. I have not been able to find another specimen for confirmation. It is said that Clarkson owned a cigar store in Bay City, Michigan. I have not been able to confirm this story nor have I ever seen any signed business-related documents. It is known that Clarkson, in the last few years of his life, suffered from severe mental illness and was committed to a psychiatric hospital. He was released sometime in 1906 as feeble minded. It is very likely he was incapable of signing his signature at this time.

Signature Population: The illustrated specimen may be the only example in existence. It is an inscription where the recipient's name was removed.

Known Forgeries: Clarkson has been forged on most mediums from photos to index cards. All forgeries vary in construction. See the stolen document section in Chapter 4.

Sales: Due to the rarity, there have been no recent sales of Clarkson's signature.

Clarkson 1: undated signature with inscription partially removed (courtesy Haulsofshame.com)

Roberto Clemente

Signature Study: Clemente's signature transformed greatly over the years. Early signatures tend to be legible and have a labored appearance. Early signatures are rudimentary in construction. Ink strokes tend to be thick and slightly shaky. As Clemente's career advanced his signature changed dramatically. What was once legible became illegible. Later signatures are very hard to read. They evidence an extremely rapid hand. Signatures tend to be a bunch of interlocking loops. Strong racing effect is evident. Clemente died in a plane crash. A genuine signature will evidence no shakiness of hand and one that does should be considered suspect and avoided.

Signature Population: The supply of Clemente material is good but not overwhelming. Demand for his signature is very strong and clearly outweighs supply. The vast majority of Clemente material in the market was signed at stadiums, hence programs, scorecards, and album pages are common mediums. There is also a good supply of team-signed baseballs in the market. Single-signed baseballs should be considered scarce but not rare. There are some nice single-signed balls in the market. Photos are uncommon but do exist in good numbers. Letters in any form should be considered rare to very rare. A few years ago some personal bank checks were released into the market, but they should be considered scarce.

Known Forgeries: Due to the lack of rapid strokes, early signatures are easy to replicate. Many well executed forgeries exist in the market. Later signatures, signed when he became a star, are much harder to forge. Well executed forgeries are very limited but they do exist. There are many forged baseballs, photos, and gum cards so proceed with caution. Over the past few years some very nice facsimile bank checks have been produced. These are typically framed under glass which makes close inspection more difficult.

Sales: 1972 National League contract counter-

Clemente 1: government postcard dated 1955

Los Nuevos Senadores, Inc. BASEBALL CLUB
Equipo

Por A. A. Saavedra Blasco, Director
Contratación de Peloteros   Presidente

Roberto Clemente   Jugador

Clemente 2: contract undated

Clemente 3: bank check dated 1972

signed by Chub Feeney sold for $15,497 (Lelands.com, November 2008). 1955 National League contract countersigned by Warren Giles sold for $27,754 (Lelands.com, June 2009). J. D. McCarthy picture postcard inscribed sold for $1,000 (Hunt Auctions, July 2010). Bank check, choice specimen, sold for $6,462 (Robert Edward Auctions, Spring 2007). Ink signature sold for $725 (eBay, November 2011).

Ty Cobb

Signature Study: Someone once said that Cobb's signature resembled a bunch of angry tangled lines. Cobb signed in a bold and confident hand that matched his personality. His signature is legible. Letters are well constructed. He essentially had two forms of the letter "T" in his first name. The most common is where the top of the "T" is separated from the stem. It almost looks like a mushroom cap. The second form of the letter "T" looks like the number "2" and is constructed all in one stroke. Cobb 3 and Cobb 6 illustrate the variant letter "T." Just about all non-document signatures were penned "Ty Cobb." Documents and checks were signed with his full name "Tyrus R. Cobb." Just about all signatures, with the exception of those penned as part of a return address on postal covers and pre–1910 contracts and letters, are finished off with a bold and flourishing paraph. Signatures through his life re-

mained fairly consistent but did go through phases of recklessness. Early signatures, those penned before 1940, tend to be neat and with precise lines. Cobb 5 shows a superior specimen with precise construction. As time went on and the demand for Cobb's signature increased, his autograph became more sloppy. The height of his signature also increases slightly. In the 1950s Cobb was bombarded with requests for his signature and autographs tend to vary and some are poorly constructed. Toward the end of his life Cobb had many health problems, among them sugar and cancer. Despite this Cobb's hand remained strong to just about the end of his life. Cobb signatures accomplished in May 1961 slowed a bit but shakiness of hand is not evident. For collecting purposes a genuine Cobb signature will exhibit no shakiness of hand and one that does should be considered suspect and avoided. Cobb did sign a few baseballs in June 1961 for Emory Hospital personnel. These do evidence a labored appearance but are limited to a few specimens.

Signature Population: Cobb is a rather common signature. The market literally has ten of thousands of signed pieces with countless more

Cobb 2: ALS dated 1916 (courtesy National Baseball Hall of Fame and Museum)

Cobb 3: TLS dated 1923, variant form of letter T

Cobb 1: contract dated 1908

Cobb 4: album page circa 1925

sitting in estates that have yet to be discovered. The demand for Cobb is simply tremendous, as only Babe Ruth has comparable demand. Cobb was a gracious signer throughout his life. Most material in the market are those items that could be signed through the mail. Government postcards, index cards, Hall of Fame plaque postcards, and exhibit cards are available. There is also a good supply of signed 8 × 10 photos and letters. In fact, Cobb was one of the most prolific letter writers of all the Hall of Famers. Starting in the late 1940s until the close of the 1950s Cobb must have had a lot of time on his hands because letters are numerous. I have probably owned 20 to 25 of these letters. I have literally seen hundreds more over the past couple of decades. Letters are well written and spelling errors are just about nonexistent. Cobb letters have great content and evidence a highly intelligent man with a powerful personality. Many letters have baseball content where Cobb is usually bashing the modern game as a perversion of what once was. Many letters with good business content are also available. They document Cobb's long running battles with state government and utility companies. One of the true gems of the field are single-signed balls. Fortunately for collectors Cobb signed many of them. Signed balls should be considered uncommon to scarce. Most Cobb-signed balls were

Cobb 7: ALS circa 1940s

Cobb 8: bank check filled out by wife, signed by Cobb

penned in the 1950s. Balls signed during his career are rare. Cobb-signed teams balls are limited to post–1920 teams and are rare. Pre–1920 team balls are very rare, in fact, I have only examined one genuine specimen from the 1910s. I had the pleasure of knowing Cobb's daughter Beverly Mc-Claren, who raised money for the Cobb Educational Foundation. Beverly would send a donor a Cobb check as a gift. Beverly told me that she handed out thousands of these checks. Cobb checks are common. About the only medium that should be considered rare are signed tobacco cards. A few exist and are true baseball treasures. According to Beverly, a few legal documents were signed in the closing days of his life but these cannot amount to more than a handful. I have never seen one of these documents in the market.

Known Forgeries: In general, Cobb's hand evidences nice strokes and is one of the tougher hands to copy. Having said that, there are many well executed forgeries in the market. The value of Cobb material is great and some auction prices have topped $50,000. Highly skilled forgers have, for years, targeted Cobb simply because there is so much money to be made in producing his signature. Most of the Cobb material found in the market is fake. Many of the Cobb signatures certified by the authentication companies are nothing more than forgeries. Cobb forgeries are everywhere and on every medium: balls, photos, baseball cards, bats, gloves, Hall of Fame plaque postcards, government postcards (complete with a postmark), and anything else you can think of. I

Cobb 5: government postcard dated 1934

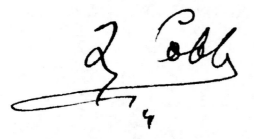

Cobb 6: ALS dated 1946, variant form of letter T

Cobb 11: forged TLS to Al Stump dated 1960

Cobb 9: circa late 1950s signature

have even examined a bowling pin complete with a forgery.

In the final years of his life Cobb gave an unknown writer a break and allowed author Al Stump to write his autobiography. When Cobb died Stump obtained a lot of Cobb's personal letterhead. Years later this letterhead was used by Stump to perpetrate one of the biggest frauds in the history of autographs. Amazing baseball content was typed on this collection of stationery and released into the market. The letters discussed Shoeless Joe Jackson, Babe Ruth, Mel Ott, and Honus Wagner, comparing skills, famous games, and the like. A crude forgery was placed at the bottom of the letters, very likely by Stump himself. The forgeries are very amateurish. Cobb 11 illustrates a Stump/Cobb forgery. Here is a good example where provenance trumped examination and allowed forged material to enter the market. If you run across any Cobb letter addressed to Stump, you should avoid it. Stump also produced forged books, photos, baseballs, and full written diaries that discussed golf and old-time baseball players. In the May 6, 2006, issue of *Sports Collectors Digest*, Jim Stinson wrote an excellent article titled *Was Cobb a Pariah or a Peach?* It details Cobb's signing habits and the fraud Stump perpetrated on the baseball world.

Just about the same time as the Stump fraud, someone got a hold of a group of vintage postcards complete with postmarks from major cities. The postmarks are dated from 1907 to 1915. The forger then would write out a letter, usually addressed to a woman. The letters have typical content about an ill friend or the offseason and coming

for a visit. Some have profanity such as "God damned" in the text. They are closed with "with kindest personal regards, Sincerely, Ty Cobb." A date is then added below the signature. These forged postcards have been around for years and fool some collectors. Upon careful examination the hand appears contrived and labored. The hand is heavy with thick ink strokes. When compared to Cobb's hand, the differences are striking. These should be considered lesser executed forgeries.

Fake handwritten Cobb letters are also in the market. Forged Cobb letters on hotel stationery exist. About 10 years ago fake Cobb letters on various old hotel stationery began to surface. They were accomplished in green fountain pen and some in green pencil. The forgeries are executed in an average fashion. Upon close inspection the hand appears labored and lacks the racing effect. This forger also went so far as to forge a couple of diaries allegedly written by Cobb in the late 1940s. They contain entries regarding business, family matters, and sports. The handwriting is labored and the grammar is poor. These diaries are also accomplished in green fountain pen. These are different than the above-referenced Stump diaries.

In the late 1940s Cobb's wife was known to pen many letters for Cobb and signed his name. From what I gather Cobb fell ill for some time between mid–1947 through early 1948 and was hospitalized for a period of time. The illustrated check dated December 30, 1947, is a key specimen (see Cobb 8). This is a check signed by Cobb. The handwriting directly above the signature is also in Cobb's hand. The rest of the check is accomplished by Mrs. Cobb. Note the hand is different than Cobb's and looks more feminine. Many Cobb letters during this period were written *and* signed by Mrs. Cobb. She became rather skilled at signing Ty's name. Cobb did have a rubber stamp of his signature that read "Tyrus R. Cobb." While he did have this stamp, it was rarely used. I have only seen one signed bank check signed with this stamp.

Cobb 10: will dated May 1961

Sales: Single-signed ball, museum grade, sold for $52,639 (Mastro April 2006). 1935 Coca-Cola signed stock certificate, signed as "Tyrus R. Cobb," sold for $11,163 (Robert Edward Auctions, Spring 2011). Single-signed baseball, signed shortly before death, sold for $6,462 (Robert Edward Auctions, Spring 2007). Hall of Fame plaque postcard sold for $3,818 (Robert Edward Auctions, Spring 2008). 8 × 10 photo, batting pose, choice specimen, sold for $11,000 (Hunt Auctions, February 2010). Bank check dated 1955 sold for $847 (RR Auctions, March 2011). Signed T-206 card, choice specimen, sold for $27,600 (Imperial Sports Auctions, October 2010).

Mickey Cochrane

Signature Study: Cochrane signed in an aggressive and angled hand. His signature is flowing with fast ink strokes. No hesitation is evident. His signature has poorly constructed letters. Legibility is somewhat impaired. Cochrane almost always signed with his nickname as "Mickey Cochrane." Documents and an authored book are usually signed "Gordon S. Cochrane." Cochrane fell victim to cancer at a relatively young age, hence infirmity of hand does not exist. A genuine Cochrane signature will exhibit no shakiness of hand and one that does should be considered suspect and avoided.

Signature Population: Demand for Cochrane material is strong. His signature is highly desired. Fortunately, Cochrane was a willing signer throughout his life which correlates into a good supply of material. Many nice items were signed during his career including index cards, album pages, scorecards, team-signed baseballs, and the like. His signature is less common on letters, Hall of Fame plaque postcards, and 8 × 10 photos. Single-signed baseballs are somewhat scarce. I have examined dozens of genuine specimens, most of which are found in the Detroit area. Years after his death

Cochrane 1: contract dated 1954

Cochrane 2: 1961 signature

Cochrane 3: undated signature

Cochrane 4: rubber stamp, circa 1930s

the family released hundreds of canceled bank checks. Signed 1933 Goudey gum cards are considered rare. In 1939, Cochrane authored a book titled *Baseball the Fan's Game*. Many signed copies of this book are available for purchase, which contain some fine inscriptions by Cochrane. Rumor has it that Cochrane fell onto hard times later in life, and that Ty Cobb would send Cochrane money on a regular basis to help out his friend financially. Though this story is likely fictitious, at least one Cobb-signed bank check made out to, and endorsed by, Cochrane does exist. This check is a priceless specimen signed by two Detroit Tigers legends.

Known Forgeries: Cochrane is a rather difficult signature to forge. Well executed forgeries are very limited. Most forgeries appear more legible and the letters are spaced apart. Forgeries are usually limited to premium items such as single-signed baseballs, Hall of Fame plaque postcards, and 8 × 10 photos. It should be noted that, in the 1930s, Cochrane was known to use a stamp, on occasion, to honor autograph requests. These were sometimes used for government postcards and index cards. The rubber stamp is illustrated in Cochrane 4.

Sales: 1926 Major League contract sold for $3,231 (Robert Edward Auctions, Spring 2011). 6 × 9 photo, in catching pose, sold for $525 (RR Auctions, March 2010). 8 × 10 photo, in catching pose, sold for $800 (Hunt Auctions, February 2010). Bank check sold for $200 (RR Auctions, November 2009). Bank check sold for $212 (eBay, November 2011).

Eddie Collins

Signature Study: Collins' signature is one of the most ornate in all of baseball. His signature is bold and striking and tends to dominate any medium it is placed upon. Letter construction is sound. The signature is legible and very busy looking. The signature has large sweeping vertical strokes and extremely flowing lines. On many occasions the hand will have noticeable pressure changes in the strokes, giving the signature a certain 3-D effect. Collins' hand remained fairly consistent, though as he became more established his hand grew bolder and more flashy. Dead Ball Era signatures are extremely rare and border on the non-existent. Early signatures are very legible. The "C" in his last name is plain. As time went on the signature becomes more bouncy. The "C" develops a nice looping cap. Collins signatures are mostly signed "Eddie Collins." "Edward T. Collins" is a much less common signature. On rare occasions he would sign business letters using his nickname "Cocky." Collins died of a heart attack at a relatively young age. Since he never reached old age, infirmity of hand does not exist. A genuine Collins signature will exhibit no signs of unsteadiness and one that does should be considered suspect and avoided.

Signature Population: Collins' signature is in strong demand and outweighs supply. Collins' signature varies in rarity depending on the medium it is found on. In general, the supply of Collins material is sound. He was receptive to autograph requests. He was, for many years, an executive for the Boston Red Sox. The most common items are letters, documents, and player

Collins, E. 1: contract dated 1907

Collins, E. 2: album page circa 1925

Collins, E. 3: TLS dated 1943

Collins, E. 4: TLS circa 1940s

releases signed as the general manager for Boston. Collins' signature is considered rare on 8 × 10 photos and handwritten letters. Government postcards are available but very scarce. Signed Hall of Fame plaque postcards are excessively rare. I have only seen one genuine specimen. The best way to obtain a Collins signature on a baseball is finding a mid– to late 1920s White Sox or Athletics signed team baseball. That is about the only way to obtain a signed ball, as single-signed baseballs border on the non-existent. I have only seen one genuine specimen in over 30 years of searching. I have never seen a signed T-card of any kind. A small cache of bank checks are in the market. Checks should be considered rare, albeit borderline. Collins was part of the most famous infield of all time. Known as the $100,000 Infield, it consisted of Frank Baker, Stuffy McInnis, and Jack Barry. If you can find this foursome signed on one item, you would have a true baseball treasure. I have never seen one but I have examined A's reunion programs signed by two or three of them. One other note, Collins' son, Eddie Collins, Jr., played with the Philadelphia A's from 1939 to 1941. He signed many items. His signature, which looks nothing like that of his Hall of Fame father, is illustrated as Collins 5.

Known Forgeries: Collins' signature is one of the most difficult to forge of all Hall of Famers. There are no well executed Collins forgeries in the market. Collins forgeries can be found on most mediums but fortunately they are always rudimentary in construction. There are many forged 1939 Hall of Fame induction photos in the market. It is a famous image with Ruth, Alexander, Speaker, Mack, and the rest. Many are signed with both fountain pen ink and white ink. I have never seen a genuinely signed 1939 class induction

Collins, E. 5: signature of Eddie Collins, Jr.

photo in my life. Many forgeries of this photo exist so caution is warranted.

Sales: 1931 Major League contract as coach sold for $2,115 (Robert Edward Auctions, Spring 2007). Signature, choice specimen, sold for $600 (Stephen Koschal Autographs, Fall 2009). 8 × 10 photo, batting pose, superior specimen, sold for $11,500 (Hunt Auctions, February 2010). 1945 baseball-related document sold for $242 (RR Auctions, July 2011).

Jimmy Collins

Signature Study: Collins' signature is flowing and his hand is bold. Letter formation is well constructed. His signature is legible. Display value is sound. Signatures are usually penned as "Jimmy" Collins with quotation marks around the first name. There seems to be great debate whether infirmity of hand existed in old age. While I do not know for certain, I believe a genuine Collins signature should not evidence a shakiness of hand. I have never examined a genuine specimen with a labored appearance.

Signature Population: This is a signature of sound demand and minute supply. Collins material is rare to very rare. I have only examined maybe 10 genuine specimens in my lifetime. Signatures are typically limited to letters, album pages, and the occasional signed legal document. I know of a nicely signed 1939 baseball first-day postal cover with a striking signature. I have never seen a genuinely signed photo, baseball, or baseball card of any kind. It is said that his will is in the market.

Known Forgeries: Collins' signature is rather difficult to forge. Given the rarity of his autograph, skilled forgers have taken up the challenge There are some nice Collins forgeries in the market so caution is warranted. A common forgery

Collins, J. 1: ALS dated 1906

Collins, J. 2: ALS dated 1906

Collins, J. 3: ALS dated 1939

Collins, J. 4: postal cover circa 1940

can be found on album pages, index cards, or lined paper. These are signed as either "James J. Collins" or "Jimmy Collins" and the phrase "3rd Sacker" is penned underneath the signature. These forgeries are usually dated with the month spelled out (i.e., "December, 20/1939"). These forgeries are well executed so careful examination is needed.

Sales: Album page, choice specimen, sold for $6,927 (RR Auctions, August 2010).

Earle Combs

Signature Study: Combs signed in a refined hand. The letter construction is strong. The signature is very legible. Good display value is noted. Combs signed with a very distinctive capital "E" in his first name. Through the years his signature changed. Early signatures tend to be more aggressive and bold. Early signatures are larger and evidence more height. Those signed in later years are much smaller. Combs' hand remained strong his entire life. A genuine signature will exhibit no shakiness of hand and one that does should be considered suspect and avoided.

Signature Population: There is an ample supply of Combs material that is balanced by demand. His signature can readily be found on index cards, government postcards, Hall of Fame plaque postcards, and photos. His signature is less common on single-signed baseballs, 8 × 10 photos,

Combs 1: undated signature

Combs 2: undated signature

Combs 3: secretarial, signed by wife

and letters. Team-signed baseballs of the Yankees during his playing days are a wonderful source of Combs signatures. After Earle's death, Mrs. Combs would honor requests for his autograph and send out bank checks to collectors. There is a small supply of Combs checks in the market but they are not common.

Known Forgeries: Combs is a difficult signature to replicate. Well executed forgeries are extremely limited. Generally, Combs forgeries are limited to premium items such as single-signed baseballs and Yankees team balls. During the final few years of his life Mrs. Combs would sign for Earle. Her secretarial signature is different as the illustration evidences. Note the capital "E" is completely different. She signed many Hall of Fame plaque postcards for her husband so caution is warranted. Mrs. Combs' work product can be seen as Combs 3.

Sales: Album page signed in pencil sold for $43 (Jim Stinson Sports, September 2011). 6 × 8 photo sold for $198 (RR Auctions, February 2011). 1928 Major League contract countersigned by Jacob Ruppert sold for $2,644 (Robert Edwards Auctions, Spring 2011). Bank check sold for $110 (RR Auctions, May 2010). Hall of Fame plaque postcard sold for $58 (eBay, November 2011).

Charles Comiskey

Signature Study: Comiskey signed in a very confident hand. His signature evidences a man of wealth and power. His signature is bold and striking. It dominates the medium it is placed upon. Early signatures are rare and very limited. The capital "C" in both the first and last name are large and dominate the signature. Just about all Comiskey signatures are signed "Chas. A. Comiskey." Some personal letters, which are very rare, are simply signed "Charlie." Comiskey's hand de-

teriorated throughout his life. Material signed after 1915 evidences a slower hand with more methodic strokes. By the early 1920s his hand slowed greatly and signatures evidence a labored appearance. Material signed in the late 1920s has little eye appeal. The signature looks very shaky and labored in appearance. The distinctive strokes exhibited in earlier signatures are no longer evident.

Signature Population: This is a signature that is in moderate demand when compared to a limited supply. Comiskey is a scarce signature but I would not consider it rare on a per se basis. Being an owner and one of the directors of the American League, he signed countless letters, documents, and checks. There is an ample supply of these items in the market and it is about the only way to obtain a Comiskey signature. Non-document related items are extremely rare and border on the non-existent. I know of only one single-signed baseball. A couple of signed presentation photos exist. A collector who wants a Comiskey signature should concentrate on signed documents or letters.

Known Forgeries: Post–1920 signatures are easy to forge. Just about all the forgeries in the market use this signature as a template. Early signatures are difficult to forge. Well executed forgeries are rare. For years many dealers sold letters

Comiskey 1: ALS circa 1890s

Comiskey 2: bank check dated 1919

Comiskey 3: circa 1925 signature

Comiskey 4: common secretarial signature

Comiskey 5: rubber stamp (courtesy National Baseball Hall of Fame and Museum)

that were secretarially signed for Comiskey. The secretarial signature looks nothing like a genuine Comiskey autograph. The secretarial signature is illustrated as Comiskey 4 and the differences are striking. In fact, some team checks that are signed by Comiskey are filled out by this same secretary so you can examine both samples of handwriting on one item. Several years ago veteran collector Ted Elmo told me that he had examined player release forms that contained a rubber-stamped signature of Comiskey. Elmo was the first to publicly identify it, which is illustrated as Comiskey 5. It should be noted that some letters addressed to August Herrmann are in the market and therefore title issues may exist. See the stolen document section in Chapter 4.

Sales: 1923 Chicago White Sox stock certificate sold for $2,115 (Robert Edward Auctions, Spring 2011). 1922 TLS sold for $900 (Hunt Auctions, July 2010). 1915 TLS sold for $847 (RR Auctions, April 2009). 1928 TLS sold for $1,250 (eBay, August 2011).

Jocko Conlan

Signature Study: Conlan signed in a bold hand. His signature is strong and somewhat reckless in appearance. Letter construction is sound but not great. The signature is legible but appears slightly choppy. His signature has only moderate display value. Most signatures are signed with his nickname "Jocko." Towards the end of Conlan's life, his hand became somewhat infirmed and thus shakiness of hand is evident.

Signature Population: The demand for um-

Conlan 1: government postcard dated 1986

pire Conlan's signature is marginal and outweighed by supply. Conlan is a common signature. His signature can be found on most mediums including baseballs, photos, Hall of Fame plaque postcards, and the like. His signature is considered uncommon on letters of any kind. Bats, Perez-Steele cards, and 1955 Bowman cards are scarce.

Known Forgeries: Replication of hand is fairly easy. Creating a well executed forgery can be accomplished with ease. Due to the nominal value of Conlan's signature, he is not the target of skilled forgers. The one exception is the Perez-Steele celebration cards that have been targeted by forgers.

Sales: Conlan's signature is available. His autograph generally sells for under $100 on most mediums. Of note: Perez-Steele celebration card sold for $299 (eBay, December 2011).

Tommy Connolly

Signature Study: Connolly signed in a flowing and pensive hand. Letter construction is marginal, resulting in a signature with impaired legibility. Connolly's refined hand lacks rapid motion. The strokes appear slower and more methodic than that of Cobb or Hornsby. The lower-case letters appear as small and abrupt ups and downs. Most signatures are signed "Thomas H. Connolly." On occasion he would sign as "Tommy Connolly." His hand slowed somewhat in later years. Material signed a few years before his death evidences a slightly labored appearance but measurable shakiness of hand is not evident.

Signature Population: The overall supply of umpire Connolly material is very limited. Demand far outweighs supply. Connolly's signature

Connolly 1: undated signature

Connolly 2: undated signature

Connolly 3: undated signature

Connor 1: ledger page circa 1895

Connor 2: common forgery

is scarce on a per se basis. Premium items are rare to very rare. Though he was a willing signer most collectors did not know his whereabouts. Most signed material in the market is limited to index cards and government postcards. Single-signed baseballs do exist but are very rare and desirable. I have only seen two or three genuine specimens in my lifetime. 8 × 10 photos are very rare. Letters of any kind are rare to very rare.

Known Forgeries: Due to the slower nature of his hand, Connolly is a rather easy signature to forge. Many well executed forgeries exist in the market. Many forgeries are signed "Tommy Connolly" and for some reason the forger would underline the signature with a single-stroke paraph. In addition, there are many well executed forged Hall of Fame plaque postcards in the market. Connolly-signed plaque postcards are very rare. If you see a signed plaque postcard, it is very likely a forgery.

Sales: Album page with William Harridge, Jack Coombs, and others sold for $473 (Lelands.com, August 2006). Ink signature sold for $267 (RR Auctions, June 2011). Banquet menu, also signed by six other Hall of Famers, sold for $1,091 (Mastronet, April 2003).

Roger Connor

Signature Study: Connor is an extremely rare signature. The illustrated example is the only specimen I could locate. His hand is legible. The display value of his signature is sound. A detailed study of his signature has never been completed. Lack of genuine material makes a signature study difficult. It is unknown whether Connor ever suffered from infirmity of hand due to illness or old age.

Signature Population: Connor is an extreme rarity. I only know of one signature in existence, accomplished in a ledger from the 1890s. I have

yet to find additional signatures to confirm the illustrated specimen. Other signatures in this ledger that are generally known by exemplars are genuine and give weight to the authenticity of the Connor signature. I know of no signed photos, baseballs, or letters in existence.

Known Forgeries: Forgeries of various construction exist. The signature illustrated as Connor 2 is a common forgery. This type of forgery has been around for many decades. Many were signed on lined paper.

Sales: Due to the rarity, there have been no recent sales of Connor's signature.

Andy Cooper

Signature Study: A search conducted by the National Archives located a World War I draft registration card. The date of birth on the card of April 24 is correct. The accepted date of his birth is 1898. The illustrated card lists the birth year as 1897. The residence listed on the card of Waco, Texas, is correct. The signature is signed in full in a rudimentary hand. This is very likely the signature of Andy Cooper. Nothing is really known about his signing habits.

Signature Population: I know of no confirmed signatures in the open market. The illustrated specimen is held by the National Archives. It is an extreme rarity.

Known Forgeries: Many forgeries exist and all vary in construction.

Cooper 1: World War I draft card circa 1917 (Record Group 163, Records of the Selective Services Division, National Archives at Atlanta)

Sales: Due to the rarity, there have been no recent sales of Cooper's signature.

Stan Coveleski

Signature Study: Coveleski signed in a very busy and jumbled hand. His signature has many non-conforming strokes. Sharp angles are limited. Coveleski's signature has limited eye appeal due to the sloppiness of hand. Signatures signed in the last five or so years of his life are affected by infirmity of hand. Signatures from this time appear labored and unsteady in appearance.

Coveleski 1: circa 1970s

Signature Population: Coveleski is a common signature. The supply outweighs demand. His signature can be found on many items including index cards, gum cards, Hall of Fame plaque postcards, photos, and the like. Signed baseballs and letters of any kind are uncommon. His signature is not considered rare in any form except for single-signed baseball bats. Material signed by both the Coveleski brothers should be considered very rare. I know of only one government postcard signed by Harry Coveleski that was later presented to Stan for signature. It is a great baseball treasure.

Known Forgeries: Coveleski's signature is rather difficult to forge. There are no well executed forgeries in the market for non-infirmed signatures. Signatures accomplished with an infirmed hand are easy to forge, so well executed forgeries of these exist in quantities. Due to the nominal value of Coveleski's signature, he is not the target of skilled forgers. Forgeries are generally limited to baseballs and Perez-Steele art postcards.

Sales: Coveleski's signature is available. His autograph generally sells for under $100 on most mediums.

Sam Crawford

Signature Study: Crawford signed in an extremely pleasing hand. His signature is marked with wonderful flow. Crawford's signature is one of the finest of all the Hall of Famers. His signature lacks hard angles and hesitation. Letter construction is very sound. This is a signature with a high degree of legibility and superior eye appeal. Crawford considered writing the cornerstone of an educated man. Crawford was a learned man and his hand evidences a great amount of sophistication. He generally signed his name as "Wahoo Sam Crawford." On occasion he would sign it as "Samuel E. Crawford." Crawford's hand remained strong his entire life. A genuine Crawford signature will evidence no unsteadiness and one that does should be considered suspect and avoided.

Signature Population: Crawford is a great name from the Cobbian era and always in demand. Fortunately the supply is sound. Crawford lived a long life and was a willing signer after his Hall of Fame induction. Crawford material is generally limited to items that could be signed in the mail. Index cards, government postcards, and Hall of Fame plaque postcards are all available. Like teammate Cobb, Crawford was a notorious letter writer. Many letters exist in the market today. His signature is considered rare on 8 × 10 photos, single-signed baseballs, and T-206 cards. I have seen one genuinely signed team ball from his days with the Tigers. An item signed by the outfield of Cobb, Crawford, and Davy Jones is an extremely rare piece. In my 30-plus years of collecting I have seen two 8 × 10 pictures signed by all three. They were both inscribed and likely signed at Crawford's Hall of Fame induction in 1957, where the three outfielders reunited for the ceremony.

Known Forgeries: Crawford's signature is one of the most difficult to forge. Well executed forgeries are limited to only one forger, who has be-

Crawford 1: ALS dated 1957

Crawford 2: 1963 signature

Crawford 3: plaque postcard circa 1960s

come rather skilled at forging Crawford's hand. This forger has produced some very nice autographed letters signed. These letters are written on blank stationery and very convincing. I have examined a few of these letters. Two of them were written to Paul S. Kerr, president of the Baseball Hall of Fame. Upon close examination the writing evidences an ever so slight labored appearance. The ink strokes lack the effortless flow of Crawford's hand. The racing effect is impaired. This forger has done an excellent job of replication. This forger has also produced forged 8 × 10 photos.

Sales: Single-signed Ralph Kiner League baseball, choice specimen, sold for $5,288 (Robert Edward Auctions, Spring 2010). Picture postcard sold for $242 (RR Auctions, February 2011). Hall of Fame plaque postcard sold for $359 (eBay, September 2011). Baseball, also signed by Davy Jones, sold for $925 (Hunt Auctions, July 2009). Hall of Fame plaque postcard sold for $265 (eBay, November 2011).

Joe Cronin

Signature Study: Cronin's signature is very flamboyant and large. His signature works well on almost any medium it is placed upon. Cronin's hand is very aggressive and flows nicely. There is no hesitation whatsoever. Letter construction is sound. The signature has sound display value. Most signatures are signed "Joe Cronin," though many documents signed as league president are signed in full. Cronin's hand remained strong his entire life. A genuine signature will exhibit no unsteadiness and one that does should be considered suspect and avoided.

Cronin 1: 1938 signature

Cronin 2: 1965 signature

Cronin 3: signature circa 1980s

Signature Population: The demand is sound for Cronin material and balanced with supply. During the 1980s Cronin cut back substantially in honoring mail requests for his signature. Cronin died just before the era of mass signing so premium items remain uncommon. His signature can be found on index cards, government postcards, photos, Hall of Fame plaque postcards, 8 × 10 photos, baseballs, and the like. His signature is considered scarce on Goudey gum cards. Single-signed baseball bats are considered rare. Cronin's position as an executive in baseball correlates into a strong supply of letters and signed league contracts. In general, Cronin is a readily available signature.

Known Forgeries: Cronin's distinct hand is very difficult to forge. No well executed forgeries exist in the market. Cronin forgeries are limited to premium items such as single-signed baseballs, 8 × 10 photos, and Perez-Steele art postcards. A common forgery that has surfaced in recent years is the 1983 Donruss Hall of Fame Heroes cards. A genuine signed Cronin card from this issue is rare. Many of the forged Cronin Donruss cards have been wrongly certified as genuine by the authentication companies so caution is warranted.

Sales: Cronin's signature is available. His autograph generally sells for under $100 on most mediums.

Arthur "Candy" Cummings

Signature Study: There is limited analysis on Cummings' signature due to the fact that so few specimens are known. He signed as "W.A. Cummings." The signature has good eye appeal. His

Cummings 1: ALS dated 1878

Cummings 2: ALS undated

Cuyler 1: circa 1930s signature

Cuyler 2: circa 1930s signature

Cuyler 3: undated signature

signature lacks rapid motion. The letters in his last name are merely up and down strokes that are not legible. It is unknown whether Cummings' hand was ever affected by infirmity due to advanced age or illness.

Signature Population: Cummings is one of those excessively rare signatures that you will likely never add to your collection. The illustrated specimens are the only two I could secure. I estimate the total population of Cummings signatures is under five. It is doubtful that signed baseballs, photos, or baseball cards exist.

Known Forgeries: Since Cummings' signature lacks rapid motion, replication of hand is very easy. Many well executed forgeries exist. Cummings forgeries are limited to some nicely executed letters signed in the same manner as the illustrated examples.

Sales: 1878 ALS sold for $22,000 (Hunt Auctions, February 2005).

Ki Ki Cuyler

Signature Study: Cuyler's has a very distinct hand with strong letter formation and wonderful flow. His signature lacks hesitation. Legibility is sound. This is a signature that has nice display value. Most Cuyler signatures are signed "'Ki Ki' Cuyler," with his nickname spelled as two words, which differs from today's generally accepted spelling of "Kiki." Autographs signed with his real name are scarce. Cuyler died at the young age of 51. He was the victim of a heart attack. Since Cuyler never reached old age, infirmity of hand was non-existent. A genuine Cuyler signature will exhibit no shakiness of hand and one that does should be considered suspect and avoided.

Signature Population: Demand for Cuyler signatures is strong and supply is limited. His signatures are mostly limited to those items signed during his playing days. Fortunately for collectors Cuyler was a gracious signer and signed much material including scorecards, team-signed baseballs, and album pages. On premium items his signature should be considered rare. Letters, 8 × 10 photos, and Goudey gum cards are few and far between. Single-signed baseballs are excessively rare. I have only seen one in 30 years of collecting. After his playing days Cuyler signed very little material as evidenced by the lack of signed material after 1938. He did sign some government postcards but those should be considered scarce. Signed bank checks are extremely rare.

Known Forgeries: Cuyler's hand exhibits nice flow. His signature is rather difficult to forge. Well executed forgeries are limited. Most Cuyler forgeries evidence thick strokes and a labored appearance. Back in the early 1990s a couple of spectacular, forged single-signed baseballs inscribed to Cuyler entered the market. One was Babe Ruth and the other was Honus Wagner. They came directly from Cuyler's estate, so the story goes. I am told a Gehrig ball exists as well, though I have never seen it. These balls were in excellent condition with bold ink signatures. The Ruth ball was inscribed as "To My Pal, Hazen Cuyler, Sin-

cerely, Babe Ruth." These forgeries are well executed and accomplished by a forger of skill.

Sales: Bank check sold for $3,952 (Lelands.
com, December 2004). Album page, with other
signatures, sold for $264 (RR Auctions, June
2009). 8 × 10 photo, batting pose, sold for $1,517
(Mastro, December 2007). Index card sold for
$390 (eBay, December 2011).

Ray Dandridge

Signature Study: Dandridge signed in an extremely legible and neat hand. Letter construction
is sound. The signature has good display value.
While his hand lacks rapid motion, it also lacks
hesitation. Dandridge's hand remained strong
for most of his life. Material signed close to his
death evidences only a slight amount of unsteadiness.

Signature Population: The demand for Dandridge material is marginal and outweighed by
supply. For many years Dandridge was considered
a prime candidate for induction into Cooperstown. Collectors had been writing him for years.
The supply of Dandridge material is strong. His
signature can be found on most items including
photos, Hall of Fame plaque postcards, balls, bank
checks, index cards, and Perez-Steele cards. His
signature is considered uncommon on baseball
bats and letters of any kind. Signatures from Dandridge's playing days are rare and limited to the
occasional letter written to a team owner.

Known Forgeries: The slower nature of Dandridge's signature makes replication of his hand
fairly easy. Due to the nominal value of Dandridge's signature, he is not a target of skilled forgers.

Sales: Dandridge's signature is available. His
autograph generally sells for under $100 on most
mediums.

**Dandridge 1: ALS circa 1940s (courtesy Newark
Public Library, The Newark Eagles Papers)**

Dandridge 2: postal cover dated 1985

George Davis

Signature Study: Davis signed in a very plain
and legible hand. The illustrated signature is the
only one I could locate. It is signed at the close of
an autographed letter signed. I contacted Amherst
College, where Davis once worked, but nothing
could be found. Further, the Davis family had
nothing signed by him. The illustrated example
comes from a baseball collection and is accepted
as a genuine specimen. It is unclear whether
Davis' hand was ever affected by infirmity. It is
said that he fell ill sometime around 1935 and was
mentally impaired until his death in 1940. His signature remains one of the great enigmas in vintage
baseball autographs. As of 2012 the illustrated
specimen should be considered unconfirmed until
other examples surface.

Davis 1: ALS undated

Signature Population: I am told there are only
two signatures in existence. Both are in letter/doc-
ument form. It should be noted that there may
be title issues associated with certain Davis signatures, so further inquiry is suggested. This signature is an extreme rarity.

Known Forgeries: Davis' rather plain hand
makes for a signature that can be replicated with
little effort. His signature was never illustrated
until recent times so forgers really had little to go
on. Most Davis forgeries that were created in the
1960s and 1970s look nothing like the illustrated
specimen.

Sales: Due to the rarity, there have been no recent sales of Davis' signature.

Andre Dawson

Signature Study: Dawson signs in a flowing
hand that has a certain uniformity to it. Letter
construction is impaired as letters blend together.
Legibility is substandard. The display value is simply average. As of 2012 Dawson's hand remains
strong. A genuine signature will exhibit no shakiness of hand and one that does should be considered suspect and avoided.

Signature Population: The demand for Dawson's signature is marginal. The supply clearly outweighs demand. His signature is common on

Dawson 1: 2011 signature

Day 2: undated signature

Day 3: secretarial signature (courtesy Newark Public Library, The Newark Eagles Papers)

index cards, photos, balls, bats, Hall of Fame plaque postcards, and the like. Letters of any kind should be considered scarce.

Known Forgeries: Dawson's signature would be moderately difficult to forge. There are no well executed forgeries in the market. Due to the nominal value of Dawson's signature, he is not the target of skilled forgers.

Sales: Dawson's signature is available. His autograph generally sells for under $100 on most mediums.

Leon Day

Signature Study: Day signed in a very plain and rudimentary hand. His signature is legible. Letter construction is sound. Display value is average. It is marked with a slight labored appearance. Since his hand evidences an unsteady appearance, signatures signed late in life vary little from earlier examples. There is no marked deterioration of hand because he died of a heart attack. This is one of the less appealing Hall of Fame signatures.

Signature Study: This is a signature of marginal demand that is outweighed by supply. Since Day was always considered a sure bet for the Hall of Fame he was targeted by collectors. Today, the supply of Day material is ample. His signature can be found mostly on index cards and photos. Single-signed baseballs and bank checks are uncommon. His signature is considered scarce on baseball bats and letters. Since Day died just days after learning of his induction into Cooperstown,

Day 1: contract dated 1943 (courtesy Newark Public Library, The Newark Eagles Papers)

no signed Hall of Fame plaque postcards exist. Any signature penned while he was a player must be considered rare.

Known Forgeries: Day's signature is very easy to replicate. It is one of the easiest of all Hall of Fame signatures to forge. Due to the nominal value of Day's signature, forgeries are generally limited to baseballs and bats. In addition, there are some Negro League era letters that are accomplished and signed by someone other than Day (see Day 3).

Sales: Day's signature is available. His autograph generally sells for under $100 on most mediums.

Dizzy Dean

Signature Study: Dean's signature went through a marked change throughout his life. Signatures from his playing days vary greatly from more modern signatures. Vintage signatures tend to be large and bold but lack the flare of modern signatures. As the years went by Dean's hand became more refined. The signature is more structured. Display value increases. Modern signatures evidence a larger "D" in both the first and last name. He also adds quote marks around the first name. Dean died suddenly of a heart attack, hence infirmity of hand is non-existent. A genuine Dean signature will exhibit no shakiness of hand and one that does should be considered suspect and avoided.

Signature Population: Dean was one of the most popular figures of the game and collectors targeted him for his autograph. The demand for

Dean 1: album page dated 1933

Dean 3: common secretarial

Dean 4: common secretarial on Falstaff Beer letters

Dean 2: 1973 signature

his signature is very high. Today, the supply of Dean material is ample and offers collectors some nicely signed items. His signature can be found mostly on index cards, Hall of Fame plaque postcards, and small book photos. Dean's signature is considered scarce on letters, 8 × 10 photos, and baseballs. Signed equipment is basically nonexistent, though I know of one signed baseball glove and one bat. In addition, Dean's brother, Paul "Daffy" Dean, was also a successful pitcher with the Cards. Anything signed by both men is in high demand and should be considered scarce.

Known Forgeries: Dean's signature is hard to replicate, so well executed forgeries are limited. Most forgeries are amateurish in appearance. Dean is one of the most commonly forged signatures of any Hall of Famer that died after 1970. He also authorized secretaries to sign for him. Many items signed through the mail in the late 1960s and 1970s were secretarially signed. The majority of signed Hall of Fame plaque postcards actually contain a secretarial signature. These signatures, as shown in Dean 3, are easily spotted as they differ greatly from a genuine signature. Another type of authorized forgery are those found on letters. For many years Dean broadcast St. Louis Cardinals baseball sponsored by Falstaff

Beer. There are many typed letters signed by Dean on Falstaff letterhead. The vast majority of these letters were secretarially signed. These signatures vary somewhat from Dean's hand and evidence a labored appearance. Dean 4 is taken from a Falstaff letter. There is a large quantity of blank Dizzy Dean/Falstaff Beer letterhead in the market. This stationery has been circulating for years and can be purchased for a couple of dollars per sheet. Many forgers purchase this stationery and either add a forged signature on it or sometimes type out an entire letter and sign it.

Sales: Single-signed National League (Warren Giles, Pres.) baseball sold for $800 (Robert Edward Auctions, May 2011). Hall of Fame plaque postcard sold for $163 (RR Auctions, October 2010). 8 × 10 photo, pitching pose, sold for $650 (Hunt Auctions, March 2009). Index card, choice specimen, sold for $200 (eBay, August 2011). Hall of Fame plaque postcard sold for $249 (eBay, November 2011).

Ed Delahanty

Signature Study: Delahanty's signature was, for decades, a great mystery to the collecting public. Many different specimens of various construction exist. An 1889 specimen from an autographed letter signed is illustrated in Delahanty 1. This signature exhibits sound letter construction and strong flow. Delahanty's signature is very legible. The display value is high. As Delahanty aged his hand became a bit more choppy as the 1903 specimen illustrates (see Delahanty 3). The letters are

Delahanty 1: ALS dated 1889

Delahanty 2: ledger circa 1895

Delahanty 3: postal cover dated 1903 (courtesy J. Casway)

more compact. Delahanty 3 compares favorably with a facsimile signature reproduced in a Stuart's Dyspepsia advertisement from 1900. The Delahanty facsimile autograph in the ad is strikingly close to the 1903 signature. Due to his untimely death, it is safe to say no infirmity of hand exists.

Signature Population: Based on my research, only three signatures exist and the title of one is openly questioned. This signature is an extreme rarity.

Known Forgeries: Delahanty's signature is fairly easy to replicate. Many forgeries were created in the 1940s and future generations of forgers used those as a template for their work. A few handwritten letters have been floating around the market that are secretarially signed. These signatures easily stand out, as the last name is spelled incorrectly and penned as "E.J. Delehanty." One of these letters sold for close to $30,000 and was accompanied by certificates of authenticity issued by two major authentication companies. In actuality, the letter was written and signed by Delahanty's manager, William Shettsline. I placed calls to both of the above-referenced authentication companies for comment, but neither returned my calls.

Sales: 1903 postal cover sold for $19,120 (Legendary Auctions, August 2012).

Bill Dickey

Signature Study: Dickey signed in a very nice and legible hand. Nice strokes make for a whimsical signature. Dickey's hand is bold and has excellent display value. His signature remained relatively constant throughout the years, though as time went on the height did decrease somewhat. In the last five or so years of his life, Dickey's hand was affected by infirmity. Signatures signed in his remaining years lack the effortless flow of earlier signatures. A labored appearance is noted.

Signature Population: The supply of Dickey signatures is very strong but demand is greater. Though he was a giant of the game Dickey remained a gracious signer throughout the 1980s. He scaled back his signing in the last three years of his life. Late in life he did engage in a few private signings. Dickey's signature is available on just about all mediums including index cards, government postcards, Hall of Fame plaque postcards, 8 × 10 photos, balls, and the like. His signature is uncommon on bats and letters. A small supply of bank checks were released into the market but today are difficult to locate. Signed Goudey gum cards are scarce. His signature is also available on many dual-signed pictures with Joe DiMaggio, Lefty Gomez, Yogi Berra, and the like.

Dickey 1: team sheet dated 1935

Dickey 2: undated signature

Dickey 3: bank check dated 1987

Known Forgeries: Dickey, in general, is a difficult signature to replicate and forgeries are generally limited to old-age signatures. Most Dickey signatures can be purchased for a nominal amount, thus forgeries are limited to premium items. There are many forged single-signed baseballs and bats in the market.

Sales: Dickey's signature is available. His autograph generally sells for under $100 on most mediums.

Martin Dihigo

Signature Study: He was born Martin Magdaleno Dihigo Llanos. Dihigo is a very controversial signature, as there seems to be two completely different signatures accepted as genuine among the various authorities in the field. The signatures illustrated are genuine and evidence a very flowing and pronounced hand. His signature exhibits wonderful flow with a good racing effect. There is no hesitation of hand evident. Letter construction is sound. Excellent display value is noted. Legibility is slightly impaired. Dihigo signatures are signed as "Martin Dihigo LL," "Martin M. Dihigo LL," or "Martin Dihigo Llanos." There is another type of signature that usually appears on index cards and signed in ball point pen. The signature is more uniform and compact, and evidences a right slant. They are said to be signed in the 1960s until death. I have never accepted these signatures as genuine as they differ greatly from the signatures illustrated. Whether infirmity of hand existed due to illness is quite possible. I have heard from more than one source that Dihigo was very ill the last decade of his life. It is also very likely he stopped signing autographs at this time as I have never examined

Dihigo 1: document dated 1939

Dihigo 2: document dated 1939

Dihigo 3: document dated 1947

Dihigo 4: undated signature

a genuine Dihigo signature that evidences a labored appearance.

Signature Population: This is a signature in good demand and of little supply. Dihigo is a rare signature. His signature is generally limited to material signed during his playing days. Signatures are typically found on album pages, documents, letters, and the occasional scorecard. Signed baseballs are very rare and are typically limited to multi-signed baseballs. I have never examined a genuine single-signed baseball or a signed index card. I have never seen a genuinely signed photo. He is also available on signed documents where he signs as a witness attesting to another player's signature. Material signed after his career ended is very rare. I can honestly say I have never seen a Dihigo signature I would feel comfortable pronouncing as genuine that was signed after the mid–1950s. Many have said that he held the official government position of minister of sports for Cuba. If this is true then there should be many signed letters from his tenure as minister, but I have yet to find one.

Known Forgeries: Given the complex nature of his signature and rapid flow, Dihigo is a very difficult signature to replicate. Well executed forgeries are rare. Dihigo is a commonly forged signature. One forger has taken it upon himself to create forged baseballs. They are more modern baseballs that have been produced in the last 30 years. The forger artificially ages them with a dark brown stain. He then places a Dihigo forgery on the sweet spot or side panel. He sometimes adds other signatures such as Luis Tiant Sr., Frank

Duncan, Alex Pompez, or the like. The forgeries easily stand out as they are signed in a slow hand evidencing a labored and shaky appearance. Another group of forged balls have been circulating for many years. They are single-signed baseballs. A forgery is placed on the side panel of the ball with an inscription in Spanish. The balls themselves are of a very inferior grade and look like a Little League style ball.

Sales: Album page sold for $1,338 (Lelands. com, December 2005). 1935 baseball contract sold for $12,902 (Lelands.com, June 2005).

Joe DiMaggio

Signature Study: DiMaggio signed in an eloquent hand. His signature is marked with effortless flow. Sound letter construction is noted. Signatures penned during his early days as a player tend to be more reckless and somewhat illegible. Letter construction of vintage signatures tend to vary more in height with a large "J," "D," and "g." As DiMaggio became established his signature became more uniform and variance in height diminished. His signature was more legible and letter construction became more pronounced. Towards the end of his life DiMaggio was diagnosed with lung cancer and basically stopped signing autographs except for close friends. Despite his illness DiMaggio's hand remained strong just about his entire life. For collecting purposes a genuine DiMaggio signature should evidence no shakiness of hand. There are a handful of genuine signatures that evidence a shaky hand but these signatures are very few and far between. There are

DiMaggio 1: circa 1940s signature

DiMaggio 2: undated signature

DiMaggio 3: government postcard dated 1987

just too many signatures in the market to fool with the tremulous specimens. Any DiMaggio signature that evidences a shakiness of hand should be avoided, as it is likely forged; even if it is real, too many people will question the authenticity.

Signature Population: The supply of DiMaggio signatures is very strong but demand is greater. He did many mass signings and also honored requests for his signature through the mail. His signature is available on just about all mediums including index cards, photos, Hall of Fame plaque postcards, balls, bats, bank checks, and Perez-Steele cards. Letters of any kind are uncommon to scarce. There are a couple of misconceptions regarding DiMaggio-signed material. First are signed baseball bats. For years dealers have advertised DiMaggio-signed bats as rare. Many signed bats exist and while uncommon they should not be considered rare. The same can be said for bank checks; like bats, they have been advertised as rare but many exist. Another type of signed photo features DiMaggio with his wife Marilyn Monroe. It is often said that DiMaggio refused to sign these pictures. While he was reluctant to do so, there are genuinely signed photos in the market. Signed photos with Monroe are uncommon.

Known Forgeries: DiMaggio's signature is very difficult to replicate; however, being the target of skilled forgers, there are many forgeries in the market. Forgeries should be considered moderate to well executed, so caution is warranted. DiMaggio is one of the most forged signatures in all of sports. Most signed baseballs and 8 × 10 photos offered in the market are forged. Chances are if you see a DiMaggio signature for sale it is a forgery. DiMaggio employed the use of secretaries throughout his career. Many signed team items and period government postcards were signed by clubhouse attendants. DiMaggio 4 illustrates a common "clubhouse" signature. DiMaggio received many requests for his autograph through the mail and in general honored requests. DiMaggio allowed both his sister and a personal assistant to sign autographs for him. Two DiMaggio sec-

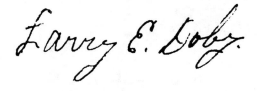

DiMaggio 4: common secretarial signature circa 1940s

Doby 1: contract dated 1946 (courtesy Newark Public Library, The Newark Eagles Papers)

DiMaggio 5: common secretarial

Doby 2: signed postal cover circa 1990

DiMaggio 6: common secretarial

retarial signatures are illustrated in DiMaggio 5 and DiMaggio 6. In the *International Autograph Collectors Club & Dealers Alliance* newsletter (Volume 5, Number 4, July/August 2001), Stephen Koschal writes in his DiMaggio signature study: "When it was called to his attention that collectors really wanted a genuine DiMaggio signature he did resume answering his mail." One of my favorite multi-signed photos features DiMaggio, Ted Williams, and Mickey Mantle. However, most of these photos in the market, upwards of 90 percent, are forgeries so caution is warranted.

Sales: Single-signed baseball sold for $289 (RR Auctions, August 2011). Baseball Legends card sold for $119 (eBay, September 2011). Bank check sold for $218 (RR Auctions, July 2011). The DiMaggio Albums, two books, one signed, sold for $200 (Hunt Auctions, September 2010). 8 × 10 photo sold for $110 (RR Auctions, January 2011). 8 × 10 photo, also signed by Mickey Mantle, sold for $324 (RR Auctions, February 2010).

Larry Doby

Signature Study: Doby signed in a rather unattractive hand. His signature has poor display value and is rudimentary in construction. The sig-

nature has good legibility. Towards the end of his life, Doby's hand was affected by infirmity, hence modern signatures evidence a fair amount of shakiness. Overall, this is one of the less appealing Hall of Fame signatures.

Signature Population: There is only marginal demand for Doby's signature. There is a good supply of material in the market. He engaged in many mass signings. His signature can be found on most mediums including index cards, photos, balls, bats, and gum cards. His signature is uncommon to scarce on letters and government postcards from his playing days. Material signed during his days in the Negro Leagues is rare.

Known Forgeries: The practical nature of Doby's signature makes replication of his hand easy. Creating a well executed forgery can be done with little effort. Due to the nominal value of Doby's signature, he is not the target of skilled forgers.

Sales: Doby's signature is available. His autograph generally sells for under $100 on most mediums.

Bob Doerr

Signature Study: Doerr signs in an extremely nice hand. His signature is very legible. It is marked with nice flowing strokes. Sound display value is noted. Doerr's signature has remained consistent throughout the years. Material signed during his playing days varies little from modern signatures. As of 2012 Doerr's hand remains strong. A genuine signature will exhibit no shakiness of hand and one that does should be considered suspect and avoided.

Signature Population: The demand for Doerr's

Doerr 1: circa 1990s signature

signature is marginal. The supply of genuine Doerr material is about limitless. Doerr has, for many years, been a gracious signer and honors all mail requests for his signature. His signature is common on index cards, photos, balls, bats, Hall of Fame plaque cards, Perez-Steele cards, and the like. Bank checks and letters are uncommon to scarce.

Known Forgeries: Doerr is a difficult signature to forge. There are no well executed forgeries in the market. Due to the nominal value of Doerr's signature, he is not the target of skilled forgers.

Sales: Doerr's signature is available. His autograph generally sells for under $100 on most mediums.

Barney Dreyfuss

Signature Study: Dreyfuss signed in a very eloquent hand. His signature contains many effortless strokes. The capital "D" in the last name dominates the entire signature. His signature has maximum display value. Letter construction is fairly sound, though portions of the signature have impaired legibility. The signature has a certain fairytale look to it. Dreyfuss died at the relatively young age of 66, hence infirmity of hand does not exist. A genuine Dreyfuss signature will exhibit no shakiness of hand and one that does should be considered suspect and avoided.

Signature Population: There is good demand for Dreyfuss material when compared to a restricted supply. Dreyfuss should be considered a scarce signature. There is a modest supply of signed Pirates documents and letters in the market. On non-document mediums his signature is very rare to non-existent. I know of only one signed photo. I have never examined a single-signed baseball.

Dreyfuss 1: document dated 1901

Dreyfuss 2: TLS dated 1912 (courtesy National Baseball Hall of Fame and Museum)

Dreyfuss 3: contract dated 1930

Dreyfuss 4: common secretarial (courtesy National Baseball Hall of Fame and Museum)

Known Forgeries: Given the complex nature of Dreyfuss' hand, it is one of the most difficult signatures to replicate. There are no well executed Dreyfuss forgeries in the market. Forgers avoid Dreyfuss' signature in favor of less complicated names to forge. A few team letters are secretarially signed, as illustrated in Dreyfuss 4. Title issues may exist with certain Dreyfuss letters. See the stolen document section in Chapter 4.

Sales: 1930 TLS, choice signature, sold for $1,875 (Lelands.com, November 2009). 1905 ALS, choice specimen, sold for $3,053 (Hunt Auctions, November 2009). 1917 baseball-related document sold for $2,150 (Hunt Auctions, July 2009).

Don Drysdale

Signature Study: Drysdale signed in a very aggressive hand. His signature is marked with bold vertical strokes and dominates the medium it is placed upon. The signature appears rapid and compact. Legibility is somewhat impaired. The uniformed look of his signature correlates into sound display value. Drysdale's signature remained relatively consistent throughout his life. Drysdale died at the age of 56 from a heart attack. Since he never reached old age, a genuine Drysdale signature will evidence no shakiness of hand

Drysdale 1: 1963 signature

Drysdale 2: common secretarial

and one that does should be considered suspect and avoided.

Signature Population: The supply of Drysdale material is strong and typically outweighs demand. He was a huge star before his induction into Cooperstown and signed countless items throughout his life. After induction he did many mass signings. Drysdale's signature is common on index cards, baseballs, photos, Hall of Fame plaque postcards, bats, Perez-Steele cards, and baseball cards. His signature is considered scarce on letters of any kind.

Known Forgeries: Drysdale's signature is difficult to replicate. There are no well executed forgeries in the market. Due to the nominal value of his signature, Drysdale is not a target of skilled forgers. It should be noted that during his playing days many autographs obtained through the mail were signed by a secretary. A common secretarial signature is illustrated as Drysdale 2.

Sales: Drysdale's signature is available. His autograph generally sells for under $100 on most mediums

Hugh Duffy

Signature Study: Duffy signed in a very rough and displeasing hand. His signature is perhaps the most unsightly signature in all of baseballdom. Duffy's signature evidences thick ink strokes and jagged lines. The display value is minimal. Letter construction is impaired. Legibility is fairly sound. Duffy's signature took a dramatic turn for the worse some time in the 1920s. There are a few

nice letters signed during the 1910s that actually have nice eye appeal but most items signed after 1920 are unsightly. Duffy 1 illustrates a rare early signature with good eye appeal. Duffy's signature remained relatively constant thereafter and evidences a slightly labored appearance. His signature looks like it was accomplished by an infirmed hand even in his younger days.

Signature Population: There is just average demand for Duffy's signature. The supply of Duffy material is ample but not great. I would consider his signature scarce, albeit borderline. His signature is generally limited to those items obtained through the mail, thus index cards and government postcards are most common. On premium items his signature should be considered rare to very rare. Multi-signed baseballs are rare while single-signed baseballs are basically non-existent. 8 × 10 photos are very rare. There is a small supply of genuinely signed exhibit cards, but these are very scarce. Letters of any kind are scarce. Team-signed baseballs from his playing days very likely do not exist.

Known Forgeries: Due to the abrupt stops in his writing, Duffy is a very easy signature to forge. Many well executed forgeries are in the market. Duffy held the positions of coach and scout with the Red Sox. Many typed letters signed by Duffy exist, complete with Boston letterhead. These letters are typically dated in the late 1940s. Many Duffy signatures on these letters look like they were signed by a child. The "y" in the last name appears large with a long and wide downstroke. Typically, Duffy-signed Red Sox letters from this era were secretarially signed, so Duffy-signed letters need to be studied carefully. Many forgeries are accomplished with breaks in the signature that a genuine autograph will not exhibit. A genuine signature will exhibit no breaks in the up and down strokes in the first letter "u" which looks like a "w." In a genuine signature the letter "u" is completed in one stroke. In some forgeries the stroke is broken at the turns of the letter and then

Duffy 1: ALS dated 1913

Duffy 2: album page circa 1925

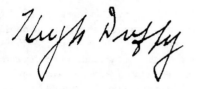

Duffy 3: will dated 1947

restarted. Under magnification the broken lines are evident. These forgeries fail on point construction.

Sales: Index card, choice specimen, sold for $433 (RR Auctions, November 2010). Album page, with Duffy Lewis, sold for $411 (Robert Edward Auctions Spring, 2009). Index card, fountain pen specimen, sold for $437 (Lelands.com June, 2011).

Leo Durocher

Signature Study: Durocher signed in a very nice and legible hand. Early signatures have excellent letter construction. Sound display value is noted. As the years progressed Durocher's hand became more flashy. He added a long line that extended from the "D" in the last name. This feature is well illustrated in Durocher 2. As Durocher entered the final years of his life, his hand became unsteady, resulting in a signature with a labored and broken appearance.

Signature Population: Durocher was a willing signer throughout the years and there is a very good supply of material. Supply is balanced with a sound demand for his signature. His signature is available on photos, baseballs, index cards, government postcards, and the like. TLsS are uncom-

![Leo Durocher signature]

Durocher 1: album page dated 1933

![Leo Durocher signature]

Durocher 2: government postcard dated 1987

![Leo Durocher signature]

Durocher 3: 1990 signature

mon. ALsS are very scarce. Signed copies of his book *Nice Guys Finish Last* are uncommon and highly collectible. Signed bats are scarce. A few signed bank checks exist but these should be considered rare. Durocher's long career in baseball correlates into a great variety of baseball cards. Signed cards exist in quantities. His signature can be found on Goudey, Bowman, Red Man Tobacco, and Topps cards.

Known Forgeries: Overall, Durocher's signature is rather difficult to replicate. Well executed forgeries are limited to old-age signatures. Forgeries are generally limited to single-signed baseballs and bats. The majority of Durocher baseballs in the market are forgeries. Many have been wrongly certified as genuine by the authentication companies. There are also forged black Louisville Slugger baseball bats in the market. They are typically signed under the facsimile signature in silver or gold sharpie.

Sales: Durocher's signature is available. His autograph generally sells for under $100 on most mediums. Of note: Rare bank check sold for $510 (RR Auctions, November 1998).

Dennis Eckersley

Signature Study: Like most modern Major League players, Eckersley signs in an illegible hand. His signature looks like a bunch of confused lines. His signature has little display value. As of 2012 Eckersley's hand remains sound. A genuine signature will exhibit no shakiness of hand and one that does should be considered suspect and avoided.

Signature Population: The demand for Eckersley material is marginal. Eckersley is a willing signer and there is a strong supply of material in the market. His signature can be found on most items including photos, baseballs, gum

Eckersley 1: circa 2005 signature

cards, and the like. Letters of any kind are considered scarce.

Known Forgeries: Given the lack of structure, Eckersley's hand is relatively easy to copy. Producing a well executed forgery would be easy. Due to the nominal value of Eckersley's signature, he is not the target of skilled forgers.

Sales: Eckersley's signature is available. His autograph generally sells for under $100 on most mediums.

Billy Evans

Signature Study: Evans signed in a very legible and sophisticated hand. His signature has nice letter construction and generally dominates the medium it is placed upon. He would typically sign items as ""Billy" Evans" with quotes around the first name. His signature is almost always finished with a nice flowing paraph. Evans' signature has excellent display value. His hand remained relatively constant throughout the years and always exhibits nice flow. Due to his sudden death, infirmity of hand was non-existent. A genuine Evans signature will exhibit no shakiness of hand and one that does should be considered suspect and avoided.

Signature Population: Evans is an uncommon signature and borders on the scarce side. The demand for his autograph is marginal. He was a willing signer throughout his life, though he received few requests for his autograph. Most signatures are document related. Were it not for his executive positions with the Tigers and Indians,

Evans would be considered a very scarce signature based simply on his umpire career. There are many letters and team-related documents in the market, which are an excellent source of Evans signatures. On premium mediums Evans is rare to very rare. I have only seen one single-signed baseball and one signed 8 × 10 photo.

Known Forgeries: Evans' signature is one of the more difficult to replicate. There are no well executed forgeries in the market. There are no specific forgeries to note. Evans forgeries are rudimentary in construction and feature an unsteady appearance, thus are easily spotted.

Sales: Signature removed from TLS sold for $268 (Lelands.com, January 2008). 1922 exhibit card, superior specimen, sold for $1,796 (Lelands.com, June 2004). Album page sold for $163 (RR Auctions, June 2009). Short TLS sold for $200 (eBay, January 2012).

Johnny Evers

Signature Study: Evers signed in a nice flowing hand that evidences choppiness in the letters. Letter construction tends to be less than sound. His signature is somewhat legible. Evers' hand has a nice flow, resulting in a signature with above average display value. Most signatures are signed as "John J. Evers" but on occasion a signature signed "J.J. Evers" will surface. I have never seen a signature where he signs with his nickname, the "Crab." Since Evers died at a relatively young age, his hand was never affected with infirmity. A genuine Evers signature will exhibit no shakiness of hand and one that does should be considered suspect and avoided.

Signature Population: There is strong demand for this Cobbian era star. Demand clearly outweighs supply. Evers is a scarce signature per se but not rare. Most Evers signatures are found on index cards, government postcards, or letters of various size. Premium items are considered very rare to extremely rare. I have only seen two genuine single-signed baseballs. I have never seen a genuinely signed 8 × 10 photo or tobacco card of any kind. There are a handful of signed bank

Evans 1: undated signature

Evers 1: bank check dated 1915

Evers 2: bank check dated 1916

checks in the market. These checks are typically dated in the late 1910s and should be considered rare to very rare. Evers business letters are scarce to rare. It seems Evers was always into some type of business venture. Letters on sporting good, camera, and shoe company letterhead exist and are a fine source of Evers signatures. Letters as early as 1910 are in the market. Evers would always go out of his way to respond to a request for his autograph, especially from a child. Many letters written to young fans are some of the finest in baseball and show the soft side (no pun intended) of the Crab. On occasion he would sign his autograph then add the inscription "Tinker to Evers to Chance." This inscription is rare and commands a substantial premium. There are only a couple of items signed by Evers, Joe Tinker, and Frank Chance. If you exclude his two very brief appearances in the 1922 and 1929 seasons, then signed team baseballs from Evers' days as a player very likely do not exist.

Known Forgeries: Due to the complex nature of his hand, Evers' signature is very difficult to replicate. Well executed forgeries are very limited in the market. Most Evers forgeries are rudimentary in construction and evidence a labored appearance. There is a grouping of forged handwritten notes in the market. They are usually one sentence long such as "Dear John Doe, Sorry for the delay — on a trip" and then signed "Yours John J. Evers" or "Sincerely John J. Evers." There are a few things to look for as these forgeries are common. First, the ink strokes are thick and labored. They lack the racing effect of a genuine signature. Second, the forger who created these notes failed to do his homework and dated them using hash marks (i.e., 12/25/34). I have never examined a genuine Evers signature where he dated a signature using this method. Evers dated many of his

signatures and almost always spelled out the month in which he signed (i.e., "Jan. 22. 1932" or "June. 3. 42"). Evers is a scarce and expensive signature so careful examination is needed as most Evers material offered in the market is fake.

Sales: 1945 ALS, choice specimen, sold for $8,813 (Robert Edward Auctions, Spring 2010). 1943 *Sporting News* questionnaire, mentions the Fred Merkle Play, sold for $11,468 (Lelands.com, June 2011). 1939 Abner Doubleday first day cover sold for $1,129 (RR Auctions, May 2009).

Buck Ewing

Signature Study: Ewing is an excessively rare signature. The only confirmed specimen I could locate is his will signed just six days before his death. The signature which appears on the will evidences a signature with good letter construction. This signature suggests that his hand remained strong until death. Ewing died at the age of 47, a victim of sugar.

Signature Population: I am told that there are a couple of genuine specimens in existence. I have never seen them. The only specimen I know of is the above-referenced will. It is not available in the open market. It is held under lock and key by Cincinnati Probate. This signature calls into question just about all Ewing signatures sold over the past 70 years, as they do not remotely resemble the signature found on the will. His signature is an extreme rarity.

Known Forgeries: The illustrated signature evidences a hand that would be rather easy to replicate. Several years ago a small group of signed pay receipts entered the market, issued by the New York baseball club. They are about the same size as a check and the signature reads "Wm. Ewing." The ink is a deep brown with thick strokes. I have only seen a couple of specimens, but it is clear that the signatures evidence bleeding of the ink into dried paper fibers. Some experts say they are real while others question the authenticity of these documents. These signatures have a material deviation from the illustrated specimen, and should be studied very carefully.

Evers 3: 1937 signature

Ewing 1: will dated 1906

Sales: Due to the rarity there have been no recent sales of Ewing's signature.

Red Faber

Signature Study: Faber signed in a very plain and legible hand. His hand tends to exhibit well constructed angles. A slight choppiness is evident. Letter construction is sound. His signature has only moderate display value. Most items are signed "U.C. Faber" or "U.C. "Red" Faber." His hand remained relatively constant throughout his life. Material signed in the last few years of his life is unsteady in appearance.

Signature Population: Faber's signature generates only average demand and is well balanced with supply. Faber material is uncommon and premium items are scarce to rare. He is one of the toughest Hall of Famers to obtain who died after 1970. His signature is generally found on index cards and vintage signed government postcards. Hall of Fame plaque postcards are available but uncommon. 8 × 10 photos are scarce. Single-signed baseballs and letters are considered rare. Team-signed baseballs are generally limited to White Sox teams of the late 1920s and early 1930s. There is also a handful of genuinely signed 1933 Goudey gum cards but these should be considered scarce to rare.

Known Forgeries: Faber's signature can be forged with moderate effort. Generally, Faber is not the target of forgers except for premium items such as single-signed baseballs. Faber's health declined in his final years. Many items signed through the mail were actually signed by Mrs. Faber. Note Mrs. Faber's hand, as exhibited in Faber 3, is more feminine and differs greatly from a genuine signature. The majority of signatures received through the mail in the late 1960s until death were actually secretarially signed. Most Hall

Faber 1: team sheet dated 1932

Faber 2: circa 1960s signature

Faber 3: common secretarial by Mrs. Faber

of Fame plaque postcards were secretarially signed.

Sales: Faber's signature is available. His autograph generally sells for under $100 on most mediums. Of note: 1926 Major League contract sold for $3,525 (Robert Edward Auctions, Spring 2011).

Bob Feller

Signature Study: Feller signed in a very nice hand. His signature has an eclectic feel. His hand lacks any hesitation and signatures are nice and flowing. Letter construction is fairly sound. The signature is legible and displays well. Feller's hand remained strong his entire life. A genuine Feller signature will exhibit no shakiness of hand and one that does should be considered suspect and avoided.

Feller 1: ALS dated 1988

Signature Population: The supply of Feller material is strong and far outweighs demand. Feller had been a willing signer for years. His signature is common on most mediums including index cards, photos, balls, bats, Hall of Fame plaque cards, and the like. Letters of any kind are uncommon to scarce. Dual-signed photos with fellow Hall of Famer Hal Newhouser exist but should be considered uncommon.

Known Forgeries: Feller's hand is fairly difficult to replicate. Creating a well executed forgery would take effort. Due to the nominal value of Feller's signature, he is not a target of skilled forgers.

Sales: Feller's signature is available. His autograph generally sells for under $100 on most mediums.

Rick Ferrell

Signature Study: Ferrell signed in a very legible and nice hand. Early signatures tend to have more

Ferrell 1: government postcard dated 1989

rapid motion. As Ferrell aged his hand slow somewhat. Letter construction became more defined. His signature has superior display value. Ferrell's hand remained strong his entire life. A genuine signature will exhibit no shakiness of hand and one that does should be considered suspect and avoided.

Signature Population: This is a signature of marginal demand that is outweighed by supply. Ferrell was a willing signer his entire life. There are countless items available in the market. His signature can be found on most mediums including photos, baseballs, index cards, Perez-Steele cards, and Hall of Fame plaque postcards. Less common are bats, letters, and bank checks. His signature is considered scarce on items signed with his brother, and fellow Major Leaguer, Wes Ferrell. Signed Goudey gum cards are scarce and desirable.

Known Forgeries: Ferrell's signature is one of the finest of all Hall of Famers and is a difficult signature to replicate. There are no well executed forgeries in the market. Due to the nominal value of Ferrell's autograph, he is not the target of skilled forgers.

Sales: Ferrell's signature is available. His autograph generally sells for under $100 on most mediums.

Rollie Fingers

Signature Study: Fingers signs in an illegible hand. Letter construction is poor but uniform. A signature with good display value. His signature evidences good flow and a rapid motion. As of 2012 Fingers suffers no infirmity of hand. A genuine signature will exhibit no shakiness of hand and one that does should be considered suspect and avoided.

Signature Population: This is a signature where supply far outweighs demand. The supply of Fingers material is strong. He is a common signature. His signature is available on baseballs, photos, Hall of Fame plaque postcards, Perez-Steele cards, gum cards, and the like. Letters of any kind are scarce.

Fingers 1: contract dated 1993

Known Forgeries: Fingers' signature is difficult to replicate. There are no well executed forgeries in the market. Due to the nominal value of Fingers' autograph, he is not the target of skilled forgers.

Sales: Fingers' signature is available. His autograph generally sells for under $100 on most mediums.

Carlton Fisk

Signature Study: Fisk signs in an extremely fast and sloppy hand. His signature has poor letter construction and is illegible. Display value is marginal at best. As of 2012 Fisk's hand is not affected with infirmity. A genuine signature will evidence no unsteadiness and one that does should be considered suspect and avoided. In general, Fisk has one of the least attractive signatures of all the Hall of Famers.

Signature Population: The supply of Fisk material is strong and far outweighs demand. His signature is common in most forms including baseballs, bats, photos, gum cards, and the like. Letters of any kind are scarce.

Known Forgeries: The unstructured nature of Fisk's signature results in a fairly easy hand to replicate. Due to the nominal value of Fisk's autograph, he is not the target of skilled forgers.

Sales: Fisk's signature is available. His autograph generally sells for under $100 on most mediums.

Fisk 1: undated signature

Elmer Flick

Signature Study: Flick signed in a plain and legible hand. His signature evidences sound letter construction. Flick's signature has moderate display value. Flick signed in a slower hand and thus his signature lacks rapid motion. As Flick entered the final decade of his life, his hand slowed greatly and infirmity is evident. Signatures penned in the last five or so years of his life are extremely unsteady and are child-like in appearance. Flick 3 illustrates a signature signed shortly before death.

Signature Population: This is a signature of average demand and well balanced with supply. Flick was one of the last remaining tobacco-card Hall of Famers when he died in 1971. He was in his mid–90s and he signed almost until the day he died. Flick simply loved to sign autographs. Today, his signature is available on index cards, Hall of Fame plaque postcards, and government postcards. Handwritten letters are also available but usually limited to those penned on government postcards or index cards. Full-page handwritten letters are rare. Flick's signature should be considered scarce on just about anything else. Single-signed baseballs are rare. Team-signed baseballs from Flick's playing days very likely do not exist. Flick is one of the few players who signed T-206 tobacco cards. While most signed T-cards are forgeries, there are a few genuine specimens in the market but they should be considered rare to very rare.

Known Forgeries: Due to Flick's more tempered hand, his signature is rather easy to forge. There are many well executed forgeries in the market though they are generally limited to premium signed items such as baseballs and 8 × 10 photos. Just about all the single-signed baseballs, 8 × 10 photos, and T-206 cards with Flick's signature are forged. Hall of Fame plaque postcards

Flick 3: circa 1960s signature

are another target of forgers and the majority of these cards offered for sale are forgeries. A common forgery of plaque postcards surfaced years ago. They were signed along the top of the card and then dated along the bottom, all purportedly in Flick's hand. The dates are all from the late 1960s. A genuine Flick signature from this time is very unsteady due to infirmity of hand. The forgeries on these postcards are clean and lack the shaky appearance of a genuine Flick signature. The forger who accomplished these forgeries does a nice job in copying Flick's hand but failed to do the proper research. Any Flick signature signed in the mid– to late 1960s should exhibit a shakiness of hand. These postcards do not and should be avoided.

Sales: 7 × 8 photo in civilian cloths sold for $121 (RR Auctions, February 2011). Index card sold for $51 (eBay, November 2011). Index card sold for $48 (eBay, November 2011). Index card sold for $60 (eBay, November 2011). Index card sold for $80 (eBay, December 2011).

Whitey Ford

Signature Study: Ford signs in a nice vertical hand. His signature tends to be illegible, at least the first name. Ford's signature exhibits nice strokes and has good display value. A genuine Ford signature will exhibit no shakiness of hand and one that does should be considered suspect and avoided.

Signature Population: Ford is a common signature. Supply is very strong and outweighs demand. He engages in mass signings. His signature is available on most mediums including photos, baseballs, Perez-Steele cards, gum cards, Hall of Fame plaque postcards, and the like. Signed letters of any kind are scarce. Ford was a member of the fabled New York Yankees teams of the 1950s and 1960s. Team balls with signatures of Berra, Mantle, Maris, and Ford are some of the finest signed balls in existence.

Known Forgeries: Overall, Ford is a fairly difficult signature to forge. There are no well executed forgeries in the market. Due to the

Flick 1: document circa 1950

Flick 2: ALS dated 1957

Ford 1: 1984 signature

nominal value of Ford's autograph, he is not the target of skilled forgers.

Sales: Ford's signature is available. His autograph generally sells for under $100 on most mediums.

Rube Foster

Signature Study: Foster signed in a nice hand. His signature is marked with nice flow and hesitation of any kind is lacking. Some signatures stand vertical with an ever so slight right slant. Letter construction is good but the "n" in the first name appears like the letter "u" and the "d" is somewhat impaired. Foster's signature has good eye appeal. Pre–1920 signatures tend to feature a more traditional letter "d." Foster died at a relatively young age, thus a genuine signature will exhibit no shakiness of hand and one that does should be considered suspect and avoided.

Signature Population: This is a signature in much demand. The supply of genuine Foster material is basically non-existent. I estimate that there are five to ten genuine specimens in the open market. All are document or letter mediums. I know of no signed baseballs or photographs in existence. Overall, this is an extremely rare and desirable signature.

Known Forgeries: Foster is a rather difficult hand to replicate. Given the extreme value of his signature, Foster has become the target of skilled forgers. Just about all of the Foster signatures in existence are forgeries. A good number of period letters and documents from the 1910s and 1920s contain secretarial signatures. Many have been incorrectly certified as genuine. One form of secretarial signature can be found on both letters and

Foster, R. 1: World War I draft card circa 1917 (Record Group 163, Records of the Selective Services Division, National Archives at Atlanta)

Foster, R. 2: document circa 1920s

Foster, R. 3: common secretarial

documents and is signed "Andrew Rube Foster" or "Andrew Foster." These secretarial signatures stand out as they appear methodic. They lack nice flow and evidence a *slight* unsteady appearance. The "d' in the first name appears like a more normally constructed letter "d" with more height than the malformed "d" of Foster's hand. Some of these signatures have been notarized. Any Foster signature that appears labored, even slightly so, should be avoided. Another type of secretarial signature can be found on "American Giants Base Ball Club" letterhead and is signed as "A Rube Foster." This signature looks nothing like a genuine signature, as illustrated in Foster, R-3.

Sales: Due to the rarity, there have been no recent sales of Foster's signature.

Willie Foster

Signature Study: Brother of Rube, Foster signed in a large and dominant hand. His signature is marked with nice bold strokes and appears hesitation free. Foster's signature is one of the few of the Hall of Fame members that slants towards the left. Most signatures are signed "Willie (Bill) Foster." On occasion he would sign as "Bill Foster" or "Willie H. Foster." Note, Foster was one the few players to sign with a parenthesis. Foster's hand remained strong his entire life. A genuine signature will exhibit no shakiness of hand and one that does should be considered suspect and avoided.

Signature Population: Foster's signature creates only moderate demand. When Foster was first inducted into the Hall of Fame in 1996, his signature was advertised as an excessively rare name. For years dealers were claiming that less than ten genuine signatures were in existence. As time went on it became apparent that the supply of genuine Foster material was much greater. Having said that, his signature must be considered

Foster, W. 1: 1974 signature

Foster, W. 2: undated signature

Foster, W. 3: undated signature

Fox 1: 1961 signature

Fox 2: bank check dated 1970

Fox 3: undated signature

rare, albeit borderline. Foster material is basically limited to index cards that he signed through the mail. I have never seen a genuinely signed baseball or photograph. About the only other mediums that Foster's signature can be found on are signed bank checks and the occasional financial document.

Known Forgeries: Given Foster's reckless use of the pen, his signature is one of the more difficult to forge. Most forgeries are amateurish in construction and evidence a labored appearance. Just about all Foster signatures in the market are forged. There are no specific forgeries to note, but many can be found on index cards and album pages.

Sales: Signed index card sold for $1,645 (Robert Edward Auctions, Spring 2009). Signed index card sold for $1,292 (Robert Edward Auctions, Spring 2008).

Nellie Fox

Signature Study: Fox signed in a nice and practical hand. His signature is flowing and legible. Hesitation is non-existent. Overall, Fox's signature has nice display value. Most signatures are signed "Nelson Fox." Some documents and bank checks are signed "J. Nelson Fox." Fox died of cancer at the young age of 47. Since he never reached old age, infirmity of hand was non-existent. A genuine Fox signature will exhibit no

shakiness of hand and one that does should be considered suspect and avoided.

Signature Population: This is a signature that has good demand and outweighs the ample supply. Most signatures were signed during his playing years. Material signed post-retirement is less common. His signature is found on material that was typically signed at the stadium such as album pages, baseballs, and scorecards. His signature is scarce on photos. Eight by ten photos are rare. Single-signed baseballs are available but should be considered very scarce. The best way to obtain a Fox signature on a baseball is to secure a signed team ball from the White Sox. Signed letters of any kind are rare. There is a good supply of signed bank checks.

Known Forgeries: Fox's hand appears to be one of the easier signatures to forge. I have seen some fairly nice forgeries in the market. Most single-signed baseballs in the market are forged and there are some convincing examples. Another common target of forgers are Topps baseball cards and exhibit cards. The majority of Fox signatures offered for sale are forgeries, so caution is warranted.

Sales: Bank check sold for $220 (RR Auctions, June 2011). 1970 Major League coach's contract sold for $437 (Lelands.com, June 2010). 1961 Topps card sold for $275 (eBay, August 2011). Choice ink signature sold for $148 (RR Auctions, May 2010). 1965 Topps card sold for $210 (eBay, November 2011).

Jimmie Foxx

Signature Study: There are essentially two forms of Foxx signatures in the market and the differences between modern and vintage signatures are striking. Material signed in the early days of his career is signed in a slower hand. When compared to modern signatures there are noted differences in just about all the letters, especially in the "J" of the first name and the "xx" in the last name. As Foxx's career progressed his hand changed markedly and remained that way until his untimely death. Modern signatures are rapid in appearance and lack the ever so slight hesitation of the earlier signatures. The letter construction is altered greatly. Note the "xx" in the last name is now separated. Many times Foxx would finish his signature with a small paraph. Both vintage and modern signatures have nice display value. There has been great controversy among collectors as to the existence of Foxx signatures where the first name is signed "Jimmy." Many dispute the authenticity of a signature signed as "Jimmy Foxx." While most Foxx signatures are signed with the more common "Jimmie" there are a few genuine examples, from early in his career, signed with the alternate first name. Why he did this I do not know. Fellow Hall of Famer Freddie Lindstrom was also known to sign his first name as "Freddy." Foxx died at the relatively young age of 59. Since Foxx never reached old age, a genuine signature will exhibit no shakiness of hand and one that does should be considered suspect and avoided.

Signature Population: Foxx is a signature

Foxx 2: circa 1930s signatureFoxx 3: 1964 signature

Foxx 3: 1964 signature

where supply is clearly outweighed by a strong demand. Foxx was a willing signer throughout his entire life. His signature is most commonly found on index cards, postcard-sized photos, government postcards, and team-signed baseballs. Less common are 8 × 10 photos and Hall of Fame plaque postcards. His signature is considered rare on letters and Goudey gum cards. Single-signed baseballs are available but should be considered rare, albeit borderline.

Known Forgeries: Due to the lack of rapid motion, replication of Foxx's hand is rather easy, at least when it comes to early signatures. Well executed forgeries exist in quantities. Modern signatures are difficult to replicate. Well executed forgeries of modern signatures are uncommon. Foxx is a highly targeted name and most Foxx signatures offered in the market are forged. Many have been incorrectly certified as genuine by authentication companies, so caution is warranted. Many forged baseball cards are in the market including Goudey gum cards and 1940 Play Ball cards. Being a member of the 500-home-run club makes Foxx a target of skilled forgers. I know of no signed items that feature just the three early 500 Home Run club members of Foxx, Babe Ruth, and Mel Ott. It is unlikely a genuine 500-home-run item exists signed by all members of this group. Several years back a small group of forged team-signed baseballs entered the market featuring the Philadelphia Athletics teams of the mid–1920s. These signed baseballs are almost comical but they still appear for sale and a few come complete with certificates of authenticity. The signatures are all in the same hand and evidence a slight shakiness of hand. The forgery is

Foxx 1: signed baseball dated 1930, variant signature

so poor that the Foxx signature is signed as "Jim-mie Fox." The explanation is given that Foxx signed with one "x" in the beginning of his Major League career, which is incorrect.

Sales: 8 × 10 George Burke photo, superior specimen, sold for $2,204 (Robert Edward Auctions, Spring 2006). 1932 postal cover sold for $525 (RR Auctions, March 2011). 1952 government postcard sold for $375 (Hunt Auctions, November 2010). 1961 postcard sold for $769 (Lelands.com, June 2010). Baseball, also signed by Ted Williams and boxer Jack Sharkey, choice specimen, sold for $4,863 (Lelands.com, June 2009).

Ford Frick

Signature Study: Frick signed in a very confined and neat hand. His signature is very flowing and lacks hesitation. Letter construction is marginal with malformed letters. The "F" in his last name is oddly formed and looks more like the letter "L." This is a signature with average display value. Frick's hand remained strong his entire life. A genuine signature will exhibit no shakiness of hand and one that does should be considered suspect and avoided.

Frick 1: undated signature

Signature Population: There is only marginal demand for Frick material. Overall, the supply is plentiful. His signature can be found on most mediums including index cards, photos, Hall of Fame plaque postcards, and gum cards. Due to his long association with the game of baseball as an executive and commissioner, many letters and baseball-related documents exist. Single-signed baseballs are considered very scarce.

Known Forgeries: Due to the various breaks in Frick's signature, it is one of the easier signatures to replicate. Given the common nature of his signature, well executed forgeries are limited to 8 × 10 photos and single-signed baseballs.

Sales: Frick's signature is available. His autograph generally sells for under $100 on most mediums.

Frank Frisch

Signature Study: Frisch signed in a very flowing and eloquent hand. Early signatures are large, bold, and dominate the medium it is placed upon. Letter construction of early signatures is sound and the capital "F"s are striking. Vintage Frisch signatures are extremely appealing to the eye and have maximum display value. As Frisch's life progressed his hand became sloppy and less legible. Later signatures lack the fine flow of early specimens. Later signatures appear choppy and have less eye appeal. Neither type of signature has any measurable hesitation in the hand. Frisch died in a car crash in 1973. Since he died a sudden death, his hand remained strong for his entire life. A genuine Frisch signature will evidence no shakiness of hand and one that does should be considered suspect and avoided.

Signature Population: There is strong demand for Frisch's signature. Fortunately, there is a good supply of his signature. Frisch material is ample as he was a willing signer throughout his entire life. His signature can be found on index cards, government postcards, Hall of Fame plaque postcards, photos, and the like. 8 × 10 photos, gum cards, and letters are scarce. Single-signed baseballs border on the rare side and most offered for sale are forged. There is a good supply of canceled bank checks in the market. Frisch was an avid reader who had a nice library of finely bound leather books from the late 1800s and mid–1900s. Frisch would sign his name and address on the inside cover. These books are sought out by book collectors as well as autograph collectors.

Known Forgeries: Frisch signatures are rather difficult to forge, especially vintage specimens. There are a few well executed forgeries in the market, which are usually limited to the more modern

Frisch 1: album page dated 1933

Frisch 2: circa 1965 signature

Frisch 3: bank check dated 1972

signatures. Frisch has generally not been targeted by forgers due to the nominal value of his signature. Forgeries are generally limited to single-signed baseballs, 8 × 10 photos, and Goudey gum cards.

Sales: 1929 Major League contract, countersigned by Branch Rickey, sold for $5,288 (Robert Edward Auctions, Spring 2011). Hall of Fame plaque postcard sold for $100 (RR Auctions, March 2011). Index card sold for $41 (eBay, September 2011). Single-signed baseball, circa 1930, museum grade, sold for $2,587 (Robert Edward Auctions, Spring 2004). First-day cover sold for $85 (eBay, January 2012).

Pud Galvin

Signature Study: Galvin's signature is one of the most unusual of all Hall of Famers. Flowing strokes give the signature a very artistic look. Letter construction is marginal. Legibility is impaired. His signature has good display value. Known specimens, what few exist, are signed "J.F. Galvin." Due to the scarce number of specimens in existence, it is unknown whether Galvin suffered from infirmity of hand. I can say that I have never seen a genuine Galvin signature that evidences an unsteady appearance. Given an early death, infirmity of hand is unlikely.

Signature Population: Galvin is an excessively rare signature. His autograph borders on the non-existent. There are only a handful of genuine specimens in existence. I know of two handwritten letters and I am told another two letters exist, though I have never seen them. I know of no other signed mediums in existence. I estimate the total population at under five signatures. This is simply an extreme rarity.

Galvin 1: ALS dated 1878

Known Forgeries: This is a signature that is reasonably difficult to replicate. Well executed forgeries are very limited. Galvin has been a rare and valuable signature for decades. Forgeries of Galvin can be found in autograph collections assembled in the 1950s. Since for years most collectors knew nothing of Galvin's hand, a common forgery surfaced in the 1960s and has been circulating ever since. Signed "Jas. F. Galvin" these forgeries look nothing like a genuine signature. Many are found as check endorsements.

Sales: 1878 ALS sold for $18,000 (Hunt Auctions, February 2005).

Lou Gehrig

Signature Study: Gehrig's signature is one of the most studied of all Baseball Hall of Fame members. Gehrig signed in a very pleasing and flowing hand. His signature evidences no hesitation whatsoever. Early Gehrig signatures, those signed in the mid–1920s, tend to be slightly larger and are more vertical in appearance. The capital "L" in the first name evidences a more blunt appearance with a smaller upper loop which differs greatly from later examples. As Gehrig's career progressed, his hand becomes more compact and exhibits faster strokes. Later signatures tend to slant to the right and the first and last name are morphed together. Material signed from the early 1930s until 1939 exhibits indistinguishable strokes. The letter construction is poor. Legibility is impaired. As Gehrig entered the 1939 season his coordination began a downward spiral. It was the beginning signs of the disease amyotrophia. Material signed in 1939 is very rare to non-existent. There are a few team-signed baseballs from that season, but for the most part material signed in 1939 is extremely difficult to locate. After 1939 Gehrig signatures are limited to legal documents. Gehrig did not sign material after 1939 for the general public. While Gehrig was severely inca-

Gehrig 1: team sheet dated 1933

Gehrig 2: circa 1930s signature

pacitated by the sclerosis, a genuine Gehrig signature should exhibit no shakiness of hand and one that does should be considered suspect and avoided. I say this because Gehrig stopped signing in 1939. Up to that time the disease had no real effect on his hand to any measurable degree. If a Gehrig signature appears unsteady, my advice is stay well away from it. There are far too many genuine signatures available to bother with the material signed in late 1939 and beyond.

Signature Population: This is a signature in very strong demand. Gehrig material is very limited. His signature should be considered scarce on a per se basis. Most items available in the market are those signed at the ballpark, such as scorecards, team-signed baseballs, and album pages. Government postcards are very scarce. Photos of any kind are very scarce. Single-signed baseballs and letters of any kind are rare to very rare. The greatest source of Gehrig signatures are Yankees team baseballs signed between 1935 and 1938. There are many specimens available and Gehrig would usually pen his name on the sweet spot. These balls are by far and away the most plentiful source of Gehrig signatures. Signed Goudey gum cards and postcard-sized exhibit cards are rare. There are also a handful of bank checks in the market but these must be considered very rare.

Known Forgeries: Gehrig is a rather difficult signature to replicate. Well executed forgeries are limited but many decent forgeries exist. Many have been incorrectly certified as genuine by authentication companies, so caution is warranted. Gehrig is one of the most forged signatures in all of autographdom, baseball or otherwise. Many skilled forgers have taken up the task and have

Gehrig 3: circa 1930s signature

Gehrig 4: team sheet dated 1937

produced some really convincing material. Forged signatures have been placed on just about all mediums from 1933 Goudey gum cards to bats to government postcards. Many forged single-signed baseballs are in the market. A common forged ball is signed on the sweet spot with an overly large signature. Gehrig signed in a confined hand. A genuine signature is small and takes up very little space on the sweet spot, as illustrated in Gehrig 7. Note the small size of the signature. The forged Gehrig signatures, on the other hand, take up the entire sweet spot and are over twice as large as a genuine signature. If you examine one of these balls with a large signature on the sweet spot, study it carefully as it is likely a forgery. Most Gehrig single-signed balls are signed *and* inscribed on the side panel. A genuine non-inscribed Gehrig single-signed baseball is extremely rare.

Another type of Gehrig forged ball is usually signed with Ruth, Miller Huggins, Christy Walsh, Herb Pennock, or a combination thereof. These forgeries were produced in the early 1990s. The balls are in excellent condition and cream white in appearance. The signatures are bold and clean with Ruth on the sweet spot. The other forgeries each occupy their own panel. The Ruth is sometimes signed with quotes placed around the first name. The forgeries are nicely executed, but while they lack a labored appearance they also lack the reckless bouncy feel of a genuine signature. There is minimal to no racing effect. The forgeries are uniform and spaced evenly apart. They are nicely placed in the center of the side panels. These balls look too spatially precise.

There are a few genuinely signed Gehrig bats in existence but they are considered extremely rare. There is a certain type of forged bat that has recently entered the market in the past few years. They are signed and inscribed in black fountain pen. The last one I examined was signed "To Frank / Best Wishes / Lou Gehrig." The forgery was well executed but again lacks the flow of a genuine signature. The racing effect was, for the most part, missing. The forgeries are parallel to the length of the bat. I have never seen a genuine

Gehrig bat signed on this angle. I have examined a few genuine Gehrig signed bats and all were signed *and* inscribed on a 45 degree angle from the length of the bat. My advice to collectors is if you happen to see a Gehrig signed bat proceed with extreme caution as it is likely a forgery.

After Gehrig left the game in 1939 he was employed by the New York City Parole Commission. A handful of letters, usually dated in 1940 and 1941, are in the market. Be warned Gehrig held this position in name only and, to my knowledge, never actually signed any of these letters. Many were secretarially signed but most were signed with a rubber stamp. The stamp is illustrated in Gehrig 6. Parole Commission letters should be avoided in total.

On occasion Mrs. Gehrig would sign autographs for her husband and many are in the market. Illustrated as Gehrig 5 is Mrs. Gehrig's signature; note the striking difference in hand. They are easily spotted as secretarial. If you would like to inspect an excellent illustration of Mrs. Gehrig's work see *The Tumult and the Shouting* by Grantland Rice (A.S. Barnes 1954). In the third picture section there is a signed and inscribed Gehrig photo to Rice penned by Mrs. Gehrig.

Sales: 1938 Major League contract, countersigned by Jacob Ruppert, sold for $70,500 (Robert Edward Auctions, Spring 2010). Small book photo sold for $3,020 (Lelands.com, June 2010). Calling card sold for $2,886 (Lelands.com, November 2008). 1935 Yankees signed team ball, with others including Dickey, Ruffing, and Lazzeri, sold for $3,403 (Lelands.com, November 2009). 1937 scorecard, with a choice ink signature, sold for $2,500 (Hunt Auctions, July 2011). Choice ink signature sold for $2,500 (Hunt Auctions, July 2011). Album page, also signed by Wal-

Gehrig 7: 1937 signed Yankees ball

ter Johnson, sold for $3,819 (Robert Edward Auctions, Spring 2009).

Charlie Gehringer

Signature Study: Gehringer has one of the finest signatures of all Hall of Famers. Gehringer's signature has amazing angles and crisp lines. It is almost machine like in appearance. Vintage signatures have a nice right slant and lack any hesitation whatsoever. Most items are signed "Chas. Gehringer." Many signatures penned in the 1920s are simply signed "C. Gehringer." As Gehringer aged his hand slow slightly, but material signed in the 1960s and 1970s still has nice flow and nice eye appeal. In the 1980s Gehringer's hand remained strong. The hand evidences a very slight unsteadiness. It remained that way until his death.

Signature Population: Demand is good for Gehringer but the extensive supply outweighs demand. Gehringer material is very common and the supply seems endless. Gehringer was a willing signer throughout his entire life. Gehringer once told me that he received about 300 letters a month requesting autographs. His signature can be found on index cards, government postcards, photos, baseballs, Hall of Fame plaque postcards, and Perez-Steele cards. His signature is less common on letters, baseball bats, and Goudey gum cards.

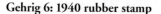

Gehrig 5: common secretarial signed by wife

Gehrig 6: 1940 rubber stamp

Gehringer 1: album page dated 1939

Signed cards from the Perez Masterworks limited edition set are uncommon. The only medium that should be considered rare are signed bank checks that are drawn on the National Bank of Detroit. There is a rather famous photo of FBI Director J. Edgar Hoover, Mickey Cochrane and Detroit G-Men of Gehringer, Greenberg, and Goslin. They are all lined up in tailored suits. What makes this picture so great is that all the men are wielding Thompson submachine guns. It is a great shot from the 1930s. Gehringer signed a few of these pictures.

Known Forgeries: Gehringer's hand is among the most difficult to replicate. There are no well executed forgeries in the market. Due to the nominal value of Gehringer's signature, he is generally not the target of skilled forgers. There are, however, some fairly nice forged items featuring all three of the Tigers G-Men of Gehringer, Greenberg, and Goslin, so caution is warranted. Another type of forgery is early American League All-Star Game balls. There are some well executed forged 1933 and 1934 All-Star Game balls, which are official American League (William Harridge, Pres.) balls. They are in nice condition and are evenly toned to a brown color. They look like they have been soaked in tea. There is an overly large Babe Ruth signature on the sweet spot and Gehringer is signed on the opposite sweet spot over the logo as "Chas. Gehringer." The forgeries are nice, except for the Gehringer, which appears labored and awkward. All forgeries are signed in black fountain pen. The forger also adds a collector's notation that reads "All Star Game — Chicago" or "All Star Game — Chicago 1933." The notation is penned around the circular Reach logo. I have seen a few of these balls. The forgeries are, for the most part, well executed.

Sales: Gehringer's signature is available. His

[signature: Chas. Gehringer]

Gehringer 2: government postcard dated 1986

[signature: Chas. Gehringer]

Gehringer 3: common facsimile

autograph generally sells for under $100 on most mediums.

Bob Gibson

Signature Study: Gibson signs in a curvy hand with vertical strokes. Letter construction is sound. The signature is legible. Display value is above average. As of 2012 Gibson's hand remains strong and evidences no shakiness of hand.

Signature Population: There seems to be a limitless supply of Gibson material that far outweighs demand. Gibson engages in many mass signings. His signature is common on most items including balls, photos, gum cards, and the like. Letters of any kind should be considered scarce.

Gibson, B. 1: undated signature

Known Forgeries: His signature is one of the easier names to forge. Due to the nominal value of Gibson's signature, he is not the target of skilled forgers.

Sales: Gibson's signature is available. His autograph generally sells for under $100 on most mediums.

Josh Gibson

Signature Study: Gibson signed in a legible hand. His signature lacks rapid motion and borders on the plain side. Most signatures, what few there are, are signed "Josh Gibson." Contracts are signed as "Joshua Gibson." Letter construction is sound. The signature is legible. Sound display value is noted. There is great debate as to whether Gibson signed in an unsteady hand in his final years, when he fell victim to a stroke induced by a brain tumor. He was diagnosed with the tumor in 1943 or 1944. This could have certainly affected

[signature: Joshua Gibson]

Gibson, J. 1: contract circa 1930s

Gibson, J. 2: contract dated 1939

his hand but there is no confirmation either way. I have seen many autographs signed in an unsteady hand but all evidenced telltale signs of forgery. Given the fact he played baseball up to the year before he died, it is unlikely that infirmity of hand existed at this time. If he had the ability to play baseball then he certainly had the ability to sign his name free from impairment. Certainly any signatures signed before 1943 should exhibit no shakiness of hand. In general, a Gibson signature with an unsteady or labored appearance should be considered suspect and avoided.

Signature Population: This is a signature of strong demand and minute supply. The population of genuine specimens is likely between 10 and 20. Just about all Gibson material is in document form. I have only seen one genuinely signed and inscribed photo. I know of only one signed baseball, a team baseball of the Homestead Grays from either 1945 or 1946. The ball originated from the estate of a team secretary who lived in Pennsylvania. Most of the signatures on this ball were accomplished in green fountain pen. I know of no single-signed baseballs. In short, Gibson is a very rare signature.

Known Forgeries: The difficulty of replicating Gibson's hand is only average. Many well executed forgeries exist in the market. Gibson has been a target of forgers for years and there are some rather convincing forgeries in the market. A common forgery is single-signed baseballs that appeared in the market in the early 1990s. They feature a grayish black or blue fountain pen signature and are signed on the side panel just under the stitching. The forgery follows the contour of the stitches. Another forgery to watch for are period secretarial

signatures on pay receipts and contracts. Just because a signature is on a contract or legal document does not guarantee the genuineness of the signature. I know of one Gibson baseball contract that features a secretarial signature of Gibson. The signature is labored in appearance. It should be noted that many forged picture postcards exist. They are signed "Joshua Gibson" along the bottom of the card or across the chest. Some contain a second inscribed signature on the reverse. These forgeries evidence a slightly labored hand but are fairly well executed.

Sales: 1939 baseball contract sold for $32,862 (Lelands.com, November 2007).

Warren Giles

Signature Study: Giles signed in a somewhat reckless hand that lacks hesitation. The signature flows well with effortless strokes. Letter construction is marginal. The signature has a degree of illegibility. The display value is limited. Giles' hand remained strong his entire life. A genuine signature will exhibit no shakiness of hand and one that does should be considered suspect and avoided.

Signature Population: This is a signature of marginal demand. Giles in a common signature and the supply of material is strong. Giles' signature is mostly found on index cards, National League letters, and documents. Less common are signed government postcards, 8 × 10 photos, and gum cards. His signature is considered scarce to rare on single-signed baseballs. Checks are also available but these should be considered scarce.

Known Forgeries: His hand is sophisticated

Giles 1: undated signature

Giles 2: common secretarial

Gibson, J. 3: letter dated 1944 (courtesy Newark Public Library, Newark Eagles Papers)

thus resulting in a signature that is difficult to replicate. There are no well executed forgeries in the market. Due to the nominal value of Giles' signature, he is not the target of skilled forgers. It should be noted that many letters and documents signed as league president are secretarially signed. The secretarial signatures, as illustrated in Giles 2, are slightly labored in appearance and appear cramped.

Sales: Giles' signature is available. His autograph generally sells for under $100 on most mediums.

Pat Gillick

Signature Study: Gillick signs in a fairly aggressive hand that lacks uniformity. Letter construction is marginal. Legibility is slightly impaired. Hesitation is lacking. This is a signature with average display value. As of 2012 Gillick's hand remains sound. A genuine signature will evidence no shakiness of hand and one that does should be considered suspect and avoided.

Gillick 1: 2011 signature

Signature Population: This is a signature where supply outweighs a marginal demand. Gillick is a willing and gracious signer. His signature is common on most mediums including Hall of Fame plaque postcards, balls, photos, business cards, and index cards. Letters of any kind are considered uncommon.

Known Forgeries: Gillick's hand is less structured. Producing a well executed forgery would prove fairly easy. Due to the nominal value of Gillick's signature, he is generally not the target of skilled forgers.

Sales: Gillick's signature is available. His autograph generally sells for under $100 on most mediums.

Lefty Gomez

Signature Study: Gomez signed in a large and flamboyant hand. His signature is bold and dominates the medium it is placed upon. Gomez's

Gomez 1: album page dated 1933

Gomez 2: circa 1980 signature

hand exhibits nice flow and lacks hesitation. Letter construction is fairly sound. The signature is, for the most part, legible.

Early signatures tend to be more vertical in nature and feature a large lower case "g" in the last name. Modern signatures tend to be more compact and develop a slant to the right. Gomez's hand remained strong his entire life. A genuine signature will exhibit no shakiness of hand and one that does should be considered suspect and avoided.

Signature Population: Gomez material is in good supply and balanced with demand. His signature is available on most mediums including index cards, government postcards, Hall of Fame plaque postcards, Perez-Steele cards, photos, baseballs, bats, gum cards, and the like. Signed letters of any kind are considered scarce. Many vintage Gomez signatures exist on Yankees team baseballs and album pages.

Known Forgeries: Gomez's signature is fairly difficult to replicate. Well executed forgeries exist but are somewhat limited. Gomez is typically not the target of forgers, as his signature has nominal value. It should be noted that many forged 1930s Yankees team balls exist with forged signatures of Gomez, Gehrig, Dickey, and the like. I have also noticed that a large group of forged single-signed baseballs has entered the market in the past couple of years.

Sales: Gomez's signature is available. His autograph generally sells for under $100 on most mediums.

Joe Gordon

Signature Study: Gordon signed in a plain and legible hand. While letter construction is sound it also lacks rapid flow. Gordon's signature has average display value. There is a good degree of legibility. In the 1960s, Gordon's hand slowed and signatures accomplished from that time until his death exhibit a fair amount of shakiness. Overall, this is a less appealing signature.

Signature Population: This is a signature where demand is in balance with supply. Gordon's signature is uncommon but by no means scarce. He had a long association with baseball. He signed many items as a manager and was responsive to mail requests. His signature can be found mostly on index cards and material signed during his playing days. Single-signed baseballs, 8 × 10 photos, and TLsS are scarce. ALsS are rare.

Known Forgeries: Due to the pensive nature of his hand, Gordon's signature is rather easy to replicate. Producing a well executed forgery can be done with little effort. Many forgeries exist, mostly on gum cards. In addition, some team baseballs signed as a manager are secretarially signed.

Sales: 1941 Major League contract, countersigned by Ed Barrow, sold for $5,350 (Lelands.com, November 2009). 8 × 10 George Burke photo, choice specimen, sold for $929 (Lelands.com. November 2009). Signed baseball, with others, sold for $103 (eBay, August 2011). 1961 Topps card sold for $275 (eBay, November 2011). 1956 government postcard sold for $156 (eBay, January 2012).

Gordon 1: circa 1940s signature

Gordon 2: circa 1960s signature

Goose Goslin

Signature Study: Goslin signed in a strong and dominant hand. His signature is marked with large capital "G"s. His signature is generally legible with good letter construction. Just about all signatures offered in the market are signed with his nickname. Signatures signed as "Leon Goslin" are rare. Most signatures are signed placing quote marks around the first name. Vintage signatures are aggressive and lack any hesitation. As Goslin aged his hand became infirmed. Modern signatures exhibit a certain amount of choppiness giving the signature a labored appearance. The hesitation of hand is illustrated in Goslin 3.

Signature Population: This is a signature of sound demand that outweighs supply. Goslin was responsive to autograph requests. There is an ample supply of genuine material in the marketplace. Most Goslin signatures are in the form of index cards and government postcards. Less common are photos and Goudey gum cards. 8 × 10 photos are very scarce. Letters of any kind are rare. Hall of Fame plaque postcards are rare and most are signed on the back. Front signed plaques are very rare. Single-signed baseballs are rare to very rare.

Known Forgeries: Vintage signatures are somewhat difficult to forge. There are a limited

Goslin 1: photograph dated 1934

Goslin 2: undated signature

Goslin 3: circa late 1960s signature

number of well executed forgeries in the market. Modern signatures are much easier to forge. Many well executed forgeries of modern signatures are in the market so caution is warranted. Most Goslin forgeries are limited to premium items such as 8 × 10 photos, Goudey gum cards, and baseballs. A common forged baseball that typically appears in the market are vintage balls The signature is usually placed on the side panel of the baseball. The forgery is labored in appearance and features overly large quotation marks. The letters "s" are elongated. A very pronounced and thick dot of the letter "i" is noted. Many of these have been certified by the authentication companies. I have never seen a genuine signed item by just the Detroit G-men of Goslin, Greenberg, and Gehringer. There are many forged book pictures and baseballs. The best way that you can obtain this trio is to find a Tigers team ball or team sheet from the 1930s.

Sales: 7 × 9 photo, signed in the 1930s, sold for $398 (Lelands.com, June 2010). 8 × 10 photo, signed in the 1930s, sold for $400 (Hunt Auctions, February 2010). Pencil signature removed from album page sold for $61 (eBay, August 2011). Choice signature sold for $85 (eBay, November 2011). Choice signature sold for $105 (eBay, November 2011).

Rich Gossage

Signature Study: Gossage signs in a very flowing hand. His signature has impaired legibility. Letter construction tends to morph into continuous loops. Gossage's signature has good display value. The signature has a nice right slant. As of 2012 a genuine Gossage signature will exhibit no shakiness of hand and one that does should be considered suspect and avoided.

Signature Population: This is a signature of marginal demand and great supply. Gossage material is very common as he is a willing signer. His signature is common on most mediums including gum cards, baseballs, photos, and the like. Letters of any kind are scarce.

Known Forgeries: The complex nature of Gossage's hand results in a rather difficult signature to forge. There are no well executed forgeries in the market. Due to the nominal value of Gossage's signature, he is not the target of skilled forgers.

Sales: Gossage's signature is available. His autograph generally sells for under $100 on most mediums.

Frank Grant

Signature Study: Due to the lack of a confirmed specimen, no signature study is possible.

Signature Population: To my knowledge there are no known signatures of Grant in existence. Autographically speaking, this is an extreme rarity.

Known Forgeries: There are no specific forgeries to note, though some do exist. Forgeries all vary in construction.

Sales: Due to the rarity, there have been no recent sales of Grant's signature.

Hank Greenberg

Signature Study: Greenberg signed in a very unusual hand. His signature is marked with nice vertical strokes and has an ever so slight back slant. Early signatures tend to exhibit very sharp angles giving the signature a somewhat jagged appearance, as illustrated in Greenberg 1. As time progressed Greenberg's signature remained reasonably constant, though later signatures do not evidence the sharp angles found in earlier signatures. Letter construction diminishes slightly. The signature looks more rounded. In general, Greenberg signatures have good display value with an artful look. Greenberg died of cancer at the age of 75, an illness he hid from the public. Despite the illness his hand remained strong. A genuine Greenberg signature will exhibit no shakiness of hand and one that does should be considered suspect an avoided.

Signature Population: This is a signature in good demand and balanced with supply. The sup-

Gossage 1: 2011 signature

Greenberg 1: 1942 signature

Greenberg 2: government postcard circa 1940s

Greenberg 3: circa 1980s signature

ply of genuine Greenberg material is sound as he was a willing signer throughout his life. He died just before the era of mass signings so supply is not nearly as great as with his counterpart Charlie Gehringer. There is an ample supply of vintage material that was signed at the ballpark. Vintage signatures can be found on scorecards, album pages, and multi-signed baseballs. Single-signed baseballs from Greenberg's playing days are very rare. Modern single-signed balls are much more plentiful. Greenberg's signature exists on most mediums most notably index cards, photos, and Hall of Fame plaque postcards. There is also a good supply of genuinely signed Goudey and Play Ball cards. His position as an executive with the Cleveland Indians correlates into many signed letters. Most are typed but some nice handwritten specimens exist. Perez-Steele art postcards are scarce and just about all were signed in black sharpie.

Known Forgeries: The complex nature of Greenberg's signature makes it difficult to forge. Well executed forgeries are limited to modern signatures. Due to the nominal value of Greenberg's signature, he is generally not the target of skilled forgers, however baseballs tend to be the one exception. There are many fairly well executed forged single-signed baseballs in the market so caution is warranted. Just about nine out of every ten signed Greenberg baseballs in the market are fake. A minority of authenticators have been erroneously pronouncing vintage signatures, as illustrated in Greenberg 1 and Greenberg 2, as secretarial. I am not sure why, as these are clearly in Greenberg's hand.

Sales: Greenberg's signature is available. His autograph generally sells for under $100 on most mediums. Of note: Single-signed ball, choice specimen, sold for $1,175 (Robert Edward Auctions, Spring 2010).

Clark Griffith

Signature Study: Griffith signed in a nice and very legible hand. Letter construction is well defined. His signature has nice display value. Early signatures lack hesitation but also lack recklessness. Griffith signed in a slower hand as evidenced by the lack of rapid flow. As Griffith aged his hand deteriorated greatly. Material signed in the late 1930s through early 1940s evidences a certain amount of hesitation in the signature. Starting about 1945 his hand exhibits infirmity and signatures accomplished from this time until his death are unsteady in appearance.

Signature Population: The supply of Griffith material is sound and balanced with moderate demand. Griffith lived a long and productive baseball life and was a willing signer throughout. His signature is generally found on items that could be signed through the mail such as index cards and government postcards. Hall of Fame plaque postcards and single-signed baseballs are rare. Signed team baseballs from Griffith's days as a player very likely do not exist. Also considered rare are signed 8 × 10 photos. His long tenure as owner of the Washington Senators correlates into many nicely signed letters, most of them typed. These are an excellent source of Griffith signatures. Autographed letters signed are considered scarce to rare. I have never seen a genuinely signed Griffith tobacco card of any kind in over 30 years of collecting.

Known Forgeries: Due to the slower nature of his hand, Griffith's signature is one of the easier names to forge. There are many well executed forgeries in the market. Most forgeries replicate the old-age signature that features infirmity of hand. A few years back a small grouping of nicely executed forged sheets featuring Griffith and Cap Anson entered the market. These are well executed forgeries and accomplished by a skilled

Griffith 1: TLS circa 1910

Griffith 2: TLS dated 1926 (courtesy National Baseball Hall of Fame and Museum)

Griffith 3: circa 1940s signature

forger. They are usually signed on small slips of paper. The Anson is signed as "A.C. Anson." To add an air of authenticity the forger also adds another signature at either the top or bottom of the sheet. He then cuts most of it off to give the appearance that it has been removed from a larger signed sheet. Overall, it is a very convincing forgery. The signatures used as a template for these forgeries were penned in a ledger from 1894 that feature many genuine ink signatures. I know of no items signed by just these two Hall of Famers, so proceed with caution. There are also a few lower-grade T-206 cards in the market featuring forged signatures of Griffith.

Sales: Index card sold for $209 (Lelands.com, January 2008). 1949 government postcard sold for $163 (RR Auctions, August 2011). 1951 baseball document, countersigned by Tom Yawkey, sold for $324 (RR Auctions, September 2011). Index card sold for $305 (eBay, November 2011). Signature removed from TLS sold for $222 (eBay, January 2012).

Burleigh Grimes

Signature Study: Grimes signed in a relatively aggressive and bold hand. His signature exhibits nice vertical strokes with an ever so slight right slant. Early signatures have a nice flow and lack hesitation. Early signatures are signed "Burleigh A. Grimes" and some are signed as "B.A. Grimes." Overall his signature is legible with sound letter

Grimes 1: team sheet circa 1930s

Grimes 2: circa 1980s signature

construction. As the years progressed Grimes' hand slowed. The signature decreases in size. Letter construction remains sound and his signature retains good display value. In the last ten or so years of his life Grimes' hand was affected with infirmity. Modern signatures tend to exhibit a labored appearance.

Signature Population: This is a signature of moderate demand. Grimes died just before the era of the mass signings; despite this the supply of Grimes material is strong. His signature is commonly found on items that were signed through the mail, thus index cards, baseball cards, and Hall of Fame plaque postcards are common. Less common are 8 × 10 photographs, baseballs, and Perez-Steele postcards. Letters and bank checks are scarce. Single-signed baseball bats are considered very scarce.

Known Forgeries: Early signatures are somewhat difficult to replicate. Modern signatures are far easier to forge. Well executed forgeries are generally limited to modern signatures. Due to the nominal value of Grimes' signature, he is generally not a target of skilled forgers. However, many forged single-signed baseballs and Perez-Steele postcards are in the market.

Sales: Grimes' signature is available. His autograph generally sells for under $100 on most mediums.

Lefty Grove

Signature Study: Vintage Grove signatures are among the finest of the Hall of Famers. They are very artistic with effortless strokes. There is no hesitation. His signature is very legible. Excellent letter construction is noted. Vintage signatures have maximum display value. As Grove aged his signature became less artistic and smaller. Modern signatures lack the flare of their vintage counterparts. In the final few years of his life Grove's hand

Grove 1: contract dated 1954

Grove 2: undated signature

Grove 3: undated signature

Gwynn 1: 2010 signature

became unsteady. Signatures from this period lack eye appeal and are less desirable. This form of signature evidences hesitation.

Signature Population: The supply of Grove material is limited. Demand far outweighs supply. Grove's signature is generally limited to items signed in the mail such as index cards, Hall of Fame plaque postcards, and 1960 Fleer cards. 8 × 10 photos and bank checks are uncommon. Letters are scarce to rare. Single-signed baseballs are scarce to rare and most in the market are forged. A nice vintage single-signed ball is among the finest signed baseballs in the field. He would pen a large flowing signature on the sweet spot. They have superior eye appeal. Vintage single-signed balls are very rare.

Known Forgeries: Grove's hand is extremely difficult to replicate and is one of the hardest Hall of Fame signatures to forge. There are no well executed forgeries in the market of vintage signatures. There are many well executed forgeries of old-age signatures in the market. Due to the nominal value of Grove's signature, he is generally not the target of skilled forgers. Forgeries are generally limited to modern single-signed baseballs.

Sales: Bank check sold for $100 (RR Auctions, July 2011). 1955 signed ball, with others, sold for $712 (Lelands.com, March 2008). 4 × 6 George Burke photo, superior specimen, sold for $838 (Lelands.com, June 2004). Index card sold for $37 (eBay, September 2011). Artvue Hall of Fame plaque postcard sold for $68 (eBay, November 2011).

Tony Gwynn

Signature Study: Like most modern ballplayers Gwynn signs in a very sloppy and illegible

hand. His signature looks like a bunch of confused lines. Display value is poor. As of 2012 Gwynn's hand lacks any hesitation whatsoever. A signature that appears labored should be considered suspect and avoided.

Signature Population: A signature of marginal demand that is outweighed by supply. The supply of genuine material is strong. His signature is very common and can be found on most mediums including gum cards, balls, photos, bats, and the like. Letters of any kind are scarce.

Known Forgeries: Due to the lack of letter construction, Gwynn's signature is easy to forge. Due to the nominal value of Gwynn's signature, he is not the target of skilled forgers.

Sales: Gwynn's signature is available. His autograph generally sells for under $100 on most mediums.

Chick Hafey

Signature Study: Hafey signed in a neat and confined hand. His signature is relatively small and works well on most mediums. Letter construction is well formed. The signature is legible. This is a signature with average display value. Hafey's hand remained strong his entire life. A genuine signature will exhibit no shakiness of hand and one that does should be considered suspect and avoided.

Signature Population: This is a signature of moderate demand that is balanced with supply. The population of genuine Hafey material is ample but not strong. He was not expected to make

Hafey 1: album page dated 1933

Hafey 2: undated signature

Haines 1: 1962 signature

Haines 2: circa 1970 signature

the Hall of Fame, so his 1971 induction was surprising to most. He was not a collected signature, to any measurable degree, prior to his induction. His signature is generally limited to signed index cards. Other mediums are scarce to rare. Signed 8 × 10 photos and letters are scarce. Single-signed baseballs are very rare. I have only seen three or four genuine specimens in my lifetime. Hall of Fame plaque postcards exist but are scarce.

Known Forgeries: The compact nature of Hafey's hand results in a signature that is rather easy to forge. There are well executed forgeries in the market. Hafey is generally not the target of the skilled forger because values are not sufficient to warrant the effort. However, there are some well executed forgeries on single-signed baseballs. Over the past few years a cache of forged 8 × 10 photographs has entered the market, which typically feature Hall of Famers that died in the early 1970s. They are signed in black or blue felt-tip pen. Forgeries include Hafey, Goslin, Traynor, Dean, Manush, and Hartnett.

Sales: Single-signed baseball, choice specimen, sold for $5,875 (Robert Edward Auctions, Spring 2010). 1929 Major League contract sold for $2,644 (Robert Edward Auctions, Spring 2011). Picture postcard sold for $134 (RR Auctions, February 2011). Hall of Fame plaque postcard sold for $240 (RR Auctions, March 2008). Hall of Fame plaque postcard sold for $300 (eBay, November 2011).

Jesse Haines

Signature Study: Haines signed in a very nice and legible hand. His signature has nice letter construction. Vintage signed Haines material has excellent display value. Most signatures are signed as "Jesse Haines." On occasion he would sign with his nickname "Pop," though this form of signature is uncommon. Haines' hand remained relatively constant throughout the years, though modern signatures tend to lack the artistic flare of vintage specimens. Material signed just before his death may evidence an ever-so-slight hesitation. A genuine Haines' signature should not evidence shak-

iness of hand, to any measurable degree, and one that does should be considered suspect and avoided.

Signature Population: Haines material has only marginal demand. Being a member of the famed Gashouse Gang, Haines was always a target of collectors even before his induction. The supply of genuine Haines material is strong. His signature is available on most mediums including index cards, government postcards, photos, and Hall of Fame plaque postcards. Letters and Goudey gum cards are scarce. Single-signed baseballs are scarce. There are quite a few genuine specimens in the market. Haines would usually sign the side panel of the ball with detailed information about his years in the big leagues. Haines' single-signed baseballs have tremendous display value. A few years back a small accumulation of canceled bank checks entered the market.

Known Forgeries: Haines' signature is fairly difficult to forge. Due to the nominal value of Haines' signature, he is generally not the target of skilled forgers. Forgeries are generally limited to single-signed baseballs.

Sales: 5 × 7 photo sold for $163 (RR Auctions, February 2011). 1935 Major League contract sold for $7,833 (Lelands.com, November 2009). 1961 Fleer gum card sold for $47 (eBay, September 2011). Index card sold for $23 (eBay, August 2011). Index card sold for $78 (eBay, November 2011).

Billy Hamilton

Signature Study: Hamilton signatures are generally limited to those penned during old age. Material signed before 1930 is just about nonexistent. I only know of three genuine signatures signed before 1930. Hamilton signed in a very legible and plain hand. His signature lacks flare and has a practical look. There are a couple of specimens that exhibit an alternate form of "H" in the last name. It is constructed using two loops. Hamilton 1 and Hamilton 2 illustrate the variant letter "H." His hand lacks rapid motion, giving the signature a somewhat pensive and labored appearance. Hamilton's hand became infirmed towards the end of his life. Signatures accomplished at this time evidence shakiness of hand.

Signature Population: Hamilton's signature is very rare and in high demand. I would say the total population of Hamilton signatures is somewhere between 10 and 20 specimens. I have never seen a genuinely signed baseball or photo. I know of one typed letter signed and one 1939 baseball first-day postal cover signed. I have never examined a genuine autographed letter signed, though many forgeries do exist.

Known Forgeries: Due to the lack of rapid motion, Hamilton's signature is very easy to forge. Just about 100 percent of Hamilton material in the market is forged. Hamilton forgeries exist on most mediums including baseballs, photos, and government postcards. There is one particular forgery to note. There is a very small grouping of forged handwritten letters in the market and they have been circulating for decades. They are on blank stationery and written to various people, among them newspaper editors. The three I have examined were signed "Very Truly Sliding Billy Hamilton." The handwriting is distinctive and evidences a slight choppiness. This forger also has created fake handwritten letters of Roger Connor

Hamilton 1: ledger circa 1890s

Hamilton 2: teamsheet circa 1930s

Hamilton 3: TLS dated 1936

Hamilton 4: postal cover circa 1940

and Sam Thompson as well as single-signed George Sisler baseballs.

Sales: Due to the rarity, there have been no recent sales of Hamilton's signature.

Ned Hanlon

Signature Study: Hanlon signed in a legible and practical hand. His signature lacks hesitation and evidences a slight choppiness. Letter construction is average. A sound display value is noted. Some signatures are signed in a hurried and sloppy hand. There is disagreement as to whether Hanlon's hand was affected by infirmity due to illness or age. I have examined many signatures that evidenced a tremulous appearance. I have yet to see a genuine specimen. I have concluded Hanlon's signature was not affected by infirmity and one that does should be considered suspect and avoided.

Signature Population: There is good demand for Hanlon material compared to a minute supply. Hanlon is a rare to very rare signature. His signature is generally limited to signed documents, letters, and pay receipts. I do know of a couple of nicely signed album pages. I have never seen a genuinely signed photo or baseball. There are probably less than 20 genuine specimens in the open market. The Herrmann Collection housed at the National Baseball Hall of Fame has many stunning Hanlon letters from the turn of the twentieth century.

Hanlon 1: ALS circa 1905 (courtesy National Baseball Hall of Fame and Museum)

Hanlon 2: TLS circa 1905 (courtesy National Baseball Hall of Fame and Museum)

Edward Hanlon

Hanlon 3: album page circa 1935

Known Forgeries: Hanlon's signature is difficult to replicate. Well executed forgeries are very limited but do exist. I have seen many forgeries, mostly on album pages and period scorecards. There is a small grouping of forgeries that exist on period cabinet team cards. The photos are of lesser known teams, such as town ball or semi-pro teams, from the 1870s through 1890s. The cards themselves are of average to lower condition. The card stock is very thick. The forger writes the names of all the players on the team in the border of the card. A forgery of Hanlon is then placed on either the lower blank border or on the reverse.

Sales: 1933 TLS, choice specimen, sold for $7,638 (Robert Edward Auctions, Spring 2010). Album page, choice specimen, sold for $15,275 (Robert Edward Auctions, Spring 2009).

William Harridge

Signature Study: Harridge signed in a very bold and confident hand. His signature is legible. A moderate display value is noted. His signature remained relatively constant throughout his life, but vintage material is signed in a heavier hand. Early signatures have a rougher look than more modern examples. As the years progressed Harridge's signature became more refined. Harridge's hand remained strong his entire life. A genuine Harridge signature will exhibit no shakiness of hand and one that does should be considered suspect and avoided.

William Harridge

Harridge 1: 1943 signature

Will Harridge

Harridge 2: undated signature

Signature Population: Demand for Harridge is marginal and outweighed by a strong supply. Due to his long tenure as a league president, Harridge-signed material is available at an affordable price. Just about all signed material is document related including checks, typed letters, league contracts, and the like. Handwritten letters are available but are considered scarce to rare. Other mediums are seldom seen and highly desirable. I have examined only a dozen or so 8 × 10 photos and single-signed baseballs, and both should be considered rare.

Known Forgeries: Harridge's signature seems to be a moderately easy name to forge, likely because of the abrupt angle changes in his hand. This signature is generally not the target of skilled forgers, due to the marginal value of his signature. Harridge forgeries are limited to single-signed baseballs and 1950s Topps cards. Secretarial-signed items are rare, as Harridge signed just about all letters and contracts personally.

Sales: 1960 TLS sold for $51 (eBay, September 2011). 1941 TLS sold for $119 (Lelands.com, January 2008). 5 × 7 photo, choice specimen, sold for $121 (RR Auctions, February 2011). 1958 government postcard sold for $70 (eBay, August 2011). Index card sold for $82 (eBay, January 2012).

Bucky Harris

Signature Study: Harris signed in a very nice and refined hand. His signature is marked with wonderful flow and striking letter construction. Legibility is sound. His signature has excellent eye appeal. As Harris aged his hand slowed a bit and the stunning flow is diminished. Material signed

"Bucky" Harris

Harris 1: government postcard dated 1938

Harris 2: document dated 1946

Harris 3: undated signature

in the 1970s exhibits a slight shakiness of hand, which has less display value. Harris' hand never produced a truly shaky signature and one that evidences an unsteady appearance should be considered suspect and avoided.

Signature Population: The supply of Harris material is ample but not great and balanced with demand. His signature is generally limited to material signed through the mail and most of those are index cards. Government postcards and Hall of Fame plaque postcards are uncommon. Letters and 8 × 10 photos are scarce. Single-signed baseballs are rare.

Known Forgeries: Early signatures are extremely difficult to replicate. There are no well executed forgeries in the market, at least when it comes to his vintage signature. Modern signatures are easy to forge, so many well executed forgeries exist. Due to the nominal value of Harris material, he is generally not the target of skilled forgers. However, there are a fair number of forged single-signed baseballs and 8 × 10 photos in the market. There is a famous photo of Harris, as manager of the Yankees, standing at the dugout steps. Many forged 8 × 10 photos of this image exist. The forger has signed these photos in felt pen or ball point across Harris' chest. Genuinely signed photos of this type are typically signed to the left of Harris' head, across the cement roof of the dugout. If you see a signed photo where Harris signed across his chest, study it carefully as it is likely a forgery.

Sales: Index card sold for $31 (eBay, September 2011). 5 × 7 photo sold for $134 (RR Auctions, February 2011). Hall of Fame plaque postcard sold for $100 (RR Auctions, March 2011). Hall of Fame plaque postcard sold for $232 (eBay, November 2011). Government postcard sold for $23 (eBay, December 2011).

Gabby Hartnett

Signature Study: Hartnett signed in a very nice and flowing hand. His signature has sound letter construction and effortless lines. His signature has stunning eye appeal. Hartnett has one of the finest signatures of all the Hall of Famers. Autographs penned during his playing days tend to be smaller than modern examples but they still evidence a very nice hand. In the 1940s his hand became bolder, resulting in a signature that is larger and usually dominates the medium it is placed upon. Signatures are usually finished with a straight line paraph. Infirmity of hand is nonexistent. A genuine signature will exhibit no shakiness of hand and one that does should be considered suspect and avoided.

Signature Population: There has always been good demand for Hartnett's signature. The supply of Hartnett material is ample but not plentiful. He was a willing signer throughout his life. His signature is generally found on index cards, Hall of Fame plaque postcards, scorecards, team baseballs, and album pages. There are also a surprising number of signed government postcards in the market. 8 × 10 photos are scarce. Letters of any kind are considered scarce to rare. Single-signed baseballs are somewhat scarce, but there are some nice examples in the market. Hartnett would add a nice inscription for maximum eye appeal. There are also many signed gum cards including 1961 Fleer and Goudey cards. There is also a decent supply of bank checks.

Known Forgeries: Hartnett's signature is very difficult to forge. Well executed forgeries are lim-

Hartnett 1: album page circa 1930s

Hartnett 2: government postcard dated 1956

Hartnett 3: circa 1960s signature

ited to one forger who signed many Artvue Hall of Fame plaque postcards. Most forgeries evidence a labored appearance and lack the flow of a genuine signature. Due to the nominal value of Hartnett's signature, forgeries are limited to premium items such as baseballs and 8 × 10 photos.

Sales: Single-signed baseball, inscribed, sold for $1,057 (Robert Edward Auctions, Spring 2008). Bank check sold for $134 (RR Auctions, July 2011). Single-signed baseball sold for $1,156 (Lelands.com, November 2009). 1960 Fleer gum card sold for $81 (eBay, September 2011). Hall of Fame plaque postcard sold for $200 (RR Auctions, March 2011).

Doug Harvey

Signature Study: Harvey signs in a very thoughtful and clean hand. His signature evidences good flow. Letter construction is sound. His signature is very legible. Display value is sound. Within the last couple of years Harvey's hand has slowed. Recent signatures evidence a shakiness of hand, so their display value is impaired.

Signature Population: This is a signature of marginal demand that is outweighed by supply. Harvey is a fairly common signature as he has been a willing signer throughout his life. His signature can be found on photos, balls, bats, Hall of Fame plaque postcards, and the like. Signed letters of any kind are scarce.

Known Forgeries: Given Harvey's rather nice hand, creating a well executed forgery would be moderately difficult. Due to the nominal value of

Harvey's signature, he is not the target of skilled forgers.

Sales: Harvey's signature is available. His autograph generally sells for under $100 on most mediums.

Harry Heilmann

Signature Study: Heilmann signed in a neat and concise hand that also incorporates a bit of whimsical flare. The big looping "H"s give the signature an artistic look. Heilmann's signature has maximum display value. Heilmann's signature remained constant throughout his life and there is little change in his hand over the years. Signatures accomplished during his playing days will sometimes be signed with his middle initial. On rare occasion, Heilmann would add a paraph to his signature. Heilmann's hand remained strong his entire life. A genuine signature will exhibit no shakiness of hand and one that does should be considered suspect and avoided.

Signature Population: This is a signature with sound demand and limited supply. Heilmann is a scarce signature. His signature is generally limited to material signed at the stadium. As such scorecards and album pages are available. Other mediums are very scarce to very rare. Government postcards are tough to locate. Bank checks are rare. There are about a dozen Heilmann bank checks dated from the mid–1940s thru 1950. They are made payable to fellow Hall of Famer Heinie Manush. Manush would endorse the reverse of the check. These checks are very rare and are a wonderful combination signed by two Hall of Famers. 8 × 10 photos should be considered very rare. Typed letters are rare and usually found on radio station letterhead, typically dated during his time as a broadcaster for the Tigers (1934–1950). The content is almost always routine. Autographed letters signed are extremely rare. Heilmann single-signed baseballs are very rare. In 30 plus years of collecting I have examined four or five genuine specimens. All the examples I have

Harvey 1: 2010 signature

Heilmann 1: undated pencil signature

Heilmann 2: bank check circa 1940s

Heilmann 3: undated signature

examined were signed on the side panel of the ball. I have never seen a genuine single-signed ball autographed on the sweet spot. The best way to obtain Heilmann on a baseball is to locate a Detroit Tigers team ball from the late 1920s. Fred Lieb published a book in 1946 titled *The Detroit Tigers*. It seems a mass signing was done because many books are signed in the inside cover by Lieb, Heilmann, and Gehringer. I do not know how many were signed, but I have seen several genuine examples in the past 30 years.

Known Forgeries: The complex nature of Heilmann's signature makes replication difficult. There are no well executed forgeries in the market. Heilmann forgeries are rudimentary in nature and exist in quantities. Numerous fake baseballs, photos, and 1940 Play Ball cards exist. There is a specific forgery worth noting because it is nicely accomplished. These are multi-signed baseballs purportedly signed in the 1920s by several stars. I have run across two of them, which tells me there is a small grouping in the market. The two I examined were forged on American League (Ban Johnson, Pres.) baseballs. They contained many nice forgeries of Hall of Famers of the day intermixed with non–Hall of Fame stars. Both balls I examined had Cobb, Ruth, Heilmann, Sisler, Walter Johnson, Connie Mack, and Miller Huggins. One had Pennock. Other forgeries included George Uhle, Howard Ehmke, Dutch Leonard, and a few others. Some of the forgeries are nicely executed, but some are not. The Mack and Cobb were poorly executed as they deviated greatly from genuine signatures. The key to both baseballs was that Ruth's signature was on the sweet spot. Babe's first name was in quotes. Heilmann was also on

the sweet spot signed as "Harry E. Heilmann." The Heilmann forgery was signed directly above the Ruth and it was signed upside down. It is such an odd way to forge a baseball that it stands out. If you see one of these baseballs you should proceed with caution.

Sales: Bank check sold for $636 (RR Auctions, July 2011). 1927 bank document sold for $581 (Hunt Auctions, November 2010). 1950 bank check, endorsed on back by Heinie Manush, sold for $2,969 (Lelands.com, June 2005).

Rickey Henderson

Signature Study: Henderson signs in a vertical and sloppy hand. His signature exhibits substandard letter construction. The signature is rather illegible. Display value is marginal at best. As of 2012 Henderson's hand remains strong. A genuine signature will exhibit no shakiness of hand and one that does should be considered suspect and avoided. Overall, this is an average and unassuming autograph.

Henderson 1: undated signature (courtesy collection of Alfred Angelo)

Signature Population: Demand is marginal and clearly outweighed by supply. Henderson's signature is common on most mediums, including gum cards, bats, baseballs, photos, and the like. Letters of any kind are scarce.

Known Forgeries: Replication of hand would be easy. Creating a convincing forgery can be done without much difficulty. Due to the nominal value of Henderson's signature, he is not the target of skilled forgers.

Sales: Henderson's signature is available. His autograph generally sells for under $100 on most mediums.

Billy Herman

Signature Study: Herman signed in a legible hand that lacks flamboyance. His signature tends to be small and compact. His signature is marked with non-uniform strokes that make for a signature with moderate display value. Signatures

Herman 1: album page dated 1933

Herman 2: circa 1990 signature

penned during his playing days evidence nice flow and lack hesitation. As Herman aged his hand slowed substantially. Signatures accomplished in the 1980s have a slightly labored look. Herman's signature is unassuming and is average among the Hall of Fame members.

Signature Population: This is a signature of marginal demand. The supply of Herman material is very strong. He was a willing and gracious signer throughout his entire life. Herman signatures exist in quantities on most mediums including photos, baseballs, index cards, bats, Perez-Steele cards, Hall of Fame plaque postcards, and the like. Letters of any kind are uncommon to scarce. Herman also is available on bank checks but these are uncommon.

Known Forgeries: Herman signatures are fairly easy to replicate. Creating a well executed forgery can be done with only minimal effort. Due to the nominal value of Herman's signature, he is not the target of skilled forgers.

Sales: Herman's signature is available. His autograph generally sells for under $100 on most mediums.

Whitey Herzog

Signature Study: Herzog signs in a fast hand that results in a signature with a slight choppiness. The signature is dominated by large sweeping tails to the letters "y" and "g." Letter construction is marginal, which creates a signature that is somewhat illegible. As of 2012 Herzog's hand is strong and should exhibit no shakiness of hand.

Signature Population: This is a signature of marginal demand. The supply of Herzog material is sound. He was willing signer through the mail before his Hall of Fame induction. His signature

can be found on gum cards, photos, baseballs, and the like. Letters of any kind are scarce. Overall, this is a very common signature.

Known Forgeries: Due to the rapid nature of his signature, replication of hand would be fairly difficult. Due to the nominal value of Herzog's signature, he is not the target of skilled forgers.

Sales: Herzog's signature is available. His autograph generally sells for under $100 on most mediums.

Pete Hill

Signature Study: Very little is known of Hill's signature. The illustrated example was located by the National Archives on Hill's World War I draft registration card. It is signed with his real name "John Preston Hill." The date of birth listed on the card is correct. Little is known of his writing.

Hill 1: World War I draft card circa 1917 (Record Group 163, Records of the Selective Services Division, National Archives at Atlanta)

Signature Population: To my knowledge there are two Hill signatures in existence. Both are held by governmental concerns. In addition to the above referenced draft card, a signed pension document also exists. I know of no signatures in the open market. This signature is an extreme rarity.

Known Forgeries: No specific forgeries are noted, though some do exist. All vary in construction.

Sales: Due to the rarity, there have been no recent sales of Hill's signature.

Harry Hooper

Signature Study: Hooper signed in a fairly legible and rather unappealing hand. It is plain in nature and is very practical in appearance. His signature has sound letter construction but evidences a slight choppiness. Hooper's signature remained relatively constant throughout the years. Vintage signatures tend to be slightly more flowing. Hooper signed in a confined hand and autographs tend to fit nicely in small spaces. Hooper's hand remained strong his entire life. A genuine signature will evidence no shakiness of hand and one that does should be considered suspect and avoided.

Signature Population: The supply of Hooper material is good and is balanced with demand. Signatures are typically limited to material signed through the mail. Picture postcards, index cards, and Hall of Fame plaque postcards are the most common. Government postcards and 8 × 10 photos are uncommon. Typed letters are scarce. Handwritten letters are much more common. Most letters have routine content. Single-signed baseballs are rare. Signed team baseballs from Hooper's playing days are limited to his days with the Chicago White Sox in the early 1920s, though these team-signed baseballs are extremely rare. Back in the mid–1980s Hooper's son would honor autograph requests from collectors by sending out signed bank checks. Today, there is a good supply of checks in the market.

Known Forgeries: His signature is one of the easier names to forge. There are many well executed forgeries in the market, though they are limited to baseballs.

Sales: Picture postcard sold for $65 (eBay, September 2011). Album page, with Duffy Lewis and Tris Speaker, sold for $477 (RR Auctions, November 2009). Hall of Fame plaque postcard sold for $100 (RR Auctions, March 2011). Picture postcard sold for $100 (RR Auctions, February 2011). Picture postcard sold for $71 (eBay, November 2011).

Rogers Hornsby

Signature Study: Hornsby had a powerful personality and his signature reflects a man of great confidence. Hornsby signed in a very aggressive and reckless hand. His signature does not stay "within the lines" and dominates the medium it is placed upon. Early signatures are signed in a wonderfully flowing hand. They exhibit a great deal of artistic tone. Sometimes he would finish off his signature with a muted paraph. Signatures accomplished during his playing career have very good eye appeal. More modern signatures do not exhibit the same level of eye appeal as the vintage specimens. Modern signatures increase in height and the powerful strokes, found in vintage specimens, are more compact. Hornsby's hand remained strong his entire life. A genuine signature will exhibit no shakiness of hand and one that does should be considered suspect and avoided.

Signature Population: This is a signature of strong demand that clearly outweighs supply. Despite his curt personality Hornsby was a willing and gracious signer throughout his entire life. There is an ample supply of Hornsby material in the market, though generally limited to items signed in the mail. His signature can be found on index cards, government postcards, and Fleer gum

Hornsby 1: document dated 1927

Hooper 1: circa 1930s signature

Hooper 2: bank check dated 1969

Hornsby 2: 1959 signature

Hornsby 3: 1962 signature

cards. His signature is considered scarce on Hall of Fame plaque postcards. Photos are uncommon and very desirable. Typed letters signed are scarce. Handwritten letters are rare. Single-signed baseballs are scarce, but I have examined a couple of dozen genuine specimens in my lifetime. I have never examined a genuine single-signed baseball from his days as a player.

Known Forgeries: Early signatures are extremely hard to forge. There are no well executed forgeries of vintage Hornsby signatures in the market. Modern signatures are much easier to forge, so well executed forgeries do exist in the market. The vast majority of Hornsby material offered in the market is forged. Forged Hall of Fame plaque postcards exist in quantities and have been circulating for years. They are easily spotted. The forgeries are signed in a slightly labored hand. The ink strokes are ever so slightly wider than what is found on a genuine signature. Many, but not all, are signed in a bright blue ball-point ink. There is also a secretarial signature from the 1920s that is circulating in the market. This signature, as illustrated in Hornsby 4, is signed by Hornsby's lawyer under a power of attorney.

Hornsby 4: common secretarial signature under a P.O.A.

Sales: Choice ink signature sold for $599 (eBay, September 2011). Single-signed baseball sold for $3,322 (Lelands.com, November 2008). 1924 Major League contract, countersigned by John Heydler and Branch Rickey, sold for $12,376 (Lelands.com, June 2011). 1952 TLS sold for $477 (RR Auctions, November 2009). 1942 TLS sold for $940 (Robert Edward Auctions, Spring 2010). Hall of Fame plaque postcard sold for $1,527 (Robert Edward Auctions, Spring 2008).

Waite Hoyt

Signature Study: Hoyt signed in a vertical hand that lacks hesitation. His signature has average letter construction. Display value is marginal at best. As Hoyt aged his hand slowed a bit. The signature becomes more legible and letter construction improves. In the last few years of his life Hoyt's hand was affected by a slight infirmity. Autographs penned in the late 1970s until death evidence a slight labored appearance and lack good eye appeal.

Signature Population: This is a signature of average demand outweighed by supply. Hoyt was a gracious signer throughout his entire life. His signature can be found on index cards, Hall of Fame plaque postcards, government postcards, photos, gum cards, and the like. Letters, single-signed baseballs, and Perez-Steele cards are scarce. Single-signed bats should be considered rare. There is a fair supply of signed bank checks in the market but they are uncommon.

Known Forgeries: Vintage signatures are hard to forge and are generally limited to forged Yankees team baseballs. Modern signatures, with their labored appearance, are easy to forge. There are many well executed forgeries in the market.

Hoyt 1: album page dated 1933

Hoyt 2: undated signature

Due to the nominal value of Hoyt's signature, forgeries are generally limited to premium items such
as baseballs, bats, and Perez-Steele cards.

Sales: Hoyt's signature is available. His autograph generally sells for under $100 on most medi-
ums.

Cal Hubbard

Signature Study: Cal Hubbard signed in a
pleasing and legible hand. Signatures have a moderate right slant. The "H" in the last name has a
strong resemblance to the letter "A." His signature
is marked with effortless lines that lack any hesitation. A strong racing effect is noted. Hubbard's
signature has good display value. It should be
noted that Hubbard often used a black felt-tip
pen to sign autographs. Hubbard's hand remained
strong his entire life. A genuine signature will exhibit no shakiness of hand and one that does
should be considered suspect and avoided.

Signature Population: Since Hubbard is a
member of both the Baseball and Football Hall
of Fame, one would think demand would be great
for his signature, but it is not. The population of
Hubbard signatures is ample. Hubbard was a willing signer throughout his entire life. His signature
is generally limited to index cards and canceled
bank checks, which there seems to be a good supply of. On any other medium his signature should
be considered scarce to rare. 8 × 10 photos due
exist but are very scarce. Letters of any kind are
also considered scarce. Single-signed baseballs are
rare and seldom surface. A medium that is a good
source of Hubbard signatures are cards from the
1975 Fleer Football Immortal Roll set. He may
have handed these out because there are a lot of
genuine specimens in the market.

Known Forgeries: Because of the complex na-

ture of Hubbard's hand, replication is difficult.
There are no well executed forgeries in the market.
Due to the nominal value of Hubbard's signature,
forgeries are generally limited to premium items
such as baseballs.

Sales: Bank check sold for $250 (RR Auctions,
June 2010). Hall of Fame plaque postcard sold for
$198 (RR Auctions, March 2011). Index card sold
for $100 (eBay, November 2011). Index card sold
for $66 (eBay, November 2011). Bank check sold
for $325 (Richard Albersheim Autographs, No-
vember 2011).

Carl Hubbell

Signature Study: Hubbell's signature went
through three distinctive phases and each style of
signature is rather unappealing. Material signed
during his early playing days evidences a signature
with good flow and no hesitation. Signatures from
this period tend to be vertical with a slight left
slant. Signatures exhibit round loops and lack
sharp breaks. During retirement Hubbell's signature went through a noticeable change. The signature now slants to the right. His hand becomes
extremely choppy with cutting angles and abrupt
breaks. His signature has a jagged appearance. In
the early 1980s Hubbell suffered a stroke, which
completely changed his hand. This form of autograph is often referred to as the "post-stroke" signature. It has little eye appeal. Post-stroke signatures revert to the left slant and become elongated.
Unsteadiness of hand is noted. The jagged sharp
angles that dominated pre-stroke signatures have
been replaced with slower less abrupt strokes.
Hubbell 3 illustrates the change in hand due to

Hubbard 1: 1967 signature

Hubbard 2: circa 1960s signature

Hubbell 1: album page dated 1933

Hubbell 2: circa 1970s signature

Hubbell 3: government postcard dated 1985, post-illness signature

illness. His hand would remain infirmed and did not change for the remainder of his life.

Signature Population: The population of Hubbell material is very strong and balanced with a sound demand. Hubbell was a willing and gracious signer his entire life. His signature can be found on most mediums including index cards, photos, baseballs, Hall of Fame plaque postcards, Perez-Steele cards, and the like. Signed baseball bats, Goudey gum cards, and letters are uncommon but do exist. Bank checks are uncommon.

Known Forgeries: Vintage signatures are very difficult to forge. Signatures penned after his stroke are very easy to forge Due to the nominal value of Hubbell's signature, he is not the target of skilled forgers. The majority of post-stroke single-signed baseballs and baseball bats in the market are forgeries.

Sales: Hubbell's signature is available. His autograph generally sells for under $100 on most mediums.

Miller Huggins

Signature Study: Huggins signed in a very consistent and refined hand. His signature is very long and lacks height. Letter construction is very good. The signature is legible. Display value is strong. He signed in a slower hand that lacks a reckless appearance. Huggins died on September 25, 1929. Since Huggins never reached old age, a genuine signature will exhibit no shakiness of hand and one that does should be considered suspect and avoided.

Signature Population: This is a signature of good demand and very limited supply. Huggins is a per se rare signature. Most of the signatures

Huggins 2: check endorsement dated 1925

Huggins 3: circa 1920s signature

in the market are document related. The most common documents are endorsed New York Yankees payroll checks. Also available are a few handwritten letters with good baseball content. A few financial-related letters penned to his business partner, and fellow Hall of Famer, Ed Barrow are in the market. Letters written to Barrow are typically signed with initials as "M.J.H." These letters contain boring investment content, usually land transactions. On non-document related items Huggins is very rare to non-existent. I have never seen a signed baseball card, single-signed baseball, or 8 × 10 photo. Though I have never examined a genuinely signed 8 × 10 photo, there are a couple of signed and inscribed presentation portrait photographs in the market. They measure 11 × 14 and have wonderful eye appeal. The safest way to obtain Huggins' signature on a baseball is to find a signed Yankees team ball from the 1920s, which is an excellent source of Huggins' signature.

Known Forgeries: Due to the less rapid nature of Huggins' hand, replication is fairly easy. It is fair to say that there are many well executed forgeries in the market. It goes without saying that most Huggins signatures offered for sale are forgeries. There are many forged photos, lesser-grade T-cards, and baseballs both as single-signed and multi-signed. There is a group of forged multi-signed Yankees balls in the market. They are signed on American League (both Ban Johnson and E.S. Barnard) baseballs. These balls contain many forged Yankees signatures with Babe Ruth

Huggins 1: ALS circa 1910 (courtesy National Baseball Hall of Fame and Museum)

Huggins 4: check endorsement circa 1925

always on the sweet spot. I have seen three of these balls and two of them have Bennie Bengough's signature accompanying Ruth on the sweet spot. The signatures are many and all jumbled together, which gives the ball a busy appearance. Some of the forgeries, such as Bill Dickey, are well executed while others, such as Tony Lazzeri, are not. The Huggins forgery looks nothing like the illustrations but rather appears small, sloppy, and very compacted. The forger signs them as "M. J. Huggins."

Sales: An 11 × 14 photo, choice specimen, sold for $4,700 (Robert Edward auctions, Spring 2010). Endorsed Yankees payroll check, countersigned by Ed Barrow, sold for $5,500 (Hunt Auctions, July 2008). 1925 real estate document sold for $4,782 (Lelands.com, Winter 2006).

William Hulbert

Signature Study: Hulbert signed in a confident and sophisticated hand. His signature is marked with bold strokes. Letter construction is sound. The signature has maximum display value. Hulbert's signature evidences a heavier hand and has dominant capital letters. The "r" in the last name is distinctive and reminds one of President Gerald Ford's hand. Hulbert ends his signature with a very muted but nice paraph. Most signatures are penned as "W A Hulbert." On rare occasion a full signature signed as "William A. Hulbert" will surface. Hulbert died at a young age. Hulbert never reached old age, so infirmity of hand is nonexistent. A genuine signature will evidence no marked shakiness of hand and one that does should be considered suspect and avoided. Overall, this is one of the more eloquent Hall of Fame signatures.

Signature Population: There is sound demand for this signature. The supply is minute. Hulbert is a very rare signature and only a handful of specimens exist. The population is limited to letters and documents or signatures removed therefrom. I have never examined a genuine non-document item. As an early executive of the National League, Hulbert signed many league documents.

Hulbert 1: ALS dated 1878

Known Forgeries: The complex nature of his hand results in a signature that is difficult to replicate. I know of no well executed forgeries in existence. Nearly 100 percent of the Hulbert signatures in the market are forgeries, but are all lesser executed forgeries.

Sales: Signature removed from letter sold for $5,500 (Hunt Auctions, August 2004). Multipage league application from 1880, which requests Detroit's entrance into National League, sold for $23,666 (Mastro, August 2007).

Catfish Hunter

Signature Study: Hunter signed in a very carefree and somewhat sloppy hand. His signature has poor letter construction. Legibility is impaired. Most signatures are penned as "Jim Catfish Hunter." Hunter's hand remained fairly consistent throughout his life. Material penned during the 1970s evidence little change from post-retirement signatures. Hunter was afflicted with a degenerative nerve disease that eventually took his life. Material signed late in his life evidences an unsteady appearance. However, Hunter basically stopped signing after his diagnosis. For collecting purposes, a genuine Hunter signature should exhibit no shakiness of hand and one that does should be avoided. There are simply too many pre-illness signatures available.

Hunter 1: 1987 signature

Signature Population: This is a signature of marginal demand that is outweighed by supply. Hunter is a common signature as he was a gracious signer throughout his life. He would honor multiple mail requests for his signature. His signature can be found on index cards, photos, baseballs, bats, Perez-Steele cards, gum cards, and the like. Letters of any kind are scarce.

Known Forgeries: Hunter's signature is hurried and busy. Replication of hand would be fairly difficult. Due to the nominal value of Hunter's signature, he is not the target of skilled forgers.

Sales: Hunter's signature is available. His autograph generally sells for under $100 on most mediums.

Monte Irvin

Signature Study: Irvin signs in a somewhat reckless hand that has limited display value. His signature is marked with large looping letters. Marginal letter construction is noted. The signature is, for the most part, legible. In the last few years Irvin's hand exhibits deterioration, so his signatures appear labored.

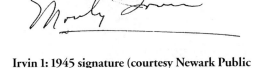

Irvin 1: 1945 signature (courtesy Newark Public Library, The Newark Eagles papers)

Monte Irvin

Irvin 2: check endorsement dated 2000

Signature Population: This is a signature of marginal demand that is outweighed by a large supply. Irvin is a very common signature as he has signed for years. His signature can be found on index cards, letters, photos, gum cards, bats, Perez-Steele cards, and the like. There is a good supply of bank checks in the market. Material signed during his days in the Negro Leagues should be considered rare. During this time he typically signed in variant as "Monty Irvin." This form of signature seldom surfaces. Irvin 1 shows a vintage signature signed as "Monty."

Known Forgeries: Irvin's hand can be replicated with little effort. Due to the nominal value of Irvin's signature, he is not the target of skilled forgers.

Sales: Irvin's signature is available. His autograph generally sells for under $100 on most mediums.

Reggie Jackson

Signature Study: Jackson signs in a flowing hand but it tends to be sloppy. Legibility is impaired. Letter construction is mediocre at best. Jackson's signature has only marginal display value. As of 2012 Jackson's hand remains strong. His signature evidences no shakiness of hand and

Jackson, R. 1: bank check dated 1991

one that does should be considered suspect and avoided.

Signature Population: There is good demand for Jackson material but the supply is much greater. Jackson engages in mass signings. The supply of Jackson material seems unending. His signature is available on just about all mediums including balls, photos, gum cards, and the like. There is a decent supply of bank checks in the market. Letters of any kind are considered scarce.

Known Forgeries: Jackson's signature is rather easy to forge. There are many well executed forgeries in the market. Jackson forgeries are common but generally limited to multi-signed 500-home-run-club items.

Sales: Jackson's signature is available. His autograph generally sells for under $100 on most mediums.

Travis Jackson

Signature Study: Jackson signed in a wonderfully flowing hand. His signature has strong eye appeal. Letter construction is sound. The signature is basically legible. His hand changed little over the years and is marked with good consistency. Vintage signatures tend to incorporate the middle initial into the autograph while more modern examples exclude it. Jackson's hand remained strong for just about his entire life, though

Travis C. Jackson

Jackson, T. 1: team sheet circa 1930s

Travis Jackson

Jackson, T. 2: government postcard dated 1985

material signed in the last months of his life tends to be more illegible and slightly sloppy in appearance. A Jackson signature will exhibit no measurable shakiness of hand and one that does should be considered suspect and avoided.

Signature Population: This is a signature of moderate demand. The supply of Jackson material is sound but not overwhelming. He was a gracious signer throughout his life and honored all mail requests for his signature. Jackson's signature is common on index cards, Hall of Fame plaque postcards, photos, and Perez-Steele cards. Also available, but less common, are baseballs and vintage signed gum cards. Letters of any kind are uncommon to scarce. There is a small cache of signed bank checks in the market but they are few and far between.

Known Forgeries: Jackson's signature is fairly difficult to replicate. Due to the nominal value of Jackson's signature, he is not the target of skilled forgers. However, it should be noted that many nicely forged New York Giants team balls from the early to mid–1920s exist with signatures of Ross Youngs, Hughie Jennings, John McGraw, Jackson, and the like. Proceed with caution as most Giants team balls from this era are fake.

Sales: Jackson's signature is available. His autograph generally sells for under $100 on most mediums.

Fergie Jenkins

Signature Study: Jenkins signs in a very unattractive hand. His signature is marked with poor letter construction. Display value and legibility are severely impaired. As of 2012 a Jenkins signature evidences no shakiness of hand and one that does should be considered suspect and avoided.

Signature Population: This is a signature of limited demand. The population of material is basically limitless as Jenkins is a willing signer for a fee, which he donates to charities. His signature

is found on most mediums including gum cards, index cards, Hall of Fame plaque postcards, baseballs, bats, and the like. Signed letters of any kind are considered scarce. Jenkins has also authored a book titled *The Game Is Easy, Life Is Hard*, of which many signed copies exist.

Known Forgeries: Given the sloppy nature of the hand, Jenkins' signature is fairly easy to replicate. Due to the nominal value of Jenkins' signature, he is not the target of skilled forgers.

Sales: Jenkins' signature is available. His autograph generally sells for under $100 on most mediums.

Hugh Jennings

Signature Study: Jennings was an intelligent man with handwriting to match. His signature is one of the finest of any member of the Hall of Fame. Jennings' hand is marked with stunning flow and effortless strokes. The capital "H" in the first name is stunningly bold. The signature evidences a nice right slant. Letter construction is fairly sound, however, the "nnin" in the last name appear as indistinguishable strokes. Material signed in the last years of his life evidence a slower, less flamboyant hand. Jennings' health began a downward spiral in the early to mid–1920s. In 1926, Jennings had retired from baseball and entered a sanitarium. In those final years he suffered a nervous breakdown. A Jennings signature will evidence no measurable shakiness of hand and one that does should be considered suspect and avoided.

Signature Population: This is a signature of strong demand with a minute supply. Jennings is a rare to very rare signature. In 30 years of collecting I have seen maybe 20 to 25 genuine specimens and just about all of them are letter/document related. I have examined a few genuine baseballs, those being a 1920 Detroit Tigers team ball and a couple of New York Giants balls from the 1920s. I have never examined a genuine single-signed baseball, photo, baseball card, or government postcard. This signature is a rarity in the autograph field.

Jenkins 1: 2008 signature

Jennings 1: TLS circa 1910

Jennings 2: album page circa 1920s

Jennings 3: ALS circa 1920

Known Forgeries: Due to the complex and flowing nature of Jennings' hand, well executed forgeries do not exist. When Jennings became a coach for the Giants, he was suffering from nervous tension and other health issues. Most Jennings-signed material from his days as a Giants coach was secretarially signed. A common Jennings forgery that has been accepted as genuine by some authenticators features a signature with a flat top style "J." This is a secretarial signature that is commonly found on Giants signed team balls. This signature has no similarities to Jennings' hand. A signature that features a flat top "J" should be avoided in total. Genuinely signed material from his days as a Giants coach is very rare. Another forged Jennings ball surfaced several years ago. There was a small cache of baseballs that feature forged signatures of Jennings and John McGraw. Each forgery occupies its own side panel. The signatures are overly large. The McGraw forgery is penned "J.J. McGraw." The caliber of the forgeries is not bad but I would not call them well executed. Given the rarity of a Jennings-signed baseball, it is highly doubtful that just these two signatures exist on a baseball. There are a few letters in existence, most of which are typed letters

signed. I know of two letters on "Jennings & Jennings" letterhead and a couple of typed letters on Detroit Tigers letterhead. Most TLsS feature a secretarial signature. They have been circulating for many decades. These signatures are easily spotted as they look nothing like a genuine signature. The signature usually features the initials "L.T." after the signature identifying the secretary who signed Jennings' name. This secretarial signature is illustrated in Jennings 5. There are many forgeries of Jennings that feature his signature with team initials under the autograph. Examples are "Det. B.B. Club," "N.Y. Giants B.B. Club," and the like. If you examine one of these signatures proceed with *extreme* caution as it is very likely forged. In fact, I have never seen an authentic Jennings signature signed with a team notation. One of these forgeries is illustrated as Jennings 4.

Sales: A 1920 Detroit Tigers signed team ball, also signed by Ty Cobb, Harry Heilmann, and Bob Veach, impaired condition, sold for $3,600 (eBay, January 2011). 1922 TLS sold for $4,700 (Hunt Auctions, July 2010).

Ban Johnson

Signature Study: Johnson signed in a very unique and artistic hand. His signature evidences very good flow. No hesitation is noted. His signature is strong in height and evidences a nice right slant. Letter construction is somewhat impaired. His signature is generally legible, though the letters tend to run into each other, giving the signature a slightly cramped appearance. Signatures generally remained consistent throughout his life, though autographs signed in the 1920s tend to be slightly smaller and a bit more compact. Just about all signatures in the market are signed as "B.B. Johnson." Johnson died at the age of 67 and though he was prone to illness in his last years, it appears not to have affected his signature. A genuine Johnson signature will evidence no shakiness of hand and one that does should be considered suspect and avoided.

Jennings 4: common forgery

Jennings 5 common secretarial

Johnson, B. 1: document dated 1908

Johnson, B. 2: TLS dated 1912 (courtesy National Baseball Hall of Fame and Museum)

Johnson, B. 3: undated signature

Signature Population: This is a signature where demand is well balanced with a limited supply. Johnson's signature should be considered scarce on a per se basis. There is a decent supply of signatures in the market. His signature is typically limited to league letters, documents, and contracts. Many nice typed letters signed exist with tremendous baseball content. His signature appears on the face of league contracts, though some are secretarially signed. These items are an excellent source of Johnson signatures. On any other medium Johnson's signature is considered excessively rare to non-existent. I have never examined a single-signed baseball. I have examined only one multi-signed baseball. I know of only one signed photo.

Known Forgeries: Due to the complex nature of his signature and the effortless strokes, Johnson's signature is very difficult to replicate. There are no well executed forgeries in the market. Forgeries tend to evidence a labored appearance and are rudimentary in construction. Many letters from his days as league president are secretarially signed. These secretarial signatures are easily spotted as they deviate greatly from a genuine signature. There are a few signed bank checks in the market, which were drawn on the First National Bank of Chicago. The specimens I have seen were dated 1929 and 1930. The checks feature an elongated signature with letters spaced much farther apart. These signatures also appear slightly labored in appearance. Some experts have pronounced them as genuine. I, for one, do not believe the

signatures are genuine. It should be noted that title issues may exist with certain Johnson letters. See the stolen document section in Chapter 4.

Sales: 1915 TLS sold for $200 (RR Auctions, July 2011). 1922 Major League contract sold for $324 (RR Auctions, September 2011). 1921 Major League contract, countersigned by Harry Frazee, sold for $391 (Hunt Auctions, November 2010). 1915 TLS sold for $294 (RR Auctions, February 2010).

Judy Johnson

Signature Study: Johnson signatures are generally limited to post-induction material. Thus more modern signatures are the target of study. Johnson signed in a very legible and plain hand. Letter construction is very sound. His signature is marked with a slight choppiness. A slight hesitation is evident. Most signatures are accomplished with his nickname. Signatures signed as "William J. Johnson" are typically limited to signed bank checks. Material signed in the last few years of his life evidence a labored appearance. Material signed just before death exhibits a very unsteady hand.

Signature Population: This is a signature of marginal demand. The supply of Johnson material is sound but not overwhelming. He did engage in some mass signings. Johnson was also a gracious signer throughout his life. He honored just about all signature requests until illness force him to stop signing in the closing days of 1988. Johnson's signature can be found on most mediums including index cards, modern government postcards, photos, baseballs, Perez-Steele cards, and the like. Letters of any kind are scarce. Single-signed bats are rare, albeit borderline. There is also a small supply of signed bank checks in the market but these to must be considered scarce. Signed material from Johnson's days as a Negro Leaguer should be considered rare.

Known Forgeries: Due to the slower nature of his signature, Johnson's autograph is one of the easier names to forge. Johnson is generally not the

Johnson, J. 1: government postcard dated 1986

Johnson, J. 2: detail of forgery

target of skilled forgers, due to the nominal value of his signature. However, there is a good supply of forged baseballs in the market, all accomplished by the same forger. Here is what to look for (see Johnson, J 2 for detail). Johnson's signature typically contains a "y" in the first name that is looped under with the stroke heading towards the first name. In later years he dropped the loop and basically signed the down stroke of the "y" with a straight line. The forged baseballs are signed on the sweet spot. They are accomplished in either blue or black ball point. For some reason the forger makes a fatal error in constructing the letter "y." The letter "y" contains a down stroke with a fairly pronounced tail that points toward the last name, something a genuine signature does not exhibit. Additionally, Johnson was featured on a Perez-Steele Celebration card. When it was issued in early 1989, Johnson had already stopped signing. I know of no genuinely signed cards in existence. In the past couple of years a few signed specimens have surfaced with the claim that they were obtained in the mail from Johnson. I have my doubts. Signed Johnson Celebration cards should be avoided in total.

Sales: Johnson's signature is available. His autograph generally sells for under $100 on most mediums.

Walter Johnson

Signature Study: Johnson's signature is dominated by sharp vertical strokes with little if any

Johnson, W. 2: 1930s signature above facsimile, variant letter J

slant. Letter construction is extremely sound. The signature is legible. Superior display value is noted. The dominant "J" in the last name only adds to the strong eye appeal. Material signed in the 1920s/1930s may, at times, evidence a more traditional letter "J" as illustrated in Johnson, W. 2. Later specimens feature a large flattop "J." Just about all signatures are signed as "Walter Johnson." I have never examined a signature where he signs with either of his nicknames. His hand remained strong his entire life. A genuine Johnson signature will exhibit no shakiness of hand and one that does should be considered suspect and avoided.

Signature Population: Demand is great for Johnson material. The supply of Johnson material is limited and it should be considered a somewhat scarce signature. His signature is generally limited to material signed after 1930. Album pages and scorecards are a good source. Government postcards and letters are very scarce. 8 × 10 photos and single-signed baseballs are rare but there are some nice examples in the market. The best source of Johnson-signed baseballs are Washington Senators team baseballs from the mid– to late 1920s. Another good source of Johnson signatures are canceled bank checks. There are many in the market. Checks are not rare by any means but should still be considered scarce. Signed Hall of Fame plaque postcards are extremely rare. I have never examined a genuine specimen in over 30 years of searching.

Known Forgeries: Johnson's hand exhibits nice flow and his signature is difficult to replicate. Only very skilled forgers have mastered his signature. Despite this, well executed forgeries exist, though

Johnson, W. 1: ledger page circa 1930s

Johnson, W. 3: government postcard circa 1940s

Walter Johnson [signature]

Johnson, W. 4: undated signature

Walter Johnson [signature]

Johnson, W. 5: undated signature

limited as they may be. Johnson forgeries are everywhere; fortunately for collectors most are poorly executed. One specific forgery to watch for are single-signed baseballs. The forgery appears on the sweet spot. The forgeries are nicely executed but there is an error. The letter "J" is defective. A genuine signature will exhibit a flat top letter "J." These forgeries feature an uneven letter "J" where the top curves up then down. The letter "J" is more angled to the right. A slightly labored appearance is noted.

Sales: Bank check sold for $1,998 (Robert Edward Auctions, Spring 2011). ALS, undated, sold for $1,555 (Lelands.com, May 2008). Index card sold for $1,000 (Hunt Auctions, November 2010). Short ALS, circa 1930, sold for $1,293 (Robert Edward Auctions, Spring 2011). Signature removed from a document sold for $636 (RR Auctions, July 2011).

Addie Joss

Signature Study: Joss' signature is an extreme rarity and causes much controversy. For years his signature was a great mystery but in recent years a signature has surfaced with sound credentials. An autographed album purportedly from the estate of Napoleon Lajoie entered the market with some rare signatures, including Hugh Jennings, Bill Armour, and Frank Navin. A signature of Joss

Addie Joss [signature]

Joss 1: circa 1910 signature

was included. The signatures in this album, where confirmed specimens existed, matched the known signatures. This gives weight to the authenticity of this Joss. To my knowledge, this Joss signature is the only known specimen to exist. It should be considered an unconfirmed signature, simply because there is nothing to compare it to.

Signature Population: Joss is an extreme rarity. One signature believed genuine exists. Back in the mid–1980s I spoke with a member of the Joss family who resided in Ohio. She informed me that the family had no signatures in their possession. I am told a couple of elementary school books signed by Joss as a young child exist. I have seen a signed McGuffey Reader with a childlike signature accomplished as "Addie Joss" in pencil. Whether these are real I do not know. They are of no value for analysis purposes.

Known Forgeries: Many forgeries are in the market. They all differ from each other, evidencing a lack of a genuine signature to use as a template. It should further be noted that there are a couple of multi-signed baseballs that were allegedly signed at the Addie Joss benefit game held in July 1911. I have seen a couple of these balls signed by Cobb, Young, Joe Jackson, Sam Crawford, and the like. I have never seen a genuine one and it is very likely they do not exist.

Sales: Due to the rarity, there have been no recent sales of Joss' signature.

Al Kaline

Signature Study: Kaline signs in a very flowing and extremely legible hand. His signature displays well. Early signatures tend to be less flowing and a bit more choppy. Modern signatures have excellent letter construction. As of 2012, Kaline's hand evidences no shakiness of hand. A genuine signature is free of any hesitation.

Signature Population: This is a signature of marginal demand outweighed by a large supply. Kaline is a willing signer and does many mass signings. His signature can be found on most mediums including baseballs, Hall of Fame plaque

Al Kaline [signature]

Kaline 1: circa 1995 signature

postcards, photos, jerseys, baseballs, bats, gum cards, and the like. Letters of any kind are scarce. Signed photos with fellow Hall of Famer and broadcast partner George Kell are uncommon and are in good demand.

Known Forgeries: The nice flow of Kaline's hand makes replication difficult. There are no well executed forgeries in the market. Due to the nominal value of Kaline's signature, he is not a target of skilled forgers

Sales: Kaline's signature is available. His autograph generally sells for under $100 on most mediums.

Tim Keefe

Signature Study: Keefe's signature is one of the great mysteries in the field of Hall of Fame autographs. I have not been able to locate a specimen for study purposes. I have never found a signature I would feel comfortable pronouncing as genuine. A search for his will proved unsuccessful.

Signature Population: I know of no genuine signatures in existence. I am told a couple of signatures were released by the Keefe estate, but I have never seen them.

Known Forgeries: All the Keefe signatures I have examined were the product of forgery. All vary in construction.

Sales: Due to the rarity, there have been no recent sales of Keefe's signature.

Willie Keeler

Signature Study: Based on the specimens illustrated, it is clear Keeler signed in a pensive and unassuming hand. His signature evidences moderate flow but lacks recklessness. Letter construction is somewhat impaired. The letters "e" in the last name appear as mere points. It is unclear whether infirmity of hand existed. The signature that appears on his will is dated in 1922 and still exhibits good flow; he died New Years' Day 1923.

Signature Population: This is a signature in

Keeler 1: signed book dated 1910 (courtesy National Baseball Hall of Fame and Museum)

Keeler 2: will dated 1922

strong demand. The more I research Keeler's signature the more I am convinced that there maybe only a few genuine specimens in existence. The 1910 specimen, illustrated as Keeler 1, is a stunning example and is the only one I could locate outside of a governmental concern. It has been accomplished in bold fountain-pen ink. This is from a presentation book signed by the members of the 1910 New York Giants. This rare piece of baseball history is currently housed at the National Baseball Hall of Fame. I know of no signed photos, cards, or baseballs.

Known Forgeries: It is clear from the illustrated specimens that replication of hand is relatively easy. Well executed forgeries exist in quantities Most forgeries I have examined are removed from a larger medium signed in either pencil or ink. The ink seems too clean and bright. Forgeries do evidence a labored appearance and are slightly choppy.

Sales: Due to the rarity, there have been no recent sales of Keeler's signature.

George Kell

Signature Study: Kell signed in a consistent and vertical hand. The hand is bold and the signature is dominated with large strokes. Letter construction is sound. Kell's signature is very legible. Sound display value is noted. Most signatures are signed as "George Kell." On occasion he would pen his name as "George Clyde Kell." In

Kell 1: government postcard dated 1954

Kell 2: government postcard dated 1986

Kelley 2: ALS circa 1910 (courtesy National Baseball Hall of Fame and Museum)

Kelley 3: ALS circa 1910 (courtesy National Baseball Hall of Fame and Museum)

Kelley 4: undated ALS (courtesy National Baseball Hall of Fame and Museum)

the last few years of his life, Kell's hand was affected by infirmity due to spinal problems. Many signatures signed at this time exhibit a shakiness of hand.

Signature Population: This is a signature of marginal demand far outweighed by supply. For many years Kell was a willing signer at baseball card shows and through the mail. His signature is very common and can be found on most mediums. Letters of any kind are uncommon. Bank checks are also available but should be considered uncommon. Signed photos with broadcast partners Al Kaline and Ernie Harwell are uncommon and highly collectible.

Known Forgeries: Vintage Kell signatures are rather difficult to replicate. Signatures with infirmity are easy to replicate. Due to the nominal value of Kell's signature, he is not the target of skilled forgers. On occasion, signatures obtained through the mail in the 1950s were secretarially signed. These signatures are small and usually signed with the phrase "Best Wishes."

Sales: Kell's signature is available. His autograph generally sells for under $100 on most mediums.

Joe Kelley

Signature Study: Kelley's hand is marked with bold strokes. Lines have noticeable variations in thickness, resulting in a signature with a medieval look. The display value of his signature is very high. The few handwritten letters that exist look like they were penned by an ancient scrivener with a highly artistic skill. Kelley's signature is vertical

Kelley 1: ALS circa 1910 (courtesy National Baseball Hall of Fame and Museum)

with a very slight back slant. There is a small supply of signatures that evidence a labored appearance and were accomplished in the last few years of his life. While shakiness of hand did exist, it is only of a limited degree, so a signature with excessive unsteadiness should be considered suspect and avoided.

Signature Population: There is sound demand for Kelley material. The supply is minute. Kelley is a signature that should be considered rare to very rare. Letters of any kind are very rare and most are held at the National Baseball Hall of Fame. There is one autographed letter signed with content that speaks of Willie Keeler and the number of hits he obtained in a game. There are a couple of endorsed payroll checks in the market, from the time Kelley worked in the front office of the New York Yankees. I know of no signed photos, tobacco cards, or baseballs. Signed team balls from Kelley's playing days very likely do not exist.

Known Forgeries: Kelley's hand is flowing, but it lacks rapid strokes, resulting in a signature that is moderately easy to replicate. Just about all Kelley signatures in the market are forgeries. There are forged letters, balls, government postcards, and the like, so proceed with caution.

Sales: 1922 Yankees payroll check, countersigned by Jacob Ruppert, sold for $11,162 (Robert Edward Auctions, Spring 2008). 1940 two-page ALS discussing Willie Keeler, superior specimen, sold for $9,987 (Robert Edward Auctions, Spring 2008). 1922 Yankees payroll check, countersigned by Jacob Ruppert, sold for $3,525 (Robert Edward Auctions, Spring 2011).

George Kelly

Signature Study: Kelly signed in a loose hand, resulting in a very unassuming signature. The hand lacks precise angles. The lines appear rudimentary in construction. The signature is generally legible, but the display value is poor. The one consistent aspect of the signature is its little change in appearance throughout the years. A signature accomplished in 1930 looks about the same as one penned in the 1980s. Kelly's hand remained strong his entire life. A genuine signature will exhibit no measurable shakiness of hand and one that does should be considered suspect and avoided.

Kelly, G. 1: signed check dated 1956

Signature Population: This is a signature of moderate demand balanced with supply. Kelly was a willing signer throughout his long life, resulting in a strong supply of signatures. In addition there are many vintage items in the market, including signed bank checks from the 1920s and 1930s. His signature can be found on photos, index cards, and Hall of Fame plaque postcards. Letters and single-signed baseballs should be considered scarce.

Known Forgeries: Do to the reserved nature of his hand, Kelly's signature is rather easy to forge. Due to the nominal value of Kelly's signature, he is generally not the target of skilled forgers. The one exception is single-signed baseballs.

Sales: Kelly's signature is available. His autograph generally sells for under $100 on most mediums.

M.J. "King" Kelly

Signature Study: King Kelly's signature is bold and dominant. His hand is marked with nice vertical strokes. Sound letter construction is noted.

Kelly, M. 1: check endorsement dated 1890 (courtesy National Baseball Hall of Fame and Museum)

Kelly, M .2: check endorsement dated 1890 (courtesy National Baseball Hall of Fame and Museum)

His signature is legible. Display value is strong. It is one of the nicer Hall of Fame signatures. The known specimens are signed "M.J. Kelly." No signatures exist signed with his nickname "King," at least to my knowledge. It is unknown whether his hand was affected by any infirmities. Given his untimely death due to pneumonia, shakiness of hand is very unlikely.

Signature Population: Kelly is an excessively

Kelly, M. 3: document dated 1890 (courtesy National Baseball Hall of Fame and Museum)

Kelly, M. 4: undated signature, commonly reproduced as a facsimile

rare signature. There are a few endorsed payroll checks from the 1890s held by the National Baseball Hall of Fame. One contract is known to exist. This is the only Kelly signature I know of in the open market. I know of no signed baseballs, photos, or nineteenth century baseball cards.

Known Forgeries: Kelly signed in a slower hand, making replication easy. There are many well executed forgeries in the market from photos to early baseball cards to fake letters. Several years ago, likely in the 1960s, a small group of forgeries entered the market. The forgeries are usually found on album pages or signatures removed from documents. These forgeries are signed as "M.J. Kelly" but unlike the genuine signature the "y" differs greatly. On the capital "K" of the last name, the forger puts a curl at the bottom of the letter. These forgeries easily stand out with examination.

Sales: Due to the rarity, there have been no recent sales of Kelly's signature.

Harmon Killebrew

Signature Study: Killebrew signed in a very distinct and attractive hand. His signature is marked with bold strokes and strong flow. His signature is generally legible, but letter construction will tend to morph into short indistinct strokes. The signature evidences a right slant. The large capital letters dominate the signature. A very strong display value is noted. Killebrew's hand remained strong his entire life. A genuine signature will evidence no shakiness of hand and one that does should be considered suspect and avoided.

Signature Population: The demand for Killebrew's signature is good but supply is greater. Killebrew is a common signature. He engaged in many mass signings for his charity. Killebrew's signature can be found on index cards, gum cards, baseballs, bats, photos, and the like. Signed letters of any kind are scarce.

Known Forgeries: His signature is difficult to replicate. There are no well executed forgeries in the market. Due to the nominal value of Killebrew's signature, he is generally not the target of

skilled forgers. Forgeries are limited to multi-signed 500-home-run-club items.

Sales: Killebrew's signature is available. His autograph generally sells for under $100 on most mediums.

Ralph Kiner

Signature Study: Kiner signs in a large and bold hand. His signature is generally vertical with a slight slant to the right. His signature is legible. Sound display value is noted. Letter construction is sound. The flow is strong, resulting in a signature that lacks hesitation. Kiner has one of the nicer signatures of the Hall of Fame members. Material signed since 2007 evidences an unsteady appearance due to infirmity of hand.

Kiner 1: circa 1980s signature

Signature Population: Demand is heavily outweighed by supply. Kiner is a very common signature and the supply seems unending. His signature is common on most mediums including index cards, photos, gum cards, baseballs, Hall of Fame plaque postcards, bats, and the like. Letters of any kind are scarce.

Known Forgeries: Replication of hand is difficult. Creating a well executed forgery would take effort. Due to the nominal value of Kiner's signature, he is generally not the target of skilled forgers.

Sales: Kiner's signature is available. His autograph generally sells for under $100 on most mediums.

Chuck Klein

Signature Study: Klein signed in a nice and flowing hand. His signature has sound display value. A good degree of legibility is noted. Letter

Killebrew 1: circa 1985 signature

Klein 1: album page circa 1930s

Klein 2: album page dated 1933

Klein 3: undated signature

construction is sound. The signature exhibits a slight right slant. Klein's signature has good flow and lacks hesitation. Klein had the habit of signing his name as "C. Klein" though this signature appears limited to material signed at the ballparks. Klein 2 illustrates the abbreviated signature. Items signed through the mail, such as government postcards, are signed in full. Klein died at a relatively young age. A genuine Klein signature will exhibit no shakiness of hand and one that does should be considered suspect and avoided.

Signature Population: There is good demand for Klein's signature that far outweighs a limited supply. Klein is a scarce signature per se. His signature is generally limited to material signed at the stadium. His signature is most commonly found on album pages, scorecards, and team-signed baseballs. Other mediums such as 8 × 10 photographs, Goudey gum cards, and letters should be considered rare to very rare. I have never seen a full-page handwritten letter nor have I examined a genuine single-signed baseball. Government postcards were signed but only sparingly.

Known Forgeries: The practical nature of Klein's hand is fairly easy to replicate. Well executed forgeries exist in quantities. Forgeries of Klein are common and found on most mediums. There is one forger that seems to produce a lot of Klein forgeries. His work product stands out as the forgeries evidence a slight labored appearance. The forgery is shorter in length, giving the letters a compacted look. Most Klein signatures in the market are forgeries, so proceed with caution.

Sales: 2 × 3 thick-stock card sold for $275 (Hunt Auctions, November 2010). 5 × 7 newspaper picture, signed by Jimmie Foxx and Freddy

Fitzsimmons, sold for $847 (RR Auctions, March 2011). 1930s baseball, with others, sold for $478 (Lelands.com, November 2007). 1930s magazine, premium photo, sold for $1,144 (Lelands.com, December 2005).

Bill Klem

Signature Study: Klem signed in one of the most unusual hands of all the Hall of Famers. His signature is marked with artistic tones and whimsical strokes of hand. His signature is one of the few that is illegible but has great display value. Klem's signature almost looks like a drawing. The signature is vertical with extremely large and dominant letters. Letter construction is very aggressive. Just about all signatures are signed "W.J. Klem." Signatures penned in full are rare and desirable. Klem's hand remained strong his entire life. A genuine Klem signature will exhibit no shakiness of hand and one that does should be considered suspect and avoided.

Signature Population: There is good demand for "the umpire of umpires." The supply is very limited. Klem is a scarce signature and generally limited to signatures removed from letters/documents and album pages. His signature should be considered rare on any other medium including photos, letters, government postcards, and single-

Klem 1: undated signature

Klem 2: undated signature

signed baseballs. Single-signed balls are signed on the side panel. I have never examined a genuine Klem-signed ball with his signature on the sweet spot.

Known Forgeries: Due to the rapid and flamboyant nature of Klem's hand, his signature is difficult to replicate. The supply of well executed Klem forgeries is very limited. Klem has been the target of forgers for years. Forged photographs, baseballs, and letters exist. I know of a couple of signed baseballs that feature forgeries of Klem, fellow Hall of Fame umpire Tommy Connolly, and usually another lesser name umpire or two. These have been circulating for years, so caution is warranted. There is a small number of Klem letters in the market which discuss protested games. Title issues may exist with these letters. See the stolen document section in Chapter 4.

Sales: 1937 government postcard sold for $700 (Hunt Auctions, July 2011). Index card sold for $294 (RR Auctions, February 2010). Index card sold for $640 (Lelands.com, June 2011).

Sandy Koufax

Signature Study: Koufax signs in a bold and moderately aggressive hand. His signature is fast on paper and lacks any hesitation whatsoever. His signature has a right slant with good letter construction. The letter "x" in the last name is large. The signature has moderate display value. As of 2012 Koufax's signature evidences no shakiness of

Koufax 1: undated signature

Koufax 2: common secretarial

hand and one that does should be considered suspect and avoided.

Signature Population: There is very good demand for Koufax material and balanced with a large supply. Koufax is a common signature. He is a gracious signer in person, though mail requests are generally ignored. His signature is common on most mediums including baseballs, photos, gum cards, Hall of Fame plaque postcards, index cards, and the like. Letters of any kind are uncommon to scarce.

Known Forgeries: Due to the flowing nature of his hand, Koufax is a difficult signature to replicate. Well executed forgeries are limited. Most forgeries are amateurish in construction and evidence hesitation. Many Koufax signatures obtained through the mail in the last 25 years were secretarially signed. Koufax 2 shows a typical secretarial signature.

Sales: Koufax's signature is available. His autograph generally sells for under $100 on most mediums.

Bowie Kuhn

Signature Study: Kuhn signed in a very distinctive hand. His signature is marked with jagged and strong strokes. His signature is vertical with a slight right slant. Letter construction is poor, resulting in a signature that is illegible. Kuhn's signature evidences a reckless appearance. Good flow is noted. Many consider Kuhn's signature unattractive. I, on the other hand, believe it is a fine display signature. Kuhn's hand remained strong his entire life. A genuine signature will evidence no shakiness of hand and one that does should be considered suspect and avoided.

Signature Population: There is good demand for Kuhn material and balanced with an ample supply. Kuhn is fairly common signature, though generally limited to photos and index cards. Letters and single-signed balls are uncommon. There is a small grouping of letters released by the Kuhn estate that are written to his mother and signed "Bowie." Some of these letters date back to the 1940s. In addition, many signatures removed from bank checks exist.

Kuhn 1: postal cover circa 1940s

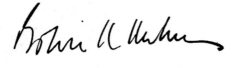

Kuhn 2: undated signature

Known Forgeries: Kuhn's signature is difficult to replicate. There are no well executed forgeries in the market. Due to the nominal value of Kuhn's signature, he is generally not the target of skilled forgers.

Sales: Kuhn's signature is available. His autograph generally sells for under $100 on most mediums.

Nap Lajoie

Signature Study: Lajoie signed in a very nice and pleasing hand. His signature is marked with strong letter construction and large well defined letters. His signature is extremely legible. It has superior display value. As nice as Lajoie's hand is, it lacks rapid flow. Strokes tend to be slower in execution. The signature illustrated in Lajoie 1 is from a contract dated 1906. Material from this date is typically not available in the market. Lajoie typically signed with his nickname "Larry." On occasion he would sign with his real name, though this form of signature is somewhat scarce. Lajoie was also fond of dating signatures, which adds to the signature's eye appeal. Lajoie's hand slowed during the final decade of his life. Signatures from this time period will evidence a slightly labored appearance. His hand never produced a truly shaky signature. One that evidences a materially unsteady appearance should be considered suspect and avoided.

Signature Population: This is a signature in

Lajoie 1: contract dated 1906

Lajoie 2: 1937 signature

Lajoie 3: album page circa 1940s

Lajoie 4: circa 1950 signature

high demand and of limited supply. Lajoie was a willing signer throughout his long life and honored all mail requests for his signature. The vast majority of Lajoie signatures are found on index cards, government postcards, and album pages. Letters of any kind and 8 × 10 photographs are very scarce. Single-signed baseballs are rare. I have examined well over 100 single-signed balls, of which maybe five or six were genuine examples. All genuine examples were signed on the side panel and dated in the 1950s. Most were signed in ball-point pen. Lajoie was one of the early converts to the technology of ball-point pens and used them often, starting in the late 1940s. Hall of Fame plaque postcards should be considered rare. I have never seen a genuinely signed T-card of any kind.

Known Forgeries: The fact that his hand lacks a reckless flow results in a signature that is rather easy to forge. Well executed forgeries exist in quantities. Lajoie is a common target of skilled forgers. Many forged baseballs, photos, and other mediums exist. Of note, forged Hall of Fame plaque postcards entered the market years ago. These forged plaque cards are fairly well executed but the forgeries appear slightly more choppy than a genuine Lajoie signature. The forger also makes an error in the "rr" in the first name. Note in the genuine signature the letters "rr" have good height and are well defined. These forgeries, as illustrated in Lajoie 5, are poorly constructed, evidencing a

Lajoie 5: detail of forgery

choppiness of hand. The height in the letters "rr" is much lower. Appearing as two small bumps, it differs greatly from a genuine signature. The forger who created these plaques also penned countless index cards.

Sales: 1950 government postcard sold for $500 (Hunt Auctions, November 2010). 1937 signature, choice specimen, sold for $932 (RR Auctions, August 2010). 1933 album page, choice ink signature, sold for $1,058 (Robert Edward Auctions, Spring 2009). 1951 ALS sold for $2,345 (Lelands.com, June 2005).

Judge Landis

Signature Study: Landis signed in a most unattractive hand. Landis' signature is basically a gibberish scrawl of ink that has no legibility. Letter construction in very poor. Most letters are pushed aside in favor of a crooked line. His signature exhibits a nice right slant. Display value is non-existent. Most signatures are signed as "K.M. Landis." On occasion he would sign his name as "Kenesaw M. Landis." This form of signature is scarce. Landis' hand remained strong his entire life. A genuine signature will exhibit no shakiness of hand and one that does should be considered suspect and avoided.

Signature Population: Landis' association with Joe Jackson and the 1919 Black Sox correlates into good demand for his signature. The supply of Landis material is limited and generally confined to signed documents and league letters. Letters exist on league letterhead and many have excellent content. There are a few letters signed as a federal judge but these are much more difficult to secure. Were it not for these letters Landis would be a very scarce to rare signature on a per se basis. On other mediums his signature is rare to very rare. Photos are rare, though a handful of presentation photos exist. These are a formal portrait pose and measure approximately 9 × 13. They are always signed underneath the image in the large lower blank portion of the photo. Baseballs are also rare. Single-signed baseballs are just about non-

Landis 1: ALS undated (courtesy National Baseball Hall of Fame and Museum)

Landis 2: TLS dated 1921 (courtesy National Baseball Hall of Fame and Museum)

Landis 3: TLS dated 1931 (courtesy National Baseball Hall of Fame and Museum)

existent. I have only examined three, maybe four, genuine specimens in over 30 years of searching. Few collectors sought out Landis for autographs. He signed relatively few mail requests. There is a small supply of government postcards and 1939 baseball first-day postal covers in the market.

Known Forgeries: Due to the rudimentary nature of hand, Landis' signature is very easy to forge. Many well executed forgeries exist in the market. Though he signed most of his correspondence, a few secretarial-signed letters will surface. The secretarial signatures evidence a choppiness that genuine signatures lack. Secretarial signatures differ greatly from genuine specimens and are exposed with little examination.

Sales: Calling card, choice signature, sold for $393 (RR Auctions, August 2010). 1922 TLS sold for $303 (Hunt Auctions, July 2010). Album page sold for $180 (RR Auctions, October 2010). Presentation photo sold for $705 (Robert Edward Auctions, Spring 2007). 1942 TLS to Walter Briggs sold for $649 (eBay, September 2011).

Barry Larkin

Signature Study: Larkin signs in a very unstructured hand. His signature has poor letter

Larkin 1: 2011 Topps limited edition card

construction. Legibility is basically non-existent. The display value is poor. As of 2012 Larkin's hand remains strong. A genuine signature will evidence no shakiness of hand and one that does should be considered suspect and avoided. Overall, this is a signature based in griffonage.

Signature Population: As of 2012 Larkin's signature had a limited population. This will certainly change with his recent induction into the Hall of Fame. Larkin will sign for years to comes and his signature will prove common on most mediums.

Known Forgeries: Larkin's signature is easy to replicate. Well executed forgeries can be produced with little effort. Due to the nominal value of Larkin's signature, he is not the target of skilled forgers.

Sales: Larkin's signature is available. His autograph generally sells for under $100 on most mediums.

Tommy Lasorda

Signature Study: Lasorda signs in a very plain and practical hand. His signature is marked with below average letter construction that has a rudimentary look. Lasorda's signature evidences a right slant. By 2012, Lasorda's hand was affected by an infirmity, so material signed in the previous few years exhibits a shakiness of hand. Overall, this is a signature with limited display value.

Signature Population: This is a signature of marginal demand. The supply of genuine Lasorda material is very strong. He is a willing and gracious signer. His signature is found on most mediums including index cards, Perez-Steele cards, baseballs, bats, photos, gum cards, and the like. Letters of any kind are scarce.

Known Forgeries: Lasorda's signature is easy to replicate. Well executed forgeries can be produced with little effort. Due to the nominal value of Lasorda's signature, he is not the target of skilled forgers.

Sales: Lasorda's signature is available. His autograph generally sells for under $100 on most mediums.

Lasorda 1: 1992 signature

Tony Lazzeri

Signature Study: Lazzeri signed in a very distinctive and crisp hand. His signature is marked with effortless flow. Well defined angles evidence a slight right slant. Letter construction is strong. The signature is legible. His signature starts with a very dominant "T" that exhibits a top and base separated from each other. Lazzeri's signature has tremendous display value. Most signatures are signed as "Tony Lazzeri." Legal and bank documents are typically signed as "Anthony M Lazzeri." In 1946, Lazzeri died at a very young age. A Lazzeri signature will exhibit no shakiness of hand and one that does should be considered suspect and avoided.

Signature Population: There is sound demand for Lazzeri's signature that outweighs supply. The population of Lazzeri material is restricted and generally limited to items signed at the ballpark. His signature is generally found on album pages, scorecards, and Yankees team baseballs. Signed photos and government postcards are very scarce. Goudey gum cards and letters are rare. I have never examined a genuine full-page handwritten letter. Single-signed baseballs are an extreme rarity. I have only examined one that I would feel comfortable pronouncing as genuine. The best way to obtain a Lazzeri-signed ball is to secure a Yankees team ball from the mid–1930s. There is a small supply of bank checks in the market.

Lazzeri 1: album page dated 1933

Lazzeri 2: government postcard dated 1938

Lazzeri 3: bank check dated 1942

Known Forgeries: The wonderful flow of Lazzeri's hand results in a signature that is very hard to replicate. Well executed forgeries are few and far between. Forgers generally avoid Lazzeri due to the complex and flowing nature of his hand. Forgeries are typically found on Yankees team baseballs and team sheets. The forgeries tend to evidence a slight shakiness of hand and lack the effortless flow of a genuine signature. There is a small grouping of forgeries that have been placed on old bank checks. The forgeries are signed on back then cut off the document and sold as signed endorsements.

Sales: 1928 Major League contract, countersigned by Jacob Ruppert, sold for $3,525 (Robert Edward Auctions, Spring 2011). Album page, choice signature, sold for $1,125 (Lelands.com, November 2010). 1934 album page, signed in pencil with others including Joe Sewell, sold for $400 (Hunt Auctions, November 2010). Bank check sold for $1,880 (Robert Edward Auctions, Spring 2009).

Bob Lemon

Signature Study: Lemon signed in a bold hand that lacks distinction. His signature is slightly sloppy. Letter construction is marginal. It has a fair degree of legibility. The "mon" in the last name appears as indistinguishable strokes. The display value of Lemon's signature is marginal. During the last few years of his life, Lemon's hand was affected by infirmity. Material signed in old age evidences a shakiness of hand.

Signature Population: Demand is far outweighed by supply. Lemon was a gracious signer throughout his entire life. His signature can be found on just about any medium including photos, Hall of Fame plaque postcards, gum cards, balls, bats, and the like. Letters of any kind are scarce. Signed photos of Lemon teaching future president Ronald Reagan how to pitch for an upcoming movie are rare and in high demand.

Known Forgeries: Lemon's signature would be moderately easy to forge. Due to the nominal value of Lemon's signature, he is generally not the target of skilled forgers.

Lemon 1: 1998 signature

Sales: Lemon's signature is available. His autograph generally sells for under $100 on most mediums.

Buck Leonard

Signature Study: Leonard signed in a very consistent and flowing hand. His signature is marked with flowing strokes. His signature is artistic in nature. Letter construction is very strong. Legibility is high. The signature evidences a very slight right slant. The display value is very high. Leonard's hand is remarkably consistent as signatures penned in the 1940s look almost identical to modern signatures. In the final years of his life, Leonard fell victim to a stroke that affected his hand greatly. Post-stroke signatures look nothing like the pre-stroke specimens. Post-stroke signatures are vertical in nature. Shakiness is well defined. Post-stroke signatures have little eye appeal. Leonard 2 illustrates a signature vitiated by illness.

Signature Population: This is a signature of marginal demand. Leonard was a willing signer throughout his life. The population of Leonard material is strong. Even after his stroke he would still honor signature requests. Leonard's signature can be found on most items including index cards, Hall of Fame plaque postcards, photos, baseballs, and the like. Letters and single-signed bats are scarce. Material from his playing days is rare and highly desirable. There is a good supply of bank checks in the market.

Known Forgeries: Leonard's signature is very complex in nature and replication is difficult. No well executed forgeries exist of pre-illness signatures. Post-stroke signatures, with a shaky appearance, are very easy to replicate. Due to the nominal value of Leonard's signature, he is generally not the target of skilled forgers.

Sales: Leonard's signature is available. His au-

Leonard 1: 1983 signature

Leonard 2: post-stroke signature

tograph generally sells for under $100 on most mediums.

Fred Lindstrom

Signature Study: Lindstrom signed in a very flowing hand with strokes that are effortless and clean. His signature has a nice right slant. Letter construction is sound, resulting in a signature that is legible. Display value is high. Early signatures, those penned during his playing days, are less uniform and are rudimentary in appearance. Early signatures are signed in a slower and less appealing hand. Vintage signatures have only marginal display value. Many vintage signatures are signed as "F. Lindstrom." Material signed in his retirement years is signed as "Freddie Lindstrom." On occasion he would sign as "Freddy Lindstrom." Lindstrom's hand remained strong his entire life. A genuine signature will exhibit no signs of shakiness and one that does should be considered suspect and avoided.

Signature Population: There is moderate demand for Lindstrom material. The supply of Lindstrom autographs is ample but not overwhelming. He died a few years before the mass signing era came into existence. Lindstrom's signature is generally limited to index cards, picture postcards, and Hall of Fame plaque postcards. His signature is scarce on 8 × 10 photos and single signed baseballs. Letters are available and are mostly accomplished on U.S. Post Office letterhead, since he was the postmaster in Evanston, Illinois. Overall, this is an affordable signature.

Known Forgeries: Lindstrom's hand is complex and replication is difficult. Well executed forgeries of his modern signatures are basically nonexistent. Signatures accomplished during his playing days are much easier to replicate. Due to the nominal value of Lindstrom's signature, he is not the target of skilled forgers. There is a small grouping of forged New York Giants team balls in the market. I have seen three. These balls are from the mid–1920s and contain many signatures including Lindstrom, John McGraw, Christy Mathewson, Hugh Jennings, Ross Youngs, Hack Wilson (signed as "L.R. Wilson"), George Kelly, and others. The forger adds the year on the ball when it was purportedly signed. The ink is very bold and striking. The Youngs' forgery is poor and looks nothing like a genuine Youngs signature. The Jennings is signed with a flat top "J" that is something a genuine Jennings signature will never exhibit. The forgeries of Wilson, McGraw, Travis Jackson, and Mathewson are fairly well executed.

Sales: Lindstrom's signature is available. His autograph generally sells for under $100 on most mediums.

John Henry "Pop" Lloyd

Signature Study: Lloyd signed in a practical hand. His signature exhibits good flow but strokes are not rapid in nature. Letter construction is strong. The signature is very legible. Lloyd's signature lacks sharp angles. Display value is marginal. As Lloyd aged, the signature becomes more rounded and flowing. The slight abruptness found in earlier signature is replaced with a more flowing hand. There is great debate as to whether Lloyd's hand was affected by infirmity due to old age. I am of the opinion it was not. A genuine signature should exhibit no shakiness of hand and I would avoid specimens that are shaky in appearance. Of the signatures I have examined all were signed as "John Henry Lloyd," or "John H. Lloyd." I have never examined a genuine signature signed with his nickname "Pop."

Signature Population: This is a signature in good demand. Lloyd is a very rare signature. The population of genuine signatures is likely between ten and twenty specimens. I have seen only four signatures that I would feel comfortable pro-

Lindstrom 1: album page dated 1933

Lindstrom 2: undated signature

Lloyd 1: World War I draft card circa 1917 (Record Group 163, Records of the Selective Services Division, National Archives at Atlanta)

Lloyd 2: undated signature

nouncing as genuine. I know of no genuinely signed baseballs, photos, letters, or government postcards. His World War I draft registration card is held by the National Archives. His signature is simply one of the rarities of the Hall of Fame members. It should be noted that Lloyd was an umpire. There is even a photo of Lloyd dressed as an umpire signing a baseball. The baseball's whereabouts are unknown.

Known Forgeries: Due to the fact that his signature lacks fast strokes, it is fairly easy to replicate. Well executed forgeries exist in quantities. Just about all Lloyd signatures ever offered for sale are forgeries. Many letters, both handwritten and typed, have been created and have circulated for years. A small grouping of forged check cuts are in the market, so caution is warranted. There is one forger that signs Lloyd's signature as "John H. Lloyd" and sometimes as "John Henry Lloyd." He places the forgery on an irregularly shaped sheet of paper. I have seen these forgeries accomplished in both black and blue ball-point pen. The forger then affixes the Lloyd forgery to larger scrapbook page. An old newspaper article about Lloyd or the Negro Leagues is glued next to the forgery. These Lloyd forgeries appear slightly choppy in appearance. The lines are abrupt and do not have the nice rounded curves of a genuine Lloyd signature. This forger has also targeted Oscar Charleston, Martin Dihigo, and Rube Foster. All forgeries evidence the same scrapbook/newsprint article approach. In addition, there are a handful of Negro League related letters that are secretarially signed. Lloyd 3 shows one of these secretarial signatures; note the

marked deviation of hand. Another group of forged letters that surfaced many years ago are written to autograph collectors. The letters state that Lloyd would be happy to autograph photos or baseballs. The letters are written in a shaky, non-flowing hand. The letters usually include the phrase "I would be honored to sign your items" or "I would be honored to have my autograph added to your collection." These forged letters should be exposed without much effort.

Sales: Due to the rarity, there have been no recent sales of Lloyd's signature.

Ernie Lombardi

Signature Study: Lombardi signed in a very nice and flowing hand. His signature evidences good flow. Hesitation is minimal. The signature has a nice right slant. Letter construction is sound. The signature is very legible and has excellent display value. This is one of the nicer Hall of Fame signatures. Lombardi's hand remained essentially unchanged throughout the years. Signatures accomplished in the 1930s look basically the same as material signed in the 1970s. Lombardi's hand remained strong his entire life. A genuine signature will exhibit no shakiness of hand and one that does should be considered suspect and avoided.

Signature Population: This is a signature where demand outweighs supply. The population of Lombardi material is ample. Many insightful collectors obtained his autograph suspecting that he would eventually be inducted into Cooperstown. Most Lombardi signatures are found on index cards and 1960s Fleer cards. Any other medium is considered scarce to rare. 8 × 10 photos and government postcards are scarce. Letters and single-signed baseballs are rare. Goudey gum cards are available but should be considered very scarce.

Lombardi 1: album page dated 1933

Lloyd 3: common secretarial (courtesy Newark Public Library, The Newark Eagles Papers)

Lombardi 2: undated signature

Known Forgeries: Lombardi's hand is difficult to replicate. Well executed forgeries are very limited, but do exist. Due to the nominal value of Lombardi's signature, he is generally not the target of skilled forgers. Single-signed baseballs are the exception. The vast majority of single-signed baseballs in the market are forged.

Sales: 1931 Major League contract sold for $2,938 (Robert Edward Auctions, Spring 2011). 8 × 10 photo, batting pose, sold for $218 (RR Auctions, July 2010). 8 × 10 photo, superior specimen, sold for $1,000 (Hunt Auctions, February 2010). Index card sold for $47 (eBay, November 2011). 1961 Fleer card sold for $75 (eBay, December 2011).

Al Lopez

Signature Study: Lopez's signature exhibits strong vertical strokes with basically no slant. His hand is bold and striking. Letter construction is very sound. His signature is legible. The display value is high. As the years progressed Lopez's signature became more pronounced and fuller. Lopez's hand remained strong just about his entire

Lopez 1: album page dated 1933

Lopez 2: circa 1980s signature

Lopez 3: common secretarial

life. Towards the very end his hand became unsteady. There are a few genuine signatures that evidence a shakiness of hand.

Signature Population: This is a signature of moderate demand. The population of Lopez material is strong. He was a willing signer in all but the last ten years of his life. He engaged in many mass signings. Lopez's signature can be found on index cards, photos, gum cards, Hall of Fame plaque postcards, baseballs, and the like. His signature is considered uncommon on baseball bats and letters. Letters tend to have good baseball content. Many Lopez letters exist where he lobbies to have Bobby Veach inducted into the Hall of Fame.

Known Forgeries: Lopez's signature is moderately difficult to replicate. Well executed forgeries are limited. Forgeries are generally limited to baseballs and bats. I have examined a few signed 8 × 10 photos that feature Casey Stengel and Al Lopez wearing suits, where Stengel is reaching into Lopez's coat pocket. They contain rather nice forgeries of both. Many team-signed baseballs from the Lopez's days as a manager were secretarially signed. Lopez 3 is a good illustration of a secretarially signed ball.

Sales: Lopez's signature is available. His autograph generally sells for under $100 on most mediums.

Ted Lyons

Signature Study: Lyons' signature went through great change over the years. Early signatures exhibit good flow and lack hesitation. Vintage signatures exhibit a "T" that is accomplished in one stroke and lacks a flat top. Letter construction is very sound. The signature is legible. The display value is high. Modern signatures exhibit an uneven appearance. Many breaks in the signature are evident. Letter construction tends to be less structured. In the final months of Lyons' life, signatures are extremely uneven. However, signatures signed late in life still evidence flow and the racing effect. Lyons' hand did not produce a truly shaky signature.

Lyons 1: team sheet circa 1930s

Ted Lyons

Lyons 2: circa 1970s signature

Signature Population: Overall, this is a common signature where supply outweighs demand. Lyons was a willing signer throughout his long life. His signature is generally found on index cards, Hall of Fame plaque postcards, and picture postcards. Baseballs, Perez-Steele cards, letters, and bank checks are uncommon. Single-signed bats are very scarce.

Known Forgeries: Early signatures are moderately difficult to forge. Well executed forgeries of vintage signatures do not exist. Modern signatures are much easier to replicate. Due to the nominal value of Lyons' signature, he is not the target of skilled forgers.

Sales: Lyons' signature is available. His autograph generally sells for under $100 on most mediums.

Connie Mack

Signature Study: Mack's signature is distinct and one of the most recognized of all Hall of Famers. His hand is bold. The signature is very legible and dominates the medium it is placed upon. Mack's signature is one that exists throughout many eras. Signatures from the turn of the twentieth century exist, though pre–1920 autographs are rare. Mack's hand remained fairly constant through the years. Early signatures tend to be slightly choppier than more modern signatures. Mack's hand exhibits excellent letter construction, The display value is high. Just about all Mack signatures in the market are signed as "Connie Mack." On rare occasions Mack signed with his real name, but this form of signature is typically reserved for legal documents. Mack's hand remained strong his entire life. A genuine Mack signature will exhibit no measurable shakiness of hand and one that does should be considered suspect and avoided.

Signature Population: A signature with sound

Cornelius McGillicuddy

Mack 1: legal document dated 1909

Connie Mack

Mack 2: TLS circa 1910

Connie Mack

Mack 3: circa 1940s signature

demand, Mack's signature is probably one of the most available of all the long deceased Hall of Famers. His signed willingly during his long life. His signature is available on most mediums including index cards, government postcards, photos, books, scorecards, and letters. Letters, both handwritten and typed, exist in quantities. Letters date from the early days of the Dead Ball Era until the 1950s. Single-signed baseballs are scarce but not rare. I have seen many genuine examples in my lifetime. Most balls were signed post–1940. About the only medium considered rare is Hall of Fame plaque postcards.

Known Forgeries: The lack of rapid motion in Mack's hand results in a signature that is easy to replicate. Well executed forgeries are in the market. Mack facsimile signatures are found in many books, including Jack Coombs' book *Baseball Individual Play and Team Strategy*. These facsimiles are typically framed under glass and sold as genuine. Facsimile signatures, two of which are illustrated as Mack 4 and Mack 5, have no value. Another common forgery are Hall of Fame plaque postcards. A small supply of these forged cards exist. They contain amateurish forgeries. The forgeries, which are accomplished in black or blue fountain pen, are shaky and elongated. The forgeries are signed on a slight downward angle. The

Connie Mack

Mack 4: common facsimile

Connie Mack

Mack 5: common facsimile

Mack 6: common secretarial from 1906

Mack 7: unused bank check, commonly used by forgers

Mackey 2: ALS dated 1945 (courtesy Newark Public Library, The Newark Eagles Papers)

Mackey 3: ALS circa 1940s (courtesy Newark Public Library, The Newark Eagles Papers)

dot of the "i" is thick and pronounced. On occasion the "e" of the first name and/or the "k" of the last name will run off the bottom of the card. These cards are exposed as crude forgeries with little examination. Another forgery is a period secretarial signature signed as "Cornelius McGillicuddy." These secretarial signatures were penned by Mack's secretary in the 1900 to 1915 era and do not resemble a genuine Mack autograph (see Mack 6). They are narrow and elongated. They are usually found on financial receipts. Mack signed most of his correspondence, but on occasion he would allow a secretary to sign for him. Secretarial signatures deviate greatly from Mack's hand. Lastly, in the past few years a group of Connie Mack Conference checks entered the market. They are unused. A specimen is illustrated as Mack 7. Forgers are placing forgeries on these checks, so caution is warranted.

Sales: Calling card, choice specimen, sold for $250 (eBay, September 2011). 1949 TLS sold for $264 (RR Auctions, July 2011). 7 × 10 book photo sold for $578 (RR Auctions, February 2011). 1950 ALS, choice specimen, sold for $200 (RR Auctions, July 2010). Biographical book, also signed by Fred Lieb, sold for $250 (eBay, November 2011).

Biz Mackey

Signature Study: Mackey signed in a very plain and deliberate hand. His hand is methodic

in construction. There is a slight hesitation noted. The signature is legible. Display value is average. There has always been great debate whether Mackey was literate. Mackey was, in fact, literate and a few handwritten letters do exist, though they are extremely rare. Mackey signed as "James R. Mackey" or "Raleigh Mackey." I have never seen a genuine signature penned with his nickname. It is unknown whether infirmity of hand affected his signature.

Signature Population: Mackey is an excessively rare signature. The total population in the market is likely between five and ten signatures. A couple of signed documents/letters exist and that is about it. I have never seen a genuine signed photo or ball of any kind. There are a few small photos signed with his last name only. I have examined two and I have concerns about the authenticity of these photos. About 15 letters and contracts are held by the Newark Public Library,

Mackey 4: ALS dated 1945 (courtesy Newark Public Library, The Newark Eagles Papers)

Mackey 5: common secretarial

Mackey 1: contract dated 1941

but these will likely never be released in the market.

Known Forgeries: The rudimentary nature of Mackey's hand results in a signature that is very easy to replicate. Well executed forgeries exist. Mackey forgeries exist mostly on album pages, small photos, and signatures removed from documents. It should also be noted that some Mackey-signed letters are accomplished and signed by someone other than Mackey, most likely a family member. Illustrated as Mackey 5 is a secretarial signature.

Sales: Due to the rarity, there have been no recent sales of Mackey's signature.

Larry MacPhail

Signature Study: MacPhail signed in a very powerful hand, resulting in a large and bold signature. His signature is marked with heavy vertical strokes. Letter construction is moderately sound. Legibility is slightly impaired. In later years MacPhail's hand evidences a slight choppiness. While a jaggedness exists, a genuine signature will exhibit no measurable shakiness of hand and one that does should be considered suspect and avoided.

Signature Population: This is a signature with marginal demand well balanced with supply. MacPhail is an uncommon signature. Many signed documents and letters exist and almost all are baseball related. Government postcards are scarce. 8 × 10 photos and single-signed baseballs are rare.

Known Forgeries: His signature is rather difficult to replicate. Well executed forgeries are limited. He is generally not the target of skilled forgers, except on premium items such as baseballs and 8 × 10 photos.

Sales: 1941 ALS, choice specimen, sold for $550 (Hunt Auctions, March 2009). 1946 TLS sold for $444 (eBay, August 2011). Index card sold for $256 (eBay, January 2012).

MacPhail, Larry 1: TLS dated 1939 (courtesy Newark Public Library, The Newark Eagles Papers)

Lee MacPhail

Signature Study: MacPhail's hand is similar to his Hall of Fame father's signature. The hand is vertical in nature and compact. Letter construction is marginal as the letters tend to run together. MacPhail's hand is very flowing. There is no hesitation. Legibility is impaired. The display value is average. Since 2002 or so MacPhail's hand exhibits infirmity. Modern signatures evidence a labored and somewhat unsteady appearance.

MacPhail, Lee 1: 1999 signature

Signature Population: This is a signature of marginal demand that is outweighed by supply. MacPhail is a common signature as he has been a willing signer his entire life. The fact that many signed documents and letters exist from his days as a baseball executive correlates into an affordable signature. His signature can be found on index cards, photos, baseballs, letters, Hall of Fame plaque postcards, Perez-Steele cards, and the like. Signed baseball bats are uncommon. Letters discussing his ruling in the infamous George Brett pine-tar game are scarce and in high demand.

Known Forgeries: His signature is fairly difficult to replicate. Producing a convincing forgery would take a good deal of effort. Due to the nominal value of MacPhail's signature, he is not the target of skilled forgers.

Sales: MacPhail's signature is available. His autograph generally sells for under $100 on most mediums.

Effa Manley

Signature Study: Manley signed in a very flowing and feminine hand. Her signature exhibits

Manley 1: document dated 1943 (courtesy Newark Public Library, The Newark Eagles Papers)

Manley 2: document dated 1943 (courtesy Newark Public Library, The Newark Eagles Papers)

effortless flow. Letter construction is strong. Her signature is very legible and has good display value. It is unclear whether infirmity affected Manley's hand. There seems to be debate on this point. Based on the material I have examined, I am of the opinion that a genuine Manley signature should not evidence any shakiness of hand simply because I have never seen a real one that appears labored in appearance.

Signature Population: This is a signature with marginal demand but very limited supply. Manley's signing habits are basically unknown. She probably received no more than a handful of requests for her autograph in the mail. I have spoken to many collectors who were active in the last 40 years. I can locate no one who wrote Manley for her signature. Manley signatures should be considered scarce to rare. Premium items should be considered very rare to non-existent. Her signature is typically limited to signed letters and documents from her days as co-owner of the Newark Eagles. Certain letters from the 1970s written to various baseball personnel also exist. I have never seen a genuinely signed 8 × 10 photo. It is my understanding that a handful of single-signed baseballs exist that were signed at a Negro League reunion in 1980. In general, a single-signed baseball of Manley should be considered very rare. I, personally, have never seen one. It should be noted that she would commonly sign letters for her husband Abe. These letters are worth just as much as a genuine Abe Manley signature, if not more.

Known Forgeries: The structured nature of Manley's hand makes for a signature that is difficult to replicate. I know of no well executed for-

Manley 3: common facsimile (courtesy Newark Public Library, The Newark Eagles Papers)

geries in the market. Forgeries can be found on index cards, balls, and Negro League related books.

Sales: Signed book on Negro League baseball sold for $3,525 (Robert Edward Auctions, April 2007). 1974 ALS, written to Joe Garagiola, sold for $2,644 (Robert Edward Auctions, Spring 2009). 1975 ALS signed as "Effa M." sold for $1,676 (Lelands.com, Spring 2006).

Mickey Mantle

Signature Study: Mantle's signature is one of the most studied of all the members of the Hall of Fame. Mantle's signature evolved greatly over the years and evidenced a marked change. Early signatures are legible and plain in construction. They evidence good letter formation but lack rapid flow. Display value is limited. Early signatures are rudimentary in construction. As the years progressed, Mantle's hand became more complex and evolved into a wonderful flowing signature. The most noted change can be found in the capital "M"s that changed completely. The hand becomes more flowing and letter construction is more artistic. Vintage signatures evidence a slight choppiness that the modern signatures have disposed of. The display value of modern signatures is extremely high. Mantle died of complications of liver disease in 1995. Mantle's hand remained strong up until the very end. A very few pieces, including a handwritten speech, were signed that evidence a shakiness of hand. These items were penned in the closing days of his life. For collecting purposes, a genuine Mantle signature should evidence no shakiness of hand and one the does should be considered suspect and avoided.

Signature Population: There is strong demand for Mantle signatures. The supply seems endless. He engaged in many mass signings. His signature is available on books, photos, gum cards, bats, baseballs, jersey, limited-edition art cards, gov-

Mantle 1: document dated 1966

Mantle 2: circa 1970s signature

Mantle 3: circa 1985 signature

Mantle 4: undated signature

Manush 1: check endorsement dated 1944

Manush 2: circa 1955 signature

ernment postcards, and the like. Letters are very scarce. Canceled bank checks are rare. I have also seen a few signed Mickey Mantle milk cartons issued in the 1950s. The supply is basically bottomless, but the demand is so great that values are not depressed by the mass quantities of signatures. One side note, Mantle was known, on occasion, to inscribe signatures with profane words. I am not sure why he engaged in this practice, but they make for crude collectibles.

Known Forgeries: Modern signatures are much more difficult to forge than vintage signatures. Given the tremendous demand for Mantle material, many forgers have targeted his signature. Well executed forgeries exist in mass quantities. Mantle forgeries can be found everywhere, especially on baseballs and bats. Also multi-signed photos are a common target. There is a famous photo that features Mantle, Joe DiMaggio, and Ted Williams all holding bats. There are many signed photos in the market. This is probably the most forged photo of all time. The vast majority of these signed photos are forgeries. Other forged multi-signed pictures exist featuring Mantle with names like Musial, Muhammad Ali, Berra, Roger Maris, Ford, and the like.

Sales: 1960 signed legal document sold for $1,129 (RR Auctions, August 2011). Single-signed baseball sold for $500 (Hunt Auctions, July 2011). Perez-Steele art postcard sold for $267 (eBay, September 2011). Autobiography, limited-edition book, sold for $355 (eBay, September 2011). 8 × 10 photo, batting pose, sold for $218 (RR Auctions, July 2011). Hall of Fame plaque postcard sold for $104 (eBay, September 2011).

Heinie Manush

Signature Study: Manush signed in an extremely powerful and rapid hand. His signature has a right slant. Letter construction is moderate,

though letters tend to blend into indistinguishable strokes. His signature lacks any hesitation and is an extremely dominant signature. His signature has sound display value. It is one of the nicer Hall of Fame signatures. Manush's hand remained strong just about his entire life. In his final year or so, his hand became infirmed. Signatures accomplished late in life evidenced a measured amount of unsteadiness. Overall, this is a very nice signature.

Signature Population: This is a signature where demand is fairly balanced with the supply. The population of Manush autographs is ample at best. He was a willing signer his entire life. Most Manush signatures are found on index cards. Manush's signature is also available on government postcards and Hall of Fame plaque postcards. Goudey gum cards and 8 × 10 photos are scarce. Both typed letters signed and handwritten letters are rare. Single-signed baseballs are also rare. A couple of vintage specimens exist with simply stunning eye appeal. There is a fair supply of signed banks checks in the market and they are a good source of Manush signatures. In addition, there are about a dozen signed Harry Heilmann checks from the mid–1940s through 1950 made payable to his fellow teammate where Manush would endorse the reverse of the check. These checks are very rare and are a wonderful combination signed by two Hall of Famers.

Known Forgeries: Due to the rapid nature of Manush's hand, his signature is difficult to replicate. Well executed forgeries are very limited. Due to the affordable nature of Manush's signature, forgeries are generally limited to premium items such as 8 × 10 photos, Goudey gum cards, and baseballs. That vast majority of Manush single-signed baseballs are forgeries, so proceed with extreme caution.

Sales: Single-signed baseball sold for $4,500 (Legedary Auctions, April 2009). Hall of Fame plaque postcard sold for $121 (RR Auctions, March 2011). 1947 Major League scout contract, countersigned by Roy Hamey, sold for $588 (Robert Edward Auctions, Spring 2011). Index card sold for $59 (eBay, December 2011).

Rabbit Maranville

Signature Study: Maranville signed in a striking and bold hand. His signature is large and flowing. His signature is vertical in nature with no measurable slant either way. Hesitation of any kind is non-existent. Maranville's signature is very pleasing to the eye and has excellent display value. He had the habit of dropping the "i" in his first name, resulting in a signature that reads as "Rabbt Maranville." Many times the "v" will be omitted from the signature. In general, the signature is legible, though letter construction is sometimes impaired. Most signatures are signed as "Rabbit Maranville" and he would add, on occasion, "Yours in Sports." Autographs signed as "Walter Maranville" are scarce and desirable. Maranville died at a relatively young age. Since he never reached old age, infirmity of hand was non-existent. A genuine signature will exhibit no shakiness of hand and one that does should be considered suspect and avoided.

Signature Population: This is a signature of good demand that outweighs supply. Maranville's signature is available but the total population is limited. While his signature per se is not considered scarce, premium items are very scarce to very rare. Most Maranville signatures are found on team-related items signed in the late 1920s and 1930s. His signature is also available on index cards, album pages, and government postcards. Photographs of any kind are very scarce. Gums cards are rare. Letters, both typed and handwrit-

Maranville 3: undated signature

Maranville 4: detail of forgery

ten, seldom surface and both are considered rare. Single-signed baseballs exist but are considered very rare. I have only examined a couple of genuine specimens in the past 30 years.

Known Forgeries: Maranville's hand is fairly difficult to replicate, but there is one forger that needs to be examined. There is a limited group of fake signatures all produced by the same forger. He has created forged baseballs, photographs, and has even gone so far as to place his work on baseball bats. There are four things to look for: (1) The forgeries usually, but not always, contain the inscription "yours in sports," (2) They are slightly labored in appearance, something a genuine signature would not exhibit, (3) the capital "R" of the first name typically tails towards the right (see Maranville 4), where on the genuine specimens the down stroke of the "R" continues straight down, (4) The first name is completely written as "Rabbit," whereas genuine specimens would omit the "i" in the first name. I have always advised collectors that if the first name "Rabbit" is completely spelled out it should be studied very carefully as it is most likely a forgery. These forgeries are very easy to spot. This forger is so bold that he has even created forged baseball bats. I have seen three in the last few years. They are on generic "Junior League" or "Semi-Pro League" bats. I have never seen a genuine single-signed Maranville bat.

Sales: 1927 Major League contract, countersigned by Branch Rickey, sold for $2,938 (Robert Edward Auctions, Spring 2011). Album page, signed in pencil, sold for $267 (RR Auctions, May

Maranville 1: teamsheet circa 1930s

Maranville 2: album page dated 1933

2011). Dinner menu, also signed by Johnny Evers, sold for $937 (Lelands.com, November 2010). Choice ink signature sold for $393 (RR Auctions, February 2010).

Juan Marichal

Signature Study: Marichal signs in a wonderfully artistic hand. His hand is basically vertical with a very slight back slant. Hesitation does not exist. Letter construction is marginal and letters tend to blend together in indistinguishable strokes. Legibility is impaired. Display value of Marichal's signature is high due to the whimsical nature of hand. His signature is basically unique in that he signs his name using a bifurcated plane. As of 2012 Marichal's hand evidences no infirmities of any kind. A genuine Marichal signature will exhibit no hesitation whatsoever and one that does should be considered suspect and avoided.

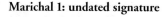

Marichal 1: undated signature

Signature Population: This is a signature of marginal demand and strong supply. His signature can be found on almost any medium including index cards, gum cards, photos, baseballs, bats, jerseys, and the like. Signed letters of any kind are scarce. As a side note, one of the umpires of the infamous Marichal/Roseboro game was Henry "Shag" Crawford. There are a few Crawford letters discussing this game in detail and his role in it.

Known Forgeries: Given the complexity of Marichal's hand, replication would be difficult. No well executed forgeries exist in the market. Due to the nominal value of Marichal's signature, he is not the target of skilled forgers.

Sales: Marichal's signature is available. His autograph generally sells for under $100 on most mediums.

Rube Marquard

Signature Study: Marquard signed in a vertical hand with a slight back slant. Letter construction is strong. His signature is very legible. He writes his name more than he signs it. The signature is

Marquard 1: book dated 1910 (courtesy National Baseball Hall of Fame and Museum)

Marquard 2: ALS dated 1932

accomplished in a slower more methodic hand. The neat appearance of Marquard's signature makes for a signature with excellent display value. Marquard's hand remained strong for just about his entire life. Material signed in the closing months of his life will evidence a fair amount of shakiness. Infirmed signatures have little to no display value. It should be noted that a signature or two accomplished around 1910 exists with a slight right slight. I know of no signatures from this era in the open market.

Signature Population: Demand for Marquard's signature appears fairly balanced with supply. The population of Marquard material is limited. He died before the baseball autograph hobby transformed into an industry. Signatures are generally limited to index cards and Hall of Fame plaque postcards. Premium items are uncommon to scarce and they include 8 × 10 photos, letters, and baseballs. There is a good supply of handwritten letters. It appears Marquard liked to pen letters to fans. Many have good baseball content. Signed T-206 tobacco cards are rare to very rare.

Known Forgeries: Marquard's signature lacks rapid flow and is easy to replicate. Creating a convincing forgery can be done with little effort. Marquard is the target of skilled forgers, but limited to the premium items such as baseballs and tobacco cards.

Sales: Marquard's signature is available. His

Marquard 3: undated signature

autograph generally sells for under $100 on most mediums.

Eddie Mathews

Signature Study: Mathews signed in a very reckless hand with many powerful strokes and compact lines. Letter construction is poor. His signature exhibits impaired legibility. Hesitation of hand is non-existent. The display value is average. Mathews' hand remained strong his entire life. A genuine signature will evidence no shakiness of hand and one that does should be considered suspect and avoided. It should be noted that while attending signings at card shows, Mathews would sometimes return from lunch slightly inebriated. This would affect the structure of his signature.

Mathews 1: circa 1995 signature

Signature Population: This is a signature of average demand but outweighed by supply. Mathews is a common signature. He engaged in many mass signings. His signature is available on most mediums including index cards, photos, gum cards, baseballs, bats, Hall of Fame plaque postcards, and the like. Letters of any kind are scarce.

Known Forgeries: Due to the poor letter construction, Mathews' hand is rather easy to replicate. Well executed forgeries exist in the market. Forgeries are limited to multi-signed 500-home-run-club items.

Sales: Mathews' signature is available. His autograph generally sells for under $100 on most mediums.

Christy Mathewson

Signature Study: Mathewson, like Honus Wagner and golfer Ralph Guldahl, had variant forms of signature, which makes study of his hand difficult. Mathewson is one of the most misunderstood signatures of any of the Hall of Famers. Mathewson's hand is complex in nature. Letter construction is strong. Legibility is high. Sound display value is noted. Mathewson's signature is very artistic and one of the nicest of any of the

Hall of Famers. His signature slants slightly to the right. His signature lacks hesitation, but it is not signed in a reckless hand like that of Cobb or Hornsby. Mathewson's signature is dominated with large letters. The capital "C" of the first name is striking as is the "M" of the last name. Mathewson would incorporate an overly large "s" in the last name that stands out. Mathewson's hand remained relatively constant throughout the years. Early signatures, circa 1905, are signed in a smaller hand and typically penned as "C. Mathewson." Signatures from this era are extremely rare. They are generally limited to a couple of endorsed New York Giants payroll checks. Mathewson had an alternative form of signature that creates much confusion. Starting in the early 1910s Mathewson would pen some signatures in a smaller more practical hand. This form of signature, as illustrated in Mathewson 6, is vertical and may, at times, exhibit a slight back slant. The hand is slower. The artistic flow is impaired. This signature has much less eye appeal. Why Mathewson signed in this fashion is unknown to me. Some have questioned the authenticity of this form of signature. Some have pronounced them as secretarial, but this is an incorrect conclusion. It is clear that both styles of signature were produced by the same hand. A couple of Mathewson handwritten letters and checks contain both types of handwriting. This dispels the theory that Mathewson 6 is a secretarial signature. Mathewson died at a very young age. Since he never reached old age, a genuine Mathewson signature will exhibit no shakiness of hand

Mathewson 1: affidavit dated 1908 (courtesy National Baseball Hall of Fame and Museum)

Mathewson 2: book dated 1910 (courtesy National Baseball Hall of Fame and Museum)

Mathewson 3: TLS circa 1913 (courtesy National Baseball Hall of Fame and Museum)

Christy Mathewson [signature]

Mathewson 4: ALS circa 1915 (courtesy National Baseball Hall of Fame and Museum)

and one that does should be considered suspect and avoided.

Signature Population: There is very strong demand for Mathewson's signature compared to a small supply. Most of the Mathewson signatures offered in the market can be found on canceled bank checks. Mrs. Mathewson would send these out to autograph collectors after her husband's death. Were it not for these checks Mathewson would be an extremely rare signature. There are a handful of letters in the market, both handwritten and typed. Letters of any kind should be considered very rare. I have examined many single-signed baseballs. I have yet to find a real one. I seriously doubt one exists. I have seen many forged single-signed balls with multiple certificates of authenticity. Signed team baseballs from Mathewson's playing days likely do not exist. In all my years of searching I have only seen one genuine Mathewson-signed ball. It was a multi-signed ball with four or five signatures with a stunning Mathewson signature. Unlike the other Mathewson "signed" baseballs I have seen, this one had a beautiful flowing signature. It was penned in the early 1920s. It is the only genuine signed Mathewson baseball I know of. Signed photos are extremely rare. I only know of one genuine 8 × 10 picture, signed in the early 1920s. It was a nice pitching pose signed and inscribed in red ink. I have never seen a genuine signed tobacco card. Signed books are excessively rare and just about all were secretarially signed.

Known Forgeries: Mathewson is a rare signature on a per se basis. Just about 99 percent of Mathewson signatures offered in the market are forged. The majority of those certified by the au-

thentication companies are, in fact, forgeries. Due to the slower nature of his hand, Mathewson's signature is one of the easier to replicate. Well executed forgeries exist in quantities. In the past few years many forged studio portrait photos on thick-stock cards have entered the market. They are anywhere from 7 × 9 up to 10 × 13. The pictures are usually affixed to a thick photographer's matte. I am not even sure if the photos themselves are genuine. The inscriptions are forged. The half dozen that I have seen feature a formal portrait of Mathewson wearing a suit and tie. There is also an image of him in a generic baseball uniform with a small turtleneck. The forgeries are amateurish. They are signed and inscribed in thick methodic fountain pen. For some reason the forger seems to favor the year 1911, as four of the six were dated 1911 in the inscription. The forger's hand is steady but slow. The racing effect is minimal.

Another controversy is signed books which Mathewson authored. *Won in the Ninth* was his most popular book, published in 1910. Many presentation copies of this book were handed out, most likely by the publisher. They feature a Mathewson signature on a bookplate affixed to the endpaper. These presentation copies are secretarially signed and not signed by Mathewson. I have seen about 15 to 20 copies and none contained a genuine signature. These signatures deviate too much from Mathewson's hand. My advice to collectors is if you see a signed Mathewson book *of any kind* proceed with *extreme* caution. I have examined dozens of Mathewson books. In over 30 years of searching I have only found a couple genuine signed books. For more information on Mathewson-signed books, see the June 12, 2005, *New York Daily News* article by Michael O'Keeffe.

There are a certain number of typed letters signed that contain a secretarial signature of Mathewson. The signatures are a bit more choppy than a genuine signature. The secretary does a decent job of replication. Fortunately, the secretary, who signed for Mathewson, places his/her initials in small print under the last name. In general, if you see initials under or next to a signature, then

Mathewson 5: bank check with both styles of writing

Christy Mathewson [signature]

Mathewson 6: bank check dated 1922 variant form of signature

Mathewson 7: circa 1920s signature

it is secretarially signed. In the last few years forged notes allegedly written by Mathewson have entered the market. They were purportedly signed while he served as an officer in the Army's poison gas division. Mathewson-signed material from his days in the military is extremely rare and limited to signed official army documents. I have examined a few of these forgeries. They are signed something to the effect "Property of Capt. Christy Mathewson" or "Capt. Christy Mathewson C.W.S." (short for Chemical Warfare Service). These forgeries appear to be on old book paper. If you come upon a Mathewson war-related signature, proceed with *extreme* caution as chances are it is a product of a skilled forger.

Sales: Bank check sold for $17,625 (Robert Edward Auctions, Spring 2008). Bank check sold for $11,357 (RR Auctions, September 2009). Bank check sold for $11,251 (Lelands.com, June 2011).

Willie Mays

Signature Study: Mays' signature is one that has gone through many phases and generally has spiraled downward in terms of legibility. Early signatures exhibit good letter construction. Legibility is high. The hand exhibits a nice right slant. Display value is good. As the years progressed, signatures are accomplished in much faster and more powerful hand. Legibility is impaired. After he retired, Mays basically settled on an illegible signature. Modern signatures are sloppy.

Signature Population: This is a signature of sound demand but outweighed by supply. Mays engages in many mass signings. The supply of Mays material is endless. His signature can be found on most mediums including photos, baseballs, bats, Hall of Fame plaque postcards, index cards, and the like. Signed letters of any kind are very scarce.

Mays 1: circa 1985 signature

Known Forgeries: Unlike earlier signatures which are rather difficult to forge, modern signatures are extremely easy to forge. Mays' signature is probably one of the easiest of all Hall of Famers to replicate. Many well executed forgeries exist in the market. Forgeries are generally limited to baseballs, bats, and multi-signed 500-home-run items.

Sales: Mays' signature is available. His autograph generally sells for under $100 on most mediums.

Bill Mazeroski

Signature Study: Mazeroski signs in a plain and legible hand. His signature is vertical in nature. Letter construction is sound. The display value of Mazeroski's signature is good. As of 2012 Mazeroski's hand remains strong. A genuine signature will exhibit no shakiness of hand and one that does should be considered suspect and avoided.

Mazeroski 1: circa 1980s signature

Signature Population: This is a signature of marginal demand clearly outweighed by supply. Mazeroski is a common signature. His signature can be found on most mediums including index cards, photos, baseballs, bats, gum cards, Hall of Fame plaque postcards, and the like. Letters of any kind are scarce. There are a limited number of items signed by both Mazeroski and Yankees pitcher Ralph Terry, who gave up Mazeroski's legendary 1960 World Series homer.

Known Forgeries: Mazeroski's signature has good flow and would be rather difficult to forge. Due to the nominal value of Mazeroski's signature, he is not the target of skilled forgers.

Sales: Mazeroski's signature is available. His autograph generally sells for under $100 on most mediums.

Joe McCarthy

Signature Study: McCarthy signs in a very practical hand. His signature lacks smooth flowing angles. There is a slight abruptness to his hand. The letter construction is strong. The signature is legible. The signature exhibits a nice right slant. His autograph works well on the various mediums it is placed upon. Due to the slight choppiness of hand, the display value is average. McCarthy's hand remained strong his entire life. A genuine signature will exhibit no shakiness of hand and one that does should be considered suspect and avoided.

Signature Population: This is a signature where demand is balanced with supply. McCarthy is one of the most common signatures of any Hall of Fame member that died in the 1970s. He was a willing and gracious signer throughout his long life. His signature exists on most mediums. Index cards and Hall of Fame plaque postcards exist in quantities. Other mediums such as 8 × 10 photos and letters are uncommon. Single-signed baseballs are somewhere between uncommon and scarce. Most single-signed baseballs are inscribed. Bank checks are scarce.

Known Forgeries: His signature is moderately difficult to replicate. Well executed forgeries are limited and mostly reserved for premium items. Due to the nominal value of McCarthy's signature, he is generally not the target of skilled forgers. However, there is a rather large grouping of forged 8 × 10 photos in the market. The photo in question is a famous image of McCarthy kneeling on the steps of the dugout with his arms folded, staring directly into the camera. The forgery is placed right across McCarthy's chest in what appears to be black sharpie and not the typical felt pen commonly found during that time frame. The forgeries per se are amateurish in construction and shaky in appearance. I have seen dozens of these photos in the last ten years, so there must be a large qauntity in the market. Many have been incorrectly certified by the authentication companies, so caution is warranted.

Sales: Bank check sold for $261 (RR Auctions, July 2011). 7 × 9 photo sold for $134 (RR Auctions, February 2011). 7 × 9 photo, also signed by Charlie Grimm, sold for $200 (Hunt Auctions, February 2010). Single-signed baseball sold for

McCarthy, J. 1: circa 1930s signature

McCarthy, J. 2: undated signature

$850 (Hunt Auctions, July 2010). Hall of Fame plaque postcard sold for $77 (eBay, November 2011).

Tommy McCarthy

Signature Study: The illustrated examples, accomplished on or about 1910, are fine examples of McCarthy's hand. The signatures have good letter construction. Legibility is high. His signature has good eye appeal. The signature is accomplished in a slower, more reserved hand. It is unknown whether infirmity of hand affected McCarthy's signature. Little is known about his writing.

Signature Population: McCarthy is an excessively rare signature. The total market population is likely under five specimens. A few letters are housed at the Baseball Hall of Fame. This is one of the rarest of all Hall of Fame signatures.

Known Forgeries: Since McCarthy signed in a more reserved hand, replication is rather easy. Many well executed forgeries are in the market. A common forgery is illustrated as McCarthy, T 3. Note the forgery is more curvy in appearance when compared to the genuine specimen. There are many forged signatures that are inscribed as "To John Doe, Best Wishes" or "Best of Luck." These inscriptions were rarely, if ever, used during McCarthy's lifetime.

Sales: Due to the rarity, there have been no recent sales of McCarthy's signature.

McCarthy, T. 1: ALS dated 1909 (courtesy National Baseball Hall of Fame and Museum)

McCarthy, T. 2: TLS dated 1910 (courtesy National Baseball Hall of Fame and Museum)

McCarthy, T. 3: common forgery

Willie McCovey

Signature Study: McCovey signs in a very bold and sloppy hand. His signature exhibits good flow. It lacks any measurable hesitation. Letter construction is poor. The signature is basically illegible. Overall, it is one of the less appealing signatures of the Hall of Fame members.

McCovey 1: circa 1985 signature

Signature Population: This is a signature of average demand that is outweighed by supply. McCovey is a common signature. He engages in many mass signings. His signature can be found on most mediums including index cards, gum cards, baseballs, photos, Perez-Steele cards, jerseys, bats, and the like. Signed letters of any kind are scarce.

Known Forgeries: McCovey's signature lacks any precision whatsoever, resulting in a signature that is easily replicated. Due to the nominal value of McCovey's signature, he is generally not the target of skilled forgers. Forgeries are limited to multi-signed 500-home-run-club mediums.

Sales: McCovey's signature is available. His autograph generally sells for under $100 on most mediums.

Joe McGinnity

Signature Study: McGinnity signed in a very neat and precise hand. His signature has good length with limited height. The signature exhibits a slight right slant. Letter construction is marginal at best. While basically legible, the "inni" in the last name is morphed into indistinguishable strokes. Despite the impaired letter construction, his signature displays well. His signature lacks rapid flow and is accomplished in a slower hand. Most McGinnity signatures are penned as "Joe J. McGinnity." There are a couple of specimens

signed as "Joseph J. McGinnity." There is no confirmation whether McGinnity's hand was ever affected by infirmity. I have never seen a genuine signature that exhibits a shakiness of hand. My opinion is that a genuine McGinnity should exhibit no shakiness of hand and one that does should be considered suspect and avoided.

Signature Population: This is a signature of sound demand and minute supply. McGinnity is a very rare signature. I estimate the total population of signatures at somewhere between 10 and 20. His signature is generally limited to documents, letters, and a stock certificate or two. I have examined one multi-signed New York banquet menu and I know of one multi-signed baseball. I have never seen a genuine signed photo or baseball card of any kind.

Known Forgeries: Due to the lack of rapid flow, McGinnity's signature is easy to replicate. Many well executed forgeries exist in the market. Most McGinnity signatures offered for sale are forged. Forgeries are found on album pages, old banquet menus, photos, tobacco cards, and the like. McGinnity had a long career in minor league baseball after his time in the big leagues. He became part owner and president of the Tacoma Tigers ballclub. A handful of letters exist and just about all of them are secretarially signed. The signatures appear smaller that a genuine signature and evidence a slow methodic hand.

Sales: Banquet menu, also signed by Rube Waddell, accomplished in pencil, sold for $17,047 (Lelands.com, November 2007).

McGinnity 1: document undated

McGinnity 2: TLS circa 1910

McGinnity 3: TLS circa 1910

Bill McGowan

Signature Study: McGowan signed in a very distinct hand. His signature is marked with bold letters. Strong letter construction is evident. His signature is very legible and dominates the medium it is placed upon. The capital letters of both the first and last name are very artful and odd looking. They give his signature good eye appeal. McGowan signed in a slower, more thoughtful hand. His signature lacks rapid flow. The racing effect is muted. McGowan's hand remained strong his entire life. A genuine McGowan signature will exhibit no shakiness of hand and one that does should be considered suspect and avoided.

Signature Population: McGowan signatures are very limited in supply, but there does not appear to be a great demand for his signature. McGowan is a scarce signature on a per se basis. It is generally limited to index cards and letters. Other mediums are rare to very rare. I have never seen a genuinely signed 8 × 10 photo. Single-signed baseballs are rare. I have only seen a few genuine specimens. There are a few multi-signed balls that contain umpiring crews of the 1940s and 1950s that McGowan was part of. These are rare but more common than single-signed baseballs.

Known Forgeries: Due to the lack of recklessness of hand, McGowan's signature is moderately easy to replicate. Well executed forgeries can be produced by a forger with limited skills. McGowan forgeries exist on photos, baseballs, and the like. McGowan owned an umpiring school in Florida. Many letters exist in the market, but some were secretarially signed. These secretarial signatures are easily identified as they look nothing like the genuine signature. Most letters were signed by McGowan himself.

Sales: Baseball, also signed by Hal Newhouser,

McGowan 1: undated signature

McGowan 2: undated signature

Hank Greenberg, and others, sold for $374 (eBay, August 2011). Index card sold for $375 (Hunt Auctions, November 2010).

John McGraw

Signature Study: McGraw signed in a very practical and sophisticated hand. His signature evidences good flow. It has only minimal hesitation in the "ohn" of the first name. Letter construction is strong. The signature is legible. McGraw's signature has superior display value. As McGraw aged his hand went through a marked change. In the 1920s his hand slowed greatly. The once flowing hand evidences more methodic strokes and a slight hesitation. McGraw died in 1934 and infirmity of hand did not affect his signature. The extent of unsteadiness is limited to that which is found in the post 1920 form of signature. His hand never produced a truly shaky signature. McGraw's nicknames were "Mugsy" and "Napoleon," but he never signed autographs with these names.

Signature Population: McGraw is a scarce signature on a per se basis. Demand is strong. The population is very limited, though rarity is restricted to premium items only. Most McGraw-signed items are limited to team-signed baseballs, album pages, and signatures removed from bank documents. Signed photographs are very rare. Single-signed baseballs border on the nonexistent. I have only examined two genuine specimens in my lifetime. The best way to obtain McGraw's signature on a baseball is to secure a Giants-signed team ball from the 1920s or 1930s. McGraw's long association with baseball correlates into a limited population of signed letters, both typed and handwritten. Many have stunning baseball content. The most common medium are signatures removed from checks. I have seen dozens in my lifetime. After his death, Mrs. McGraw would graciously honor requests from collectors by cutting off McGraw's signature from a check. Full-signed checks are extremely rare. I

McGraw 1: letter dated 1917 (courtesy National Baseball Hall of Fame and Museum)

McGraw 2: document dated 1920 (courtesy National Baseball Hall of Fame and Museum)

McGraw 3: team sheet circa 1920s

McKechnie 1: circa 1930s signature

McKechnie 2: circa 1960s signature

have only seen one in my lifetime. I have never examined a genuine signed baseball card.

Known Forgeries: Due to the complex nature of McGraw's hand, vintage signatures are difficult to forge. Well executed forgeries are very limited. Signatures accomplished after 1920 are much easier to replicate and many well executed forgeries of these exist. Forgers typically target the post–1920 signature. Forgeries can be found on baseballs, album pages, scorecards, and the like. A common forgery are dual-signed baseballs by Mathewson and McGraw. Each forgery occupies its own panel, with an overly large McGraw signature. The McGraw signature is usually dated. Sometimes two McGraw forgeries appear on the ball. This forger has accomplished other forged balls, of note dual-signed McGraw and Jennings balls. Most McGraw signatures offered in the market are forgeries, so proceed with extreme caution. Title issues may exist with certain McGraw signed letters; see the stolen document section of Chapter 4.

Sales: Signature removed from a check sold for $1,129 (RR Auctions, May 2007). Signature removed from a check sold for $771 (Lelands.com, January 2008). Signature removed from a check sold for $1,026 (RR Auctions, January 2006).

Bill McKechnie

Signature Study: McKechnie signed in a plain and practical hand. His signature evidences good letter construction. Legibility is sound. The signature has a slight right slant. His signature is penned in a slower hand that lacks reckless flow. Display value is marginal. Early signatures are typically penned as "W.B. McKechnie." Material signed later in life is usually signed as "Bill Mc-

Kechnie." McKechnie's hand remained strong his entire life. A genuine signature will exhibit no shakiness of hand and one that does should be considered suspect and avoided.

Signature Population: This is a signature where an ample supply is balanced with demand. The supply of genuine McKechnie material is sound. McKechnie was a willing signer his entire life and honored all requests for his signature. His signature is generally limited to index cards and government postcards. Premium items such as 8 × 10 photos, Hall of Fame plaque postcards, and baseball cards are scarce. Single-signed baseballs are rare. Many Cincinnati Reds signed team baseballs from the 1930s exist, which are an excellent source of McKechnie signatures.

Known Forgeries: The slower nature of McKechnie's hand results in a signature that is moderately easy to replicate. Forgeries are generally limited to premium items such as baseballs, Hall of Fame plaque postcards, and the like. Forged plaque cards exist in quantities. The forgeries are fairly well executed. They are signed in a slighty choppy hand. The forgeries appear vary small and take up only a small portion on the lower border of the plaque. McKechnie 4 illustrates a forged

McKechnie 3: signature of Bill McKechnie, Jr.

McKechnie 4: forged Hall of Fame plaque postcard

plaque postcard. Bank checks signed by McKechnie's son, Bill McKechnie Jr., are in the market. They are easily spotted as his hand deviates greatly from his father's signature. His son's autograph is illustrated as McKechnie 3. I have never seen a bank check signed by Hall of Famer McKechnie.

Sales: 4 × 6 George Brace photo sold for $220 (RR Auctions, February 2011). Hall of Fame plaque postcard sold for $300 (Hunt Auctions, March 2009). Index card, superior specimen, sold for $365 (eBay, January 2012).

Bid McPhee

Signature Study: McPhee's signature appears to have transformed little throughout the years. Early signatures are very flowing and penned without hesitation. The signature evidences a slight right slant. Letter construction is strong with wonderfully precise lines and beautiful curves. Early signatures have maximum eye appeal. Material signed in the 1930s still exhibits wonderful flow. Display value remains high. It is unknown whether infirmity of hand affected his writing in old age. Material signed in the mid–1930s evidences no shakiness of hand. He died in 1943.

Signature Population: This is a signature of sound demand and very minute supply. McPhee is a very rare signature. I estimate a total population of signatures in the market at under five. There are a few signed documents and contracts that are housed at the Cincinnati Museum Center. These will likely never be released into the market. I am told that a signed government postcard exists, though I have not seen it. I know of no signed photographs or baseballs.

Known Forgeries: Due to the artistic nature of McPhee's signature, replication of his hand is difficult. Well executed forgeries are non–existent. Just about all McPhee signatures in the market

McPhee 2: signed contract circa 1890 (courtesy Cincinnati Base Ball Club Records, Mss c574bas, box 1, folder 12, Cincinnati Museum Center)

McPhee 3: ALS circa 1930s

are forgeries. There are forged letters in the market written on 5 × 7 blank stationery. These forgeries are fairly well executed but the handwriting exhibits a labored appearance.

Sales: 1938 ALS, choice specimen, sold for $78,000 (Legendary Auctions, August 2007).

Joe Medwick

Signature Study: Medwick's signature is one that evolved over time. Medwick signed in a very pleasing and legible hand. His signature evidences good letter construction. An ever so slight right slant is evident. Early signatures tend to exhibit a slower hand. The letters are slightly ajar. As the years progressed Medwick's hand became more refined. The signature is much more precise and flowing. Hand strokes become faster. The letters are more uniform, making for a signature that is complex in nature. He would sometimes add a paraph under the autograph. Medwick died suddenly of a heart attack. Since he never reached old age, infirmity of hand was non-existent. A genuine Medwick signature will exhibit no shakiness of hand and one that does should be considered suspect and avoided.

Signature Population: This is a signature of sound demand that is balanced with supply. There are many find specimens from various eras

McPhee 1: check endorsement dated 1886 (courtesy of Cincinnati Base Ball Club Records, Mss C574bas, Box 1, Folder 12, Cincinnati Museum Center)

Medwick 1: album page dated 1933

Medwick 2: undated signature

in the market. His signature is available on most mediums including index cards, photos, Hall of Fame plaque postcards, and government postcards. Single-signed baseballs are scarce. Typed letters signed are scarce. Autographed letters signed are rare.

Known Forgeries: Modern signatures are more difficult to forge than their vintage counterparts. Well executed forgeries are generally limited to vintage specimens. Due to the affordable nature of Medwick signatures, forgeries are generally limited to premium items such as 8 × 10 photos and single-signed baseballs.

Sales: Single-signed baseball sold for $705 (Robert Edward Auctions, Spring 2008). Index card sold for $66 (eBay, September 2011). Government postcard sold for $44 (eBay, September, 2011). Hall of Fame plaque postcard sold for $56 (eBay, November 2011). Hall of Fame plaque postcard sold for $100 (eBay, November 2011).

Jose Mendez

Signature Study: Mendez's signature is well constructed and evidences good flow. The illustrated example is signed "Jose del Villi (or Ville) Mendez." Nothing else is really known about his signature.

Signature Population: The illustrated signature is from Mendez's World War I draft registration card. The date of birth listed on the card is not what is generally reported as his birth date. The place of birth listed on the card is correct. Mendez lists his occupation as a cigar maker. His employer listed on the card is fellow Hall of Famer Rube Foster. Foster's address listed on the card is

Jose del Valle, Mendez

Mendez 1: World War I draft card circa 1917 (Record Group 163, Records of the Selective Services Division, National Archives at Atlanta)

correct. To my knowledge this is the only known signature in existence. It is held by the National Archives. I know of no signatures in the open market.

Known Forgeries: Forgeries of various construction exist.

Sales: Due to the rarity, there have been no recent sales of Mendez's signature.

John Mize

Signature Study: Mize signed in a very powerful hand. His signature is accomplished with strong and heavy strokes. The hand is very flowing and lacks hesitation. Letter construction is sound but slightly reckless. Legibility is still evident. Overall, this is a signature with good display value. The letter "i" is typically dotted with a dash. Mize's hand remained strong his entire life. A genuine Mize signature will evidence no shakiness of hand and one that does should be considered suspect and avoided.

Signature Population: This is a signature of marginal demand that is outweighed by supply. Mize is a common signature. He was a gracious signer throughout his entire life. His signature can be found on most mediums including index cards, Hall of Fame plaque postcards, photographs, baseballs, and gum cards. Less common are baseball bats. Letters of any kind are scarce.

Known Forgeries: Mize's hand and its rapid nature makes for a signature that is difficult to replicate. Due to the nominal value of Mize's signature, he is not the target of skilled forgers.

Sales: Mize's signature is available. His autograph generally sells for under $100 on most mediums.

Mize 1: circa 1950s signature

Mize 2: circa 1985 signature

Paul Molitor

Signature Study: Molitor signs in a large and dominant hand. His signature evidences good flow. There is no hesitation. Letter construction is marginal to poor, which greatly impairs legibility. The signature is marked with a large capital "P." Letters are generally morphed together, which results in a signature with marginal display value. As of 2012 Molitor's hand remains strong. A genuine signature will exhibit no shakiness of hand and one that does should be considered suspect and avoided.

Molitor 1: undated signature

Signature Population: This is a signature of marginal demand that is outweighed by supply. Molitor engages in mass signings. His signature is generally found on baseballs, bats, photos, and gum cards. Letters of any kind are scarce.

Known Forgeries: Due to the poor letter construction, his signature is easy to replicate. Producing a well executed forgery can be accomplished with little effort. Due to the nominal value of Molitor's signature, he is not the target of skilled forgers.

Sales: Molitor's signature is available. His autograph generally sells for under $100 on most mediums.

Joe Morgan

Signature Study: Joe Morgan signs in a very unattractive hand. His signature evidences good flow. Hesitation is minimal. Letter construction is poor resulting in a signature that is illegible. Display value is poor. As of 2012 Morgan's hand is strong. A genuine signature will exhibit no shakiness of hand and one that does should be considered suspect and avoided.

Signature Population: This is a common signature where supply outweighs demand. His signature is generally found on index cards, photos,

Morgan 1: undated signature

gum cards, baseballs, bats, and the like. Letters of any kind are scarce.

Known Forgeries: The non-uniform nature of Morgan's hand makes for easy replication. Due to the nominal value of Morgan's signature, he is not the target of skilled forgers.

Sales: Morgan's signature is available. His autograph generally sells for under $100 on most mediums.

Eddie Murray

Signature Study: Murray signs in a very practical hand. His signature is large with good letter construction. The well formed letters result in a signature that is legible. Display value is sound. Murray signs in a slower hand. The signature lacks rapid flow. His signature exhibits a marked back slant. As of 2012 Murray's hand remains strong. A genuine signature will exhibit no shakiness of hand and one that does should be considered suspect and avoided.

Signature Population: This is a very common signature where supply clearly outweighs demand. Murray's signature can be found on most mediums including index cards, gum cards, baseballs, bats, photos, and the like. Letters of any kind are scarce.

Known Forgeries: The slower nature of Murray's hand makes replication easy. It would not be difficult for a forger to create a convincing forgery. Due to the nominal value of Murray's signature, he is generally not the target of skilled forgers.

Sales: Murray's signature is available. His autograph generally sells for under $100 on most mediums.

Murray 1: undated signature

Stan Musial

Signature Study: Musial signs in a very distinctive and attractive hand. His signature is vertical in nature with no measurable slant. Musial's hand exhibits powerful and effortless strokes. The signature has good letter construction. The signature has no hesitation whatsoever. Early signatures tend to be slightly less flamboyant. The height of the letters is shorter and the signature tends to be longer than more modern examples. As of 2012 Musial's hand is affected with a slight infirmity. Recently signed material evidences a more methodic hand with a labored appearance.

Signature Population: This is a common signature but balanced against a good demand. Musial has been a gracious signer throughout his life. The supply of Musial material is very strong. His signature can be found on most mediums including photos, Perez-Steele cards, baseballs, jerseys, bats, gum cards, and the like. Letters of any kind are scarce and desirable. There is a small supply of "Stan The Man Inc." bank checks in the market, though they should be considered uncommon. Musial is also a fairly skilled harmonica player. A certain number of harmonica-related items have been signed by Musial, which make an interesting collectible.

Known Forgeries: Due to the complex and flowing nature of Musial's hand, his signature is difficult to replicate. There are no well executed forgeries in the market. Due the nominal value of Musial's signature, he is generally not the target of skilled forgers.

Sales: Musial's signature is available. His autograph generally sells for under $100 on most mediums.

Musial 1: government postcard dated 1954

Musial 2: government postcard dated 1986

Hal Newhouser

Signature Study: Newhouser's signature went through a marked evolution. Early signatures are fairly well constructed. They evidence good flow. Material signed during his playing days has good display value. In retirement the signature still evidences good flow. The letter construction found in vintage signatures is gone, resulting in a signature that is basically illegible. The capital "H" in the first name is impaired and affects display value. After his Hall of Fame induction Newhouser's hand further eroded. Material signed post-induction is illegible. A slight hesitation is evident. Signatures accomplished in the last five or so years of his life have poor eye appeal. In 1939, Newhouser signed a few autographs as "'Lefty' Newhouser." This form of signature, illustrated as Newhouser 1, is scarce. In the last few years of his life some collectors requested him to sign with this nickname, to which he obliged.

Signature Population: The population of Newhouser signatures is sound and balanced with demand. He was a willing signer for years. After induction he did many mass signings. His signature is generally found on index cards, baseballs, photos, gum cards, Hall of Fame plaque postcards, and the like. Signed bats are uncommon. Letters in any form are scarce. Newhouser released a small amount of canceled bank checks, but they are considered uncommon and desirable.

Known Forgeries: Vintage signatures are flowing and rather difficult to replicate. Post-induction signatures are easy to replicate. Producing a well executed forgery would be rather easy. Due to the nominal value of Newhouser's signature, he is not the target of skilled forgers

Sales: Newhouser's signature is available. His autograph generally sells for under $100 on most mediums.

Newhouser 1: album page dated 1939

Newhouser 2: circa 1970s signature

Newhouser 3: 1987 signature

Charles "Kid" Nichols

Signature Study: Nichols' signature is one of limited study because just about all the signatures in existence were signed in old age and thus affected by infirmity of hand. I only know of two or three specimens signed before 1920. Nichols signed in a very practical and neat hand. His signature evidences a nice right slant. Letter construction is sound. A high degree of legibility is noted.

Signature Population: This is a signature where demand clearly outweighs a small supply. Nichols is a scarce signature per se and premium items are rare to extremely rare. Most Nichols signatures are removed from bank checks. Were it not for the supply of check cuts he would be considered a rare signature. Photos of any kind are rare. 8 × 10 photos are basically non-existent. I have only examined two genuine specimens in close to 30 years of searching. Handwritten letters exist but are very rare. I have never seen a genuine single-signed baseball. Signed team balls from Nichols' playing days very likely do not exist. Complete bank checks are considered very rare.

Known Forgeries: Due to the lack of flow and the slower nature of Nichols' hand, his signature is easy to forge. Well executed forgeries exist in quantities. Forgeries exist on Hall of Fame plaque postcards, check cuts, photos, and baseballs. There is a small grouping of forged baseballs accomplished by one forger. Basically, these are newer baseballs that have been artificially aged using dirt. The baseballs are brown toned but

Nichols 1: ALS dated 1915 (courtesy National Baseball Hall of Fame and Museum)

Nichols 2: circa 1940s signature

Nichols 3: bank check undated

evenly so and appear dull. The hide is ever so slightly rough. The forgery is placed neatly on the sweet spot and signed as "Charles "Kid" Nichols," "Charles A. "Kid," Nichols," or "Charles A. Nichols." The signatures are accomplished in black ink but the process used to age the balls has affected the ink, so the signatures are slightly blurred.

Sales: Bank check sold for $3,210 (Lelands.com, November 2007). Government postcard sold for $582 (Lelands.com, November 2010). Souvenir Kid Nichols Day card sold for $849 (Lelands.com, May 2008).

Phil Niekro

Signature Study: Niekro's signature evidences good flow and lacks hesitation. His signature features a back slant and effortless lines. Letter construction is marginal at best. Legibility is somewhat impaired. As of 2012 Niekro's hand remains sound. A genuine signature will evidence no shakiness of hand and one that does should be considered suspect and avoided.

Niekro 1: circa 1980s signature

Signature Population: Overall, this is a common signature where supply outweighs demand. His signature is typically found on most mediums including index cards, photos, gum cards, baseballs, Hall of Fame plaque postcards, and bats. Less common are signed jerseys. Signed letters of any kind are scarce.

Known Forgeries: Niekro's signature, with its flowing hand, is rather difficult to replicate. Due to the nominal value of Niekro's signature, he is not the target of skilled forgers.

Sales: Niekro's signature is available. His autograph generally sells for under $100 on most mediums.

Walter O'Malley

Signature Study: O'Malley signed in a very pleasing hand. His signature has effortless flow. Hesitation is non-existent. Letter construction is impaired. The signature is somewhat illegible. Overall, his signature is very nice and the display value is high. O'Malley's hand remained strong his entire life. A genuine signature will evidence no shakiness of hand and one that does should be considered suspect and avoided.

Signature Population: This is a signature of sound demand and limited supply. It is clear that most signatures are found on team-related documents and typed letters. There also seems to be a limited supply of signatures removed from bank checks. 8 × 10 photos, single-signed baseballs, government postcards, and handwritten letters should be considered rare.

Known Forgeries: Due to the complex and flowing nature of O'Malley's hand, his signature is difficult to replicate. Well executed forgeries are non-existent. Forgeries, which evidence a labored hand, can be found on most mediums.

Sales: 1962 TLS sold for $162 (eBay, September 2011). 1963 TLS signed with first name only sold for $200 (Lelands.com, June 2010). 1957 TLS sold for $460 (eBay, December 2011).

O'Malley 1: document dated 1947

O'Malley 2: bank check dated 1962

O'Malley 3: TLS dated 1978

Jim O'Rourke

Signature Study: O'Rourke signed in a very pleasing hand. His signature evidences strong flowing lines. Hesitation is trivial. The signature evidences a right slant. Letter construction is sound. O'Rourke's signature is legible. It has good display value. He pens his autograph as either "Jas. H. O'Rourke" or "J.H. O'Rourke." Most signatures I have examined were signed in the early to mid–1910s. Anything signed before 1900 is excessively rare. There is no confirmation whether infirmity of hand affected his signature in his later years. Given the fact that I have never seen a genuine signature that evidences a shakiness of hand and coupled with the fact that he fell victim to an aggressive form of pneumonia, infirmity of hand is unlikely.

Signature Population: O'Rourke is a very rare signature. The total population is likely under ten genuine specimens in the open market. Most are associated with his tenure as secretary of the Eastern Association. Years after his death the O'Rourke family released a few signatures to collectors. These were signatures removed from documents or letters. I have never examined a genuine signed photo, baseball, gum card, or government postcard. Title issues may exist with certain letters in the open market. See the stolen document section of Chapter 4.

Known Forgeries: O'Rourke's hand is complex in nature, thus replication is difficult. Well executed forgeries are rare but do exist. Most O'Rourke signatures offered for sale are forgeries. There is only one forger that seems to have mastered O'Rourke's hand and produces some fairly convincing forgeries. He signs them as "Jas. H.

O'Rourke 1: ALS dated 1911 (courtesy National Baseball Hall of Fame and Museum)

O'Rourke 2: ALS dated 1911 (courtesy National Baseball Hall of Fame and Museum)

O'Rourke 3: ALS dated 1914

O'Rourke." These forgeries exhibit decent flow. The forgeries evidence a very slight choppiness. For some reason the forger adds a straight line paraph under the forgery. I am not sure why the forger adds a paraph as a genuine O'Rourke signature will not exhibit this mark, at least I have never seen it associated with a genuine signature. I have seen these forgeries on two types of mediums, album pages and on the inside end paper of books.

Sales: 1914 ALS, with baseball content, sold for $10,440 (Robert Edward Auctions, Spring 2006).

Mel Ott

Signature Study: Ott's signature is wonderfully precise and clean. Ott signed in a crisp flowing hand. His signature evidences strong lines. There is no hesitation whatsoever. Ott's signature has superior letter construction. Legibility is very high. Ott's hand remained consistent over the years. Material signed during his early playing days varies little when compared to post-retirement signatures. Most signatures are signed "Mel Ott" but some early specimens were signed as "Melvin Ott." A choice early signature is illustrated as Ott 2, which is a form of signature he, in later years, reserved for bank and legal documents. On November 21, 1958, Ott was killed in a car accident, hence infirmity of hand is non-existent. A genuine Ott signature will exhibit no shakiness of hand and one that does should be considered suspect and avoided.

Signature Population: Ott material is in high demand, clearly outweighing the supply. The supply of Ott material is sound. He signed countless items during his playing days and in retirement. His signature is generally found on index cards,

Ott 1: album page dated 1933

Ott 2: circa 1930s signature

Ott 3: undated signature

album pages, government postcards, and team-signed baseballs. Single-signed baseballs are very scarce and border on the rare side. Most were signed in the 1950s during Ott's days as a broadcaster for the Detroit Tigers. There are a few dual-signed balls with fellow broadcaster Van Patrick in the market. Ott signed balls on both the sweet spot and the side panel. Single-signed examples from the 1940s are very rare and are typically signed on the side panel. 8 × 10 photographs and Hall of Fame plaque postcards are very scarce to rare. Letters of any kind are rare. In the 1980s, Mrs. Ott would send collectors signatures of her husband that she would cut from a check. Unfortunately, she would cut the signature in half removing the last three letters of the name "Melvin" and tape them together to read "Mel Ott." These are of little value. Full checks are extremely rare, as only a handful were released by the family.

Known Forgeries: One would think that Ott's signature would be easy to forge, since it is only six letters long. But, in fact, Ott's signature is extremely difficult to replicate. Well executed forgeries are very limited. There are a couple of common Ott forgeries to watch for. Several years ago forged Ott single-signed baseballs entered the market. They are penned on "Reach Official League" balls. The balls are clean with a light cream color tone. These balls are signed in jet black fountain pen. The forgeries are most always placed on the top part of the side panel, just under the sweet spot stitching. These balls have been around for 20 years. Many have been incorrectly certified as genuine by the authentication companies. The forgeries are fairly well executed but evidence a slight amount of hesitation in the ink strokes. Forged letters have also been around for years. In general, Ott letters are considered rare, both typed and in handwritten form. These forged letters are fairly well executed. The handwriting has a slight variance from Ott's hand. The angle of the hand is slanted more to the right than the genuine signature. Many of these forgeries are accomplished in green fountain pen. I think what is fooling most people is the rapid nature of the handwriting.

Sales: Government postcard sold for $435 (RR Auctions, August 2011). 8 × 10 photo, batting pose, sold for $1,998 (Robert Edward Auctions, Spring, 2010). Album page sold for $549 (eBay, September 2011). Single-signed baseball, choice specimen, sold for $10,057 (Lelands.com, Winter 2006). 7 × 9 photo, batting pose, choice specimen, sold for $5,000 (Hunt Auctions, February 2006). 1943 TLS sold for $2,510 (Legendary Auctions, August 2011). Index card sold for $711 (Legendary Auctions, May 2010).

Satchel Paige

Signature Study: Paige signed in a practical hand. His signature is flowing but intermixed with sharp turns. The signature lacks hesitation and appears fast on paper. Letter construction is sound but slightly muted. The signature has slightly impaired legibility. His signature is usually finished with a straight paraph. Early signatures are accomplished in a slower, more legible hand. Early signatures appear rudimentary in construction. Most signatures are accomplished with his nickname. Signatures penned with his real name "Leroy" are uncommon. Paige's hand remained strong his entire life. A genuine Paige signature will exhibit no shakiness of hand and one that does should be considered suspect and avoided.

Signature Population: Paige's signature has always been in demand and balanced with supply. Paige was an erratic signer throughout his life. Many mail requests for his signature went unanswered. He is an uncommon signature per se and generally limited to items signed through the mail. Most Paige signatures are found on index cards, Springfield Redbirds business cards (where Paige held the title of vice president), and Hall of Fame plaque postcards. 8 × 10 photos and single-

Paige 2: undated signature

Paige 3: common secretarial

signed baseballs are scarce. Letters of any kind are rare, especially handwritten specimens. Signatures accomplished during his days as a Negro Leaguer are rare and generally limited to letters penned to baseball clubs.

Known Forgeries: Paige's signature is fairly complex in nature, thus replication of hand is somewhat difficult. Well executed forgeries are limited but do exist. Vintage signatures are much easier to replicate. Paige has been the target of forgers for years, though most forgeries are limited to premium items such as baseballs and 8 × 10 photos. Many post-induction signatures obtained through the mail were signed by someone other than Paige. A common secretarial signature can be seen in Paige 3. Note the signature varies greatly from the genuine specimen. Some of the secretarial signatures are signed incorrectly as "Satchell Paige."

Sales: Business card sold for $198 (RR Auctions, July 2011). Hall of Fame plaque postcard sold for $149 (eBay, September 2010). 1939 baseball contract, countersigned by Bill Perkins, sold for $8,748 (Lelands.com, November 2007). 8 × 10 photo, pitching pose, sold for $350 (Hunt Auctions, November 2010). Signed postcard sold for $115 (eBay, November 2011).

Jim Palmer

Signature Study: Palmer signs in a fast and reckless hand. His signature is very flowing. There is no hesitation. Letter construction is marginal. The first name usually appears as the letter "J" followed by a sloppy trail of ink. The last name is fairly legible, but the last three letters are morphed together as indistinguishable strokes.

Paige 1: circa 1970s signature

Palmer 1: bank check dated 1988

Pennock 1: album page dated 1923

Pennock 2: government postcard dated 1945

Overall, this is a rather unappealing signature. As of 2012 Palmer's hand remains strong. A genuine signature will exhibit no shakiness of hand and one that does should be considered suspect and avoided.

Signature Population: Palmer is a very common signature. Supply clearly outweighs demand. Palmer engages in mass signings. His signature is found on most mediums from index cards to photos to baseballs and the like. Letters in any form are scarce. A few years back many canceled bank checks were released in the market.

Known Forgeries: Palmer's hand is easy to replicate. Due to the nominal value of Palmer's signature, he is not the target of skilled forgers.

Sales: Palmer's signature is available. His autograph generally sells for under $100 on most mediums.

Herb Pennock

Signature Study: Pennock signed in a very flowing and pleasing hand. His signature is marked with effortless strokes. The signature evidences a slight right slant. Letter construction is sound, resulting in a very legible signature. The overall display value of Pennock's signature is sound. Pennock's hand seems to have gone through a marginal change through the years. Early signatures tend to be short in height while length is dominant. As the years progressed the signature becomes more compact and the height increases. Material signed as general manager of the Philadelphia Phillies tends to lack the artistic flow of earlier signatures. Most are simply signed as "Herb Pennock" in a rather unattractive hand. Pennock died suddenly in 1948, thus infirmity of hand is non-existent. A genuine signature will exhibit no shakiness of hand and one that does should be considered suspect and avoided.

Signature Population: This is a signature of limited population where demand far outweighs supply. Pennock is a scarce signature on a per se basis and premium items are rare to very rare. His signature is generally found on material signed at

the stadium such as album pages, scorecards, and the like. Yankees team-signed baseballs are also a good source of Pennock signatures. It is about the only way to obtain Pennock on a baseball. I have never seen a genuine single-signed baseball in my life. Photographs of any kind are very scarce. 8 × 10 photos are rare to very rare. There is a decent supply of bank checks. Another good source of Pennock's autograph are letters signed as GM of the Phillies. Many typed letters are in the market, most with good baseball content. ALsS should be considered very rare.

Known Forgeries: Pennock's signature is very complex in nature. There are no well executed forgeries in the market, at least when in comes to the earlier signatures. Signatures accomplished later in life lack flow and are easier to forge. There are some nicely executed forgeries of Pennock's later style of signature. There are some well executed forged Yankees team baseballs in the market. The forgeries are evenly spaced apart. Forgeries are signed using the same pen pressure. All the signatures appear uniform. For the most part, the forgeries lack the racing effect. Some forgeries evidence an ever so slightly labored hand. Another trademark of this forger is that sometimes he will sign one panel of the ball on a different plane. He will place four or five forgeries on a upward slanting 30 to 40 degree angle. If you see this trait on an early Yankees team ball, proceed with extreme caution.

Sales: 1924 endorsed Yankees payroll check

Pennock 3: undated signature

sold for $533 (Legendary Auctions, November 2010). 1947 TLS sold for $950 (Hunt Auctions, April 2011). 1920 Major League contract, countersigned by Ban Johnson, sold for $2,938 (Robert Edward Auctions, Spring 2011). Bank check sold for $924 (RR Auctions, June 2006). Ink signature sold for $350 (eBay, January 2012).

Tony Perez

Signature Study: Perez signs in a flowing hand with nice effortless ink strokes. His signature is vertical in nature with no measurable slant. Letter construction is sound. The signature is, for the most part, legible. Perez's signature works well on paper. The display value is high. As of 2012 Perez's hand remains strong. A genuine signature will exhibit no shakiness of hand and one that does should be considered suspect and avoided.

Perez 1: document dated 2000

Signature Population: This is a signature of great supply and marginal demand. Perez's signature can be found on most mediums including index cards, baseballs, gum cards, photos, bats, jerseys, and the like. Signed letters of any kind are scarce.

Known Forgeries: Perez is one of the easier signatures to replicate. Due to the nominal value of Perez's signature, he is not the target of skilled forgers.

Sales: Perez's signature is available. His autograph generally sells for under $100 on most mediums.

Gaylord Perry

Signature Study: Perry signs in a very eclectic hand. His signature exhibits flowing lines but the hand lacks precision. Letter construction is marginal. The signature is somewhat illegible. The sloppy nature of Perry's hand limits the display value. As of 2012 Perry's hand remains sound. A genuine signature will exhibit no shakiness of

Perry 1: bank check dated 1981

hand and one that does should be considered suspect and avoided.

Signature Population: This is a signature of marginal demand outweighed by supply. His signature can be found on most mediums including index cards, baseballs, gum cards, photos, bats, jerseys, and the like. There is also a good supply of canceled bank checks in the market. Letters of any kind are scarce. Perry did, at one time, own a peanut farm. He signed a limited number of small burlap sack peanut bags for collectors. They are great conversation pieces. The former pitcher often accused of throwing a spitball will also, on occasion, sign jars of Vaseline, which make for a fine collectible.

Known Forgeries: The lack of structure of hand makes Perry's signature easy to replicate. Creating a well executed forgery would be rather easy. Due to the nominal value of Perry's signature, he is not the target of skilled forgers.

Sales: Perry's signature is available. His autograph generally sells for under $100 on most mediums.

Eddie Plank

Signature Study: Plank signed in a very practical and neat hand. His signature is flowing in nature but lacks flair. Letter construction is sound. His signature has a high degree of legibility. The signature evidences a slight right slant. The rather plain nature of his hand impairs display value. Plank had essentially three ways of signing his name: "E.S. Plank," "Eddie S. Plank," and "Edward S. Plank." Plank died at a relatively young age from a stroke. A genuine signature should evidence no measurable shakiness of hand and one that does should be considered suspect and avoided.

Signature Population: This is a signature of strong demand with a minute supply. Plank is a very rare signature. I estimate that there are under 20 specimens in the market. There are a couple of signed banquet dinner menus. Years ago there was a Philadelphia Athletics program in pencil

Plank 1: will dated 1915

signed by multiple Athletics. This program contained two genuine Plank signatures. One of the signatures was partially signed over a dark portion of the program which impaired display. The two signatures were removed from the program and sold separately. I have never seen a genuine signed photo or single-signed baseball. I know of only one genuinely signed baseball. It was autographed in the mid–1920s and contains many signatures including one "E.S. Plank." I have never seen a signed team baseball from Plank's playing days. The chance that one exists is unlikely. A couple of letters, written to his wife and dated in the 1910s, exist but are signed with the first name only. In retirement Plank returned to his native Gettysburg, Pennsylvania, and opened a garage. Though many business-related documents must have been signed, I have never seen one. Plank is simply a rare signature where supply is just about non-existent.

Known Forgeries: Given the lackluster hand, Plank's signature can be replicated with ease. Many well executed forgeries exist the market, so caution is warranted. Nearly all Plank signatures offered in the market are forged. Many forged photographs, old currency, generic rent receipts, and baseballs exist. Back in the early 1990s, forged single-signed baseballs entered the market. I have seen a handful in the past ten or so years. They are all accomplished by the same forger. They are signed on period American League, Pioneer League, or Federal League baseballs. All were signed as "E. S. Plank" on the side panel. The forgeries are nicely executed but they do evidence an ever so slight unsteadiness in the lines. Another group of forgeries entered the market decades ago and, to this day, are still being offered as genuine. They are cut signatures signed as "E.S. Plank." I have seen them accomplished in both fountain pen and pencil. The forgeries are amateurish. They evidence a labored appearance. The letter

Plank 2: World War I draft card circa 1917 (Record Group 163, Records of the Selective Services Division, National Archives at Atlanta)

"P" is elongated. They are affixed to old index cards. "Eddie Plank — Hall of Famer" or something to that effect is typed across the top. The date of his death or the year of his induction into the Hall of Fame is also added. They are rudimentary in construction and are easily spotted as fake. Another type of forgery are forged bank checks. It is apparent that a forger obtained some period unused checks from The Pacific Bank out of New York. The check is made payable to Plank. It has been filled out either by hand or typewriter. A pencil forgery of Plank is added on the reverse as an endorsement. The forgeries are rudimentary in construction. In addition, the checks lack the proper bank cancellations but rather have a couple of holes applied using a hand held hole-punch.

Sales: 1916 three-page ALS, signed with first name only, sold for $27,469 (Lelands.com, May 2008).

Alex Pompez

Signature Study: Pompez signed in a flowing hand. His signature exhibits fine strokes and lacks hesitation. The signature evidences a nice right slant. Letter construction is moderately sound but lines tend to morph together. Legibility is impaired. Display value is average. It is unclear whether infirmity of hand existed. I have only examined a handful of genuine specimens. None evidenced a shakiness of hand.

Signature Population: Pompez is a rare signature and the supply is extremely small. Pompez proved elusive and generally his whereabouts were unknown. Associated with mobster Dutch Schultz, it is said that Pompez was a target of a New York rackets investigation and fled to Mexico for many years. He returned to the United States in the few remaining years of his life. Though he died in 1974, it may well have been 1874 since his signatures surface only rarely. It is usually on Negro League related letters and contracts. I have never

Pompez 1: signed postcard dated 1941 (courtesy Newark Public Library, The Newark Eagles papers)

Pompez 2: TLS dated 1944 (courtesy Newark Public Library, The Newark Eagles Papers)

Pompez 3: TLS dated 1944

Pompez 4: undated signature

seen a genuinely signed photo or baseball. Overall, this is a rare and desirable Negro League signature.

Known Forgeries: Pompez's signature lacks precise angles, thus replication of hand is fairly easy. Since his Hall of Fame induction, forgeries have entered the market so caution in warranted. Most forgeries are found on album pages and unused government postcards. Forgeries evidence a labored appearance with thick unsteady lines. These forgeries are amateurish in construction and can be exposed with little effort. Pompez was the business manager for the New York Cubans baseball club. A few signed letters exist, but some were secretarially signed.

Sales: Due to the rarity, there have been no recent sales of Pompez's signature.

Cum Posey

Signature Study: Posey signed in a flowing and aggressive hand. The signature is practical in nature and lacks flamboyance. His signature evidences a nice right slant. The strokes are fast and the racing effect is strong. Letter construction is sound, though the "um" in the first name is blended into indistinguishable strokes. Posey had essentially two ways of signing his name, "Cum Posey" and "C.W. Posey." Posey made liberal use of the pencil while writing letters. It is unclear whether

his signature was affected by infirmity of hand due to illness.

Signature Population: This is a signature of average demand that outweighs a restricted supply. Posey is a somewhat rare signature but a good number of specimens exist. Posey's signature is generally limited to league-related letters, documents, and the occasional endorsed check. I have never examined a genuinely signed photo or baseball. It should be noted that a small grouping of Homestead High School diplomas bear the signature of Posey as a director of the school. Diplomas are all dated in the late 1930s or 1940s. While only a couple of dozen exist, he could have signed hundreds of them. These diplomas will adversely affect rarity as more enter the market. The Newark Public Library does have many nice letters in their Newark Eagles collection, but these will likely never be released to the general public.

Known Forgeries: Posey is an easy signature to replicate. There are well executed forgeries in the market. Forgeries of Posey exist on most mediums. Album pages are a common target. There

Posey 1: ALS dated 1943 (courtesy Newark Public Library, The Newark Eagles Papers)

Posey 2: ALS circa 1940s (courtesy Newark Public Library, The Newark Eagles Papers)

Posey 3: ALS circa 1940s (courtesy Newark Public Library, Newark Eagles Papers)

Posey 4: common secretarial (courtesy Newark Public Library, The Newark Eagles papers)

Posey 5: common secretarial (courtesy Newark Public Library, The Newark Eagles papers)

Puckett 1: undated signature

are many baseball-related Homestead Grays letters and documents, but many were secretarially signed (see Posey 4 and Posey 5). Note the signatures look nothing like a genuine Posey signature. Additionally, there are a few Homestead Grays season passes in the market. I have examined a few of them. Most were signed by Posey's secretary. The majority of the above referenced diplomas were secretarially signed.

Sales: Signed diploma sold for $1,247 (Lelands.com, June 2010). Signed diploma sold for $950 (Hunt Auctions, July 2010).

Kirby Puckett

Signature Study: Puckett signed in a very flowing hand with many curves. His hand is reckless in nature. Hesitation is non-existent. Letter construction is poor as individual letters are basically indistinguishable. Puckett's signature is illegible. Display value is impaired. Puckett died suddenly of a stroke, hence his hand remained strong his entire life. A genuine Puckett signature will exhibit no shakiness of hand and one that does should be considered suspect and avoided.

Signature Population: The supply of Puckett material is strong and outweighs demand. Puckett engaged in many mass signings. His signature should be considered common, though certain premium items are tough to locate. His signature is generally found on baseballs, gum cards, photos, index cards, and the like. Bats and Perez-Steele cards are uncommon. Letters of any kind are scarce.

Known Forgeries: Given the illegible nature of Puckett's hand, his signature can be replicated with little effort. Due to the nominal value of Puckett's signature, he is not the target of skilled forgers.

Sales: Puckett's signature is available. His autograph generally sells for under $100 on most mediums.

Hoss Radbourn

Signature Study: Radbourn signed in a very plain and legible hand. He wrote his name more than signed it. Letter construction is sound. Average display value is noted. Radbourn signed in a slower hand that lacks recklessness. From the illustrated specimens, Radbourn had the habit of omitting the letter "e" from his first name; therefore it reads as "Charls." This habit can be clearly seen in Radbourn 1 and Radbourn 2. The signature on his will, dated 1895, evidences an excessive amount of shakiness due to infirmity of hand. Shakiness is due to partial paralysis. He accidentally blew off part of his head with a shotgun while hunting, which led to an untimely death shortly thereafter.

Signature Population: This is a signature of strong demand with no supply. There are only a handful of signatures in existence. The illustrated specimens, dated in 1890, are from the Frederick Long Collection housed at the Baseball Hall of Fame. The only other specimen I know of can be found on his will, which is currently held under

Radbourn 1: check endorsement dated 1890 (courtesy National Baseball Hall of Fame and Museum)

Radbourn 2: check endorsement dated 1890 (courtesy National Baseball Hall of Fame and Museum)

lock and key at the McLean County Clerk's Office in Illinois. I know of no Radbourn signatures in the open market, thus making this signature an extreme rarity.

Known Forgeries: The slower nature of Radbourn's hand makes replication easy. Radbourn forgeries exist in quantities and can be found on most mediums. There is one Radbourn document to note. Several years ago a contract dated in 1879 by and between Radbourn and the Dubuque Baseball Club surfaced. It is signed as "Chas. Radburn." It was held out as a genuine signature. Upon examination, the contract is what is known as a "file copy contract" and is not the genuine contract. The entire contract is filled out all in the same hand and the "signature" is also in the same hand as found the body of the document. Also note the last name is misspelled omitting the letter "o." The signature on this contract is illustrated as Radbourn 4.

Sales: Due to the rarity, there have been no recent sales of Radbourn's signature.

Radbourn 3: will dated 1895

Radbourn 4: file contract with secretarial signature

Pee Wee Reese

Signature Study: Reese signed in a remarkably consistent hand that deviated little throughout the years. His signature evidences wonderful flowing lines. There is no hesitation. The signature has a slight right slant. Letter construction is strong. The signature is very legible. The signature is dominated with large capital letters that only enhance the display value. Reese's hand remained strong his entire life. A genuine signature will exhibit no shakiness of hand and one that does should be considered suspect and avoided.

Reese 1: 1946 signature

Reese 2: circa 1990 signature

Signature Population: This is a signature of good demand but outweighed by supply. Reese was a willing signers for many years. He also engaged in many mass signings. His signature is found on most mediums including Hall of Fame plaque postcards, Perez-Steele cards, bats, gum cards, photos, baseballs, and the like. Letters in any form are uncommon to scarce. Letters are usually signed as "Pee Wee." Checks are also available but are considered uncommon.

Known Forgeries: Due to the excellent flowing lines and clean sweeping motions, Reese's signature is difficult to replicate. No well executed forgeries exist. Due to the nominal value of Reese's signature, he is not the target of skilled forgers.

Sales: Reese's signature is available. His autograph generally sells for under $100 on most mediums.

Jim Rice

Signature Study: Rice signs in a fast and fairly legible hand. His signature exhibits good flow.

Rice, J. 1: check endorsement dated 1980

Racing effect is pronounced. There is nothing really fancy about his signature. As of 2012 Rice's hand remains strong. A genuine signature should not exhibit any shakiness of hand.

Signature Population: This is a signature where supply outweighs demand. Rice is a very common signature that can be found on index cards, photos, baseballs, bats, and the like. Letters of any kind are scarce.

Known Forgeries: Replication of hand would take some effort. Due to the nominal value of Rice's signature, he is not the target of skilled forgers.

Sales: Rice's signature is available. His autograph generally sells for under $100 on most mediums.

Sam Rice

Signature Study: Rice signed in a nice and bold hand. His signature is marked with thick, dominant lines and powerful strokes. The signature is generally vertical in nature. Sound letter construction is evident. The degree of legibility is high. The signature has good eye appeal. As Rice aged his hand remained fairly constant. Deviation of hand over time is minimal. Early signatures, those penned in the 1920s, evidence the capital "R" in the last name that is separated from the first name. Later in life the "m" in the first name is usually linked to the "R." In the 1960s, Rice's hand became infirmed due to age. Signatures accomplished in the last ten or so years of his life evidence a shakiness of hand.

Signature Population: Overall, this is a signature where demand is balanced with supply. Though a willing singer throughout his life, the total population of Rice signatures is limited. Premium items are scarce to rare. Most Rice signatures are found on index cards or Hall of Fame plaque postcards. 8 × 10 photos are scarce. Signed Goudey gum cards are also very tough to secure. Letters of any kind are considered rare. Single-signed baseballs are rare to very rare. I have only

Rice, S. 1: team sheet circa 1920s

Rice, S. 2: circa 1930s signature

Rice, S. 3: undated signature

examined three or four genuine specimens in my life.

Known Forgeries: Well executed forgeries exist in quantities though the more modern, infirmed, signature is targeted by forgers. Forgeries of Rice do exist, though generally limited to premiums items such as single-signed baseballs. Forged Artvue Hall of Fame plaque postcards entered the market with some very convincing forgeries. The forger places the forgery across the image of Rice, right over the collar of the uniform. Many are signed in felt tip and evidence a fast signature with no hesitation. The forgery appears bunched together, which shortens the length of the signature. The strokes appear a bit more sharp and jagged, as especially seen in the letter "m" of the first name. Rice was inducted into the Hall of Fame in 1963 and his hand became infirmed shortly thereafter. One would expect a genuine signature to evidence a measured amount of shakiness. These forged plaque postcards do not exhibit such. Proceed with caution.

Sales: 4 × 6 photo sold for $218 (RR Auctions, February 2011). Hall of Fame plaque postcard sold for $134 (RR Auctions, March 2010). Index card sold for $34 (eBay, November 2011). Limited-edition baseball insert card sold for $68 (eBay, November 2011).

Branch Rickey

Signature Study: Rickey signed in a very powerful and dominant hand. His signature evidences strong flow that borders on the reckless side. The signature lacks hesitation. The rapid motion of his hand marginalizes letter construction. The legibility is impaired though only slightly. Overall, the signature has good display value. As Rickey aged his hand changed slightly. Signatures accomplished later in life tend to be a bit on the sloppy side. Rickey's hand remained fairly strong his entire life. A genuine signature will exhibit only slight shakiness of hand and this is limited to material penned late in life. A signature with material unsteadiness should be considered suspect and avoided.

Signature Population: This is a signature where supply is balanced with mediocre demand. The supply of Rickey material is sound due to his long association with baseball, mostly as an executive. Most Rickey signatures are found on team-related letters, documents, and contracts. There are several Major League contracts from the early 1930s signed by Rickey and typically countersigned by then National League President John Heydler. Non-document related signatures are generally limited to album pages and scorecards signed at the stadium. Premium items such as 8 × 10 photos are rare. Single-signed baseballs are very rare. Rickey's grandson, Branch B. Rickey, served as president of the Pacific Coast League. His signature is also in the market.

Known Forgeries: Well executed forgeries are few and far between because of Rickey's complex and flowing hand. There are many forgeries in

Rickey 3: signed document dated 1944

the market. They are mostly limited to premium items such as his 1915 Cracker Jack card, 8 × 10 photos, and baseballs. Most forgeries are amateurish in appearance and are exposed with little effort. It should be noted that secretaries would, on occasion, sign Rickey's name to letters.

Sales: 4 × 6 photo sold for $393 (RR Auctions, February 2011). Signed document, baseball related, sold for $220 (RR Auctions, June 2009). Government postcard sold for $275 (Hunt Auctions, September 2010). Index card sold for $325 (Hunt Auctions, March 2009). Limited-edition baseball insert card sold for $575 (eBay, November 2011).

Cal Ripken

Signature Study: Ripken signs in a rudimentary and sloppy hand. His signature is one of the poorest of all Hall of Fame signatures. Display value is weak. The letter construction is very poor. His signature reads as "Car Ri J." As of 2012 Ripken's hand remains strong. A genuine signature will exhibit no shakiness of hand and one that does should be considered suspect an avoided.

Signature Population: Ripken is an extremely common signature. He has been a willing signer for years. He would graciously sign for hours at the ballparks and also engages in mass signings. His signature is found on most mediums especially photos, gum cards, and baseballs. Letters in any form are scarce.

Known Forgeries: The hurried nature of Ripken's hand makes for a signature that is easy to

Rickey 1: signed document dated 1916

Rickey 2: TLS dated 1920 (courtesy National Baseball Hall of Fame and Museum)

Ripken 1: undated signature

forge. His signature is one of the easiest of all Hall of Famers to forge. Due to the nominal value of Ripken's signature, he is not the target of skilled forgers.

Sales: Ripken's signature is available. His autograph generally sells for under $100 on most mediums.

Eppa Rixey

Signature Study: Rixey signed in a practical and calculated hand. His signature is confined. It is accomplished in a slower hand. Hesitation is minimal. The signature lacks reckless flow. The signature, which exhibits no measurable slant, has excellent letter construction. Legibility is high. Rixey's hand remained remarkably consistent throughout the years with little deviation of hand. Material signed later in life does evidence slight hesitation. Shakiness is noted but at a very measured degree. Rixey's hand never produced a truly shaky signature.

Signature Population: This is a signature of average demand that is balanced with supply. Rixey is an uncommon signature. Were it not for a large supply of signed bank checks he would be considered a scarce signature. Back in the 1980s his family graciously released many checks into the market to satisfy collectors' requests for his signature. Many hundreds are in the market. His signature is also found on album pages and team-signed items accomplished in the late 1920s until retirement. 8 × 10 photographs are very rare. Single-signed baseballs are very rare. I have only examined two or three genuine specimens in my lifetime. There is a limited supply of letters in the market. Handwritten letters are more common

![Eppa Rixey signature]

Rixey 1: TLS dated 1925 (courtesy National Baseball Hall of Fame and Museum)

![Eppa Rixey Jr signature]

Rixey 2: bank check dated 1959

Rixey 3: undated signature

than typed letters. Signed 1933 Goudey gum cards are also rare but a few nice examples exist.

Known Forgeries: The slower nature of Rixey's hand results in a signature that is easy to replicate. Well executed forgeries exist in quantities, so caution is warranted. Forgeries exist on just about all mediums.

Sales: Bank check sold for $121 (RR Auctions, May 2010). 1932 ALS sold for $325 (Hunt Auctions, November 2006). Signature removed from a check sold for $110 (RR Auctions, March 2008). Bank check sold for $178 (Legendary Auctions, August 2009). Signed check sold for $287 (eBay, November 2011).

Phil Rizzuto

Signature Study: Rizzuto signed in a wonderfully flowing and artistically whimsical hand. His signature evidences wonderful flow. A strong display value is noted. The signature is somewhat legible but construction is impaired. It is one of the nicer Hall of Fame autographs. In the last ten or so years of his life Rizzuto's hand became slightly infirmed. Signatures accomplished at that time evidence an unsteady appearance.

Signature Population: This is a signature of average demand outweighed by supply. Rizzuto is a very common signature. He was a willing signer for years and engaged in many mass signings. His signature can be found on most mediums including index cards, gum cards, bats, baseballs, photos, Hall of Fame plaque postcards, and the like. There are some nice handwritten letters in the market and many are signed with his nickname "Scooter."

Known Forgeries: Due to the complex nature of Rizzuto's hand, his signature is difficult to replicate. Well executed forgeries do not exist for non-infirmed signatures. Signatures, where infirmity is present, are easier to forge. Due to the nominal value of Rizzuto's signature, he is generally not the target of skilled forgers. Many signatures obtained through the mail were secretarially signed, presumably by a family member. The secretarial

Rizzuto 1: circa 1980s signature

Rizzuto 2: circa 1990s signature

Roberts 2: government postcard dated 1986

erts' hand makes replication fairly difficult. Producing a well executed forgery would take effort. Due to the nominal value of Roberts' signature, he is not the target of skilled forgers.

Sales: Roberts' signature is available. His autograph generally sells for under $100 on most mediums.

signature deviates in that the letters "zz" are longer and extend far below the signature. These are quite common.

Sales: Rizzuto's signature is available. His autograph generally sells for under $100 on most mediums.

Robin Roberts

Signature Study: Roberts signed in a flowing and vertical hand. His signature evidences no measurable slant. Hesitation is non-existent. Letter construction is below average. The signature is basically illegible. Though a marginal looking signature, the hand is rapid in nature with clean lines. In the last few years of Roberts' life, his hand slowed somewhat but not to the point of unsteadiness.

Signature Population: This is a signature of marginal demand. Roberts is an extremely common signature. He had been a willing and gracious signer for years. The supply is basically limitless. His signature is found on most mediums including baseballs, photos, gum cards, bats, Perez-Steele cards, and the like. Signed letters of any kind are scarce.

Known Forgeries: The rapid nature of Rob-

Brooks Robinson

Signature Study: Robinson signs in a very unique and whimsical hand. His signature is marked with broad strokes and nice sweeping curves. The signature exhibits no hesitation whatsoever. A trivial back slant is noted. Letter construction is fairly sound, though some letters in the last name are blended together. Overall, an oddly attractive signature. As of 2012 Robinson's hand remains strong. A genuine signature will evidence no shakiness of hand and one that does should be considered suspect and avoided.

Signature Population: This is a signature of marginal demand. Robinson is an extremely common signature. The supply of Robinson signatures is basically limitless. He has been a willing signer for years and engages in many mass signings. His signature can be found on most mediums, though letters of any kind are scarce. There is also a decent supply of signed bank checks in the market.

Known Forgeries: Robinson's signature is rather difficult to forge. There are no well executed

Robinson, B. 1: 1995 signature

Roberts 1: government postcard dated 1950

forgeries in the market. Due to the nominal value of Robinson's signature, he is not the target of skilled forgers.

Sales: Robinson's signature is available. His autograph generally sells for under $100 on most mediums.

Frank Robinson

Signature Study: Robinson signs in a fairly aggressive hand. His signature exhibits good flow. Hesitation is lacking. Letter construction is marginal, at best, which impairs legibility. His signature has average display value. In recent years his signature evidences a bit more choppiness. As of 2012 Robinson's hand remains strong. A genuine signature will evidence no shakiness of hand and one that does should be considered suspect and avoided.

Robinson, F. 1: 1975 signature

Signature Population: This is a signature of marginal demand that is outweighed by supply. Robinson is a common signature. He engages in mass signings. Robinson's signature can be found on index cards, gum cards, baseballs, photos, bats, Hall of Fame plaque postcards, Perez-Steele cards, and the like. Letters of any kind are scarce.

Known Forgeries: Replication of his hand is moderately difficult, but there are some nice forgeries in the market. Due to the nominal value of Robinson's signature, he is generally not the target of skilled forgers. The one exception is forged 500-home-run items that exist in quantities.

Sales: Robinson's signature is available. His autograph generally sells for under $100 on most mediums.

Jackie Robinson

Signature Study: Robinson signed in a very practical hand. His signature lacks rapid motion and is accomplished in a slower hand. Reckless flow is lacking, which impairs the racing effect. There is even a slight hesitation in the very early signatures, those which were signed in the 1940s. The signature evidences a right slant. Sound letter

construction is evident. Robinson's signature is extremely legible. Display value is sound. Most signatures are signed as "Jackie Robinson." He would, on occasion, sign as "Jack Robinson." In the mid- to late 1950s Robinson's signature evolved in a measured way. His hand became more compact, resulting in a signature that is tighter. Hand speed increased. Material signed from this period until his death appears much cleaner and more flowing than early specimens. Robinson died at a relatively young age. A genuine signature will exhibit no shakiness of hand and one that does should be considered suspect and avoided.

Signature Population: Robinson's signature is in strong demand and outweighs supply. Robinson is an uncommon signature. On premium items his signature is scarce. Robinson's signature can be found on album pages, scorecards, and index cards. Signed photos are uncommon and 8 × 10 photos are scarce. Handwritten letters are rare. Typed letters signed are much more common. Robinson worked at Chock Full O' Nuts and many letters exist, usually with routine content. An excellent source of Robinson signatures is Brooklyn Dodgers signed team baseballs. Single-signed baseballs are scarce to rare. Most offered in the market are forgeries. Several years

Robinson, J. 1: 1951 signature

Robinson, J. 2: circa 1960s signature

Robinson, J. 3: undated signature

Robinson, J. 4: undated signature

ago the family released a good supply of canceled bank checks into the market. There is a small supply of President Richard Nixon related material that Robinson had signed. In 1960, Robinson supported Nixon for president. Every once in a while a signature will surface where Robinson adds the inscription "Vote for Nixon." Robinson-signed Nixon material is rare and is highly treasured by both baseball and presidential collectors alike.

Known Forgeries: Due to the lack of rapid motion, Robinson signatures accomplished in the 1940s and early 1950s are relatively easy to forge. Many well executed forgeries exist. The modern signature is much more difficult to replicate, though a few skilled forgers have mastered his signature. One common forgery that has entered the market in the past few years exhibits a signature that is very sloppy with a good degree of choppiness. The legibility is impaired. The forgeries deviate greatly from a genuine Robinson signature. I have seen this forgery on many items, especially on colored index cards. The forger tries to enhance the authenticity of his work by adding spurious collector's notations on the back, such as where and when the signature was supposedly obtained.

Sales: Bank check sold for $650 (RR Auctions, June 2011). Signed book sold for $1,763 (Robert Edward Auctions, Spring 2009). 1952 TLS sold for $1,812 (Lelands.com, November 2010). Index card sold for $500 (Hunt Auctions, November 2010). Single-signed baseball, superior specimen, sold for $14,400 (Mastro, December 2008).

Wilbert Robinson

Signature Study: Robinson signed in a very rudimentary hand. His signature is slow. Recklessness of hand is lacking. His hand is marked by slightly labored lines. The racing effect is basically non-existent. Letter construction is fairly sound. The signature is legible. The display value is marginal at best. About the only signatures available are those accomplished after 1920. Robinson's hand, which was not too great to begin with, became increasingly unsteady in the mid– to late 1920s. Overall, this is a simple signature with limited appeal.

Signature Population: This is a signature where the small supply is clearly outweighed by demand. Robinson is a rare signature on a per se basis, albeit borderline. His signature is generally limited to signed documents and the occasional album page. Being a member of management for the Brooklyn Dodgers, Robinson signed many letters, contracts, and other team-related documents. A few survive today and are an excellent source of Robinson signatures. Other mediums are rare to non-existent. Government postcards are very rare. I have only examined two in my life. Both were signed across the top, just under the edge of the card. I have never seen a genuinely signed 8 × 10 photo, baseball card, full-page autographed letter signed, or single-signed baseball. Signed baseballs of any kind are rare, but there are handful of Brooklyn team baseballs from the mid–1920s where Robinson signed as manager.

Known Forgeries: Given the slower nature of Robinson's hand, his signature is very easy to replicate. Well executed forgeries exist in quantities. Many forgeries exist on old scorecards, album pages, and the like. One needs to examine his signature carefully as there are many convincing forgeries.

Sales: 1930 Major League contract, signed as

Robinson, W. 1: TLS dated 1922 (courtesy National Baseball Hall of Fame and Museum)

Robinson, W. 2: TLS dated 1927

Robinson, W. 3: signed document circa 1930

president of the club, sold for $7,569 (Lelands.com, November 2010). 1930 TLS sold for $3,020 (Lelands.com, June 2011). 1929 Major League contract, signed as president of the club, counter-signed by Val Picinich, sold for $1,500 (Hunt Auctions, February 2010).

Wilber "Bullet" Rogan

Signature Study: Rogan's signature is the center of much debate. Many different examples, of various construction, exist in the market. There is one signature that is generally accepted as genuine, which was signed on a real estate document from the 1960s. This signature is illustrated as Rogan 1. The hand is rudimentary. The signature is accomplished in a slower hand. Letter construction is sound. I have not been able to determine whether infirmity of hand existed later in life.

Rogan 1: signed document dated 1960 accepted as genuine

Signature Population: Rogan is an extremely rare signature. The population of genuine signatures may be only a few. I know of no letters, photos, baseballs, or bank checks. I know of no signatures signed with his nickname "Bullet." This is an extreme rarity among Hall of Fame signatures.

Known Forgeries: It is clear that Rogan's signature is very easy to replicate. Creating a well executed forgery would not be a difficult task. There are many Rogan forgeries in the market. They are generally found on album pages and as signatures removed from postal covers. These are typically signed as "Wilber Rogan, RR 2 Duncan Point, Edwards, Mo."

Sales: Due to the rarity, there have been no recent sales of Rogan's signature.

Edd Roush

Signature Study: Roush signed in a very odd and eclectic hand. His signature is very reckless in appearance. No hesitation is evident. The signature is choppy yet flowing. It is one of the strangest of all Hall of Fame signatures. There is a certain geometric appearance noted. There are many breaks in the first name. The first name is basically printed. Just about all signatures are penned as "Edd J. Roush." As Roush aged his signature went through a marked change. The signature becomes very uniformed. The hand slowed greatly. The signature appears methodic and more labored. Roush's hand remained labored until his death but did not really deteriorate. Material signed towards the end of his life evidences a labored appearance but shakiness of hand is limited. Overall, this is a nice Hall of Fame signature.

Signature Population: This is a signature of sound demand slightly outweighed by supply. Roush was a willing and gracious signer throughout his long life. The population of Roush material is strong. His signature is commonly found on index cards, photos, Hall of Fame plaque postcards, 1961 Fleer cards, and Perez-Steele cards. Single-signed baseballs are uncommon. Signed bats are fairly scarce. Letters of any kind should be considered scarce and are highly desirable. There is a good supply of canceled bank checks in the market.

Known Forgeries: Despite the breaks in the first name, his signature is difficult to forge. Creating a well executed forgery would be a task. Modern signatures, with the labored appearance, are much easier to replicate. Many forged baseballs exist, so caution is warranted.

Sales: Roush's signature is available. His autograph generally sells for under $100 on most mediums.

Roush 1: TLS dated 1920

Roush 2: 1985 signature

Red Ruffing

Signature Study: Ruffing signed in a strikingly bold and clean hand. His signature is marked with powerful lines. A nice flow is evident. The signature is dominated by large capital letters. Letter construction is sound. Ruffing's signature is very legible. Display value is sound. Vintage signatures are typically signed with his first name and not the nickname. As Ruffing aged his hand changed markedly. The signature is less flamboyant. Modern signatures are much smaller. The flowing nature is replaced with a more conservative and pensive hand. The hand lacks the reckless appearance of a vintage signature. Legibility and display value remain high. Modern signatures are almost always signed as "Red Ruffing." Ruffing's hand deteriorated slightly in the last few years of his life, hence signatures will evidence a slight hesitation of hand but not true shakiness.

Signature Population: This is a signature where demand is balanced with supply. The population of Ruffing material is sound but not overwhelming. He died just before the era of mass signings. In addition, Ruffing was a highly erratic signer in the mail. The majority of mail requests for his autograph went unanswered. Ruffing's signature is generally found on index cards, Hall of Fame plaque postcards, photos, and Fleer cards. Less common are 8 × 10 photos and single-signed baseballs. Letters of any kind are scarce. Signed bats are scarce.

Known Forgeries: Due to the complex nature of Ruffing's hand, well executed forgeries are nonexistent, at least when it comes to vintage specimens. Modern signatures are much easier to forge. Many well executed forgeries exist. Due to the

nominal value of Ruffing's signature, he is generally not the target of skilled forgers. However, premium items such as single-signed baseballs are the exception. Most Ruffing-signed baseballs are forgeries. A common forged card is the Donruss Hall of Fame Heroes card issued in 1983. This card is tough to locate signed and the majority of these cards are forged.

Sales: Ruffing's signature is available. His autograph generally sells for under $100 on most mediums.

Amos Rusie

Signature Study: Rusie signed in a very practical hand that lacks any sort of flair. His signature is accomplished in a slower hand. Reckless flow is lacking. The signature evidences a very slight choppiness. Trivial hesitation is evident. Letter construction is sound. The signature is very legible. Display value is impaired due to the simple nature of the hand. It is unclear whether infirmity of hand existed. Overall, this is one of the less appealing Hall of Fame signatures.

Signature Population: Rusie is a very rare signature. I estimate the population somewhere between 10 to 20 genuine specimens. His signature is generally limited to the occasional signed document or cut therefrom. There are a couple of genuine index cards. I am told that an authentic government postcard exists, though I have never seen it. I have never examined a genuinely signed baseball, letter, or photo of any kind.

Known Forgeries: Due to the slower nature of the hand, Rusie's signature is easy to replicate. Well executed forgeries exist in quantities. His signature has been forged on just about all mediums including fake government postcards complete with postmarks. One forger has created some single signed baseballs all with the same modus operandi. The balls are heavily toned a deep rustic brown. An amateurish forgery is placed on the side panel or sweet spot. A small obituary or box score of Rusie, removed from a newspaper, is glued onto the ball. These balls are exposed as obvious forgeries with little examination.

Ruffing 1: circa 1930s signature

Ruffing 2: undated signature

Rusie 1: signed document undated

Rusie 2: circa 1930s index card

Sales: Due to the rarity, there have been no recent sales of Rusie's signature.

Babe Ruth

Signature Study: Ruth's signature is one of the most studied of all Hall of Famers. Ruth signed in a powerful and bold hand. His signature evidences very strong flow and thick effortless strokes. The signature evidences no hesitation whatsoever. Material signed in the early 1920s tends to be a bit smaller and less dominant than later specimens. Early examples tend to be ever so slightly choppy. They are sometimes mistaken for clubhouse signatures. His signature has one of the finest construction of letters of any of the Hall of Famers. The signature is legible. Ruth's signature also has superior display value. The large capital letters in the first and last name further enhance eye appeal. During the 1920s Ruth would signed with quotes around the first name, a habit he would drop in later years. Ruth's hand remained fairly constant, though the signature becomes larger and more powerful looking. It would remain this way until the closing days of his life. Throughout the 1930s and 1940s his hand evidences no measurable change. In late 1947, Ruth's health began a steady decline when he was diagnosed with cancer. Despite this, Ruth's hand remained strong his entire life. Signatures accomplished in the closing days of his life still evidence good flow. The overall size of the signature decreased. A genuine signature will evidence no shakiness of hand and one that does should be considered suspect and avoided.

Signature Population: This is a signature of the highest demand. Only Cobb has comparable demand. Though Ruth has been dead for more than 60 years, the supply of genuine material is sound. His signature is most commonly found on album pages, scorecards, baseballs, and other ma-

Ruth 2: album page dated 1927

terial that could have been signed at the ballpark. 8 × 10 photos are also available but less common. Typed letters signed are scarce. Full-page handwritten letters are rare and highly treasured. Ruth signed many baseball bats but only a scarce few survive to this day. Signed bats are an extreme rarity. Signed Goudey gum cards are rare. Hall of Fame plaque postcards are extremely rare. I have seen one genuine specimen. While signed bank deposit slips are rare, canceled bank checks are not. Many exist and are signed as "G.H. Ruth." There is a variant form of check in the market that is signed by both Ruth and his wife Claire. They are known as trustee checks, which were signed in the last few months of Ruth's life. This form of check is very rare and highly treasured as Ruth signed his name as "George Herman Ruth." I have only seen half a dozen of these checks in my life. Ruth was one of the few players asked to sign bizarre items. Softballs, bowling pins, cricket bats, and at least one shoe for broadcaster Ernie Harwell were signed. Material signed in combination with fellow Hall of Famer Lou Gehrig is rare and highly treasured. Material signed with fellow immortal Ty Cobb is even more rare and more treasured.

Known Forgeries: Though his hand is flowing, it lacks complexity. Replication of his hand is fairly easy. Well executed forgeries exist in mass quantities. Ruth forgeries cover a broad spectrum, with most falling in the amateurish category. While most are rudimentary, there are some fabulous forgeries in the market that fool most experts. Just about all of the museum-grade single-signed Ruth baseballs that sell for $40,000 and up are well executed forgeries. One forger has created some very convincing forgeries with baseballs and 8 × 10 photographs his favorite target. The famous image of Ruth swinging and facing

Ruth 1: team sheet dated 1922

Ruth 3: 1930 signature

Ruth 4: album page dated 1933

Ruth 5: government postcard dated 1936

directly into the camera is one of his favorites. He signs the forgery as "Sincerely, Babe Ruth" across the chest. He has Ruth's hand almost down to the fine points. Letter construction is very good but unlike a true master forger, he does not have the right speed. The forgeries are clean but methodic. The hand does not evidence a shakiness nor does it have the fast bouncy feel of a genuine Ruth. The lines are uniform and lack variant pressure. He has gone so far as to create a forged 8 × 10 photo inscribed to movie star Gary Cooper. Overall, these forgeries are very nice but they look too perfect.

There is a fairly good test to determine if that museum-grade Ruth-signed baseball or photo is genuine or not. It is not full proof but it is accurate most of the time. Because the forgeries are signed in a methodic way, the signature lacks the nice up and down bouncy strokes of a genuine Ruth. If you examine the bottom of the last name, the forgeries will exhibit a leveled appearance. They look written on a straight line. See Ruth 10 for an illustration. Note the forgery is uniform. Compare it with a genuine signature, note the

Ruth 6: bank check dated 1937

Ruth 7: government postcard dated 1938

Ruth 8: common secretarial

Ruth 9: common secretarial

Ruth 10: forgery, leveled appearance

variations in height and the nice flowing strokes with variant thickness.

One forgery that has been circulating in the market for many years are 1939 Baseball Centennial postal covers. Some are postmarked, some are not. This forger signs Ruth's name along with his address across the front of the cover, as "Babe Ruth, 173 Riverside Drive, New York City, N.Y." in fountain pen. The forgeries are fairly decent but evidence a slightly labored appearance. The racing effect is greatly impaired. Another very well executed forgery can be found on Hotel Astor–Mayor's Naval Committee ballroom tickets. Ruth forgeries are on the reverse of the tickets. I have seen a few of them signed in blue and black fountain pen. Again, very nice forgeries but too precise and too mechanical to be genuine. For years postcard-sized pictures with the famous Ruth batting pose have been circulating. They contain an odd looking signature. They are dated 1948. The explanation forwarded for this malformed looking signature is that Ruth was in ill health. These photos are secretarially signed and should be avoided in total.

Sales: 6 × 8 portrait photo, superior specimen, sold for $4,506 (RR Auctions, August 2011). Trustee bank check sold for $15,037 (RR Auctions, February 2011). Bank check sold for $3,250 (Hunt Auctions, July 2011). Single-signed baseball sold for $7,260 (Hunt Auctions, November 2010). Single-signed baseball sold for $10,025 (Mastro, December 2007). Oversized photo, action shot, choice specimen, sold for $29,586 (Mastro, December 2006). Signed 8 × 10 portrait photo sold for $5,453 (RR Auctions, June 2011). Choice ink signature sold for $3,200 (eBay, December 2011).

Nolan Ryan

Signature Study: Ryan signs in a very flowing hand. His signature evidences reckless flow. The signature dominates the medium it is placed upon. Letter construction is poor. Legibility is impaired. The signature does retain good display value. As of 2012 his hand remains sound. A genuine signature will exhibit no shakiness of hand and one that does should be considered suspect and avoided.

Signature Population: This is simply a common signature where demand is outweighed by supply. His signature can be found on most mediums from gum cards to baseballs to photos. Signed letters of any kind are scarce.

Known Forgeries: Due to the impaired letter construction and lack of precise lines, his signature would be rather easy to replicate. Due to the nominal value of Ryan's signature, he is not the target of skilled forgers.

Sales: Ryan's signature is available. His autograph generally sells for under $100 on most mediums.

Ryne Sandberg

Signature Study: Sandberg signs in a rapid hand. His signature is accomplished with indistinguishable strokes. The signature lacks legibility.

Ryan 1: 1991 signature

Display value is marginal. It is one of the poorer Hall of Fame signatures. As of 2012 Sandberg's hand remains strong. A genuine signature will exhibit no shakiness of hand and one that does should be considered suspect and avoided.

Sandberg 1: circa 1995 signature

Signature Population: This is a signature where supply clearly outweighs demand. Sandberg is a very common signature that can be found on most mediums. There is a good supply of signed copies of his book *Second to Home* in the market. Letters of any kind are scarce.

Known Forgeries: His signature would be fairly difficult to replicate. Due to the nominal value of Sandberg's signature, he is generally not the target of skilled forgers.

Sales: Sandberg's signature is available. His autograph generally sells for under $100 on most mediums.

Ron Santo

Signature Study: Santo signed in a fairly aggressive hand. His signature lacks hesitation. Letter construction is marginal. Legibility is slightly compromised. The "R" is distinctive in an otherwise average signature. Santo's hand remained strong his entire life. A genuine signature will evidence no shakiness of hand and one that does should be considered suspect and avoided.

Signature Population: This is a signature of marginal demand that is outweighed by a strong supply. Santo's signature can be found on most mediums including gum cards, photos, bats, balls, and the like. TLsS are scarce. ALsS are rare. The

Santo 1: 2004 signature

famous photo of Santo in the on-deck circle with a black cat walking by him is always in high demand by collectors.

Known Forgeries: Santo's signature has loose structure. Producing a well executed forgery can be done with little effort. Due to the nominal value of Santo's signature, he is not the target of skilled forgers.

Sales: Santo's signature is available. His autograph generally sells for under $100 on most mediums.

Louis Santop

Signature Study: Santop signs in a practical hand. Letter construction is sound. The signature is legible. Reckless flow is lacking. Because of the reserved nature of Santop's hand, the display value is impaired. The racing effect is muted. It is unknown whether infirmity of hand existed.

Santop 1: World War I draft card circa 1917 (Record Group 163, Records of the Selective Services Division, National Archives at Atlanta)

Santop 2: circa late 1930s signature

Signature Population: Santop is an extremely rare signature. It is safe to say less than five genuine examples exist in the market. I have never seen one offered for sale. His World War I draft registration card is held by the National Archives.

Known Forgeries: Many forgeries exist that all vary in construction. They are typically penned on scorecards and album pages.

Sales: Due to the rarity, there have been no recent sales of Santop's signature.

Ray Schalk

Signature Study: Schalk signed in a very practical hand that is just average in nature. His signature changed very little throughout the years.

The signature is signed in a confined hand. It lacks reckless flow. Schalk's signature has strong letter construction. The signature is very legible. The plain nature of Schalk's hand creates a signature with limited display value. Most signatures are penned as "Ray Schalk." On occasion he would sign his autograph with his nickname "Cracker" but this form of signature is uncommon. Schalk's hand, which was never very fast to begin with, slowed ever so slightly in the last years of his life. Signatures accomplished in the 1960s until his death appear slightly more methodic. While the hand appears slower, a genuine Schalk signature will evidence no measurable shakiness of hand and one that does should be considered suspect and avoided.

Signature Population: This is a signature where demand and supply are well balanced. Schalk was a willing signer throughout his life. The supply of genuine material is strong, though limited to items signed through the mail. His signature is common on index cards, picture postcards, government postcards, and Hall of Fame plaque postcards. 8 × 10 photos are scarce. Letters are limited to short writings penned on postcards and the like. A full-page handwritten letter is rare. Single-signed baseballs are rare and most in the market are forgeries. Signed team balls are generally limited to post–1920s teams.

Known Forgeries: A Schalk signature from any era is relatively easy to replicate. Producing a well executed forgery can be done with little effort. Schalk forgeries are generally limited to premium items such as baseballs. Schalk was a member of the infamous 1919 Chicago Black Sox. I have seen many signed team balls of the 1919 and 1920 White Sox teams that include Schalk, Eddie

Schalk 1 album page circa 1930s

Schalk 2: undated signature

Collins, Dickie Kerr, and the rest. I have never seen a genuinely signed ball from either year. It is very doubtful that a team ball for either team exists. One forger has created a couple of 1919 team balls. He places a forgery of manager Kid Gleason on the sweet spot. Hap Felsch's signature is in printed script. All signatures appear labored.

Sales: Hall of Fame plaque postcard sold for $180 (RR Auctions, January 2011). Index card sold for $44 (eBay, September 2011). Index card sold for $100 (RR Auctions, February 2010). Hall of Fame plaque postcard sold for $248 (RR Auctions, August 2011). Hall of Fame plaque postcard sold for $245 (eBay, January 2012).

Mike Schmidt

Signature Study: Schmidt signs in a very pleasing and flowing hand. His signature is artistic in nature. Letter construction is poor, resulting in a signature with impaired legibility. The display value is nice due to the whimsical nature of the hand. As of 2012 Schmidt's hand remains strong. A genuine signature will exhibit no shakiness of hand and one that does should be considered suspect and avoided.

Signature Population: A signature where supply clearly outweighs demand. Schmidt is a very common signature that can be found on most mediums including gum cards, photos, bats, and balls. Typed letters signed are uncommon. Handwritten letters are scarce.

Known Forgeries: Schmidt's signature is difficult to replicate. Well executed forgeries do not exist. Due to the nominal value of Schmidt's signature, he is generally not the target of skilled forgers. Forgeries are generally limited to 500-home-run-club items.

Sales: Schmidt's signature is available. His autograph generally sells for under $100 on most mediums.

Schmidt 1: undated signature

Red Schoendienst

Signature Study: Schoendienst signs in a powerful and aggressive hand. His signature is marked with thick bold lines. No hesitation of hand is evident. Letter construction is sound but tends to appear a bit sloppy. The signature has average display value. As of 2012 Schoendienst's hand remains fairly strong but hesitation of hand does exist. Signatures accomplished over the previous year or so will exhibit some shakiness of hand.

Schoendienst 1: circa 1955 signature

Schoendienst 2: circa 1985 signature

Signature Population: This is a signature of marginal demand that is outweighed by supply. Schoendienst is a very common signature. His signature can be found on most mediums including gum cards, baseballs, bats, photos, jerseys, and the like. Signed letters of any kind are scarce.

Known Forgeries: Replication of hand would be rather difficult. Creating a well executed forgery would be hard. Due to the nominal value of Schoendienst's signature, he is generally not the target of skilled forgers.

Sales: Schoendienst's signature is available. His autograph generally sells for under $100 on most mediums.

Tom Seaver

Signature Study: Seaver signs in a very flowing and aggressive hand. His signature is marked with fast lines. Hesitation is non-existent. Letter construction is substandard. It is basically an illegible signature. Display value is average. As of 2012 Seaver's hand remains strong. A genuine signature will exhibit no shakiness of hand and one that does should be considered suspect and avoided.

Signature Population: This is a very common autograph where supply outweighs demand. Seaver's signature can be found on most mediums

Seaver 1: circa 1990 signature

including gum cards, baseballs, bats, photos, jerseys, and the like. Signed letters of any kind are scarce.

Known Forgeries: Since letter construction is poor, replication of hand would be fairly easy. Due to the nominal value of Seaver's signature, he is generally not the target of skilled forgers.

Sales: Seaver's signature is available. His autograph generally sells for under $100 on most mediums.

Frank Selee

Signature Study: Selee signs in a very unique and distinctive hand. The signature is marked with choppiness. Multiple break in the strokes are noted. Letter construction is sound. The signature has a good degree of legibility. The choppiness of hand impairs display value. It is unknown whether infirmity of hand affected his writing.

Signature Population: The total population of Selee signatures is likely under five specimens. The illustrated letter is housed at the National Baseball Hall of Fame. The signature from 1895 is only one of two specimens I know of in the open market.

Known Forgeries: Given the slower nature of Selee's signature, replication of hand would only

Selee 1: ledger page circa 1895

Selee 2: ALS circa 1900 (courtesy National Baseball Hall of Fame and Museum)

be a small challenge. Creating a well executed forgery should prove fairly easy. Just about all of the Selee signatures in the market are forged.

Sales: Due to the rarity, there have been no recent sales of Selee's signature.

Joe Sewell

Signature Study: Sewell signed in a very refined and pleasing hand. His signature evidences wonderful flow. Hesitation is non-existent. Letter construction is superior. Individual letters are well defined, resulting in a signature that is very legible. The display value of Sewell's signature is high. His signature varies little throughout the years. Vintage examples tend to exhibit a softer capital "S" and are usually signed in a larger scale. As the years progressed his signature decreased in size. Sewell's hand remained strong his entire life. A genuine signature will exhibit no shakiness of hand and one that does should be considered suspect and avoided. Overall, this is one of the finer Hall of Fame signatures.

Signature Population: This is a signature of average demand that is clearly outweighed by supply. Sewell was a very accommodating signer throughout his life. His signature can be found on most mediums. Signed letters are uncommon and typically limited to ALsS. Sewell loved to write about baseball and many good content letters exist. Sewell letters are a good source of information from the Ruthian era of ball. Sewell wrote with a cutting pen and was opinionated. He has been known to write letters about Hank Aaron's pursuit of Ruth's home run record. Sewell would write how black pitchers eased up on Aaron to allow him to pass the Babe. Letters with such content are highly valued from both a collection and research standpoint. There is also a good supply of signed bank checks in the market. Signed baseballs are uncommon but there is still a decent supply. Anything signed with his brother Luke Sewell should be considered scarce.

Known Forgeries: Due to the precision of Sewell's hand, his signature is difficult to replicate. Creating a well executed forgery would be a hard

Sewell 1: ALS dated 1988

task. Due to the nominal value of Sewell's signature, he is generally not the target of skilled forgers. Well executed forgeries are generally limited to forged Yankees team balls of the early 1930s.

Sales: Sewell's signature is available. His autograph generally sells for under $100 on most mediums.

Al Simmons

Signature Study: Simmons signed in a flowing and uniformed hand. His signature evidences good flow. Hesitation of hand is not evident. Letter construction is marginal at best. Legibility is impaired. The "immon" in the last name appears as letters morphed together. His signature changed little throughout the years. He does have a habit of utilizing variant forms of the capital letter "S" in the last name. Of note, Simmons used a hurried form of signature that he would pen at the ballparks. Simmons 2 illustrates this variant signature. This form of signature is reckless in appearance and extremely illegible. Overall, Simmons' signature has nice display value and is sought after by collectors. Simmons died suddenly of a heart attack. A genuine signature will exhibit no shakiness of hand and one that does should be considered suspect and avoided.

Signature Population: There is very good demand for Simmons material. The supply is lim-

Simmons 1: 1932 signature

Simmons 2: 1942 hurried signature

Simmons 3: bank check circa 1950s

Simmons 4: undated signature

Simmons 5: common forgery

ited. His signature is generally found on mediums signed at the ballpark. Album pages and scorecards are good sources for his signature. Signed team balls are also available and are the best way to obtain his signature on a ball. Single-signed baseballs are considered rare to very rare. I have seen only a few genuine examples. Letters are rare in any form. Hall of Fame plaque postcards are very rare. There is a small supply of canceled bank checks in the market.

Known Forgeries: Due to the lack of sound letter construction, Simmons' signature is fairly easy to replicate. Well executed forgeries exist in the market. Simmons forgeries are common and found on most mediums especially Artvue Hall of Fame plaque postcards, Goudey cards, and baseballs. Forged Hall of Fame plaque postcards exist in quantities. They exhibit a labored signature with a large and elongated capital "S" in the last name. The forgeries are rudimentary at best (see Simmons 5).

Sales: Bank check sold for $321 (RR Auctions, July 2011). Single-signed baseball sold for $2,232 (Robert Edward Auctions, Spring 2008). 1948 government postcard sold for $429 (RR Auctions, April 2011). Ink signature sold for $198 (RR Auctions, August 2011). 1932 signed postal cover sold for $393 (RR Auctions, March 2011).

George Sisler

Signature Study: Sisler signed in a very unattractive hand. His signature is marked with abruptness and jagged lines. The signature is basically vertical in nature. While no hesitation is evident, neither is there effortless flow. The choppiness of the hand impairs legibility. Display value is limited. Letter construction is just average. Vintage signatures are more appealing, evidencing faster flow. The jagged edges are smoother and muted. Vintage signatures have sound display

Sisler 1: 1922 signature

Sisler 2: bank check dated 1955

value. Sisler's hand remained strong his entire life. A genuine signature will exhibit no shakiness of hand and one that does should be considered suspect and avoided. Overall, this is one of the less appealing Hall of Fame signatures.

Signature Population: This is a signature of strong demand and limited supply. Sisler signatures are generally found on index cards, government postcards, and Hall of Fame plaque postcards. Gum cards from his playing days and 8 × 10 photos are scarce. Typed letters signed are scarce. Autographed letters signed are rare, albeit borderline. Single-signed baseballs are rare and highly desirable. Team balls from his playing days exist, though limited to post–1920 teams. There is a small supply of canceled bank checks in the market. In recent years checks have become very difficult to locate. At least one bank check exists written out to and endorsed on back by Football Hall of Famer Don Faurot.

Known Forgeries: Due to the choppiness of hand, Sisler's signature is easy to replicate. Well executed forgeries are common. The vintage signature is much more difficult to replicate, therefore forgers avoid earlier Sisler signatures. There are many forged single-signed baseballs in the market including many with inscriptions. These are accomplished by one forger. The forger places the signature on the sweet spot. He adds the inscription either "to my friend John Doe from" or "to my good friend John Doe from" on the side panel of the ball just above the sweet spot. This forger has used American League baseballs from all eras from E. S. Barnard to Joe Cronin.

Sales: 8 × 10 portrait photo sold for $297 (RR

Sisler 3: circa 1965 signature

Auctions, February 2011). Hall of Fame plaque postcard sold for $152 (eBay, September 2011). Exhibit card sold for $110 (RR Auctions, July 2011). Short ALS sold for $110 (RR Auctions, June 2010). TLS, with baseball content, sold for $477 (RR Auctions, March 2007).

Enos Slaughter

Signature Study: Slaughter signed in a very nonconforming and sloppy hand. The signature has good flow. Hesitation is lacking. Letter construction is marginal at best. Legibility is impaired. The signature is of limited display value. Most signatures are accomplished as "Enos Slaughter." On request he would sign autographs with his nickname "Country." This form of signature is uncommon. Slaughter's hand remained strong his entire life. A genuine signature will exhibit no shakiness of hand and one that does should be considered suspect and avoided.

Slaughter 1: 1992 signature

Signature Population: This is a signature of average demand that is outweighed by supply. Slaughter was one of the most gracious of signers. His signature is very common and can be found on most mediums including baseballs, bank checks, photos, bats, and the like. Signed letters of any kind are uncommon.

Known Forgeries: The reckless and flowing nature of Slaughter's hand makes replication difficult. Creating a well executed forgery would be hard. Due to the nominal value of Slaughter's signature, he is generally not the target of skilled forgers.

Sales: Slaughter's signature is available. His autograph generally sells for under $100 on most mediums.

Hilton Smith

Signature Study: Smith signed in a practical hand. His signature is marked with a nice right slant and cutting angles. The signature has choppiness which impairs flow. Letter construction is moderately sound. The signature has good legibility. In the last few years of Smith's life his hand slowed. The signature becomes more muted in appearance. The letters are more uniform in size. The entire signature evidences a slightly labored appearance. Smith had the habit of crossing the letter "t" at the very top of the letter. He did this on many occasions but not always. Smith's hand never produced a truly shaky signature. Much of his written correspondence contains spelling errors.

Signature Population: There is sound demand for Smith material. The supply is very limited. Smith is a scarce signature per se and mostly found on index cards. On any other medium his signature should be considered rare to very rare. I have never seen a genuinely signed 8 × 10 photo. A few smaller signed photos do exist. I have never seen a full-page handwritten letter. He was known to pen many short notes, usually listing facts about his career. Single-signed baseballs do exist but are rare to very rare. His signature is more common on multi-signed baseballs but these to should be considered rare. Signatures accomplished during his days in the Negro Leagues are very rare.

Known Forgeries: Due to the slower nature of his hand, Smith's signature is fairly easy to replicate. Well executed forgeries exist, so caution is warranted. Most Smith signatures offered for sale are forgeries. Forgeries can be found on album pages, index cards, baseballs, and the like. Proceed with caution.

Sales: Signed ball, with other Negro League players, sold for $646 (Lelands.com, May 2008). Index card sold for $294 (RR Auctions, January 2010). Government postcard sold for $475 (Hunt Auctions, November 2010). Index card sold for

Smith, H. 1: circa 1970s signature

Smith, H. 2: circa 1980 signature

Smith, H. 3: undated signature

$250 (Hunt Auctions, November 2010). Index card sold for $324 (RR Auctions, September 2009).

Ozzie Smith

Signature Study: Smith signs in a confined and neat hand. His signature evidences good flow and effortless lines. Letter construction is sound. The signature is, for the most part, legible. Display value is average. As of 2012 Smith's hand remains sound. A genuine signature will exhibit no shakiness of hand and one that does should be considered suspect and avoided.

Smith, O. 1: undated signature

Signature Population: Supply clearly outweighs demand. Smith is an extremely common signature. He engages in mass signings. His signature can be found on most mediums including gum cards, photos, balls, bats, and the like. Letters of any kind should be considered scarce.

Known Forgeries: Smith's hand would be fairly easy to replicate. Creating a well executed forgery can be done with little effort. Due to the nominal value of Smith's signature, he is generally not the target of skilled forgers.

Sales: Smith's signature is available. His autograph generally sells for under $100 on most mediums.

Duke Snider

Signature Study: Snider signed in a very distinctive hand. Early signatures tend to be very plain looking and are vertical in nature. Letter construction is sound. The legibility is high. Early signatures are accomplished in a slower hand. As the years progressed Snider's hand evolved. The hand speed increased. The signature also develops an uncommon left slant. Letter construction becomes obscured, which impairs legibility. His signature does have nice display value. On rare oc-

Snider 1: government postcard dated 1949

Snider 2: 1990 signature

casion, Snider was known to sign on a bifurcated plane. Snider's hand remained strong his entire life. A genuine signature will exhibit no measurable shakiness of hand and one that does should be considered suspect and avoided.

Signature Population: This is a signature of sound demand but outweighed by a large supply. Snider had been a willing and gracious signer throughout the years. His signature can be found on most mediums including gum cards, photos, bats, baseballs, jerseys, Perez-Steele cards, and the like. Letters of any kind should be considered scarce.

Known Forgeries: Given the slower nature of the hand, Snider's signature is easy to replicate. Producing a well executed forgery can be done with little effort. Due to the nominal value of Snider's signature, he is generally not the target of skilled forgers.

Sales: Snider's signature is available. His autograph generally sells for under $100 on most mediums.

Billy Southworth

Signature Study: Southworth signed in a very nonconforming and artistic hand. His signature is marked with good flow. The signature has wonderful letter construction. Legibility is high. His signature evidences a right slant. Display value is superior. One of the finer Hall of Fame signatures. As Southworth aged he signed in a slower, more poignant, hand. The hand still flows nicely. Southworth's hand remained strong his entire life. A genuine signature will exhibit no measurable shakiness of hand and one that does should be considered suspect and avoided.

Southworth 1: bank check dated 1942

Southworth 2: 1962 signature

Signature Population: This is a signature of limited demand and supply. Southworth's signature is found on index cards and government postcards. 8 × 10 photos, letters, and single-signed baseballs should be considered rare. Signed teams balls from his days as a manager are a good source of Southworth autographs. There is a good supply of bank checks in the market.

Known Forgeries: Given the slower nature of Southworth's hand, his signature should be easy to replicate. Forgeries exist mostly on baseballs and photos.

Sales: Short ALS sold for $823 (Robert Edward Auctions, Spring 2010). 8 × 10 photo, superior specimen, sold for $3,250 (Hunt Auctions, February 2010). 8 × 10 photo, also signed by Frank Frisch, sold for $500 (Hunt Auctions, February 2010). 4 × 5 newspaper picture sold for $200 (RR Auctions, December 2008). Signature removed from a check sold for $93 (eBay, December 2011).

Warren Spahn

Signature Study: Spahn signed in a powerful and reckless hand. His signature is vertical in nature with strong flowing lines. There is no evidence of hesitation. Letter construction is marginal. Some letters appear as indistinguishable strokes. Legibility is average, but the signature does have good display value. Spahn's hand remained strong for most of his life but in the last couple years his hand became infirmed. Signatures accomplished at this time evidence moderate to heavy shakiness of hand.

Signature Population: This is a common signature where demand is outweighed by supply. Spahn was a willing and gracious signer throughout his long life. Spahn's signature can be found on index cards, gum cards, bats, baseballs, photos,

Spahn 1: album page dated 1946

Spahn 2: 1986 signature

Perez-Steele cards, and the like. Letters of any kind are scarce. There is a small grouping of signed bank checks in the market. These checks are typically from the 1950s and signed "Warren Edward Spahn." Anything signed with fellow Braves pitcher Johnny Sain is uncommon and highly desired.

Known Forgeries: Due to the rapid nature of Spahn's signature, replication of his hand is difficult for non-infirmed signatures. Creating a well executed forgery would take effort. Due to the nominal value of Spahn's signature, he is generally not the target of skilled forgers.

Sales: Spahn's signature is available. His autograph generally sells for under $100 on most mediums.

Albert Spalding

Signature Study: Spalding signed in a very no-nonsense hand. The signature evidences good flow but is accomplished in a slower hand. Letter construction is very sound. The signature has good legibility. Spalding's signature has good eye appeal and displays well. In the last five or so years of his life his hand became infirmed, so the signature evidences a shaky appearance. Towards the end of his life his hand deteriorated. Signatures accomplished in the last year of his life evidence heavy unsteadiness.

Signature Population: Spalding is a rare signature per se and mostly limited to signed documents and letters. Both typed letters and handwritten letters are available. There is a very small grouping of Spalding letters written to fellow Hall of Famer Henry Chadwick, though title issues may exist with these letters. I have never seen a

Spalding 1: ALS dated 1885 (courtesy National Baseball Hall of Fame and Museum)

Spalding 2: TLS dated 1905 (courtesy A.G. Spalding Collection, Manuscripts and Archive Division, The New York Public Library, Astor, Lennox, and Tildon Foundations)

Spalding 3: TLS dated 1906

Spalding 4: circa 1915 signature

signed photograph or baseball. In 1911 Spalding published *America's National Game*, considered one of the most important books ever written on baseball. Fortunately, Spalding signed many copies of this book, usually, with fine inscriptions. These books are a fine source of Spalding signatures.

Known Forgeries: Due to the slower nature of his hand, Spalding's signature, from any era of his life, is easily replicated. Well executed forgeries exist in quantity, so caution is warranted. Most of the Spalding signatures in the market are forgeries. Forgeries have been placed on most mediums including baseballs, cabinet photos, album pages, and the like. Some typed letters signed on A.G. Spalding letterhead have a variant form of signature. The signature appears smaller than most Spalding signatures I have examined. The letters are more tightly compacted giving the signature a slightly squeezed look. These are secretarially signed and not signed by Spalding himself.

Sales: 1909 TLS, Abner Doubleday as father of baseball content, sold for $4,930 (Robert Edward Auctions, Spring 2006). Signed book sold for $1,854 (RR Auctions, May 2008). 1911 ANS sold for $3,210 (Lelands.com, November 2008).

Tris Speaker

Signature Study: Speaker signed in a very precise and mechanical hand. His signature is one of the oddest of all Hall of Famers. Early signatures exhibit good flow. Hesitation is lacking. The signature has nicely rounded corners. Letter construction is sound. A signature with good legibility. His signature changed throughout the years. By the 1940s the once flowing hand becomes slower and more methodic. Later signatures tend to look very choppy and less appealing than vintage specimens. The "p" in the last name evolves to the point that it becomes the most dominant feature of the signature. Consistency among more modern signatures is amazing. The deviation of hand is slight as if signatures almost look like carbon copies of each other. Speaker died at the age of 70 from a massive heart attack. His hand remained strong his entire life. A genuine signature will exhibit no shakiness of hand and one that does should be considered suspect and avoided.

Signature Population: This is a signature with strong demand that clearly outweighs a limited supply. Speaker material is limited but it should not be considered scarce, at least on a per se basis. Most Speaker signatures were obtained through the mail, hence index cards, government postcards, and picture postcards are the most common. Signed 8 × 10 photos and typed letters signed are scarce. Autographed letters signed and Hall of Fame plaque postcards are rare. Speaker's signature is available on team-signed baseballs, though limited to post–1920s teams. Single-signed baseballs are rare but a good number do exist. He is one of the easier names to obtain on a ball among the original 1939 Hall of Fame members. Signed gum cards are very rare. I have never seen a genuine signed T-card.

Known Forgeries: Early signatures, those signed in the 1920s, are difficult to replicate. Well executed forgeries of this form of signature are rare. Later signatures, with its slower construction, are rather easy to replicate. Well executed forgeries

exist in quantities. Philadelphia Athletics team baseballs purportedly signed by the 1928 team have surfaced in the past ten years. They are fairly well executed and upon first glance look genuine. The person forging these baseballs has a fair amount of skill. The Speaker and Cobb forgeries are well executed. Like most forged team balls, the signatures are evenly spaced from each other, giving the ball a neat and uniform look. While the Speaker and Cobb are well executed forgeries, the other signatures are less convincing. The Lefty Grove, typically but not always on the sweet spot, is the weakest of the forgeries. Mickey Cochrane and Jimmie Foxx are executed in an average fashion. Most are signed on American League balls. Some, but not all, are signed on William Harridge American League baseballs, which did not exist until the 1930s. Sometimes they are sold as Philadelphia A's "reunion" balls to overcome the inconsistency of being signed on a Harridge baseball. In recent years signed "dream" outfield items have surfaced, signed by what many consider the all-time dream outfield of Cobb, Ruth, and Speaker. This trio is commonly forged on album pages, balls, pictures, old tickets, and scorecards. I have seen only three genuinely signed Cobb, Ruth, Speaker combination items in over 30 years of looking. They are excessively rare.

Another forgery that has been circulating for years is a certain single-signed baseball. The forgeries are placed on the sweet spot. The balls appear artificially aged with soil. As baseballs age they develop nice tones. Depending on where and how they are stored the ball can be toned a light cream color or a dark brown. The hide develops a certain patina that only time can create. A telltale sign that a ball has been artificially aged can be seen in the hide. They don't appear evenly

Speaker 1: 1923 signature

Speaker 2: contract dated 1928

Speaker 3: album page dated 1937

Speaker 4: 1950 signature

Speaker 5: undated signature

toned. They appear dirty and grimy. It looks as if dirt or some other substance was rubbed into the leather. Baseballs aged with dirt will have what I call a "cracked" appearance. The ball will have thin dirty lines that run randomly on the surface of the ball. This is usually a sign that some foreign substance has been rubbed hard into the ball. The lines are actually the twine underneath the hide that ever so slightly ripple the surface. The substance collects in these elevated areas causing the lines. If you see these lines, examine the ball carefully as it is likely a forgery. The above referenced Speaker baseballs have this "cracking" effect. The forger basically obtained a bunch of baseballs from the past 30 years and simply rubbed them down. He then placed the Speaker forgery on the sweet spot. The forgeries are poorly executed with a slight labored appearance throughout. The first name is poorly constructed with a muted and malformed "r" in the first name. Speaker would dot his "i" with a little circle. The circle on the forgeries are lopsided and look almost like a little heart above the signature. Overall, this is a rudimentary forgery but I see many of these baseballs offered for sale.

Sales: Exhibit card sold for $357 (RR Auctions, July 2011). Single-signed baseball, choice specimen, sold for $4,993 (Robert Edward Auctions, Spring 2008). 1951 government postcard sold for $416 (eBay, September 2011). 1952 TLS to Connie Mack sold for $508 (Legendary Auctions, March 2011). Team-issued picture postcard sold for $474 (Legendary Auctions, August 2010). Album page sold for $256 (eBay, December 2011).

Willie Stargell

Signature Study: Stargell signed in a very unique and non-conforming hand. His signature evidences a noticeable back slant. Breaks in the signature are noted. Letter construction is marginal at best. The signature is on the illegible side. Overall, this is a signature with limited display value. Stargell died of a stroke at the age of 61. Since he never reached old age, infirmity of hand was non-existent. A genuine Stargell signature will

Stargell 1: 1988 signature

exhibit no shakiness of hand and one that does should be considered suspect and avoided.

Signature Population: This is a common signature where demand is far outweighed by supply. His signature can be found on most mediums including index cards, photos, bats, baseballs, Hall of Fame plaque postcards, and the like. Letters of any kind are scarce.

Known Forgeries: Replication of hand would be moderately difficult. Creating a well executing forgery would take some effort. Due to the nominal value of Stargell's signature, he is generally not the target of skilled forgers.

Sales: Stargell's signature is available. His autograph generally sells for under $100 on most mediums.

Turkey Stearnes

Signature Study: Stearnes signed in a very pensive hand. The signature evidences average flow. Recklessness of hand is lacking. Letter construction is marginal, evidencing weak formation. Letters appear as indistinguishable bumps. Stearnes signed with an odd looking capital letter "S" in the last name, which displays more like the letter "B." Stearnes' signature has marginal legibility. Stearnes' hand remained consistent throughout the years, evidencing little change. Signatures accomplished in the last few years of his life evidence a labored appearance with a good amount of unsteadiness. Overall, this is a plain and unassuming Hall of Fame signature.

Signature Population: This is a signature of average demand that outweighs a limited supply. When Stearnes was inducted into the Hall of Fame in 2000, his signature was offered by dealers as very rare. "Only a few exist" they claimed. Over

Stearnes 1: circa 1970s signature

Stearnes 2: circa 1970s signature

Stearnes 3: circa late 1970s signature

time it has become apparent that Stearnes signed many index cards and was a willing signer through the mail. His signature should be considered scarce on a per se basis but by no means rare. Premium items are considered rare to very rare. I have never seen a genuine signed 8 × 10 photograph. I have never found a single-signed baseball I would feel comfortable pronouncing as genuine. I have examined a handful of genuine multi-signed baseballs over the years. A few signed letters exist but these also should be considered rare. Material signed during his days in the Negro Leagues borders on the non-existent.

Known Forgeries: The slower nature of Stearnes' hand makes for easy replication. Many well executed forgeries exist in the market, so caution is warranted. Forgeries are mostly found on index cards. The general rule is if the letter "S" looks like a "S" the signature should be avoided.

Sales: Index card sold for $940 (Robert Edward Auctions, Spring 2008). Index card sold for $889 (Legendary Auctions, May 2010).

Casey Stengel

Signature Study: Stengel signed in a very nice and clean hand. His signature evidences good flow. Hesitation is lacking. Letter construction is very sound. The signature is highly legible. Material signed during his days as a player tends to be smaller in size and less flamboyant than later signatures. Material signed in the 1950s tends to be larger with bold letters. Due to the high legibility, Stengel signatures have good display value. Stengel's hand remained strong his entire life. A signature will exhibit no shakiness of hand and one that does should be considered suspect and avoided.

Signature Population: Stengel's signature is

Stengel 1: 1965 signature

popular among collectors. Demand is balanced with supply. The supply of Stengel material is sound but not overwhelming. He was a willing and gracious signer throughout his life. His signature is available on most mediums including photos, index cards, government postcards, Hall of Fame plaque postcards, gum cards, and the like. Since he was closely associated with the game for so many years, material signed at the stadium is also available. Scorecards, album pages, and a good number of single-signed baseballs exist. Typed letters signed are uncommon. Handwritten letters are scarce. There is a decent supply of canceled bank checks in the market.

Known Forgeries: Stengel is a relatively easy signature to replicate. Many well executed forgeries exist in the market, so caution is warranted. Stengel forgeries are generally limited to premium items such as baseballs and 8 × 10 photos. In the late 1940s and early 1950s the Yankees would send out typed letters signed by Stengel on team letterhead. They are not addressed to a particular person by rather simply addressed to "My Dear Friend." The letter advises autograph collectors to send money to a company that will send a complete set of signed pictures of the Yankees (no doubt facsimile signed). The Stengel signature affixed to the letter is signed in a slower more labored hand. They are secretarially signed. Should you see one of these letters, examine it carefully as it is most likely a secretarial signature.

Sales: Bank check sold for $134 (RR Auctions, March 2011). Bank check sold for $138 (eBay, September 2011). Signed Mets calling card sold for $88 (eBay, September 2011). Hall of Fame plaque postcard sold for $134 (RR Auctions, March 2011). Index card sold for $101 (eBay, November 2011).

Stengel 2: undated signature

Bruce Sutter

Signature Study: Sutter signs in a bold and sloppy hand. His signature evidences large sweeping strokes. It is reckless in appearance. There is no hesitation whatsoever. The signature is basically vertical in nature. Letter construction is poor. The signature is illegible. Due to the poor penmanship, his signature has limited display value.

Sutter 1: Donruss-Panini baseball card dated 2010

Signature Population: This is a signature where supply clearly outweighs demand. Sutter is a common signature and can be found on most mediums including baseballs, gum cards, photos, Hall of Fame plaque postcards, and the like. Letters in any form are scarce.

Known Forgeries: Sutter's signature would be somewhat difficult to replicate. Due to the nominal value of Sutter's signature, he is generally not the target of skilled forgers.

Sales: Sutter's signature is available. His autograph generally sells for under $100 on most mediums.

George "Mule" Suttles

Signature Study: Suttles signed in a very hesitant and rudimentary hand. His signature is marked by much shakiness. Uneven letter construction is noted. The signature lacks good flow. It is marked with a choppy appearance. The signature is somewhat illegible. It is very likely that the infirmed appearance of his signature was evident his entire life. Former Negro League pitcher Cecil Kaiser once told me that Suttles was illiterate. Overall, this is one of the lesser appealing Hall of Fame signatures.

Signature Population: Suttles is an extremely rare signature. His autograph is limited to team-related documents. I know of no non-document related signatures in existence. A few Suttles sig-

Suttles 1: circa 1930s signature (courtesy Newark Public Library, The Newark Eagles papers)

Suttles 2: contract dated 1941 (courtesy Newark Public Library, The Newark Eagles papers)

Suttles 3: contract dated 1944 (courtesy Newark Public Library, The Newark Eagles papers)

Suttles 4: secretarial signature (courtesy Newark Public Library, The Newark Eagles papers)

natures are held at the Newark Public Library. I have never seen a genuine signature in the open market.

Known Forgeries: Due to the slow nature of Suttles' hand, replication is very easy. Many well executed forgeries exist. It should be noted that one letter exists with a secretarial signature (see Suttles 4). The hand appears more feminine and does not, in any way, resemble a genuine Suttles signature. Effa Manley was known to sign documents for Suttles. Several years ago, and well before his Hall of Fame induction, Suttles forgeries entered the market. They are signed on album pages or book pages. All the forgeries are accomplished by the same forger. They evidence the unsteady appearance of a genuine signature and are rather convincing. The forgeries are signed as "George (Mule) Suttles" with parentheses.

Sales: Due to the rarity, there have been no recent sales of Suttles' signature.

Don Sutton

Signature Study: Sutton signs in a very artistic and pleasing hand. His signature is marked with excellent flow. There is no hesitation whatsoever. Letter construction is sound. The signature is legible. The display value is high. The signature is vertical in nature. Measurable slant is lacking. As of 2012 Sutton's hand remains sound. A genuine signature will exhibit no shakiness of hand and one that does should be considered suspect and avoided.

Sutton 1: contract dated 1975

Signature Population: This is a signature where supply clearly outweighs demand. Sutton is a common signature. It can be found on most mediums including baseballs, gum cards, photos, Hall of Fame plaque postcards, and the like. Letters of any kind are scarce.

Known Forgeries: Sutton's hand is fairly difficult to replicate. Creating a well executed forgery will take a good amount of effort. Due to the nominal value of Sutton's signature, he is generally not the target of skilled forgers.

Sales: Sutton's signature is available. His autograph generally sells for under $100 on most mediums.

Ben Taylor

Signature Study: Taylor signs in a practical hand. The strokes are heavy and bold. Letter construction is sound. The signature is legible. Average display value is noted. As Taylor aged his hand appears to have become a bit more haphazard. Letter construction of more modern signatures exhibits impaired legibility. I have been unable to confirm whether infirmity affected his hand later in life.

Signature Population: This is a signature of average demand. The supply of Taylor material is minute. The letter illustrated in Taylor 2 is one of only a few in existence. The World War I draft card is held by the National Archives. I estimate a total population of under ten specimens in the open market. This signature is an extreme rarity.

Taylor 1: World War I draft card circa 1917 (Record Group 163, Records of the Selective Services Division, National Archives at Atlanta)

Taylor 2: TLS circa 1930s

Known Forgeries: The signature suggests a hand that is practical in nature, so replication of his hand would be rather easy. Taylor forgeries exist and are typically limited to album pages and scraps of old book paper.

Sales: Due to the rarity, there have been no recent sales of Taylor's signature.

Bill Terry

Signature Study: Terry's signature went through a very noticeable change through the years. Early signatures, those penned during his playing days, exhibit wonderful flow. Sound letter construction is evident. Material penned during this time has excellent display value. In the 1940s, Terry's hand changed somewhat and produced a signature that is more slanted to the right. The signature appears more rapid on paper. It has less eye appeal than its vintage counterparts. In old age, Terry's hand became infirmed. The once flowing signature is replaced by an aged signature. It has a labored appearance. This form of signature is signed in a slower and more choppy hand. The letters become more uniform in size. Terry signed basically until the very end of his life. Material signed in the last few months of his life exhibit a noticeable shakiness.

Terry 1: album page dated 1933

Terry 2: circa 1960 signature

Terry 3: 1986 signature

Signature Population: Overall, this is a common signature but one that seems to be in demand. Terry was a willing and gracious signer throughout his long life. The supply of material is strong and generally limited to photos, Hall of Fame plaque postcards, index cards, and commemorative gum cards. Less common are single-signed baseballs, letters, and Perez-Steele cards. Signed baseball bats are fairly scarce and highly desirable. There is a small supply of bank checks in the market, both personal and business. Signed 1933 Goudey gum cards are scarce. Material signed by both Terry and Ted Williams, the last two .400 hitters, is scarce and in much demand.

Known Forgeries: In general, Terry's signature is difficult to replicate. Only modern signatures, with a labored appearance, are easy to replicate. Due to the nominal value of Terry's signature, he is generally not the target of skilled forgers. However, there is a good supply of forged single-signed baseballs in the market. Moreover, many forged bats, baseballs, and photos in combination with Ted Williams exist, so caution is warranted.

Sales: Terry's signature is available. His autograph generally sells for under $100 on most mediums.

Sam Thompson

Signature Study: Thompson's signature is one of the least studied of all Hall of Famers simply because the specimen population is so small. His handwriting, as illustrated in Thompson 2, can be analyzed from a postcard that was postmarked

Detroit, Michigan, March 21, 1913. This card evidences a nice hand with good letter construction. This specimen was obtained directly from the Thompson family. I combined the "Sam" and the "Thompson" to create a post–1900 signature for illustration. His hand is distinctive. The 1894 specimen is a nice ink signature, as shown in Thompson 1. This signature has nice letter construction. It is also legible. Both signatures have good display value. It is unknown whether infirmity of hand existed due to old age.

Signature Population: Thompson is an excessively rare signature. To my knowledge, only one genuine specimen exists in the market. The above referenced postcard exists only in Xerox copy form. The original has been lost. A search for his will at Wayne County Probate Court turned up empty. It is said that Thompson became a federal marshal in Detroit. The U.S. Marshal's Service has no record of Thompson serving as a marshal. Period press reports from that time state that he was a marshal. It is also said that Thompson served as a bailiff for Arthur J. Tuttle, federal judge

Thompson 1: ledger dated 1894

Thompson 2: postcard dated 1913

Thompson 2a: generated signature from postcard

for the Eastern District of Michigan. A search of Tuttle's papers housed at the Bentley Library, University of Michigan, turned up no Thompson signatures.

Known Forgeries: There are a few signatures of Thompson that are purportedly removed from the end of handwritten letters signed as a U.S. marshal. I have always questioned these signatures, as the hand deviates from the illustrated specimens. Just about all signatures of Thompson in the market are forgeries.

Sales: Due to the rarity, there have been no recent sales of Thompson's signature.

Joe Tinker

Signature Study: Tinker signed in a very pensive and thoughtful hand. His signature is compact. It lacks reckless flow. The signature is basically vertical in nature. Letter construction is sound. A high degree of legibility is evident. His signature has average display value. As time went on Tinker's hand slowed even more. Material signed in the 1940s evidences a slight hesitation, which impairs the flow. Starting in the 1930s Tinker would, on occasion, add the word "Cubs" underneath his signature.

Signature Population: Tinker is a signature of sound demand with a restricted supply. Tinker should be considered a very scarce signature. Just about all Tinker signatures found in the market are on index cards or government postcards. Any other medium should be considered rare to very rare. Signed letters are available but are rare to very rare. Signed photos of any kind should also be considered rare. I have never examined a gen-

Tinker 1: TLS dated 1913 (courtesy National Baseball Hall of Fame and Museum)

Tinker 2: ALS circa 1915 (courtesy National Baseball Hall of Fame and Museum)

Tinker 3: government postcard circa 1940s

Tinker 4: common secretarial (courtesy National Baseball Hall of Fame and Museum)

uinely signed 8 × 10 photo in my lifetime. Signed baseballs are extremely rare. I have seen only a couple of multi-signed baseballs that contained a genuine Tinker signature. I have never seen a single-signed baseball. Signed team balls from his days as a player very likely do not exist. Moreover, I know of no signed Hall of Fame plaque postcards. Every once in a while an index card will surface that is signed by both Tinker and teammate Johnny Evers. These should be considered very rare and are highly treasured. Material signed by the infield trio of Tinker, Evers, and Chance are limited to a couple of banquet programs. These are excessively rare.

Known Forgeries: A Tinker signature, from any era, is signed in a slower hand. It is a signature that is easily replicated. Many well executed forgeries exist, so caution is warranted. Tinker forgeries are prevalent and there are some convincing examples in the market. Tinker managed for the Chicago Cubs and the Federal League Chicago Whales. A few letters exist in the market from these years, but many are signed by his secretary (see Tinker 4). Title issues may exist with certain Tinker letters.

Sales: Ink signature sold for $1,026 (RR Auctions, January 2011). *The Sporting News* questionnaire sold for $2,411 (Lelands.com, June 2011). Album page, signed with Johnny Evers, sold for $2,077 (Lelands.com, December 2004). Ink signature, choice specimen, sold for $1,067 (Legendary Auctions, November 2009).

Cristobal Torriente

Signature Study: Little is known of his writing habits. From the illustrated specimen, it appears that Torriente signed in a tempered hand. The

Crustobal Torriente

Torriente 1: World War I draft card circa 1917 (Record Group 163, Records of the Selective Services Division, National Archives at Atlanta)

signature lacks reckless flow. Sound legibility is noted. It is unknown whether infirmity of hand existed.

Signature Population: The illustrated specimen is Torriente's World War I draft registration card. There is a second draft card but it is signed in printed script. This, too, could have been written by Torriente. His signature is one of the great mysteries of the Hall of Fame members. One, possibly two, signatures are known to exist.

Known Forgeries: No specific forgeries are known. Forgeries do exist and all vary in construction.

Sales: Due to the rarity, there have been no recent sales of Torriente's signature.

Pie Traynor

Signature Study: Traynor signed in an unassuming and plain hand. Letter construction is fairly sound. Some of the letters in the last name will blend together, especially the "nor." This habit slightly impairs legibility. Over the years Traynor's hand went through a noticeable change. Early signatures tend to flow better and have a more bouncy feel to them. Traynor 1 is a superior vintage specimen from 1934. Material signed later in life appears more practical. The hand becomes slightly more abrupt. Letter construction, in more modern signatures, is sound. A good degree of legibility is noted. Traynor's hand remained strong his entire life. A genuine signature will exhibit no shakiness of hand and one that does should be considered suspect and avoided.

Signature Population: This is a signature where sound demand outweighs the supply. The population of Traynor material is limited. He was a good signer through most of his life. In the 1960s he curtailed honoring requests and proved an erratic signer at best. There is a decent supply of index cards and government postcards in the market. There is good supply of vintage material from team-signed baseballs to album pages. Single-signed baseballs are scarce. These are typically limited to baseballs signed after retirement. Traynor had a bad habit of inscribing balls on the

Traynor 1: postal cover 1934

Traynor 2: government postcard dated 1937

sweet spot, which made for a small and cramped signature. Single-signed baseballs from his playing days border on the non-existent. 8 × 10 photos are very scarce. Letters of any kind should be considered scarce. Signed 1933 Goudey gum cards are rare. There is a small supply of canceled bank checks in the market. In recent years these checks have been absorbed into collections.

Known Forgeries: Due to the practical nature of Traynor's hand, his signature is rather easy to replicate. Many well executed forgeries exist, so caution is warranted. One common forgery can be found on black and white Hall of Fame plaque postcards. Most genuinely signed black and white plaque cards are signed at the bottom of the card. These forged plaques are signed at the top. The forgery is signed in a rapid hand. The top of the letter "T" in the last name is elongated. The letter "P" in the first name is oddly formed. The head of the letter is larger and more pointed at the end. There is another forgery that surfaces every now and then and it is worth more than a genuine Traynor signature. The legendary Honus Wagner coached for the Pittsburgh Pirates after his retirement. He signed many items. Wagner had a bad habit (or good depending on how you look at it)

Traynor 3: undated signature

Traynor 4: forged signature accomplished by Honus Wagner

Vance 1: album page circa 1930s

Vance 2: album page dated 1933

Vance 3: circa 1950s signature

of signing autographs of the Pirates players. Illustrated as Traynor 4 is a Traynor forgery accomplished by Wagner. It is a great collectible.

Sales: 1934 Major League contract sold for $4,406 (Robert Edward Auctions, Spring 2011). Hall of Fame plaque postcard sold for $240 (RR Auctions, September 2010). Bank check sold for $300 (Legendary Auctions, June 2009). Bank check sold for $275 (Hunt Auctions, March 2009). 8 × 10 photo sold for $477 (RR Auctions, February 2011).

Dazzy Vance

Signature Study: Vance's signature is marked with wonderful flow and bold thick lines. Letter construction is sound. The signature is very legible. The signature is usually finished off with an elongated letter "e." Vance's signature has excellent display value. Most signatures are signed with his nickname. Vance's hand remained strong his entire life. A genuine signature will evidence no shakiness of hand and one that does should be considered suspect and avoided.

Signature Population: Overall, this is a signature where demand and supply work well together. Vance's signature is mostly found on album pages, index cards, and government postcards. Signed 8 × 10 photos are scarce but a good number exist. Single-signed baseballs are rare. Letters of any kind are rare to very rare. I have never seen a genuine full-page handwritten letter. Hall of Fame plaque postcards are also rare. After his death, the family would release signatures removed from bank checks to satisfy requests from autograph collectors. Complete bank checks are very rare.

Known Forgeries: As wonderful as Vance's hand is, it does have one major flaw, that being the many breaks in the signature. This allows for fairly easy replication of his hand. Many well executed forgeries are in the market, so caution is

warranted. Vance forgeries are found on most mediums including single-signed baseballs, photos, Hall of Fame plaque postcards, and the like. One forger has created many forged baseballs. Note on the genuine signature the end of the capital "V" in the last name points to the right. The forged baseballs in question feature a signature where the "V" does not tail but continues straight up with no deviation. On many baseballs the forger adds an inscription of "To my friend, Joe Doe, from A.C. 'Dazzy' Vance" or "To my good friend." The handwriting evidences a slightly labored appearance. The forgeries are actually amateurish in appearance, but some have been incorrectly certified as genuine by the authentication companies.

Sales: 8 × 10 photo, pitching pose, sold for $1,058 (Robert Edward Auctions, Spring 2010). 1949 government postcard sold for $294 (RR Auctions, August 2011). 1951 government postcard sold for $248 (Hunt Auctions, November 2010). 5 × 7 photo sold for $840 (Mastro, August 2007). Single-signed baseball, choice specimen, sold for $4,281 (Mastro, April 2005).

Arky Vaughan

Signature Study: Vaughan's signature is one that went through a noticeable change over time. Early signatures are accomplished in a very plain, almost labored hand. Early signatures evidence thicker lines and slower flow. The racing effect is muted. Letter construction is strong. The signature is very legible. Most signatures that were penned during the first few years of his playing career are usually signed as "F. Vaughan" or "Floyd Vaughan." As Vaughan attained stardom in the big leagues his signature changed significantly. His signature became more flowing and artistic in nature. The slow lines of earlier signatures are replaced by a more reckless flow. The eye appeal increases greatly. Vaughan was killed in a boating accident and never reached old age. His signature remained strong his entire life. A genuine signature will exhibit no shakiness of hand and one that does should be considered suspect and avoided.

Signature Population: Demand clearly outweighs supply. Vaughan is a scarce signature. His signature can be found on album pages, team-signed baseballs, and scorecards. Premium items are rare to very rare. Signed 8 × 10 photos do exist but are considered rare. Signed gum cards of any kind should also be considered rare. Single-signed baseballs are very rare. I have examined only one genuine specimen ever. Letters are also very rare.

Vaughan 1: album page dated 1933

Vaughan 2: undated signature

Vaughan 3: forged signature accomplished by Honus Wagner

I have never seen a full-page handwritten letter in my life.

Known Forgeries: Early signatures lack rapid flow. They are very easy to replicate. Many well executed forgeries exist. Modern signatures are much more difficult to replicate, so well executed forgeries of these are extremely limited. Vaughan is a commonly forged name and fakes can be found on most mediums. Honus Wagner would, on occasion, sign Vaughan's name. Illustrated as Vaughan 3 is a Vaughan forgery penned by the great Wagner.

Sales: Index card sold for $321 (RR Auctions, July 2009). Album page sold for $704 (Lelands.com, June 2011). 1939 World's Fair card sold for $350 (Hunt Auctions, July 2009). 1940 Play Ball gum card sold for $1,001 (eBay, November 2011).

Bill Veeck

Signature Study: Veeck signed in a strong and fast hand. His signature evidences bold strokes and powerful lines. Letter construction is marginal. Impaired legibility is noted. The display value of Veeck's signature is just average. Veeck's hand remained sound for most of his life. However, material signed in the last year or so of his life appears sloppy with a slightly labored appearance.

Signature Population: The demand for Veeck's signature is limited at best. The supply is ample. Veeck is a fairly common signature as he was a willing and gracious signer throughout his life. His signature is most commonly found on index cards and team-related letters, which exist in quantities. Signed 8 × 10 photos do exist but are considered scarce. Handwritten letters of any kind are rare. Single-signed baseballs are scarce but many fine specimens exist. Veeck signed many copies of his autobiography titled *Veeck, as in Wreck*. In addition, Veeck's father, William L. Veeck, Sr., was president of the Chicago Cubs from 1919 until his death in 1933. Veeck Sr. signed many items. His signature is sometimes incorrectly sold as that of his more famous son. Illus-

Veeck 1: circa 1960 signature

Waddell 2: legal document signed dated 1909

Veeck 2: signature of Bill Veeck, Sr., circa 1920

trated as Veeck 2 is a signature of Veeck Sr. Veeck Sr.'s autograph is of comparable value to that of his son.

Known Forgeries: Given the lack of precision in the hand, his signature is easy to replicate. Creating a well executed forgery should not be a difficult task. Due to the nominal value of Veeck's signature, he is generally not the target of skilled forgers. However, signed baseballs are the one exception.

Sales: Signed book, limited edition, sold for $121 (RR Auctions, February 2011). 1976 TLS sold for $100 (RR Auctions, February 2011). 8 × 10 photo sold for $121 (RR Auctions, February 2010). 1965 Topps White Sox team card sold for $120 (eBay, December 2011). 1924 bank check signed by William Veeck Sr. sold for $121 (RR Auctions, September 2009).

Rube Waddell

Signature Study: A few years back I wrote an article for the *Sports Collectors Digest* and pronounced that there were no known Waddell in the market. Those who owned or authenticated Waddell material disagreed vehemently. For years Waddell's signature has caused great debate. Many Waddell signatures have been bought and sold and have appeared in auctions. For years I have been telling people that these were forged and that no known specimens exist. For years I have tried to locate a genuine Waddell signature. I even went so far and contacted family members but with no success. After much work and a bit of luck, Waddell's divorce file from 1909 has been recently located. It had been quietly resting in the sub-basement of a St. Louis circuit courthouse for the past 100 years. The legal file contained a total of

Waddell 1: legal document signed dated 1909

three Waddell signatures. The Waddell signatures that had been sold as genuine and pronounced as such by the experts do not match the Waddell signatures held in the St. Louis court records. The court documents invalidate every Waddell signature I have seen for sale except for one specimen. There is a banquet program from 1910 that has been around for years. It contains many signatures including a "G.E. Waddell" accomplished in pencil. Also on this program is a Joe McGinnity signature. It is the only Waddell signature I know of in the open market. It is not known whether infirmity of hand was caused by his illness. Waddell died at a young age from consumption.

Signature Population: There is strong demand for Waddell's signature. Based on my research, there are a total of four Waddell signatures known to exist. Three are held by a governmental concern and will never be offered for sale. Therefore, Waddell should be considered an extremely rare signature in the market.

Known Forgeries: Waddell forgeries exist in quantities. Forgeries can be found on baseballs, T-206 baseball cards, photos, and letters. I know of no genuine signatures that exist on any of the above referenced mediums. Many old cabinet cards, usually in less than desirable condition, have been utilized by forgers. Many forged examples exist, typically signed "Compliments of G. E. Waddell," "Geo. Waddell," or "G.E. (Rube) Waddell." Some are signed in fountain pen while others are in pencil. I have seen them signed on both the front and on the reverse. These forged cabinet photographs surfaced over the past 15 to 20 years. Another common forgery is handwritten letters. These are actually freehand forgeries and are accomplished in a nice flowing hand. The writing lacks hesitation. I have examined at least half a dozen. Some are multi-paged letters, while others are penned on a single sheet. These letters were signed "Your Friend, G.E. Waddell" or "Yours Sincerely, G.E. Waddell." Under the signature, the forger adds the name of the town where the letter was allegedly written. The forgeries don't really look anything like the illustrated signatures. The forgeries contain a very fancy and artistic capital "W" in the last name.

Sales: 1910 banquet menu, also signed by Joe McGinnity, accomplished in pencil, sold for $17,047 (Lelands.com, November 2007)

Honus Wagner

Signature Study: Wagner's signature is very complex. He had many different ways of signing, which makes authentication a nightmare. Wagner's hand had many changes throughout his long life. No matter when a Wagner signature was penned, letter construction is sound and legibility is high. Early signatures are signed in a very flowing and artistic hand. Material signed in the 1910s and 1920s is among the finest of any signature. Vintage signatures have a whimsical and almost fairytale look to them. The fine strokes and swinging curves make for a signature with maximum eye appeal. In the 1930s Wagner's hand slowed somewhat. Signatures from this decade are still flowing. The display value is still strong. On a whim, Wagner would change the slant of his signature, as seen in Wagner 2. While most signatures exhibit a right slant, some are vertical and others evidence a slight back slant. Why Wagner did this is a mystery but it causes much confusion. During the 1940s, especially late in the decade, Wagner's hand slowed. Signatures accomplished during this time evidence a slower and slightly labored hand. The once flowing curves and effortless strokes are replaced by jaggedness. In the 1950s Wagner's hand was affected by infirmity. Material signed during this period evidences a moderate amount of shakiness. Display value is severely impaired. Wagner had variant ways of signing his name, including: "Honus Wagner," "J. Honus Wagner," "John H. Wagner," "J.H. Wagner," and "J. Hans Wagner." Wagner's hand

Wagner 3: government postcard dated 1934

Wagner 4: circa 1930s signature

exhibits significant evolution throughout the years and is one of the most challenging Hall of Fame signatures to study.

Signature Population: The demand is strong for Wagner material and clearly outweighs supply. Wagner is a signature of limited population. Wagner was a good signer throughout his life. From the early 1930s until the early 1950s he was a coach for the Pirates, sometimes in name only. This gave collectors access to him. Most Wagner signatures are limited to lesser grade mediums such as index cards, government postcards, album pages, and scorecards. Single-signed baseballs are available but should be considered rare. Balls were generally signed during his tenure as a coach. Most of the time Wagner would sign baseballs on the side panel. If you examine a single-signed Wagner ball where the signature appears on the sweet spot, it is most likely a forgery. Rarely did he sign on the sweet. It is highly unlikely a signed team ball from his days as a player exists. Wagner letters are scarce

Wagner 1: ALS dated 1918

Wagner 5: government postcard dated 1946

Wagner 2: album page dated 1933 variant signature

Wagner 6: circa 1950 signature

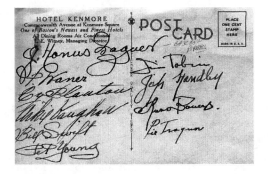

Wagner 7: undated signature

Wagner 8: team postcard accomplished entirely by Wagner

but a decent supply exists. He loved to write letters to fans. Many typed letters signed with business content are available. Handwritten letters are tougher to locate than their typewritten counterpart. Handwritten letters usually contain routine content. Spelling errors are common. In late 1980s, Wagner bank checks surfaced. When these checks first entered the market they were advertised as rare. In reality, they are not. There is a good supply in the market. A Wagner item that seems to be on every collector's want list is a signed Hall of Fame plaque postcard. I have never seen a genuine example signed on the front. There is one or two genuinely signed on the reverse.

Known Forgeries: Signatures accomplished before 1930 are very difficult to replicate. Well executed forgeries are extremely limited. Signatures accomplished after that time are much easier to replicate, so well executed forgeries exist in quantities. Like Cobb and Ruth, Wagner is one of the most targeted signatures. A few years back a forger got a hold of a small number of American League (William Harridge, Pres.) baseballs. The baseballs were in excellent condition and just about snow white. Forged Wagner signatures were placed on the sweet spot of the baseball. The ones I have examined were signed in blue ball-point pen. The forgeries are not that convincing as the signature appears cramped. The "er" in the last name reads as "uu." The beginning of the "W" appears as a

cursive capital "J." These forgeries stand out with little examination. Other common forged single-signed baseballs are those signed on the sweet spot with an overly small signature. The forgeries are rudimentary in construction. The forgeries appear fuzzy, evidencing new ink placed on an old ball. This is a good example of the bleeding effect. One final comment about Wagner and forgeries, when Wagner was a coach for the Pirates he was *notorious* for signing autographs of the players. The postcard illustrated as Wagner 8 was signed entirely in Wagner's hand. He did this on many occasions. These are odd baseball treasures that retain strong value.

Sales: 1947 government postcard sold for $636 (RR Auctions, January 2011). 1930 signed album page, choice specimen, sold for $1,410 (Robert Edward Auctions, Spring 2009). Bank check sold for $1,645 (Robert Edward Auctions, Spring 2009). Bank check sold for $1,050 (Hunt Auctions, November 2009). 1917 real estate document sold for $3,909 (Lelands.com, April 2007). 1940 Pirates team ball, also signed by Arky Vaughan and Lloyd Waner, sold for $2,200 (eBay, November 2011).

Bob Wallace

Signature Study: Wallace signed in a very pleasing and confined hand. His signature evidences good flow. The signature is accomplished in a slower hand. Reckless lines are lacking. The hand is refined and letter construction is sound. Wallace's signature is very legible. The display value is high. Wallace's hand slow slightly in old age. Material signed in the 1950s until his death is signed in a slightly slower hand. A somewhat labored appearance is noted. Display value is still sound. Wallace's hand remained relatively sound his entire life. The labored appearance never reached a point that the hand appears truly shaky.

Signature Population: This is a signature of limited population where demand outweighs supply. Wallace is an uncommon signature and premium items are rare to very rare. His signature is generally found on index cards and government postcards. Photos of any kind are scarce. 8 × 10 photos are very rare. Letters are typically limited to short writings penned on government postcards. Full-page typed or handwritten letters are rare to very rare. Single-signed baseballs of Wallace do exist but they should be considered very rare. I have only examined a couple of gen-

Wallace 1: check endorsement dated 1924

Wallace 2: undated signature

uine examples in my life. Hall of Fame plaque postcards are rare. While no personal bank checks are known to exist, there is a small supply of Chicago Cubs payroll checks made out to Wallace. His signature appears on the reverse as an endorsement. These checks are especially nice as they are signed on front by William Veeck Sr.

Known Forgeries: Wallace's signature from any period is fairly easy to replicate. This is due to the lack of rapid flow of hand. Many well executed forgeries exist, so caution is warranted. Many forged Hall of Fame plaque postcards exist. These forged plaques are nicely executed but the forger makes one key mistake in the middle initial "J." Note the genuine signatures exhibit a very distinctive letter "J" with a flat looking top. The forgeries exhibit a more conventional letter "J," as illustrated in Wallace 4, which deviates greatly from the genuine signature to tip off these forgeries.

Wallace 3: undated signature

Wallace 4: detail of forgery

Sales: Index card, choice specimen, sold for $423 (Lelands.com, January 2008). Social Security card sold for $425 (Hunt Auctions, November 2010). Index card sold for $350 (Hunt Auctions, November 2010). Index card sold for $354 (RR Auctions, January 2009).

Ed Walsh

Signature Study: Walsh signed with a fairly practical and non-conforming hand. His signature evidences good flow. Recklessness of hand is lacking. Letter construction is sound. Walsh's signature is legible. The display value is average. His signature is usually marked with thicker lines and dominates the medium it is placed upon. Walsh's hand remained fairly consistent throughout his life. Signatures from various eras evidence little change. Material signed in the 1950s is accomplished in a slightly slower hand. There is an ever so slight labored appearance.

Signature Population: Overall, this is a signature where supply and demand are balanced. Walsh is an uncommon signature per se. Most signatures offered in the market are found on index cards and government postcards. Photos of any kind are scarce. 8 × 10 photos are rare to very rare. Hall of Fame plaque postcards are rare, albeit borderline. Letters of any kind are rare. Most are usually penned on blank stationery. Single-signed baseballs are rare. Most were signed in the 1950s and in ball-point pen. Signed team balls from Walsh's days as a player very likely do not exist. Walsh's son, Ed Walsh, Jr., played four years of Major League baseball. His signature is sometimes confused with that of his famous father.

Known Forgeries: Due to the lack of rapid flow and precise angles, Walsh's signature is fairly easy to replicate. Many well executed forgeries exist, so caution is warranted. Walsh forgeries are typically limited to photos, baseballs, and Hall of Fame plaque postcards.

Sales: 1949 government postcard sold for $267 (RR Auctions, August 2011). Hall of Fame plaque postcard sold for $830 (Legendary Auctions, November 2010). Index card sold for $294 (RR Auctions, August 2010). Choice signature sold for

Walsh 1: circa 1920s signature

Walsh 2: album page circa 1925

Walsh 3: team sheet circa 1930s

$284 (eBay, November 2011). Hall of Fame plaque postcard sold for $306 (eBay, November 2011). Index card sold for $256 (eBay, January 2012).

Lloyd Waner

Signature Study: Waner's signature is very plain and unappealing. His signature evidences flowing lines but there is a slight choppiness evident. Letter construction is sound. The signature has a high degree of legibility. Display value is marginal at best. Waner's hand remained fairly consistent his entire life. Signatures accomplished later in life appear a bit more cramped. On rare occasions, Waner would finish a signature with a paraph but this is typically limited to vintage specimens, as noted in Waner, L 1. On occasion, Waner would sign with his nickname "Little Poison." Waner's hand remained strong his entire life. A genuine signature will evidence no measurable shakiness of hand and one that does should be considered suspect and avoided.

Signature Population: Waner's signature is of average demand that is outweighed by supply. Waner was a willing signer throughout his life. His signature can be found on most mediums including index cards, photographs of various size, Hall of Fame plaque postcards, gum cards, and government postcards. There is a good supply of letters, mostly handwritten. Bank checks are also available but are somewhat scarce. Single-signed baseballs are scarce. Signed team balls from Waner's days as a player exist in quantities, which are an excellent source of vintage Waner signa-

Waner, L. 1: album page dated 1933

Waner, L. 2: circa 1970s signature

tures. Waner is considered rare on single-signed baseball bats. Waner is considered very rare on Perez-Steele art postcards. It is one of the modern rarities in the field of autographs, sports or otherwise. Waner is the rarest of all Perez-Steele cards to obtain signed. The total population is unknown. I have seen many signed but none of them I believe were genuine. In addition, famed golfer Paul Runyan, who captured the 1934 and 1938 PGA Championships, was also nicknamed "Little Poison." In the 1990s Runyan was presented with a handful of Waner signed index cards to sign but these are rare.

Known Forgeries: A Waner signature from any era is rather easy to forge. Well executed forgeries exist, though limited to premium items. Due to the nominal value of Waner's signature, he is generally not the target of skilled forgers. However, many well executed forged single-signed baseballs and Perez-Steele cards exist.

Sales: Waner's signature is available. His autograph generally sells for under $100 on most mediums. Of note: 1938 Major League contract sold for $3,819 (Robert Edward Auctions, Spring 2011).

Paul Waner

Signature Study: Waner signed in a very nice and flowing hand. His signature is marked with effortless lines. Hesitation of any kind is lacking. Letter construction is sound. The signature is fairly legible. Display value is sound. Early signatures tend to exhibit longer scale than more modern signatures. Material signed in the 1950s appears a bit more compact. Waner died at a relatively young age and his hand remained strong his entire life. A genuine signature will exhibit no shakiness of hand and one that does should be considered suspect and avoided.

Signature Population: Overall, this is an uncommon signature that is in high demand. Waner was a good signer throughout his entire life. The supply of genuine material is ample. Most signa-

Waner, P. 1: album page dated 1933

tures in the market are found on index cards and government postcards. Photos of any kind are scarce. 8 × 10 photos are rare. Letters and Goudey gum cards are scarce and highly desirable. Signed Hall of Fame plaque postcards are rare. The best way to obtain Waner on a baseball is to locate a team-signed baseball from late in his career. There is a good supply in the market. Single-signed baseballs are considered rare. I have seen less than 10 genuine specimens in my lifetime. I have never seen any medium signed by just the two Waner brothers. Waner published a 36-page booklet on batting, titled *Paul Waner's Batting Secrets*, a how-to book on the science of hitting. Waner would usually sign these books on the cover in bold red ball-point ink. He would then sign a second autograph on the back cover.

Known Forgeries: Waner's signature is smooth and complex in nature. Replication of hand is difficult. Well executed forgeries exist but are very limited. Many Waner forgeries exist on baseballs, Hall of Fame plaque postcards, 8 × 10 photos, and the like. A Paul Waner forgery is typically added to a genuinely signed index card of his brother Lloyd. These are tricky because there is a genuine signature along side the forgery.

Sales: 1944 Major League contract, counter-signed by Ed Barrow, sold for $3,819 (Robert Edward Auctions, Spring 2011). 1949 government postcard sold for $240 (RR Auctions, July 2011).

Waner, P. 2: circa 1960s signature

Waner, P. 3: 1962 signature

Index card sold for $175 (RR Auctions, June 2009). Hall of Fame plaque postcard sold for $1,200 (Hunt Auctions, November 2007). Batting booklet sold for $375 (eBay, December 2011).

John Ward

Signature Study: Ward signed in a very pensive and deliberate hand. His signature evidences good flow. Reckless strokes are lacking. Letter construction is fairly sound but some of the letters are muted in appearance. His signature is legible. Average display value is noted. The capital "J" exhibits a distinctive curve. The "d" in the last name is unfinished and tails off before completion. It is unclear whether his hand was affected by infirmities late in life.

Signature Population: Ward's signature is of great rarity. I know of only a few letters in existence and that is about it. I know of no signatures that exist outside of letters. I estimate the total population to be under five authentic specimens in the open market. This is an extreme rarity among autographs.

Known Forgeries: Due to the slower nature of Ward's hand, his signature is very easy to copy. Many well executed forgeries exist in the market. Just about 100 percent of Ward signatures in the market are forgeries. Many period letters are signed by Ward's secretary. Secretarial signatures,

Ward 1: ALS dated 1905

Ward 2: TLS dated 1911 (courtesy National Baseball Hall of Fame and Museum)

Ward 3: TLS dated 1912 (courtesy National Baseball Hall of Fame and Museum)

Ward 4: common secretarial (courtesy National Baseball Hall of Fame and Museum)

as seen in Ward 4, deviate greatly from the genuine signature. Title issues may exist with some Ward letters, so caution is warranted.

Sales: Due to the rarity, there have been no recent sales of Ward's signature.

Earl Weaver

Signature Study: Weaver signs in an aggressive hand. Ink strokes are rapid. Hesitation is non-existent. Letter construction is marginal at best. Legibility is slightly impaired. Material signed in recent years evidences an ever so slight unsteadiness. Overall, this is just an average signature.

Weaver 1: document dated 2002

Signature Population: This is a signature where supply vastly outweighs demand. Weaver's signature is very common. His signature can be found on most mediums including baseballs, photos, gum cards, and the like. Letters of any kind are scarce.

Known Forgeries: Replication of his hand would be moderately easy. Creating a well executed forgery would not take much effort. Due to the nominal value of Weaver's signature, he is not the target of skilled forgers.

Sales: Weaver's signature is available. His autograph generally sells for under $100 on most mediums.

George Weiss

Signature Study: Weiss signed in a very bold but unstructured hand. His signature evidences good flow. Hesitation is lacking. Letter construction is marginal where letters are somewhat muted. As such legibility is impaired. The "W" in the last name displays more like the letter "U." Early signatures tend to be somewhat more defined and legible. Weiss's hand remained strong

his entire life. A genuine signature will evidence no shakiness of hand and one that does should be considered suspect and avoided.

Signature Population: Weiss is a signature of limited population and demand. He was not a target of most autograph collectors. He signed relatively little material outside of business-related documents and letters. There is a good supply of TLsS in the market. Full-page ALsS are very rare. There is also a good supply of personal bank checks in the market. Non-document signatures are considered scarce to rare. Government postcards are scarce and seldom surface. I have never seen a genuinely signed 8 × 10 photo or Hall of Fame plaque postcard. Signed baseballs are rare. Single-signed baseballs border on the nonexistent. I have only seen a couple in my entire life. Signed documents exist from his pre–Major League days when he was involved with the New Haven club. A very small supply of New Haven signed documents came out of the estate of Yankees owner Jacob Ruppert. These early Weiss documents are rare and desirable.

Known Forgeries: Weiss' hand is moderately easy to replicate. Well executed forgeries exist. Weiss is not commonly forged due simply to the weak demand for his signature. There is one controversy that involves Hall of Fame plaque postcards. Weiss died shortly after his induction so there is great debate as to whether a genuine specimen exists. For years a small group of signed plaque postcards have been circulating. It is said that collectors received them directly in the mail from Weiss. Whether this is true or not, I do not know. I have seen a few of these signed plaque postcards. The signatures deviate greatly from the accepted specimens. They have strong letter construction. The letter "W" actually looks like a "W." The theory to explain the deviation of hand is that Weiss's health was failing. The flaw with the explanation is that the signature evidences no shakiness of hand. In addition the signature is nicely centered on the top of the card and uniform throughout. If declining health were evident, then infirmity of hand would manifest itself with shak-

Weiss 1: undated signature

iness. The signature would likely be off centered and penned on an uneven plane. I have concluded that no genuine signed Hall of Fame plaque postcards exist. My advice is to avoid them in total. Weiss signed typed letters exist in good numbers. While the vast majority are signed by Weiss, there is a small percentage that are secretarially signed. These easily standout as the signature deviates greatly from genuine specimens.

Sales: 1949 signed document sold for $100 (RR Auctions, December 2010). Bank check sold for $178 (eBay, September 2011). Index card sold for $102 (eBay, December 2011).

Mickey Welch

Signature Study: Welch signed in a very plain and tempered hand. His signature evidences marginal flow. His signature lacks reckless lines, which gives it a slightly muted appearance. The "W" exhibits a distinctive loop in an otherwise unassuming hand. Letter construction is sound. His signature has a high degree of legibility. The few Welch signatures in the market are signed as "M. Welch." I know of two genuine letters signed with his nickname "Mickey." It is unclear whether infirmity of hand affected his signature in later years.

Signature Population: Welch is an extremely rare signature. It is limited to just a few signatures, mostly removed from documents. I have never seen a genuinely signed photo, baseball, government postcard, or other non-document signed item. I estimate the market population of Welch signatures to be under five specimens.

Known Forgeries: Since Welch signed in a slower hand, his signature is rather easy to forge. Well executed forgeries exist in quantities. Just about 100 percent of Welch signatures offered in the market are forgeries. Forgeries are found on most mediums including ledger pages, album pages, government postcards, scorecards, and the like. There are a few forged album pages to note, all created by the same forger. He signs Welch's signature as "Smiling Mickey Welch" or "Mickey Welch" across the top of the page. He then signs eight to 12 forgeries of common players from a particular team, such as the 1934 Athletics, 1935

Welch 2: undated signature

Tigers, or 1936 Indians. The Welch forgery is rudimentary in construction. I see these sheets offered for sale every now and then.

Sales: Due to the rarity, there have been no recent sales of Welch's signature.

Willie Wells

Signature Study: Wells signed in a very practical and unassuming hand. His signature exhibits good flow. Hesitation of any kind is lacking. Letter construction is sound. The signature is legible. Wells' signature remained fairly constant throughout his life. Material signed from the 1940s until the early 1980s evidences little deviation. Modern signatures tend to be a little more sharp in appearance. In the early to mid–1980s Wells' eyesight began to fail. Signatures accomplished during the last years of his life are signed in a sloppy and illegible hand. Signatures evidence uneven construction and are misspaced. These signatures have little in common with earlier specimens. The general rule is if you examine a level and nicely spaced signature signed in the mid–1980s it is forged. Wells 3 is a good illustration of an elderly signature. Despite the sloppy appearance of his hand, I have never run across a Wells' signature that evidences true shakiness of hand.

Signature Population: Overall, this is a signature of very limited population that is outweighed by demand. Wells was a willing signer throughout his life. He even signed after his eye sight failed. He would seek the assistance of a neighbor to help him mail back the autographs. The problem is very few collectors wrote Wells for his signature. Today it is considered a scarce signature per se. Premium items are rare to very rare. The vast majority of Wells signatures in the market are on index cards. The occasional first-

Welch 1: pay receipt circa 1880s

Wells 1: ALS circa 1940s (courtesy Newark Public Library, The Newark Eagles papers)

Willie Wells

Wells 2: contract dated 1944 (courtesy Newark Public Library, The Newark Eagles Papers)

Willie Wells

Wells 4: common secretarial (courtesy Newark Public Library, The Newark Eagles papers)

Wells 3: circa 1980s signature

day cover surfaces but these are rare. Signed photos of any kind are rare. A small number of 8 × 10 photos featuring Wells in a Winnipeg Buffaloes uniform exist. I have never seen a single-signed baseball that I would feel comfortable pronouncing as genuine. Multi-signed baseballs exist but are rare. Handwritten letters are available but these are also considered rare and highly desired.

Known Forgeries: Well's signature from any era is fairly easy to replicate. Well executed forgeries exist in quantities. The majority of Wells signatures in the market are forged. There are two vintage signatures that stand out. A few handwritten letters from the 1940s exist, but the letters are written and signed by someone other than Wells, likely his wife. The signature appears very feminine and deviates greatly from a genuine signature, as shown in Wells 4. Another signature that has been circulating for years can be found on pay receipts. There are a few in the market. These have been sold as genuine but I do not believe they are in Wells' hand. Wells' signature exhibits a right slant, a characteristic that can be found in all signatures signed before his blindness. The pay receipts are signed in a hand that exhibits a slight left slant. This type of signature deviates from the 1940s specimens. Save old-age signatures, I advise collectors to avoid Wells signatures that exhibit a left slant of any degree. They deviate too much from genuine specimens. Another forgery that has recently entered the market are single-signed National League (Bart Giamatti, Pres.) baseballs. They are signed on the side panel of the ball in slightly faded black or blue felt-tip pen. This is a telltale sign the balls have been left in direct sunlight. The balls are usually dated with the years 1986, 1987, or 1988 under the signature. The signatures are overly large and uniform in na-

ture. Wells, who was blind at this time, could not accomplish a uniform and neat signature.

Sales: Ink signature, choice specimen, sold for $525 (Lelands.com, May 2008). 1941 baseball contract sold for $2,770 (Lelands.com, December 2005). ALS, choice specimen, sold for $812 (Robert Edward Auctions, Spring 2006).

Zack Wheat

Signature Study: Wheat signed in a very bold and powerful hand. His signature lacks hesitation. His hand evidences cutting lines and angles. Letter construction is marginal at best. Letters will sometimes morph into non-conforming lines that impair legibility. Wheat's hand remained fairly constant throughout his life. Wheat's hand remained strong his entire life. A genuine signature will evidence no shakiness of hand and one that does should be considered suspect and avoided. Overall, this is just an average signature with marginal display value.

Signature Population: This is a signature where supply and demand are fairly balanced. Wheat is a fairly common signature as he was a willing signer throughout his life. Most signatures are limited to index cards. Premium items should

Best Wishes Zack D Wheat

Wheat 1: 1962 signature

Sincerely Zack D Wheat

Wheat 2: undated signature

be considered scarce which include 8 × 10 photos and Hall of Fame plaque postcards. Signed letters of any kind are very scarce. Single-signed baseballs are rare. Team-signed baseballs from his days as a player are rare, and are limited to post–1920s teams. There is a good supply of canceled bank checks.

Known Forgeries: Wheat is a fairly easy signature to replicate. Many well executed forgeries exist, so caution is warranted. Forgeries are generally limited to premium items such as baseballs and 8 × 10 photos. Many well executed forged Hall of Fame plaque postcards exist. These were produced several years ago when a forger secured many blank plaques. The Wheat forgeries are signed in a slightly neater and slightly slower hand. Many contain various inscriptions such as "Best Wishes, Zack D Wheat, Hall of Fame 1959" or "Sincerely, Zack D Wheat, Brooklyn Dodgers." These forged cards have been circulating for years, so caution is warranted.

Sales: 4 × 6 photo, batting pose, choice specimen, sold for $264 (RR Auctions, February 2011). Bank check sold for $115 (eBay, September 2011). 1927 Major League contract sold for $2,644 (Robert Edward Auctions, Spring 2011). Hall of Fame plaque postcard sold for $200 (RR Auctions, March 2011). Index card sold for $157 (eBay, December 2011).

Sol White

Signature Study: Little is known of White's hand. The illustrated specimen is from an ALS dated January 1940. It is written to White's longtime friend, Philadelphia Giants owner H. Walter Schlicter. It has been in the market for many years and is believed to be genuine. I have found no other White signatures for comparison. The signature has sound legibility. The hand evidences a slight hesitation. I have been told that White, on occasion, would sign autographs as "King Solomon," but I have no confirmation of this fact.

Signature Population: Given the fact that

White 1: ALS dated 1940 (courtesy FC Associates, www.fcassociates.com)

White was a writer and author would naturally lead you to believe many signed items exist. In fact, White is an extremely rare signature. I have been told a couple of signed letters exist. The illustrated specimen matches the description of a letter auctioned off by Sothebys that originated from the Barry Halper collection.

Known Forgeries: No specific forgeries bear note. All forgeries in the market vary in construction.

Sales: Due to the rarity, there have been no recent sales of White's signature.

Hoyt Wilhelm

Signature Study: Wilhelm signed in a very sloppy and unattractive hand. His signature is marked with wavy lines. Precision is very limited. Letter construction is marginal. Wilhelm's signature has poor legibility. Display value is substandard. Wilhelm's hand remained strong his entire life. A genuine signature will evidence no shakiness of hand and one that does should be considered suspect and avoided.

Wilhelm 1: undated signature

Signature Population: This is a very common signature where supply far outweighs demand. His signature can be found on most items including photos, gum cards, baseballs, bats, Hall of Fame plaque postcards, and the like. Letters of any kind are considered scarce.

Known Forgeries: His signature would be easy to replicate. Producing a well executed forgery can be done with ease. Due to the nominal value of Wilhelm's signature, he is not the target of skilled forgers.

Sales: Wilhelm's signature is available. His autograph generally sells for under $100 on most mediums.

J.L. Wilkinson

Signature Study: Wilkinson signed in an extremely attractive hand with lines of effortless flow. Letter construction is very sound. Both legibility and display value are high. He signed his name as "J.L. Wilkinson," "J. Leslie Wilkinson," or "Less Wilkinson." It is apparent by the specimens illustrated that his hand remained relatively constant throughout the years. In old age his eye sight failed. He was known to write in crayon in the last years of his life. Wilkinson material signed in the last few years of his life will evidence a shaky and labored appearance.

Signature Population: I only know of few genuine specimens. All are in the form of documents or letters. The 1919 Kansas City Monarchs

Wilkinson 2: circa 1920s signature

Wilkinson 3: signed document dated 1954

Wilkinson 4: common secretarial circa 1920s

incorporation papers, which are countersigned by Thomas Baird, co-owner of the Monarchs, exist. I know of no signed photos, gum cards, or baseballs. This is an extremely rare Negro League autograph.

Known Forgeries: Due to the wonderful hand and precise letter formation, Wilkinson is an extremely difficult signature to replicate. Well executed forgeries do not exist. Many signatures in the market are signed as "James Wilkinson." Wilkinson was not named "James" but was born as "J Leslie" and thus without a first name. Any signatures signed with "James" or "Jim" should be avoided as forgeries. You will note that his Hall of Fame plaque reads as "J Leslie." There is no reference to the name Jim, nor did he adopt a first name of any kind during his life. There are a few Negro League related documents signed by Wilkinson in the market. The signatures deviate from the illustrated specimens (see Wilkinson 4). The documents in question feature a signature signed in a shaky and slower hand. They lack the strong flow of Wilkinson's signature. These are secretarially signed and of no value.

Sales: Early Negro League document sold for $35,000 (private sale, Winter 2011).

Billy Williams

Signature Study: Williams signs in a very fast hand. His signature evidences rapid flow. Hesitation is non-existent. Letter construction is marginal at best. The signature has impaired legibility. Williams tends to drop the letter "i" from his first

Wilkinson 1: ALS dated 1909

Williams, B. 1: undated signature

Williams, D. 2: 2007 signature

and last name. The display value of Williams' signature is just average. As of 2012 Williams' hand remains strong. A genuine signature will exhibit no shakiness of hand and one that does should be considered suspect and avoided.

Signature Population: Overall, this is a very common signature where supply far outweighs demand. Williams' signature can be found on most items including photos, gum cards, baseballs, bats, Hall of Fame plaque postcards, and the like. Letters of any kind are considered scarce.

Known Forgeries: Due to the rapid nature of his signature, replication of his hand would take some effort. Due to the nominal value of Williams' signature, he is not the target of skilled forgers.

Sales: Williams' signature is available. His autograph generally sells for under $100 on most mediums.

Dick Williams

Signature Study: Williams' signature is accomplished in a bold hand. His signature evidences good flow and tight letter construction. The signature is fairly legible. Display value is average. The signature lacks any measurable slant and is signed in a vertical hand. Material signed in the last few years of his life is penned in a slower and labored hand. The overall scale of the signature has decreased.

Signature Population: Overall, this is a very common signature where supply far outweighs demand. Williams had been a gracious signer for many years. His signature can be found on most items including photos, gum cards, baseballs, bats, Hall of Fame plaque postcards, and the like. Letters of any kind are considered scarce.

Known Forgeries: Vintage signatures are rather difficult to forge. Modern signatures, with infirmity, are easy to replicate. Due to the nominal value of Williams' signature, he is not the target of skilled forgers.

Sales: Williams' signature is available. His autograph generally sells for under $100 on most mediums.

Joe Williams

Signature Study: From the illustrated specimen it is clear that Williams signed in a rudimentary hand. Letter construction is marginal. Display value is limited. The World War I draft registration card differs from his accepted birth date. The month and day are correct but the year is one year off. He lists his occupation as a baseball player.

Williams, J. 1: World War I draft card: circa 1917 (Record Group 163, Records of the Selective Services Division, National Archives at Atlanta)

Signature Population: I know of two signatures in existence, both military-related documents. I know of no other signatures in existence. This is an extreme rarity.

Known Forgeries: There are many forgeries in the market, all vary in construction. A few forged handwritten letters have surfaced signed as "Smokey Joe" Williams.

Sales: Due to the rarity, there have been no recent sales of Williams' signature.

Ted Williams

Signature Study: Ted Williams signed in a very aggressive and attractive hand. There is no evidence of hesitation. Letter construction is sound. The signature is legible. The display value

Williams, D. 1: circa 1970s signature

is superior. Towards the end of his life his hand changed to a measurable degree. Signatures accomplished late in life lack strong flow. They tend to be smaller. Despite this Williams never produced an unsteady signature. A genuine signature will evidence no shakiness of hand and one that does should be considered suspect and avoided.

Signature Population: This is a very common signature but demand is sound for Williams. His signature will always be treasured by collectors. The supply of Williams material seems endless as he signed countless items. Williams did many mass signings and did so for many years. He also would, on occasion, honor autograph requests through the mail. Williams' signature can be found on most mediums including gum cards, photos, baseballs, bats, Perez-Steele cards, Hall of Fame plaque postcards, and the like. Letters are borderline scarce in any form. There is a decent supply of typed letters signed in the market.

Known Forgeries: Williams is a rather difficult signature to replicate, however, many nice forgeries do exist. Williams has long been targeted by skilled forgers. Williams forgeries can be found on most mediums, especially on 500-home-run multi-signed items. The majority of all multi-signed photos of Williams, Mickey Mantle, and Joe DiMaggio are forgeries. In the late 1950s and 1960s many mail requests sent in care of the Red Sox were signed using a rubber stamp. The stamp is illustrated as Williams, T. 5. Further, many mail

Williams, T. 1: circa 1940s signature

Williams, T. 2: undated signature

Williams, T. 3: undated signature

Williams, T. 4: common secretarial

Williams, T. 5: common rubber stamp

requests signed in the 1980s until death were secretarially signed (see Williams, T. 4). These secretarial signatures are accomplished in a slightly jagged hand. The "T" in the first name usually has an abrupt stop at the bottom of the letter. The capital "W" in the last name is connected with the first name and exhibits a large odd loop at the top of the letter.

Sales: Vintage album page sold for $63 (Jim Stinson Sports, September 2011). Single-signed baseball sold for $275 (eBay, September 2011). Perez-Steele art postcard sold for $200 (eBay, September 2011). 1960 Fleer gum card sold for $180 (eBay, September 2011). 1954 TLS sold for $436 (RR Auctions, May 2011).

Vic Willis

Signature Study: Willis signed in an aggressive and bold hand. His signature is marked with thick lines and effortless flow. The signature evidences no hesitation whatsoever. The letter construction is sound. The signature has a high degree of legibility. Sound display value is noted. Willis either signed as "Victor G. Willis" or "Vic Willis." I have never seen a signature accomplished with either of his nicknames. I have been unable to determine whether infirmity of hand affected Willis' signature in later years. Since I have never examined a genuine specimen signed in a labored hand, it is unlikely infirmity existed.

Signature Population: Willis is a very rare signature. Only a handful of specimens exist. A couple of signed index cards that originated from the Peggy Dannehy collection surfaced in the late 1980s. A couple of handwritten letters and one signed business card also exist. I would estimate the population of Willis signatures is somewhere between 10 and 20 specimens. I have never exam-

Willis 1: undated ALS

Willis 2: business card

ined a genuinely signed photo, T-card, or baseball of any kind.

Known Forgeries: Willis' hand is rather difficult to forge. Well executed forgeries are very limited but do exist. Willis forgeries are typically found on index cards, old album pages, and scorecards. Forgeries typically evidence a shaky appearance.

Sales: Business card sold for $9,705 (Lelands.com, November 2008).

Hack Wilson

Signature Study: Wilson's signature is powerful and striking. His signature evidences thick and dominant lines. The signature evidences good flow. Hesitation is minimal. Letter construction is sound. Wilson's signature is legible. The display value is high. Most signatures are signed with his nickname. Wilson died at the young age of 48. Since he never reached old age, infirmity of hand is non-existent. A genuine signature will evidence no shakiness of hand and one that does should be considered suspect and avoided.

Signature Population: Wilson is a scarce signature on a per se basis. Premium items should be considered rare to very rare. Most Wilson signatures are found on album pages, scorecards, and multi-signed baseballs. Government postcards are rare. Signed letters of any kind are very rare. I have never seen a genuine full-page handwritten letter. Team-signed baseballs are a good source for Wilson's signature, especially the Brooklyn teams of the early 1930s. Single-signed baseballs

Wilson, H. 1: bank check dated 1931

Wilson, H. 2: album page dated 1933

Wilson, H. 3: government postcard dated 1935

should be considered very rare. I have only seen three genuine specimens in my lifetime. Back in the 1980s, a dealer walked into a card show in Plymouth, Michigan, with several Wilson canceled bank checks signed as "Lewis R. Wilson" or "L.R. Wilson." Based on my conversation with the seller, I estimate about 300 checks were released into the market. Today signed checks are rare, albeit borderline.

Known Forgeries: Due to the powerful nature of Wilson's signature, replication of his hand is very difficult. There are no well executed Wilson forgeries in the market. Wilson forgeries will exhibit a labored appearance and unsteady lines. About 15 years ago a forger secured some old baseballs. He forged Wilson's signature on the sweet spot. These forgeries are rudimentary in construction with shakiness of hand evident. These forgeries are misscaled as they appear smaller. They lack the boldness of a genuine Wilson signature. All forgeries were accomplished in green fountain pen ink. Every once in a while one of these spurious Wilson balls turn up in auction with a certificate of authenticity. Most Wilson signatures offered in the market are forgeries.

Sales: Bank check sold for $3,231 (Robert Edward Auctions, Spring 2010). Bank check sold for $1,560 (RR Auctions, May 2011). Album page with others sold for $932 (RR Auctions, April 2011). 1934 Major League contract sold for $12,533 (Lelands.com, November 2010). Album page sold for $950 (eBay, November 2011).

Jud Wilson

Signature Study: Wilson's signature causes much controversy as there is great debate as to what his signature looks like. For many years signatures signed in a vertical and simple hand have been accepted as genuine by some experts. They

Wilson, J. 1: ALS dated 1945 (courtesy Newark Public Library, The Newark Eagles papers)

are signed as "J. Wilson" or sometimes "Jud Wilson, Bainbridge Street, Phila, Penna." Is does not make sense to me why Wilson would sign autographs as "J. Wilson." He could not have received many autograph requests. The mere fact that a signature is accomplished with just the first initial raises concerns. For years I have been trying to locate a confirmed Wilson signature. After much searching I did locate a specimen that calls into question the authenticity of those signatures that have been accepted as genuine. The signature, illustrated as Wilson, J 1, is from a two-page ALS dated March 30, 1945, written to Newark Eagles owner Abe Manley. The letter asks for a tryout with the Eagles as Wilson has not heard from Cum Posey of the Homestead Grays for the 1945 season. The letter is signed "Jud Wilson" and addressed in Washington, D.C. I spoke with a member of Wilson's family who confirmed that Wilson was living in D.C. at the time this letter was written. The Manley letter signature evidences a nice right slant and strong flowing lines. This signature is in stark contrast to the other Wilson signatures in the market. This letter is currently housed at the Newark Public Library as part of the Newark Eagles collection.

Signature Population: I know of two signatures in existence, the above referenced letter and a signed military document from World War I. Both are held by governmental concerns. To my knowledge, there are no signatures in the open market. This signature is an extreme rarity.

Known Forgeries: Many Wilson forgeries exist. All vary in construction. Many forged picture postcards are in the market. They feature Wilson in a Grays uniform leaning on a bat. Some are signed as "J. Wilson" others as "Jud Wilson." All are accomplished by the same forger.

Sales: Due to the rarity, there have been no recent sales of Wilson's signature.

Dave Winfield

Signature Study: Winfield signs in a very rapid and unattractive hand. His signature evidences good flow. Hesitation is lacking. Letter construc-

Winfield 1: undated signature

tion is weak. The signature has poor legibility. Display value is marginal, at best. Winfield will typically sign his autograph as either "Dave Winfield" or "D. Winfield." As of 2012 Winfield's hand remains sound. A genuine signature will evidence no shakiness of hand and one that does should be considered suspect and avoided.

Signature Population: This is a very common signature, where supply clearly outweighs demand. His signature can be found on most mediums including photos, gum cards, bats, baseballs, and the like. Letters of any kind should be considered scarce.

Known Forgeries: Winfield's signature is easy to replicate. Creating a well executed forgery can be done with little effort. Due to the nominal value of Winfield's signature, he is generally not the target of skilled forgers.

Sales: Winfield's signature is available. His autograph generally sells for under $100 on most mediums.

George Wright

Signature Study: Wright signed in an extremely flowing and beautiful hand. Early signatures evidence wonderful lines. Effortless and wavy strokes are noted. Letter construction is sound, though some choppiness is noted. The signature has a marginal degree of legibility. Display value is sound. Signatures accomplished later in life are signed in a slower and labored hand. The nice flow of vintage signatures is replaced with an elderly and less attractive hand. All genuine specimens I have examined are signed as "Geo Wright."

Signature Population: Most Wright signatures offered in the market, what few there are, were signed in the last few years of his life. Wright is a rare signature. I estimate a total population of somewhere between 20 to 30 specimens in the open market. Signatures are generally limited to documents and typed letters signed. A few smaller-sized index cards exist. I have never seen a genuinely signed photo or baseball.

Wright, G. 1: TLS dated 1904

Wright, G. 2: TLS dated 1905

Wright, G. 3: will dated 1934

Wright, H. 1: ALS dated 1871

Wright, H. 2: ALS dated 1871

Wright, H. 3: ALS circa 1875 (courtesy National Baseball Hall of Fame and Museum)

Known Forgeries: Vintage signatures are very difficult to replicate. The elderly signatures are extremely easy to replicate, so well executed forgeries exist in quantities. Wright forgeries are generally limited to album pages, scorecards, and other generic material. I have also examined forged baseballs and cabinet photographs. The majority of all Wright signatures offered in the market are forgeries. Title issues may exist with certain Wright letters.

Sales: 1894 ALS sold for $17,925 (Legendary Auctions, August 2012).

Harry Wright

Signature Study: Harry Wright's signature is one of the finest of all the Hall of Famers. It is right up there with Charlie Gehringer, Barney Dreyfuss, and Alexander Cartwright. The signature is wonderfully flowing with finely crafted lines. Letter construction is superior. The signature has maximum display value. The signature is distinctive with dominant capital letters that enhance any medium it is placed upon. At times, Wright would sign

in a more pensive hand. These signatures lack the panache of his more ornate signatures. Some experts have pronounced these as secretarial but when examining the bodies of autographed letters

Wright, H. 4: ALS circa 1875 (courtesy National Baseball Hall of Fame and Museum)

signed it is clear the same hand penned both. The question of whether infirmity of hand existed due to old age is still unanswered. I have never examined a genuine signature that exhibits shakiness of hand. Given the fact that he died at the age of 60, infirmity is unlikely but still unconfirmed.

Signature Population: The demand is strong for Wright-signed material. The supply is minute. Wright's signature is very rare. His signature is basically limited to handwritten letters and documents. Most letters are written on team letterhead and have good baseball content. Wright letters are a significant part of nineteenth century baseball. I have never examined a genuinely signed baseball or photo of any kind.

Known Forgeries: Due to Wright's flowing hand, his signature is one of the most difficult, if not the most difficult, to forge. There are no well executed forgeries in existence. Wright forgeries do exist but all are rudimentary in nature. They have a measurable degree of deviation from a genuine signature. Many forged cabinet photographs exist. These are signed in pencil or ink across the bottom of the card. These were accomplished by one forger. Title issues may exist with certain Wright letters.

Sales: 1878 ALS sold for $6,500 (Hunt Auctions, February 2005).

Early Wynn

Signature Study: Wynn signed in a powerful and non-conforming hand. His signature evidences strong flow. Thick bold lines are evident. The racing effect is very noticeable. Letter construction is marginal, where letters tend to appear sloppy. The overall result is a signature with impaired legibility. Wynn's hand remained strong his entire life. A genuine signature will exhibit no shakiness of hand and one that does should be considered suspect and avoided.

Signature Population: This is a signature with marginal demand that is clearly outweighed by supply. Wynn was an erratic signer at best. He was known for his combative attitude towards autograph collectors. He was a willing signer for a fee. His signature is common and can be found on most mediums including gum cards, baseballs, Perez-Steele cards, Hall of Fame plaque postcards, photos, and the like. Signed letters of any kind are scarce.

Known Forgeries: Wynn's hand is fairly easy to replicate. Creating a well executed forgery can

Wynn 1: undated signature

be done with little effort. Due to the nominal value of Wynn's signature, he is not the target of skilled forgers.

Sales: Wynn's signature is available. His autograph generally sells for under $100 on most mediums.

Carl Yastrzemski

Signature Study: Yastrzemski signs in a very bold hand that lacks precision. The signature is signed in a reckless fashion. Good racing effect is noted. The dominant feature of his signature is the large "Y" of the last name. Letter construction is poor. The signature is basically illegible. The display value is impaired. As of 2012 Yastrzemski's hand remains sound. A genuine signature will evidence no shakiness of hand and one that does should be considered suspect and avoided.

Signature Population: This is a signature where supply outweighs demand. His signature is very common and can be found on most mediums including photos, gum cards, bats, baseballs, and the like. Letters of any kind should be considered scarce.

Known Forgeries: Due to the lack of precise angles, replication of his hand is easy. Creating a well executed forgery would take little effort. Due to the nominal value of Yastrzemski's signature, he is generally not the target of skilled forgers.

Yastrzemski 1: undated signature

Sales: Yastrzemski's signature is available. His autograph generally sells for under $100 on most mediums.

Tom Yawkey

Signature Study: Yawkey signed in a very powerful and dominant hand. His signature exhibits thick strokes. Excellent flow is noted. Letter construction is sound with good formation. The resulting signature evidences a high degree of legibility. Display value is sound. It is simply one of the nicer Hall of Fame signatures. Yawkey's signature evidences a man of confidence and thus complex in nature. Yawkey's hand remained sound his entire life. A genuine signature will exhibit no shakiness of hand and one that does should be considered suspect and avoided.

Signature Population: This is a signature with marginal demand. Yawkey is an uncommon signature on a per se basis. It is generally limited to signed letters and team-related documents. The occasional signed scorecard and album page does surface but not often. 8 × 10 photos are somewhat scarce. Yawkey did hand out nice portrait 8 × 10 photos. These are usually inscribed. They are typically signed in light ball-point ink. Single-signed baseballs are rare. I have only examined a handful in the last 30 years. Autographed letters signed are rare and most are signed with just his first name.

Known Forgeries: His signature is difficult to replicate. No well executed forgeries exist in the market. Forgeries are typically limited to premium items such as baseballs and 8 × 10 photographs.

Sales: 1966 TLS sold for $220 (RR Auctions, July 2011). Index card sold for $235 (eBay Sep-

tember 2011). Picture postcard sold for $444 (Hunt Auctions, September 2010). 1951 TLS, choice specimen, sold for $477 (RR Auctions, November 2009). Choice ink signature sold for $250 (Stephen Koschal Autographs, Fall 2009).

Cy Young

Signature Study: Young signed in a very meaningful and pensive hand. His signature evidences good flow. It is not signed in a rapid or reckless fashion as one would find in a signature of Hornsby or Cobb. Letter construction is very pronounced. The "n" in the last name appears more like the letter "u." Overall, the signature is legible. Display value is high. Signatures accomplished before 1940 tend to be compact with letters signed closer together. As Young aged his signature changed slightly. The length increases, resulting in a longer, more drawn out, signature. The hand slows ever so slightly but display value is still sound. On many occasions Young would add "Peoli, O" or "Peoli, Ohio" under his signature. Just about all signatures are signed as "Cy Young." Locating an autograph signed with his real name is a very difficult undertaking. As Young entered the late 1940s his hand became infirmed. Signatures accomplished in the last few years of his life evidence an unsteady appearance with uneven letter construction. This form of signature is of limited eye appeal.

Signature Population: This is a signature where demand greatly outweighs supply. Young was a willing signer throughout his life. There is an ample supply of signatures in the market. His signature is mostly found on index cards and government postcards. Premium items are rare to very rare. 8 × 10 photos seldom surface. Signed letters are rare in any form. There are few specimens

Yawkey 1: undated signature

Young 1: government postcard dated 1935

Yawkey 2: undated signature

Young 2: ALS dated 1942

Young 3: government postcard dated 1943

Young 4: album page circa 1940s

from the 1950s which are drafted on personal letterhead that simply reads "Cy Young" at top. These letters are signed by Young but the body of the letter is accomplished in the hand of another. Autographed letters signed are considered rare to very rare. Young had an odd habit of changing the scale of his hand when writing long letters. As the body of the letter progresses the handwriting becomes larger. This habit is typically limited to multi-page letters. Single-signed baseballs are rare. Just about all were signed post–1950. They are typically signed in a labored hand. Signed team baseballs from Young's playing days likely do not exist. I have never examined a genuinely signed tobacco card of any kind.

Known Forgeries: Young never signed in a fast hand and because of this his signature is rather easy to replicate. Many well executed forgeries are in the market. I estimate that 90 percent of the Young signatures offered for sale are forged. One common forgery is signed Hall of Fame plaque postcards. While genuine signed plaque cards do exist they are rare. The majority offered in the market are forgeries. The forged cards are too clean and neat, or the corners are sharp and evidence no measurable aging or wear. This is likely due to the fact they were in storage undisturbed for years. The forgeries exist in blue and purple ball-point pen and fountain pen. The forgeries lack the distinctive loop at the bottom of the two letters "Y"s and the "g" in the last name. The lack

Young 5: circa 1950s signature

Young 6: rubber stamp

of the loops is not conclusive that the signature is forgery but the genuine signed cards seem to have the loops present. Young had a rubber stamp made of his signature (see Young 6). While he rarely, if ever, use this stamp to respond to autograph requests, he did make liberal use of it on his personal items. Many personal photos that derived from the Young estate feature this stamp on the back of the photo. Stamp signatures have entered the market, so caution is warranted.

Sales: Single-signed baseball sold for $3,616 (RR Auctions, November 2009). Government postcard sold for $800 (Hunt Auctions, November 2010). Index card sold for $800 (Hunt Auctions, July, 2010). 1952 LS written to Connie Mack sold for $1,912 (Legendary Auctions, March 2011). 1950 government postcard sold for $1,016 (RR Auctions, August 2011).

Ross Youngs

Signature Study: Youngs' hand is quite distinctive. His signature exhibits rapid flow with bold thick strokes of hand. The signature evidences a nice right slant. Hesitation of any kind in lacking. The racing effect is muted. Letter construction is sound. The signature has acceptable legibility. Sound display value is noted. Youngs' hand varied little in the decade or so that he was signing autographs. Most signatures are signed as "Ross 'Pep' Youngs." Youngs died of kidney disease at a very young age, hence infirmity of hand does not exist. A genuine signature will evidence no shakiness of hand and one that does should be considered suspect and avoided.

Signature Population: This is a signature with good demand and minute supply. Youngs' signature is considered very rare. Only a handful of genuine specimens exist, mostly on team-signed New York Giants baseballs. The occasional album page also surfaces now and then. The pages are usually signed with other Giants. I have never seen a genuinely signed photo, single-signed baseball, letter, or baseball card.

Known Forgeries: The complex nature of his

Youngs 1: album page 1920s

Youngs 2: circa 1920s signature

hand makes replication difficult. There are no well executed forgeries in the market. Youngs forgeries appear on most mediums. Just about all the Youngs signatures in the market are forgeries. Proceed with extreme caution.

Sales: Album page sold for $6,346 (Mastro, April 2001).

Robin Yount

Signature Study: Yount signs in an extremely sloppy and unattractive hand. Letter construction

Yount 1: undated signature

is poor. The signature is mostly illegible. Display value is marginal. This is simply one of the less appealing Hall of Fame signatures. As of 2012 Yount's hand remains sound. A genuine signature will evidence no shakiness of hand and one that does should be considered suspect and avoided.

Signature Population: Yount is a common signature where demand is far outweighed by supply. His signature is found on many mediums including photos, balls, bats, and gum cards. Letters of any kind are scarce.

Known Forgeries: Given the rudimentary nature of Yount's hand, producing a well executed forgery can be done with ease. Due to the nominal value of Yount's signature, he is not the target of skilled forgers.

Sales: Yount's signature is available. His autograph generally sells for under $100 on most mediums.

Index